D1281381

RHODIAN
FUNERARY MONUMENTS

RHODIAN FUNERARY MONUMENTS

BY

P. M. FRASER

OXFORD
AT THE CLARENDON PRESS
1977

Oxford University Press, Walton Street, Oxford OX2 6DP

OXFORD LONDON GLASGOW
NEW YORK TORONTO MELBOURNE WELLINGTON
IBADAN NAIROBI DAR ES SALAAM LUSAKA CAPE TOWN
KUALA LUMPUR SINGAPORE JAKARTA HONG KONG TOKYO
DELHI BOMBAY CALCUTTA MADRAS KARACHI

© Oxford University Press 1977

British Library Cataloguing in Publication Data
Fraser, Peter Marshall
    Rhodian funerary monuments
    Index
    ISBN 0-19-813192-5
    1. Title
    731'. 76'093916   NB1800
    Rhodes – Sepulchral monuments

Printed in Great Britain
at the University Press, Oxford
by Vivian Ridler
Printer to the University

Στή μνήμη τοῦ φίλου
Λουκᾶ Μπενάκη
† 28. 10. 76
ἥλιον ἐν λέσχηι κατεδύσαμεν

PREFACE

STUDENTS of the history and archaeology of the ancient city of Rhodes
are faced with a difficulty which increases rather than decreases with
the passing years: the absence of systematic specialized studies of the
different types of archaeological material, both in the immediate
context of archaeological discovery and excavation and also typologically and historically. The material of the later hellenistic period,
both from residential areas and from cemeteries, is probably more
abundant than that yielded by any other Greek city, including Athens,
and, in view of the outstanding commercial importance of Rhodes in
the history of the Aegean at that time, the basis for the detailed study
of a major feature of the hellenistic world is potentially available. In-
evitably, however, in almost every field detailed study must lag far
behind discovery,* and the continual spate of new material, particularly
from building-sites, increases the gap, in spite of the valuable progress
made by the Greek Archaeological Service, since the Dodecanese passed
to Greece, in recording all new discoveries. At a time when vast quantities
of fragments of domestic ware, glass, etc., excavated in the last sixty years
are still largely unstudied, any attempt to write the economic and commercial history of Rhodes would be premature. What is true in the field
of common manufactured objects is true also, *mutatis mutandis*, in the
field of epigraphy, and particularly that of funerary monuments. Large
numbers of these—by far the largest class of inscribed monument
from the city of Rhodes—are preserved in the Museum and elsewhere,
but no recent general publication of them exists, and at the same time
most of the inscriptions seen by Hiller von Gaertringen in and around
the city when preparing the Corpus of Rhodian inscriptions at the end of
the last century have disappeared, leaving only one or two chance survivors. Until these monuments are classified and identified, and then
studied chronologically, our understanding of many aspects of Rhodian
life, and especially the evolution of its social life, must be very incomplete.

The present monograph is an attempt to remedy one particular
aspect of this general problem. In it I have tried on the one hand to
describe the main types of Rhodian funerary monuments, mostly of the

* Obvious exceptions to this are provided by the coinage of Rhodes, which was syste-
matically studied by B. V. Head, whose catalogue of Caria and the Islands (1897) remains
fundamental, and by the stamped Rhodian amphora-handles to which Miss V. Grace has
devoted a lifetime of hard labour; but the latter are only in part a problem of Rhodian
archaeology.

later hellenistic age; and on the other to place them in the context of other similar or comparable hellenistic funerary monuments, and in particular those of the other Dorian communities of Asia Minor and of the islands dependent on Rhodes. At the same time I have attempted to identify the monuments in Rhodes Museum by their location in the Museum; this may be of service in any more extensive exercise in identification in the future.* In the second part I have analysed various aspects of the funerary inscriptions and attempted to indicate the light thrown by them on the religious practices of the population of Rhodes in connection with the commemoration of the dead. I have concentrated on the hellenistic age, in which I am most at home, and to the later part of which most of the monuments seem to belong, and I have given only the briefest references to the funerary monuments of the period before the synoecism, and to those of the fourth century. An exhaustive analysis of these must be left to specialists in that field.

Studies analogous to the present work in the many branches of Rhodian archaeology for which material exists will, it may be hoped, one day provide the necessary background for a detailed history of all aspects of Rhodian life, and thus fill one of the main lacunae in our knowledge of the hellenistic age.†

P. M. FRASER

Oxford, 1975

---

* This task will now be much simplified by the recent publication (1977) of Dr. Konstantinopoulos's Μουσεῖα τῆς Ρόδου, I, Ἀρχαιολογικό Μουσεῖο (II, Πινακοθήκη, Μουσεῖο Λαϊκῆς Τέχνης, Καστέλλο), in which the monuments (including many of the inscriptions discussed and illustrated in the present work) are described according to their location in the Museum. I regret that I have not been able to include references to this useful work in the notes.

† I may call attention in this connection to the recent essay of Gloria S. Merker, *The Hellenistic Sculpture of Rhodes* (Stud. Medit. Archaeol. 40, Göteborg, 1973), in which the author sets herself a similar task for the free-standing hellenistic sculpture.

CONTENTS

x   *Contents*

ACKNOWLEDGEMENTS

I MUST first and foremost express here my warmest thanks for their continual and unselfish co-operation to the staff of the Greek Archaeological Service of the Dodecanese, and in particular Dr. G. Konstantinopoulos, its Director from 1964 until 1973, from whose great familiarity with all aspects of Rhodian and Dodecanesian antiquities I have greatly profited. It was only through his generous and friendly help that I was able to collect and study the Dodecanesian material published here. His successor as Director of the service in the Dodecanese, Dr. Chr. Doumas, also gave generous help during my visits in 1974–5.

I also owe a great debt to the authorities of the Danish National Museum, and in particular to Dr. Steffen Trolle, Assistant Keeper, who helped me greatly in my study of the Lindian material in the Museum, and also generously authorized my publication of the hitherto unpublished Rhodian monuments in the Museum.

I must also record my debt to Dr. Eberhard Erxleben, *Custos* of the *Inscriptiones Graecae* Department of the Berlin Akademie der Wissenschaften, who permitted me to study the Rhodian squeezes in the collection in March 1972 and to the British Academy which provided the funds for my visit.

My thanks are also due to the following Museums and institutions, as well as individuals, for providing me with photographs for reproduction in this work.

Fig. 15: Arkeoloji Müzesi, Istanbul
    16, *b*: Ny Carlsberg Glyptothek, Copenhagen
    17, *a*: Rhodes Museum
    17, *b*: Arkeoloji Müzesi, Istanbul
    17, *c*: Danish National Museum, Copenhagen (Dept. of Near Eastern and Class. Art)
    21, *c–d*: Kestner-Museum, Hanover
    22: Kunsthistorisches Museum, Vienna (Antikensammlung)
    25, *a–b*: Mr. M. Lowe
    28: Dr. P. Roos
    29, *a*: Staatliche Museen zu Berlin, Berlin (Antiken-Sammlung)
    30: Trustees, British Museum, London
    33, *a–b*: Danish National Museum, Copenhagen (Dept. of Near Eastern and Class. Art)
    34, *a–b*: Danish National Museum, Copenhagen (Dept. of Near Eastern and Class. Art)
    36: Musée du Louvre, Paris

40, *d*: Dr. Chr. Doumas
41, *a–b*: National Museum, Athens
44, *a*: Professor G. E. Bean
46, *a–d*: Kunsthistorisches Museum, Vienna (Antikensammlung)
47, *a*: Rhodes Museum
47, *b*: Danish National Museum, Copenhagen (Dept. of Near Eastern and Class. Art)
48, *a–b*: Dr. G. Konstantinopoulos
50, *a*: Staatliche Antikensammlungen und Glyptothek, Munich
52, *a*: Deutsches Archäologisches Institut, Athens
55: Trustees, British Museum, London
56, *a*: Trustees, British Museum, London
56, *b*: Dr. Chr. Doumas
58, *d*: Dr. Chr. Doumas
65, *a*: Professor James R. McCredie
69: National Museum, Athens
71, *a, c–d*: Staatliche Museen zu Berlin (Antiken-Sammlung)
72, *a–b*: Trustees, British Museum, London
73, *a*: Trustees, British Museum, London
73, *b*: Musée du Louvre, Paris
74, *g*: Musee d'archéologie, Château Borely, Marseilles
74, *h*: Professor A. Orlandos
75, *b*: Mr. T. L. Shear, Jr.
75, *c*: Museo Archeologico, Venice
75, *d*: Mr. R. N. L. Barber
76, *c*: Mr. C. K. Williams, Jr.
76, *d–e*: Department of Antiquities, Nicosia
76, *g*: Professor R. Ghirshman
80, *e*: Arkeoloji Müzesi, Istanbul
80, *f*: Professor G. E. Bean
81, *a–h*: Professor K. Jeppesen
81, *j*: Trustees, British Museum, London
82, *a–b*: Trustees, British Museum, London
82, *d*: Visitors, Ashmolean Museum, Oxford
83, *a–c*: Miss D. Chatzi
83, *e*: Arkeoloji Müzesi, Istanbul
83, *j–k*: Department of Fine Art, University of Glasgow
85, *b–c*: Arkeoloji Müzesi, Istanbul
85, *d–e*: Archäologisches Seminar der Universität Marburg
85, *g–h*: Arkeoloji Müzesi, Istanbul
86, *b*: Kunsthistorisches Museum, Vienna (Antikensammlung)
91, *d*: Dr. W. Mallwitz
91, *e–f*: Museo Archeologico, Venice
91, *g–h*: Arkeoloji Müzesi, Istanbul
92, *c*: Kunsthistorisches Museum, Vienna (Antikensammlung)
92, *d*: Danish National Museum, Copenhagen (Dept. of Near Eastern and Class. Art)

92, *e*: Staatliche Museen zu Berlin (Antiken-Sammlung)
93, *a*: Danish National Museum, Copenhagen (Dept. of Near Eastern and Class. Art)
93, *d*: Rhodes Museum
94: Danish National Museum, Copenhagen (Dept. of Near Eastern and Class. Art)
95: Ny Carlsberg Glyptothek, Copenhagen
96, *c*: Museo Nazionale, Naples
97: Staatliche Museen zu Berlin (Antiken-Sammlung)
98: Rhodes Museum
99: Trustees, British Museum, London
101, *b*: Professor G. E. Bean
101, *f*: Dr. P. Roos
103: Trustees, British Museum, London
104: Trustees, British Museum, London
106, *a–c*: Mr. R. E. Allen
109, *a*: Arkeoloji Müzesi, Istanbul
111, *b*: Mr. C. K. Williams, Jr.
111, *c*: Mrs. B. Drushell
112, *d*: Trustees, British Museum, London
113, *a–d*: Museo Archeologico, Venice
114, *a–b*: Professor Werner Peek
115, *a–c*: Trustees, British Museum, London
118, *f–g*: Dr. B. F. Cook

The following figures are taken from the publications indicated:*

49, *d*: *Ann.* N.S. 1–2, pl. xi, no. 12
57: *Napiski Olbia*, pl. xiii, no. 24
61, *a*: *Supp. Rod.* fig. 45
62, *a–b*: *Tit. Cam.* figs. 24, 37
62, *c–d*: *Inscr. Lind.* nos. 91 and 105
85, *g*: Lawrence, *Later Greek Sculpture*, pl. 45
86, *a*: *Cl. Rh.* 5(2), p. 94 f
96, *a*: *Cl. Rh.* 2, p. 66, fig. 34
96, *b*: *Cl. Rh.* 2, no. 30 and fig. 35
113, *e–f*: *NS* 45
114, *g*: *Ann.* N.S. 1–2, pl. vi, no. 11

* For abbreviations see Introduction to Notes, below, pp. 83–4.

PART I

THE MONUMENTS

My aim in this study is to describe the main classes of funerary monuments found in Rhodes, and to investigate some social and religious questions raised by them—what personal details were recorded on them, what ceremonies were held in the necropoleis, and so on. I am concerned primarily with the city of Rhodes, Rhodos, founded in 408/7 B.C., and thus only with monuments of the Classical and subsequent periods. Although I have not excluded in principle funerary monuments from the three old cities, Ialysos, Kamiros, and Lindos, the number of post-Archaic monuments from these sites is very small, and the main hellenistic and later cemeteries have not been discovered.[1]

I may begin with a brief general description of the necropoleis of the ancient city, from which the monuments ultimately come. I leave for consideration elsewhere many questions relating to the topography and antiquities of the city.

I. THE URBAN NECROPOLEIS

Although the main necropoleis of Rhodos have been known since before the middle of the last century, no detailed account of them has been published. In the following brief account I have used largely my own observations, but I have been considerably helped by various partial accounts by earlier travellers, notably Ross and Newton, by the reports of the Italian Archaeological Service, and, for the period after 1947, by those of the Greek Archaeological Service. The accompanying plan serves to indicate the main necropolis areas against the background of the ancient city wall, where the course of this is known, and against the modern town plan.[2] To those unfamiliar with the subject and the terrain a particular problem is created by the changes in nomenclature which the whole area has undergone during and since the Turkish period, and I have tried to give the different names for the various localities, where this is possible.[3] Unfortunately in many cases the names are used in a very vague manner, and it is not possible to determine precise locations very closely.

The main necropolis zone lay south of the city, and stretched from the south-western end of the Acropolis Hill of Monte Smith (St. Stephen's Hill; San Stefano) on the west to the coastal belt of Cova (Acandia; Marino) and Karakonero on the east. The whole area lay outside, i.e. to the south of, the city walls, which ran north of the two ravines which separated, for the most part, the necropolis area and the *chora* of the city from the city itself. These two ravines are of fundamental importance to the understanding of the necropolis zone, and their course must be kept in mind. As may be seen from the plan, the more northerly of the two, Makry Steno, starts in the high land south of Monte Smith, where the road to Sandurli (Sandruli; Sandyrli) descends from the plateau to the coast at Trianda, and follows a winding course through the area of the suburb of Agios Ioannes (or Ai Yanni, as it is generally known), down to the sloping terrain on the eastern side of the island, where, at a distance of about a kilometre from the coast at Cova, it is joined by the second ravine, that of Rhodini (Simbulli; Sümbüllü; Sambylli; Zimburli (*turcicé*; i.e. 'Place of Hyacinths'); *ital.*: Rodino), which rises in the high ground above Rhodini, then descends a steep terraced waterfall stretch, converted into a public resort by the Italians, and then, after crossing the Koskinou road, flows more gently north-eastwards to the point of junction. The common bed then narrows to pass under the ancient bridge on the Cova (Acandia) road by the British War Cemetery, and thence flows in a narrow, modern, channel into the sea. In its upper reaches the wide bed of the Ai Yanni ravine is now largely occupied by houses, but its natural features remain clearly evident, and its course still dominates the whole area; further down, after it turns east, roads have been built both across it and down its length, principally the newly constructed Hodos Vasilissis Annas Marias, which runs down the centre of the ravine until it joins the Hodos Lindou, which, in its turn, has run down the centre of the Rhodini ravine, from the turn in the road at the entrance to Rhodini park, to reach the point of junction. In the area between the Ai Yanni ravine and the course of the city wall, a belt of varying width, isolated tombs and groups of tombs may still be seen in the fields and farmyards of the upper region and among the houses in its lower reaches.

The whole necropolis zone may be conveniently divided into three sectors, a western, a central, and an eastern, which in antiquity no doubt formed a continuous belt.

(i) The western sector consists of (*a*) the area at the south end of Monte Smith, and still on the slope of the hill, above the ravine, immediately outside the city wall, a stretch of which is preserved at this point (plan; figs. 1–3), (*b*) the suburb of Ai Yanni itself, and more especially its southern extension within the ravine, in the locality now called τοῦ Ἄϊ Ἰάννι τά Λαϊκά (i.e. Makry Steno), containing workers' houses, and (*c*), the high broken ground south of (*b*) called Kizil Tepé (Chizil Tepé; Qyzyl Tepé; 'The Red Hill') by the Turks, through which runs a narrow footpath which, after a kilometre or so largely along the line of an ancient way once flanked by rock-cut tombs of which occasional traces survive, below the modern settlement of Agia Triada built on the edge of the ravine, reaches the hilly ground above Rhodini, where, on the edge of the Rhodini ravine, there are isolated monuments, notably the 'Ptolemaion'. This track once evidently ran across the ravine from the city to the south, and there is natural access past the 'Ptolemaion' across the head of the ravine, both to the south, and to the cliffs above Trianda Bay on the west.[4] It is a source of confusion that the terms Kizil Tepé and Makry Steno are found used of a wider area including the region north-west of the ravine up to the summit of Monte Smith; I confine the former to the area between the two ravines and the latter to that of the Ai Yanni ravine. Area (*a*) contains tombs of the early fourth century, in both its western and eastern sectors, and it appears that the stretch of hellenistic city wall at this point is built either over or very close to graves of the early and middle fourth century (figs. 2, 3);[5] there can be little doubt that this was the first burial area of the new city. All the graves are simple pit-graves sunk in the rock. Both (*b*) and (*c*) are rich in ruined hypogaea and rock-cut structures with loculi and chambers, facing on to open courts delimited by surrounding walls cut from the living rock (fig. 4), and frequently approached by external staircases. The most notable enclosure in this area, found by the Italians, lies on the southern side of the modern road through the ravine of Ai Yanni. Here, in addition to groups of rock-cut and stone-built façades surmounted by terraced platforms and pierced by rows of vaulted and rectangular loculi (fig. 5) there is a large hypogaeum consisting of several chambers. Unfortunately the original form of the hypogaeum has to some extent been destroyed by subsequent medieval quarrying, and the basis of the Italian restoration of the hypogaeum, which was never fully published, is not known. Nevertheless, the core of the hypogaeum at least preserves its original form.[6] This consists of two main chambers, no doubt originally approached by an external staircase, the walls of which are pierced by rows of triangular loculi, set behind continuous projecting ledges, while, in the manner familiar elsewhere, other passages tunnelled deeper into the rock contain more loculi (fig. 6).

(ii) The central sector consists of the tombs found lower down the ravine of Ai Yanni before its junction with the Rhodini ravine; its course here ran very close to the city wall (see plan). Of particular importance are two recently discovered groups of pit-graves found just north of the Hodos Lindou and in the Hodos Gregoriou E′, which lie just within the line of the surviving stretch of the hellenistic city wall; the graves, like those close to and under the wall at the western end of the necropolis zone, contain material of the early fourth century.[6a]

(iii) At the eastern end of the belt the material is rich, but apparently all of later hellenistic and Roman date. From the line of the ravine bed at the ancient bridge (see plan) starting at the British War Cemetery (opposite the new Orthodox Cemetery), for approximately a kilometre on the western side of the road to Kallithea, there extends a series of rock-cut tombs, mostly now at road level, but originally at a lower level; these are evidently the surviving remains of a large necropolis area which extended from the higher ground to the west as far as the shore.[7] Two or three sections of the necropolis (the Cova or Acandia, or south-eastern, necropolis) are excellently preserved. The whole area, originally no doubt used as a quarry, was terraced in the rock, above the tombs, and at some points the funerary altars found by the Italians have been set in position on the terraces above the loculi, and the original appearance of the area may be easily comprehended (figs. 7, 8). The most conspicuous feature on the west side of the road is an open rock-cut court on the back and side walls of which are carved in deep relief, apparently against a background of hanging draperies or a tent, a series of funerary subjects.[8] The central feature is the figure of a rider on a horse or other quadruped, in a deep recess, with (later?) loculi behind, carved in high relief, and facing outward; it is natural to suppose that he is the person buried in the tomb. The whole figure is badly weathered and details are hardly distinguishable, but he appears to be wearing armour (fig. 9). On the left, as we face him, are other figures and objects, including a figure pouring a libation into a kantharos (fig. 10), below which is a small cavity for offerings, and a circular funerary altar encircled by a wreath or a snake, while on the right wall there is a conspicuous relief of a snake, and on the left side there are female figures in movement.[9] There is no satisfactory means of dating this monument, but both snakes and kantharoi play a prominent part in hellenistic funerary cults, and there is no reason why it should not be of that period; unfortunately it is not possible to associate any grave furniture, small finds, or funerary inscription with the monument. Very slightly further south, on the eastern side of the road, on the sea-shore, there is a further group of funerary emplacements in the sand, apparently of late date in their present form, since they embody reused late hellenistic monuments (fig. 11). This group extends to the small cove known as Karakonero, where there is a cafe-restaurant in which there are a number of circular funerary monuments acting as supports for the terrace.[10] All this area, and the higher ground above it, has yielded large numbers of tombstones.

In addition to this main necropolis there is (iv) a further group of isolated funerary monuments on the high ground above Rhodini, near the head of the ravine. Of these the best preserved is the so-called Ptolemaion, a large rectangular chamber-tomb with an imposing exterior, with undecorated pilasters on all sides (fig. 12) and a rock-cut staircase to an upper storey; the top is not preserved, but it seems likely that it was originally pyramidal in form (fig. 13).[11] The date of the tomb, which was restored in 1924, is quite uncertain. Its pyramidal structure and design have some affinity with Carian monuments, and it is possible that the monument was erected for some eminent Carian individual or family of the period of Carian rule in the middle of the fourth century.[12] Another, newly discovered, tomb in the area consists of a large hypogaeum with a Doric façade of the familiar type.

There is every reason to suppose that this large, connected region of necropoleis continued further south. Five miles from the city, the area of the Turkish village of Asguru (Asgourou; Sgourou; Asgurdu; Svuru), on the southern part (Mangavlí) of the undulating plateau which on the north commences in the Makry Steno area, was a source of numerous tombstones in the last century, and recently a fine isolated hellenistic funerary precinct has been found in the terraced agricultural land lying between the Lindos road and the sea—as the crow flies, a line due east of Asguru hits the coast about 2 km south of Karakonero. The area, once again, gives the impression of terracing, fundamentally natural, but no doubt also man-made in part, in the same way as the area of the eastern necropolis and the city area and the acropolis.

This elaborately planned and widely spread region of tombs and necropoleis indicates that, like some other ancient communities (for example the Cyrenaeans), the Rhodians paid great heed to the disposition and arrangement of their cemeteries, and that on the south-eastern side in particular they took advantage of the natural lie of the land to accommodate funerary monuments in the whole park-like area from the central plateau to the sea; on the west side the steep slope above Trianda Bay did not offer the same opportunities.[12a]

Most of the monuments studied here undoubtedly come from this great necropolis zone. However, it is rarely possible to determine the exact provenance of any particular stone. Neither Hiller von Gaertringen nor the Italian editors of inscriptions were in a position to state precisely where the many hundreds of tombstones discovered or seen between 1890 and 1945 were found, and the published information mostly consists of a general reference to a locality.[13] With the enormous development of Rhodes as a holiday resort since 1950 the situation has changed: land development, especially for the construction of hotels, has been continuous, and modern methods of sinking foundations have brought to light innumerable remains of the ancient city (mostly not tombstones) in the central areas of Mandraki and Neochori, and all such remains, and their associated finds, have been studied by the Greek Archaeological Service, and published, where possible with full details, in the *Archaiologikon Deltion*. (There remain, scattered about the town in the courtyards of private houses, etc., particularly in the old Greek suburbs, and in the surviving older houses of Mandraki and Neochori, a number of funerary monuments, which I have, whenever possible, studied.)

So much by way of preface regarding the topography of the necropolis, and the provenance of the material. There remains to note one preliminary fact of considerable general interest regarding the date of most of the material. Although the total number of recorded tombstones from Rhodes is among the largest, if not the largest, of those found in any Greek city other than Athens, they are mostly of the later hellenistic period. Fourth-century graves are rare, and the surviving tombstones of the fourth century can be counted on the fingers of one hand, and those of the early hellenistic period, in so far as they can be identified as such by their letter forms—say, down to the latter part of the third century— are scarcely more common; those of the later hellenistic age are innumerable. It is true that we must make some allowance for fourth- and third-century material among recorded but lost inscriptions, and that the rendering of letter forms given in Hiller's *Corpus* is frequently extremely misleading, but at the same time Hiller's own remarks on the inscriptions—based on the observations of an extremely acute and already experienced pair of eyes—make it quite clear that very few of the inscriptions he saw within the area of the Turkish city and its environs (including the necropoleis) were in his opinion of the fourth century or of the early hellenistic period. My own study of Hiller's squeezes in Berlin amply confirms that impression on the whole and the accuracy and precision of his dating.

How are we to explain this lack of early material, which was already noted by Maiuri?[14] Is it purely casual and of no significance at all? That does not seem very likely, given the richness of the material of the later period. Is it to be explained on demographic grounds, namely that the population of the city itself was small, and that these early monuments have indeed survived in proportion to the size of population? That is unsatisfactory, for not only have fourth-century graves, in modest numbers, been found, though with no accompanying tombstones, but by the middle of the fourth century Rhodes was already among the leading powers of the eastern Aegean, able to challenge both Athens and Maussollus; and by the middle of the third century she was well on her way to maritime supremacy, and occupied a central economic position in the Aegean world. Such a position was not won and held by a city without adequate resources in manpower—at no time, we may add, does Rhodes seem to have employed mercenaries, and, at the same time, Rhodians did not emigrate in large numbers. The number of Rhodians buried in Athens and Alexandria for instance—a rough indication of this aspect of ancient life—is singularly small.[15]

Two alternative explanations suggest themselves. (i) Extensive pre-hellenistic necropoleis of the city exist, as yet unlocated. This is possible, but unlikely, since they could hardly have been located elsewhere but outside the walls, in the same general area as the later necropolis belt, and in this area, although a certain number of fourth-century tombs have been found, no fourth-century tombstones have come to light. The area further south, around Asguru, may still contain tombs, but those known in that area seem to have been isolated tombs on private properties, and not within regular necropoleis; and in any case, the region is too far from the city to have constituted a main burial area. Alternatively (ii) many of the monuments of the fourth and earlier third century may have been destroyed in antiquity, perhaps at an early date. This seems to me the most likely explanation, though other factors no doubt also contributed. It is well established that funerary monuments were reused for secular purposes after a lapse of time, perhaps of two or three generations; we may recall in this connection the large series of Eretrian tombstones of the late fourth and early third centuries which were reused in the early second century as cover-plates of a very secular drainpipe,[16] and the painted stelai of Pagasae which were reused as packing in the towers of Demetrias at about the same time.[17] Once the tombstones had been removed from the necropolis the chances of their survival obviously diminished. Two occasions in Rhodian history present themselves as particularly suitable occasions for the reuse of such slabs. First, the great tidal wave of 316 B.C. (the third since the foundation of the city in 408),[18] which we know to have flooded, if not submerged, the lower part of the town and to have caused great damage to public and private buildings; and, second, the earthquake of *c.* 225, which again caused very great damage and occasioned rapid rebuilding with outside help.[19] Either or both of these disasters might have led to the use in rebuilding of all available material, including tombstones. This hypothesis seems plausible, and may be tentatively advanced as the main reason for the virtually total disappearance of all Classical and early hellenistic tombstones. If we are to give weight to the comparative absence of third-century tomb-stones as well, we must regard the earthquake as responsible, and not the tidal wave.

A word as to the chronology of the hellenistic monuments. It is evident that some guidance as to dating may be provided by the style both of their decoration, mouldings, bucrania, etc., and of the lettering of the inscriptions. One may be sceptical about the degree of precision of

either criterion, for many of the monuments are crudely worked, and in-
elegantly inscribed, as one might expect in the middle and later hellenistic
periods. I have found it impossible to trace any constant stylistic development in the decorative elements, and attempts to establish a chronology
based on the 'development' of garlands, etc., are of little help when
faced with the quantity of indifferent material available in the Dorian
islands. I have therefore relied more on the lettering to give an approximate date. In any case, in the absence of particular features, I feel it is
hardly possible to date the bulk of the monuments more precisely, on any
criterion, than to 'early' (if any), 'middle', and 'late' hellenistic, and
similarly with the Imperial period. It is regrettable both that Rhodos
should not provide us with regularly dated series of monuments which
reveal the development of epigraphical style, such as exist at both Lindos
and Kamiros, and also that the epigraphical style of the city itself is for
the most part undistinguished, humdrum work which does not allow
precise dating. That may well be a result of the size of the city, and the
consequent development of its social and commercial life; whereas in the
old cities there might be one or two stonemasons who executed both
public and private epigraphical work for a generation or more, in
Rhodos there was, no doubt, a μαρμαρᾶς at every street corner; and the
large and mixed foreign population of the later hellenistic period was
probably not for the most part particular as to the quality of the decoration or of the inscriptions carved on the tombstones. This is one respect in
which the loss of the earlier material makes itself particularly felt, but the
wealth of new material continuing to emerge from the soil of the city
encourages the hope that the gap before the middle and later hellenistic
periods may one day be filled in some measure.

2. THE EARLY MONUMENTS (FIFTH TO THIRD CENTURIES B.C.)

The only archaic monument discovered within the city area is the roughly
inscribed tombstone, probably of the early fifth century B.C., found on
the upper part of Monte Smith, commemorating Charonidas, the son of
Xenotimos (fig. 14).[20] This tombstone may point to an early settlement
at this end of the island, within Ialysian territory; there is no reason why
the Ialysians should have avoided the area later occupied by the city of
Rhodos for normal occupation.[21] A fragmentary but well-executed
funerary stele with a representation of a seated woman, found on the
north coast of the island in the last century, and now in Istanbul (fig.
15),[22] if it is to be dated to the fifth rather than to the fourth century,
may belong to the same settlement; the flowing and plastic lines of the

drapery seem clearly to place it earlier than the famous stele of Krito and Timarista from Kamiros, the inscription of which can itself hardly be earlier than the early years of the fourth century (fig. 16, *a*).[23] There are reports that the line of the city wall, itself of fourth- and third-century construction in its present form, at one point on Monte Smith overlay graves of the fifth century, and that material of the Classical period was found in excavation. However, the material has not been published, and the brief description of it does not clinch the matter, for fifth-century objects may well be found in tombs of the early and middle fourth century.[24] The small but remarkable archaic relief of a bearded man sitting on a stool, now in the Ny Carlsberg Museum, was acquired by Kinch in the city of Rhodes, but no information exists as to its original provenance (fig. 16, *b*).[25] It clearly belongs to the tradition of Archaic art, but it is perhaps not certain that it is funerary rather than dedicatory.[26]

The first funerary relief of the new city of roughly determinable date seems to be the small, but excellently carved, funerary naiskos of Kalliarista, found in Makry Steno in 1931 (fig. 17, *a*).[27] This, the sole surviving complete example of a fourth-century Rhodian funerary relief—probably of the middle of the century—has close links with contemporary Athenian reliefs, and in the softness of line and feature shows Praxitelean influence. The dead woman is shown in the traditional attitude, seated on a klismos, in a relaxed and natural pose, while her serving maid stands facing her; the epigram of three hexameters and two pentameters (carved in two lines on the epistyle) records, without much literary pretension, that the monument was erected by her husband, Damocles.[28] Other reliefs, tentatively dated to the fourth century and of unknown provenance within the city, save for one found 'on Monte Smith', are too damaged for any firm conclusions regarding their style or date to be drawn.[29] A damaged relief of two figures, a seated man and a standing woman, now in Istanbul (fig. 17, *b*), and a representation in Copenhagen of a seated woman holding a curved object, her feet on a footstool, and a smaller standing female figure, below which, in letters of the earlier third century B.C., is the incomplete inscription Χρυσὼ Τιμάνακ[τος] (fig. 17, *c*), are probably the latest examples of the third century of the purely Classic funerary relief.[30]

Some time in the later fourth century a quite different type of funerary monument makes its appearance: the plain stele without relief. Several of these can be dated by their letter forms to the later fourth or early third century. These are sometimes as much as 1·30 m high, but the tendency to carve small monuments, already noticeable in the stele of Krito and Timarista and of Kalliarista, and later so conspicuous in Rhodes in an exaggerated form, is evident, and some of these pieces are hardly more than 0·50 m high. Some have a simple horizontal moulding at top and bottom (fig. 18, *a*, *b*),[31] while others terminate in a triangular pediment with three acroteria, or one central acroterion (fig. 19, *a*, *b*).[32] All stood on rectangular bases with a central cutting to receive the tang of the stele,[33] and the amount of tapering from top to bottom varies considerably.[34] It is a striking feature of these plain, late classical and early hellenistic stelai that they are frequently inscribed unsymmetrically, often towards the bottom of the stone. One example with the inscription *Τίμαρχος*/*Δαμομένευς* (fig. 18, *a*) is inscribed almost casually about one-third below the top of the stele, in small letters which are well off-centre. It is to be noted that the practice of inscribing the name of the deceased towards the lower margin of the stele continued on undecorated stelai down into the later hellenistic period, though the style becomes more formalized and regular in the course of time (fig. 21, *a–d*).[35] The bases themselves are, in the earlier period, plain rectangular blocks, but those inscribed in letters of the second century and later have multiple mouldings on front and side. The receiving bases are, as often as not, inscribed with a complete inscription, and when they are it is natural to suppose that the (lost) stele was not. One or two instances in which a base and stele belonging to each other have been found together show that the reverse was certainly the case; when the stele was inscribed the base was not, unless the inscription was actually completed on the lower member.[36]

Most of the stelai are of a slightly fawn stone distinct from the familiar grey-veined 'Lartian' stone, of which the great majority of funerary monuments of the hellenistic and Roman periods are made. One, of the later fourth century, with an extremely finely cut, symmetrical inscription low on the face, is of a sparkling white marble very rare in Rhodes (fig. 19, *a*).

The fact that most of the plain stelai are inscribed towards the bottom of the stone, and at times unsymmetrically, might lead one to suppose that they originally carried a painted representation of the deceased on the upper part of the stele. There is, however, not the slightest trace of colour on any of the many limestone or marble stelai seen by me, but since one limestone stele (fig. 22) once carried traces of colour, it would be rash to conclude that more may not have done so.[37] An interesting variation of material, and thence of style, is provided by two pedimental stelai (one with acroteria) of poros (fig. 23, *a*, *b*), made in one piece with their bases, which are covered with a rose stucco.[38] Though no trace of a representation survives on either, it is of course probable that these both originally carried a figure or figures in different coloured stuccoes.

As already indicated, only a few tombstones of the third century survive, but those that can be assigned to that period by reason of their letter forms are for the most part plain stelai of the type already described as originating in the fourth century. At present it is not possible to give a general picture of the funerary monuments of the third century, and it is to be hoped that chance will bring to light a necropolis of this period.[39]

3. THE LATER HELLENISTIC AND EARLY IMPERIAL MONUMENTS

The funerary monuments of the later hellenistic period, when Rhodes had become a city with a very large urban population, are very numerous. The large necropoleis in and beyond the ravines south of the city on the east all belong to this period, and most of the monuments now to be considered come from tombs in that area, where the caskets were placed in loculi and the monuments were set above the rock-cut façades in the manner already described. I have not thought it necessary to state the actual provenance of individual monuments (where that is known), but where the information is significant, I have noted it.

In assigning the stones to 'the later hellenistic and early Imperial' periods, I have been guided solely by internal considerations, style, and, above all, letter forms, and have paid no heed to political epochs. The division in the political history of the city, caused by her submission to Rome in 166 B.C., had no effect on her funerary customs, or, for the most part, on other aspects of social life, and may be disregarded in the present context. Even the economic consequences of that event seem to have been slight, in spite of the gloomy announcements of Rhodian politicians at the time, for the Rhodian export trade, in at least one major item—the export of domestic pottery, notably storage amphorae—far from having suffered a serious setback, seems to have developed, as Mediterranean trade in general expanded under Roman influence.[40] Most—but certainly not all—of the monuments here to be considered are probably to be dated after about 150 B.C., and thus belong to the period after Rhodian political ascendancy in the Aegean had lapsed. A very few of them belong to the Imperial period—the first two centuries A.D. and even the third century—and very few are the monuments of Roman citizens, Italian or Greek. This reflects that absence of permanent Roman settlement on Rhodes which is in marked contrast to their presence in large numbers on Cos.[41]

The three main groups, (a) stone cinerary caskets, (b) rectangular monuments, and (c) cylindrical monuments, survive in very large numbers. There are also to be considered two smaller groups; later types of figured and plain stelai, and miscellaneous items (see below, pp. 33 ff.).

For classes (b) and (c) I use either the generic term 'monument' or the more specific term 'altar', for these monuments must be regarded both as inscribed tombstones in the normal sense, like stelai, and also as altars at which offerings for the dead were made in one form or another. That the rectangular altars had this dual function is clear from the fact that they are, save in one respect, of exactly the same design as the votive 'epistatai-altars' of Lindos (see below, pp. 14–15), and may indeed have been transferred to funerary use from the sphere of votive dedications; moreover their design and structure can only be understood in terms of the rituals which were held in the burial areas (see below, pp. 62 ff.). There is no indication of the noun used to describe the rectangular monument; the only reference to one, which occurs in the description of such rituals to be held 'at the monument' of Dionysodoros of Alexandria (below, p. 61), describes it in general terms as τὸ μνημεῖον. For the cylindrical monuments we have the specific testimony of a Coan dedication inscribed on such a monument, that it was called a βωμός (see below, p. 51, and note 278),[41a] and this too corresponds with the rituals that centred round the anniversaries of the dead, ἐπὶ τῶν τόπων—'among the burial-grounds'.

(a) *Cinerary Caskets.*[42] These are normally of white limestone, less frequently of 'Lartian' stone. They invariably have the form of rectangular containers with lids of triangular section, and are thus, on a small scale, of the same shape as the large sarcophagi which are occasionally found in the city (fig. 25, *b*). The surface is worked, but not highly finished. The walls are rather thick (fig. 25, *a–b*), with a rim for the lid to sit on. They stand on short, approximately square feet. Average dimensions are: height (including lid) 0·20–0·25 m, width (long side) 0·35–0·50 m, depth 0·30–0·35 m, height of median of triangular section of lid, 0·07–0·11 m. A large example is 0·41 m high, 0·515 m wide, 0·54 m deep (fig. 26, *b*). There are many hundreds of these containers, and nothing is gained by publishing a full list of the inscribed items;[43] for some characteristic examples see fig. 27, *a, b, c, d*. The caskets are inscribed either on the lid,[44] or (most frequently) on the short side,[45] but not on the long side; many are uninscribed. They are all entirely plain, and, though some are better executed than others (particularly in respect of the lid) they show no development of any sort. As to their date, a few are, to judge by their lettering, of the third century B.C.,[46] and one or two record the names of Roman citizens,[47] but the vast majority are of the later hellenistic period, and at that time they were certainly the regular containers of the ashes of cremated Rhodians alongside the various types of monument used for interment burials. Naturally, the caskets were always placed in the loculi or in chamber-tombs in the necropoleis along with the rest of the funerary furniture and with sarcophagus burials, if any, and not above the loculi or chamber, as were the monuments properly so called, to be considered below. We shall see that this is a fact of some significance in interpreting the inscriptions (see below, pp. 52 ff.).

The distribution of these small caskets is strictly limited. A few examples (but only a few) have been found in the neighbouring Rhodian islands, and in the Peraea (fig. 28), but that is all.[48] Similar, but not identical, caskets occur in small numbers in some cities of Asia Minor, notably Pergamon and Sardis (figs. 29, *a–c*, 30),[49] but the Rhodian variant is recognizable by its complete lack of decorative elements.[50] There is no reason to suppose a link between the various regions in this respect, for the employment of this shape of casket for ashes clearly derives from the use of the sarcophagus for inhumation; it evidently developed subsequently on its own, in places where, as at Rhodes, the sarcophagus was not in general use in the post-Classical period. The familiar ash-casket of Imperial Rome differs fundamentally in shape, for it is far more cubical, and rarely gable-lidded, to say nothing of the invariably ornate decoration.[51]

(*b*) *Rectangular Altars.*[52] This class of monument must be considered from various points of view. We may begin with a general description of the basic form and dimensions of the altars.

The form is the same, whatever the size. The front face of the rectangular block is divided horizontally into four almost unvarying sections: (*a*) a lower multiple moulding and fascia with spreading foot and sides, (*b*) the main body of the monument, carrying the inscription and decorative elements, if any, (*c*) an upper multiple moulding and fascia corresponding closely to the lower, crowned by (*d*) an architecturally formed upper surface, which has been hollowed to leave on three sides a deep wide margin terminating in the front in a projecting double cornice as on an aedicula. In the better-executed pieces there is often a faint, smooth, narrow margin, *c*. 0·01–0·02 m deep, along the front edge of the upper surface and around the inner side and back faces of the raised margins. In addition to the frontal decoration, the sides are usually decorated with a pediment terminating in a central palmette-acroterion the top of which lies flush with the upper cornice of the margin. Such is the basic form of the altars. Their dimensions vary considerably, and they may be classed as 'small', 'medium', and 'large', their approximate dimensions being (*a*) small, height 0·35 m, width 0·40–0·45 m, depth 0·20–0·25 m, (*b*) medium, height 0·45 m, width 0·50–0·55 m, depth 0·30 m, (*c*) large, height 0·50 m, width 0·65 m, depth 0·35 m. The total range of monuments is therefore roughly between 0·35 and 0·50 m in height, 0·40 and 0·65 m in width, and 0·20 and 0·35 m in depth. Some even larger monuments of this class were constructed with a separate upper member, of which several survive

(though none of the corresponding lower members) (fig. 31, *a*, *b–c*).[53]
These upper members have a width of up to 1 m and a depth of 0·70 m.

The physical aspect of the stones varies little. They are mostly of dark or mottled grey 'Lartian' stone, while a few of the largest size are of the white marble, which existed, and still exists, in small quantities in the island, and others are of the almost rose-red stone found on Mount Profiti Elia, and called, or once called, σωμακί.[54] The front and sides of all monuments are worked to a uniform smoothness, while the back is carefully rough-picked, but is not smooth. Under surfaces are smoother than the back, with either a small rough-picked rectangular area or a clamp-hole in the centre. The stones therefore rested on a lower member, and since not a single rectangular base with a central rough-picked area or a clamp-hole corresponding to a rectangular monument survives, it is possible that the monuments were mostly placed not on a base, but on a larger architectural member, i.e. on the prepared terrace on which they rested. Nevertheless, the fact that some of the altars are uninscribed is an indication that, like the circular monuments shortly to be discussed, they at least stood on an inscribed base; and two examples on which the base is actually formed in one piece with the altar itself (fig. 32, *a*, *b*), serve to show the appearance of the complete monument.[55]

Rectangular altars of this general type seem to have been used both as dedicatory and as funerary monuments. Though there is no example of the former class from Rhodos, Lindos provides numerous examples of it. There, rectangular altars with the upper surface hollowed out, leaving a margin, and with pedimental sides, are not infrequent as dedicatory monuments from the early second century B.C. onwards. They are almost invariably employed for one type of dedication, those made by epistatai to Athana Lindia and Zeus Polieus, and perhaps to other gods,[56] at the end of their annual period of office, 'on behalf of themselves and of those serving with them'. Although other forms of dedication are made by epistatai—plain rectangular and cylindrical altars[57]—no other form of epistatai-dedication can be said to constitute a regular series, and at the same time there are only three dedications of such altars by persons other than epistatai—one by two nakoroi, and two by officials described as ὁ ἐπὶ τοῦ δοχείου.[58] We may therefore accept the description of these altars used by the Danish excavators of Lindos, and call them 'epistatai-altars'.[59] I illustrate as examples of this class of Lindian monument, *ILind.* 209, of *c.* 160 B.C. (fig. 33, *a*), and 230 of 134 B.C. (fig. 33, *b*). It is further to be observed that on the earliest epistatai-altar, *ILind.* 149, of 198 B.C., the sides have only the continuation of the upper and lower front mouldings, and have no pediment (fig. 34, *a*). The same feature recurs on another relatively early piece, no. 195, of 169 B.C. which is also without upper margins (fig. 34, *b*).[60]

So much for the Lindian altars. We may note here that there is evidence for only one similar altar at Kamiros, an altar dedicated to Apollo Apotropaios and Hekate Propylaia (fig. 35, *a*, *b*).[61] It possesses all the features of the Lindian altars, though it is more nearly cubical than most of them (height 0·48 m, width 0·39 m, depth 0·29 m). The absence of a series at Kamiros similar to that at Lindos is not surprising,[62] for on the whole the votive monuments of the two cities differ; at Lindos, apart from the epistatai-altars, the cylindrical predominates, at Kamiros the rectangular base.[63] In particular, the dedications by Kamiran epistatai and strategi were usually carved on votive stone shields (fig. 36),[64] a type of monument which is also, though less frequently, used for military dedications at Lindos.[65]

In Rhodos the same rectangular altars with upper and lower profiles and pedimental sides are found in abundance, but with this fundamental difference, that there the type of altar seems, on the present evidence, to have been used exclusively as a funerary monument, and never for votive purposes. This restriction of use must be considered together with one particular feature of the Rhodian monuments: the presence of one or two circular bosses on the hollowed-out upper surface of a large number of them. I illustrate a representative selection of these monuments in figs. 37, *a–d*, 38, *a–d*. Of this remarkable feature no satisfactory explanation has been given, and it will be considered here in some detail, even if its significance cannot be determined beyond a doubt. Only one monument with a boss (an upper member only) is known from Lindos (fig. 31, *b*, *c*); it was probably not found on the acropolis, but in the outskirts of the lower town, and may be regarded as a funerary monument; it has a single boss.[66]

A representation of one such rectangular altar with bucrania and garlands may be seen on a recently found monument with a representation of a 'Totenmahl' (fig. 50, *b*).[66a] The altar is placed in the left corner of the relief, behind the usual seated figures, and seems to be decorated with one bucranion and one stag's head (as on some surviving examples); above it, an upper element consists of an arched offering-niche of the type familiar from many surviving examples, and a tree and snake are represented across the arch and the altar. Although the offering-niche does not occur on surviving rectangular funerary monuments, it is evident that the monument portrayed is of the same basic type as those studied here.

First, it is to be emphasized that by no means all the funerary altars have the boss, though they all have the margins and architectural design. Out of a total of some seventy-five monuments of this class that I have studied (probably most of the surviving material), the largest single group (30) has no bosses at all (figs. 37, *d*, 39, *b–d*), though those with two bosses are almost equally numerous (28), while there are sixteen with one boss, and one sport with three. As the examples reproduced here show, the bosses stand either centrally, when only one (fig. 38, *a–d*), or symmetrically when there are two (fig. 37, *a–c*), on the upper surface; like the surrounding margins, they are carefully cut, but not, like the front and side faces, worked smooth with an abrasive. The base of the boss is a true circle, and the sides are slightly sloping (fig. 40, *a*); it is therefore a truncated cone; the top surface is unbroken save for a small pin-sized hole (fig. 40, *a*) which is not always discernible. The bosses naturally vary in size according to whether they are one or two, and according to the size of the actual monument. According to the three divisions into 'large', 'medium', and 'small' monuments above (p. 13), the average circumference varies from *c.* 0·070 m on the small monuments with two bosses, to 0·18 m on large altars with one boss; their height is always the same as that of the surrounding margin, with which they are flush (fig. 40, *b*), having, like them, been left when the rest of the upper surface was cut away. They thus have nothing in common, beyond their basic circularity, with the much larger, almost flat, circular cushion on the upper surface of a rectangular altar in Athens, which has careful picking and anathyrosis on its upper surface, and was evidently the base for another, smaller circular stone, which crowned the monument (fig. 41, *a–b*),[67] or with another, similar epithema on a circular altar of the age of Augustus with triglyph-frieze on Thera (fig. 40, *d*).

One other, less basic difference from the Lindian votive altars lies in the fact that although most of the funerary altars have only the simple decoration of mouldings and side pediments (fig. 40, *b, c*), others are more richly decorated. The simplest form of decoration is to be seen on a well-executed piece in white marble with two bosses (figs. 37, *b*, 40, *b*), on which one of the upper profiles on front and sides consists of a careful dentil-moulding;[68] it is surprising that this decoration occurs on only one of the otherwise plain pieces, although it is also found on one or two isolated upper members. One or two others have honorific wreaths carved on them, representing the honours paid during life or after death to the deceased (fig. 42, *a–b*), but this decoration is representational, and will be considered later (below, p. 68).

One large group of monuments has bucrania with suspended wreaths and pendent fillets on front and sides (figs. 42, *c–d*, 43, *a–d*). On these, which, by chance of survival perhaps, are all of 'Lartian' stone, the execution and the amount of decorative detail vary considerably. The bucrania are more frequently of the later, narrow, skeletal type than of the full fleshed type and the garlands are rather meagre: see further the discussion of the bucrania on the circular altars, below, pp. 27 ff. Not all are inscribed, but among those that are is one piece with two bosses,

carrying the inscription Καρποφόρου καὶ τῶν αὐτοῦ ζών(τω)ν, which is
among the latest of the whole series of surviving funerary altars, being
hardly earlier than the third century A.D. (fig. 43, *b*).[69] On this piece,
alone among surviving rectangular examples, the bucrania have no
fillets, though this is not infrequent on circular ones.

Another small class consists of those altars with a recessed rectangular
panel on which is carved in relief a funerary scene. The relief panels
occupy differing amounts of the front face; sometimes there is only
a narrow margin on either side, whereas on others the panel and the
margins each occupy about half the total area. There are four or five simple
scenes of parting in which the deceased is represented sitting on a chair
or lying on a couch, taking farewell of one or more figures (figs. 44, *a*,
45, *a*, *b*).[70] In another instance a full funerary banquet scene is represented
(fig. 45, *c*),[71] while in a third, the deceased, a kitharode, is represented
alone, sitting on a chair and playing on his lyre (fig. 45, *d*).[72] One or two
of these stones are uninscribed, but it is evident from the style of the relief
no less than from those inscriptions which survive, that they are not earlier
than the later hellenistic age. The free-standing funerary banquet-relief
plaque is not a frequent type of monument at Rhodes,[73] and it appears
that the present type, in which the relief is subordinated to the design of
the altar, was more in vogue. It is noteworthy that in a few pieces—one
rectangular altar, and two circular ones, all uninscribed—the relief panel
has been fully cut and smoothed, but left without relief, though in other
respects the monuments are complete.[74]

Three rectangular altars, all of late hellenistic date, stand alone by
reason of their ornate decoration. One, with two bosses and a dentilled
upper moulding, is the tombstone of Komos of Laodicea (fig. 46).[75] On
the front, (fig. 46, *a*), between the upper and lower mouldings and two
filleted laurel wreaths to left and right, a scene of parting is carved on a
projecting ledge; the deceased man, behind whom stands the figure of a
child, is bidding farewell to a woman seated on a draped chair, with her
feet on a footstool; behind her stands another child; the inscription,
Κώμου Λαοδικέως, is engraved on the lower moulding, below the projecting ledge. The back of the monument carries a virtually identical
scene, but no inscription (fig. 46, *b*). The left and right sides are identical
the one to the other. They are pedimental, the central acroterion being
(uniquely among surviving rectangular altars) of the palmette type, and
the dentilled moulding is continued from the front face (fig. 46, *c*, *d*). In
the field on either side, a female figure is dancing or running towards the
right, holding in her right hand, extended naturally behind her, an
object which is damaged in both representations, and in her no less
naturally raised left hand a circular object, perhaps a castanet, which she
is clasping by means of a grip or handle on the inner side. The figures

closely resemble those on the rock-cut funerary peribolos of the Rider at
Cova, already described (p. 4), and also the winged figures on some of the
large, ornamental circular altars (see below, pp. 31–2). They are therefore probably a recognized funerary motif. Here, however, they may also
constitute, in part at least, a deliberate play on the name of the deceased,
Komos, the Revel.[76] The piece as a whole is a fair specimen of hellenistic
Rhodian funerary art at a modest level, its Classical models still clearly
visible alike in theme and in execution.

The second piece, in Rhodes, a well-preserved monument of white
marble, is the most elaborate specimen of this type of altar, and very
different from the classical style of the Vienna piece (fig. 47, *a*).[77] It is
uninscribed, and must be dated by the decoration and by the style of the
figures. The upper surface carries two fully preserved bosses, and the
usual margins. The front and sides are richly moulded above, with an
Ionic frieze consisting of ovolo, astragal, and dentils, with, below them, a
fascia containing on the front three double rosettes, alternating with two
bucrania, all joined by swags. Below this is a naiskos-form composition
consisting of two antae, the left hollowed out and occupied by a female
figure in high relief, in a position of mourning, the right un-hollowed and
carrying two olive wreaths in relief, one below the other. The sunk field
between the antae is occupied by a bed with tall legs on which is stretched
out the figure of the dead man in high relief, represented naked to below
the waist, lying facing the onlooker, with the right arm raised behind his
head, the left extended over the edge of the bed clutching loosely a
kantharos from which he may be supposed to have been drinking. Below
the bed on the main surface of the altar are two further wreaths which
extend over the lower fascia. Below the fascia is an elaborate Ionic
moulding. The sides are plain. The approximate date of the piece is
sufficiently indicated by the slack, loosely formed body of the dead man
and the elongated figure of the mourner, and by the general composition,
as of the later hellenistic period; the carefully executed and elaborate
mouldings are characteristic of this date.

The third ornamented piece is from the Rhodian incorporated island,
Nisyros, and in some ways closely resembles the previous piece (figs. 48,
a, *b*, 49, *a*).[78] It has one central boss, instead of two, but its mouldings
and friezes are similar in detail to those of the Rhodian pieces. The upper
member of the cornice, immediately below the upper surface, normally
left plain, is here uniquely occupied by a triglyph-frieze (the metopes,
now damaged, were probably left empty), below which is a cyma
reversa, consisting of ovolo, astragal, dentils, and bucrania-frieze, as on
the previous piece; all these features, except the triglyph-frieze, being
continued on the pedimental short side(s) (only the left side survives,
fig. 48, *b*). The pediment and atticas of the side face are masterpieces of

minute carving; in the centre of the pediment is a bucranion, to left and right of which are running tendrils, while in each corner of the lower attica is a rosette with tendrils running towards the centre, and in the upper attica, to left and right of the central acroterion, are, on the left, a linked rosette and bucranion, and, on the right, a bucranion and a rosette (see the details in fig. 48, *b*). The lower mouldings of the front face are as on the other piece, astragal, cyma reversa, and guilloche mouldings, but the plain fascia is replaced by a square meander. The centre of the monument is occupied by a simple circular wreath, perhaps of laurel, behind which is placed obliquely a long, pole-like object, which appears to be a spear or a shepherd's staff.[79] Below the wreath is inscribed un-symmetrically, in letters of late hellenistic date, Μέναν δρε χρηστὲ χαῖρε, above which, at a later date, was inscribed in an irregular, cursive hand —ηρος / Ἀφροδίσιος.

One detail of decoration, which stands by itself, may be noted here. One altar, erected in memory of a Galatian named Πάρνασσος, without bosses, but with an elaborate and well-executed design of one bucranion and one stag's head respectively on front and sides (fig. 43, *c–d*),[80] carries on the front faces of the upper surrounding margin, which is normally left plain between its upper and lower projecting fasciae, small representations of a Rhodian rose on the left, and a head of Helios on the right. Not only is the piece unique among surviving examples in being decorated in this position, but the representations themselves are worthy of consideration (fig. 44, *b*, *c*, enlarged). These are the only simple, popular representations of the symbols of Rhodes known, other than those on the stamps of amphorae,[81] which, in the case of Helios at least, are very crude, and these small pieces of sculpture thus provide an indication of what ordinary masons, as opposed to more lavishly patronized sculptors, produced in this field. It is also of interest to compare them with the representations of the same objects on Rhodian coins; the rose resembles that of contemporary coins fairly closely, but the head of Helios, chubby and overblown, almost childish, with snub nose and rather straight locks, is quite different from the Helios of the coins.[82] It is noteworthy also that the surviving relatives of the Galatian, who was not a Rhodian citizen, should have felt inclined to ornament his tombstone with these symbols. It may be an indication of the attachment that the large foreign population of the city may have felt to their adopted home; it can hardly be dismissed as conventional decoration.

These pieces apart, the rectangular funerary altars are plain and simple monuments, and their most remarkable feature is undoubtedly the boss(es) on the upper surface. No adequate explanation of these has been offered as yet, and further consideration of them is desirable. Those who were first confronted with them were evidently unwilling to speculate about their significance. Hiller von Gaertringen, who published at least two altars of this group,[83] described the pedimental decoration of the sides, but omitted all mention of the bosses or the surrounding margin. His formula is: 'ara rectangula . . . cuius latera aetomatis sunt ornata', and 'ara rectangula a dextro sinistroque latere aetomatis ornata', and he does not distinguish them from another example with pedimental sides and no bosses.[84] Maiuri, who published some sixteen of these altars, normally made no reference either to the pedimental sides or to the bosses.[85] His only clear statement as to their significance was in his publication of the marble decorated piece (fig. 47, *a*), of which he said,[86] 'dal piano superiore, incassato e contornato da tre lati, sporgono due piccole basi cilindriche, destinate probabilmente a fissare l'incastro della mensa lignea delle offerte funebri'. Subsequently, L. Laurenzi, in republishing the same stone, spoke of the presence 'delle zone più alte' on the upper surface, but made no attempt to explain them.[87] Finally, G. Susini, in his recent publication of two altars with two bosses from Telos,[88] described the bosses, 'due cippetti troncoconici', as 'una singolare sopravvivenza del più semplice segnacolo funerario entro l'architettura dell'ara'.

These explanations hardly grasp the problem, and certainly do not solve it. The possibilities are in fact strictly limited, and may be considered in general terms: are the bosses purely decorative, in the way, for example, that frieze or garlands may be so described; are they functional, i.e. do they fulfil a practical function, as suggested by Maiuri, who (as quoted above) claimed that they were supports for a wooden sacrificial table or, we may add, for a fire-grate, or perhaps for something different; or are they representational, that is, do they represent something, some object, and, if so, are they purely representational, or are they symbolic of some state or condition? In considering these possibilities we must bear in mind that the bosses are not essential features of these altars; many, like the Lindian epistatai-dedications, are without bosses, which were therefore not an essential part of the structure of the monument as such.

First, there is no rigid correspondence between the number of bosses on the altar and the number of people commemorated in the accompanying inscription. It is true that a majority of the altars commemorate a husband and wife, and equally that a majority have two bosses; but the two sets of figures do not tally precisely, and the approximation must be judged fortuitous. Thus, leaving on one side those instances in which the presence or absence of one (or two) bosses is uncertain owing to damage to the stone, or to later deliberate removal of the boss (which seems to have occurred quite often), and also those in which the number of persons commemorated is uncertain, we find several instances in which more than two persons are recorded on a stone with two bosses, and even on a stone with one boss.[89] Thus the bosses cannot be regarded as corresponding precisely to the number of persons; in other words, they do not 'stand for' the deceased. Similarly, physical reasons apart, they cannot be interpreted, as has been suggested,[90] as the bases for small statues or protomae.

The second possibility is that they were functional. It has been suggested that they formed the permanent supports of a sacrificial table, or some similar object, for example a brazier or oven or a fire-brick, for burnt sacrifices. Such objects are known from sacrificial scenes on vases,[91] and it is evident that the braziers, normally of terracotta, might be set on the upper surface of the altar; and when seen in side view, as on a vase, they bear a resemblance to the appearance that would be presented by the bosses if they were surmounted by a fire-brick and seen in profile. Nevertheless, unless we take refuge in the supposition that our bosses are connected, in some unexplained way, with the use of braziers in sacrifice, this solution is not very satisfactory. Granted that brazier-supports or fire-bricks, usually made of terracotta with an insulating layer of crushed fireproof wood and mortar, were placed on altars in this way, we must ask first of all, why it is that the votive epistatai-altars from Lindos, all dedicated to Athana and Zeus, were not furnished with them. And if it be answered that such brazier-supports were used especially for burnt offerings to the dead, then why do not all the Rhodian funerary altars have them? And again, it is not easy to conceive of a local output of braziers, some of which required but one boss to support them, and others two, and others yet again even three. Such variation in manufacture is hardly conceivable for a stereotyped, mass-produced object. And yet again, what practical purpose would be served by constructing a fire-pan, or other object, of such shape as to sit over these low bosses, when it would sit perfectly well on the margins without the bosses, as can be seen on vases on which the fire-brick rests on volutes?[92]

These considerations (and others) reveal the difficulty of explaining the bosses as supports of a fire-brick or of a portable sacrificial table; the hypothesis, attractive in its practical simplicity, seems to raise more problems than it solves. It is, of course, possible that the Rhodian style of fire-pan was, in spite of these objections, so constructed, and we cannot exclude this solution categorically. It is equally difficult to regard them as simple decorative elements. They certainly do not belong to the common repertoire of decoration found on stelai and altars, and though, once more, it is not possible to deny categorically that they may have had a decorative value for the ancient Rhodian, this is not evident to the modern observer. Moreover, as a general practice, decorative features on monuments are not free-standing but carved in relief. The Rhodian altars of this class certainly have one invariable decorative feature, the pedimental sides, but the bosses, as their frequent absence indicates, were not an obligatory addition to it.

An alternative functional explanation presents itself, namely that they served as collars round which to hang wreaths. At first sight the bosses may seem rather small for this purpose—the small bosses, it will be recalled, have a diameter of *c.* 0·07 m—and also in some instances rather close-set, but much must have depended on the type of wreath. This interpretation finds considerable support in the discovery at Kamiros of a small free-standing circular boss (fig. 49, *d*), standing on a base and surrounded by an olive wreath; the inscription records the honours bestowed by a koinon on an individual, 'praising him and crowning him', and the boss here, surrounded by the wreath, no doubt represents the act of crowning.[93] It seems likely that there is a link between this honorific monument and our bosses, and that the bosses are in fact collars for vegetal or artificial funerary wreaths. This is supported by the traces—very faint traces, save in one instance[94]—half-way down some of the bosses of a slight projection or rim right round them, which was certainly insufficient to grip any substantial artefact or utensil, but which might nevertheless serve as an effective seat for a small wreath or fillet. I am inclined to regard this as the most probable use of the bosses.

One alternative explanation must also be considered. It is possible that the bosses are in one way or another representational, either in the simple sense that they represent an object, either in or for itself, or as having symbolic reference to life after death, to the underworld, or even to death itself. We enter here a world of thought and feeling in which, before the development of the explicit funerary symbolism of the Imperial period, it is extremely hazardous to identify the intentions of the individual concerned in the commissioning of the monument; for, quite apart from the representation of objects for their own sake, conscious symbolism may be succeeded by a repetitive and conventional use of the same symbol, in which the symbolic value of the object represented has been forgotten. Thus the two notions of pure decoration and symbolism, which seem at first sight to be fundamentally opposed to each other, may nevertheless in some cases have been unconsciously merged.

Among symbolic objects in the present context it is natural to think of cones, which occur frequently as funerary epithemata, or even as complete monuments, in various parts of Greece and Italy.[95] Such objects, of which there may be examples from Rhodes itself (see below), are, however, quite different in appearance from our bosses and it would need much ingenuity to associate them or their symbolism (phallic, chthonic, or whatever it may be) with them. As symbols, the bosses resemble nothing so much as simple representations of a class of objects closely associated with chthonic and funerary rites, circular sacrificial cakes. These went by many names and were of as many varieties as names, and it is not always possible to decide what the form of any particular cake was.[96] However, it seems clear that, of those called by the most familiar names, the πελανός, the πόπανον, and the πυραμίς, the first was for the most part liquid meal, and might be said to be poured, the second was a cake made of honey and meal and basically circular,[97] while the third derived its name from its shape.[98] Scholiastic and lexico-graphical sources make it clear that these cakes were placed on the altars used in funerary and chthonic cults,[99] and correspondingly they appear regularly in many different shapes on the table laid before the deceased on 'Totenmahl' reliefs.[100] That such cakes were used in Rhodian funerary cults is clear from the epitaph of the Platonist Arideikes, who died *c.* 200 B.C. This states that μείλια and πελανοί would be offered at his grave in burnt offerings,[101] and though, as always, it is difficult to know exactly what is meant by πελανοί, it is evident that rituals for the dead of the type under discussion were celebrated.[102] Could our bosses represent, in a very formal way, such cakes? I do not think so, but the answer does not consist of an easy negative. A 'Totenmahl' relief from Ainos of the mid fourth century, now in Istanbul (fig. 52, *a*), carries, beneath or in front of the table with cakes and fruits, a representation of a rectangular altar with volutes, forming a sunken upper surface as on the Rhodian altars, with four or five cakes and fruits of various shapes placed in the sunken area. The altar might almost be Rhodian, save that the rectilinear margins are apparently replaced by curved volutes; the back margin is clear.[103] There is, however, a real difference between the bosses on the Rhodian altars and the representation of cakes and fruits in general, and in particular on the relief from Ainos; whereas the cakes and fruits are for the most part very naturalistically portrayed in different shapes, the Rhodian bosses are very rigid and geometrical, and monotonously similar in appearance, and as representations of the cakes they simply do not convince. Nevertheless, the Ainian altar is important, for it enables us to see that the upper sunken surface was naturally used as a receptacle, and was not merely a form of ash-grate. Returning, therefore, to our earlier hypothesis that the bosses were stands or collars for chaplets, we may see how the idea of having a boss, or bosses, in the upper surface would arise naturally: if fruits and cakes, why not something more permanent? As we shall see in more detail below (pp. 61 ff.), the Rhodians were particularly fond of honouring both the living and the dead with wreaths, and this practice was frequently expressed, when an especial honour bestowed by a corporate body was involved, by carving crowns and wreaths on tombstones. The bosses served a similar purpose, with the difference that actual wreaths were placed on them on commemorative occasions. We can now understand why the Lindian epistatai-altars, which are votive, do not have the bosses: gods were not crowned at sacrifices. At the same time the Ainian parallel shows us that the original use of the upper surface was as a receptacle for gifts, and both at Lindos and Rhodos it may have been used for sacrificial offerings and libations of one sort or another. This explains why on the better-executed pieces, the upper surface of the altar slopes down towards the front edge; it was to allow the libation to flow away easily.[104] We can also understand why not all the funerary altars have the bosses; the presence or absence of these collars was obviously a matter of choice for the survivors, and the decision was dictated probably by financial considerations; there must have been a considerable expense involved in the working of the upper surface in such a way as to leave the bosses.

Finally we can now see why, far from being a survival of an earlier form of funerary monument, the bosses only make their appearance along with the rectangular altars themselves; they were a natural response to the existence of the sunken 'sacrificial' area, if we may so describe it, and developed from it; in this development the mason's *horror vacui* may have played no less decisive a part than the necessity of providing a permanent feature for the commemorative purpose indicated. It is natural that the bosses occur only on the rectangular altars with the recessed upper surfaces, and do not occur on the other large class of monument, the circular altar about to be discussed; the circular surface of the cylindrical monument did not provide a suitable location for them, in the same way that the upper surface of the altar did.[105]

Distribution of the rectangular altar. Whether we choose to regard the bosses as brazier-supports or as wreath collars, the exclusively Rhodian nature of the funerary altars is borne out and emphasized by their distribution.

It has wrongly been stated that the altars have only been found on Rhodes itself.[106] They are in fact known, as might be expected, from both the Incorporated Peraea and the Incorporated Islands. Examples survive from the Peraean regions of Bozburun and Karaça and Loryma (figs. 52, *b* (drawing); 44, *a*; 54, *c*),[107] and also from Telos (fig. 53, *a*, *b*; cf. 49, *b*, *c*),[108] Nisyros (figs. 48, *a*, *b*, 49, *a*; 53, *c*, *d*; 54, *a*),[109] Chalke,[110] and, perhaps, Syme (fig. 54, *b*).[111] There can thus be no doubt that the usage extended over the Rhodian state as a whole. This is of some interest, since Telos does not appear to have been incorporated until the late third, or early second century B.C.,[112] and Nisyros probably became Rhodian in 200 B.C.;[113] before that, both were independent, and their links were rather with Cos than with Rhodes.[114] It is then likely that this type of funerary monument spread to these islands after their incorporation in the Rhodian state.[115] They are not survivals of the pre-Rhodian period, and their introduction to these islands and to the

Peraea must be added to the list of those features of Rhodian life which that state exported, consciously or unconsciously, to its dependencies and incorporated territories. On the other hand, the only example now in Cos (fig. 54, *d*) is almost certainly of Rhodian origin, being, it seems, of 'Lartian' stone; it presumably reached Cos casually at some time, from Rhodes or Nisyros.[116] A well-preserved example in the British Museum (figs. 55 and 56, *a*), stated on dubious evidence to be from Iasos, may also have come originally from the Peraea.[117] The exclusively Rhodian character of this type of monument marks it off from the other large group, the cylindrical altars, and emphasizes its especial link with the Rhodian funerary cult.[118]

(*c*) *Cylindrical Monuments.* These are the commonest of all hellenistic funerary monuments on Rhodes, and, though the size and decoration varies slightly, they are fundamentally all very similar, and their basic form is invariable. They stand normally on a simple, unprofiled rectangular base terminating in a low circular projection with a simple moulding, the trochilus, with an anathyrosis on which the altar itself stands (figs. 59, *c*, 60, *a–c*, etc.).[119] At times the base consists of a profiled block of two stages, either of a simple form (fig. 58, *a*), or of a more complex type in which the upper block is recessive to the lower, the profiles either simple or multiple (fig. 58, *b–d*);[120] and in some instances the circular monument stands on a circular multi-profiled lower member (fig. 59, *a*, *b*).[121] The base normally bears the inscription, though the simplest blocks are sometimes uninscribed. It is only rarely that monument and base are found together (fig. 59, *c*),[122] and numbers of unassociated bases and monuments may be seen in the museum at Rhodes. Sometimes the two original elements have been assembled, but for the most part the association is modern, and the individual monuments must be considered without reference to the base on which they now stand.[123]

The altars themselves normally have a multiple moulding at the base, next to the trochilus—usually a plain cyma recta and cyma reversa with undecorated mouldings between—and a similar moulding either at the top (figs. 58, *b*, 60, *a*), or, more frequently, a short distance below the top; in the latter case, there is a further plain cavetto moulding and profile at the top (figs. 59, *a*, *c*, 60, *b*, *c*).[124] The upper surface is smooth and flat, with no provision for further attachment. As already noticed, the bosses, which are so conspicuous a feature of the rectangular altars, are never found on the circular ones.

The cylindrical monuments may have their prototypes in the plain forms of votive monuments. These are not particularly frequent at Rhodos,[125] where rectangular votive monuments predominate, but they were

employed at Kamiros, along with rectangular monuments, for the normal collective dedications by the Kamiran colleges of magistrates—the
eponymous damiourgoi, the hieropoioi, and the archieristas—of which a
long series survives from the third and second centuries B.C. (fig. 61, *b*).[126]
The latest example at Kamiros is the dedicatory base of a statue of
Trajan (fig. 61, *c*). At Lindos they appear frequently as bases of votive
monuments from about the mid third century B.C. onwards.[127] Such
cylindrical bases are invariably plain, while the funerary monuments in
Rhodos are almost as invariably decorated, principally with bucrania,[128]
and similarly on the votive monument the inscription normally occupies
the main field of the cylinder, the lower member remaining uninscribed,
whereas on the tombstone the decoration on the body restricted the
space available for the inscription, and the inscription is almost always
engraved on the rectangular base.

Decoration: Mouldings. The simple upper and lower mouldings are
sometimes replaced by more elaborate profiles. These may take various
forms. Especially noteworthy is a group of mouldings of large altars, of
which in almost every instance there survives only the upper or the lower
moulding; these were often later hollowed out and adapted for use as the
basin of Turkish fountains. Like the upper members of the large rectangular altars (above, pp. 13–14), these large epithemata were made
separately and attached by a clamp, and their separation from the main
cylinder was not difficult. The large altars were mostly of white marble,
like the larger rectangular altars, and the profiles and mouldings are of
very high quality (fig. 64, *a–c*).[129] A typical altar, of the 'Nike' group
discussed below, has the following decoration from the top downwards
(fig. 84, *a*, *b*): (*a*) above, cavetto moulding with palmette frieze; cyma
recta; ovolo; astragal; dentils; fascia with bucrania and rosettes linked
by festoons; (*b*) below, rectangular meander; fascia; astragal; cyma
reversa. Another, considerably larger (diam. 1·03 m), now forming
the basin of the Turkish fountain in the corner of the garden of the
Metropolitan of the Dodecanese (fig. 64, *b*),[130] has a similar lower
moulding consisting of a rectangular rosette-meander below which are an
astragal, a cyma recta, a cavetto cornice, and a cyma reversa. One large
upper element of red stone (see p. 14) has only dentils as a moulding,
a consequence perhaps of the very hard stone. An intermediate stage
between the simple and the elaborated mouldings is represented by an
altar of 'Lartian' stone with the normal bucrania, but with the simple
upper mouldings replaced by dentils, below which is a fascia with rosettes
(fig. 64, *d*).[131]

In one or two instances the mouldings of the altars show clear traces of
colour, and it is probable that at least on those of the usual grey 'Lartian'
stone the decorative elements were regularly picked out in colour (fig.

60, *c*).[132] The only surviving colour is white, but polychromy, so widely spread in Greek funerary art, seems likely.

Body decoration. In general limits the body decoration of the monument consists of three or four bucrania with or without fillets, connected by swags or other linking elements.[133] The bucrania, occasionally replaced by very similar looking skeletal, or semi-skeletal, deer's heads with antlers, are mostly naturalistically portrayed as short and broad, with clearly marked features—nostrils, eyes, central tuft of hair, ears, and horns (sometimes with a string of pearls across the forehead, and with pendant fillets and pearls)—which is the characteristic form in the second and first centuries B.C.; the earlier, elongated form of semi-skeletal head found on architectural friezes at Samothrace (fig. 65, *a*),[134] and Pergamon (fig. 66, *a*, *c*)[135] in the third century, and the later fully skeletal type (see above, p. 16, for such variations on the rectangular altars) are less frequent. It seems probable that this naturalistic development may itself have originated in monumental architecture at Pergamon, for such bucrania alternating with eagles, along with garlands, are found there on the Temple of Athena Nikephoros in the early second century;[136] but in any case it was widely dispersed in the course of the second century. On the Pergamene friezes along with the bucrania we find also the various other elements, the fillets and the garlands, as on the Rhodian altars, in contrast to the earlier Samothracian friezes where the bucrania are, as in the fourth century, represented in isolation.[137] In general the Rhodian garlands conform to the same style; they are naturalistically divided at their point of lowest gravity, frequently indicated by a suspended bunch of grapes, the leaves of the left half opening towards the right, those of the right towards the left. The leaves are for the most part of ivy and laurel, the fruit most commonly grapes, apples, and pomegranates (figs. 60, *b*, *c*, 67, *a*, *b*).[138] The field between the suspended garlands and the upper moulding may at times be filled by a wreath (fig. 67, *b*).[139] On architectural friezes, rosettes and phialai are so used (as occasionally on smaller monuments, including altars, but not at Rhodes), as on some Pergamene examples (fig. 66, *c*, *d*),[140] but not wreaths. On the altars it is probable that a crown or wreath either refers to the honours bestowed in life on the deceased, as on other Rhodian tombstones, or alternatively stands for the wreath as an object of funerary practice and cult (see above, pp. 23–4, below, pp. 61 ff.).

One conspicuous variation of the naturalistic garland of fruit and leaves is the tubular type of garland consisting solely of graduated laurel leaves having the appearance of a rope or scales (fig. 68, *a*, *b*).[141] This rather stylized form of garland, also found on Pergamene architraves and occasionally on altars elsewhere, has been said to indicate a later date than the naturalistic;[142] but at Pergamon it occurs with skeletal bucrania on the architrave of the early temple of Demeter (269–263 B.C.) (fig. 66, *a–c*),[143] and on the Rhodian altars at least there seems little sign of a difference in date. The tubular garland occurs with both naturalistic and skeletal bucrania, and the inscriptions on one or two altars with this type of garland (fig. 68, *a*, and *b*, top) seem to be among the earliest on a circular altar.[144] In one instance, the stylized garland, without any pendants or attachments, embraces the altar, which is otherwise entirely plain, in such a way as to resemble a snake (fig. 60, *a*).

Origin and distribution of cylindrical altars with bucrania and garlands. It is not part of this study to analyse in further detail the innumerable variations on the theme of bucrania and garland in the late hellenistic and Roman periods, but it is necessary to consider the place of the Rhodian altars in the general context of this type of monument.[145] Although, in effect, the circular altar with garlands and bucrania (or, especially in the Imperial period, other linking elements such as figures of Erotes) constitutes a distinct class of monument, and may justly be considered as such, we may repeat at the outset that these decorative features, which became so closely associated with the altars, were probably first used in architectural contexts—and probably separately. In the third century, on the monuments of Samothrace and Delos, the bucranion occurs alone as a metopal decoration, and not as a garland-supporter as at Pergamon. Though the establishment of an exact chronological relationship between the Pergamene architraves with bucrania and garlands and the Rhodian and other circular altars is not possible, since the latter can only be dated by letter forms, which allow a considerable margin, there can be no doubt that the majority, if not all, of the altars are later than the third-century Pergamene friezes. It is only natural that the introduction of the architectural decoration led without undue delay to its adaptation to private monuments, especially (but not exclusively) to cylindrical altars, and, granted the general influence of Pergamene artistic styles in the later hellenistic period, and their particular influence in the cities of Asia Minor and the eastern Aegean, it is extremely likely that the bucrania and garland decoration in the form which concerns us owes its ultimate origin to Pergamon. It is at the same time quite clear that the style became overwhelmingly fashionable, and it would be unrealistic to attribute each instance of its use to conscious imitation of Pergamene prototypes. We may then suppose that the decoration of the Rhodian and other funerary altars derives at least ultimately from Pergamene architectural models.[146] This is borne out by the very close resemblance of the type of many of the bucrania and garlands both to the mature Pergamene architectural types, and also to the decoration of a votive altar of the reign of Eumenes II (fig. 71, *a*).[147] It is noteworthy in this connection that no architectural fragments with this decoration have, to the best of my knowledge at least, been found in Rhodes.

The problem of distribution must, however, be considered not only in terms of the decoration but also in terms of the unified product, the cylindrical monument with bucrania and garlands, or similar decoration. Here a fundamental question arises. Monuments of this type are widely dispersed in the later hellenistic period, occurring not only in Pergamon, and on Delos, in the eastern Aegean and the Greek mainland,[148] but also in Republican Italy,[149] and we cannot hope to assign a single direct source to such a fashionable class of monument. Rather, just as, for example, the more we learn about the hellenistic antecedents of the 'First Style' of Pompeian wall-painting, the less inclined we are to assign it to a single source, Delos or elsewhere, so here too we are in the presence of a general fashion, the origin of which it is dangerous to assign to one centre. Nevertheless, while monuments of this class are found throughout the Aegean, they are overwhelmingly frequent in the Dorian cities of the south Carian coast and the adjacent islands, especially Cos and Rhodes. Thus at Rhodes the number in the Museum and scattered about the city, especially in the old suburbs outside the medieval walls, probably exceeds 200,[150] and many more have been found in the Rhodian islands, and on Cos the number certainly exceeds 50, while both Cnidos and Halicarnassos have yielded a number of similar pieces.

Given this distribution, we are clearly justified in regarding Rhodes, Cos, and the opposite Carian coast as the main area of production of this class of altar. But to go further and to assume that this area, either as a whole, or a particular part of it, was the single centre from which the type spread to Delos, where there are numerous examples,[151] and to Italy, would be unwise.[152] The composite design of bucrania and garlands may indeed have originated in, or gained renewed impetus from, the architectural decoration of Pergamene public monuments, but it was evidently found suitable for, and transferred with local variations to, smaller monuments as a matter of fashion over a wide area in the later hellenistic age, and that fashion became especially popular in the region in question. At Delos in particular it is used for a variety of domestic objects, as at Pompeii. The popularity of the circular funerary monument itself, as of the rectangular altar, was no doubt increased by its eminent adaptability to the type of terraced and rock-cut necropolis, itself dictated by topographical considerations, prevalent at Rhodes and elsewhere in the region.[153]

Nevertheless, in spite of the numerical preponderance of the Rhodian pieces, there are grounds for doubting whether even in the Rhodian area they represent the normative and original type of altar thus decorated. First and foremost, the Coan examples,[154] which, like the Rhodian, are of late hellenistic and Roman date (though the Roman inscription often belongs to a reuse of the altar), are of far finer workmanship than the Rhodian; certainly the Coan mason started with one great advantage, the abundant availability of a fine, malleable white marble, which gave the decoration a high degree of plasticity; but, over and above that, the ornamentation, while still within the recognized limits imposed by the theme, has a naturalistic life and vigour, as well as an elegance, rarely found on the Rhodian pieces. A comparison of a characteristic group of altars from both places reveals at once the difference in general workmanship and style (fig. 77, *a, b*). We may note particularly, on representative Coan pieces, the frequent tapering of the cylinder, the deep chiselling and under-cutting leading to high relief, and, in the decorative motifs, the development of the use of the cornucopia, or rather twin cornucopiae, as a divider in the centre of the garlands, the individuality and extreme naturalism of leaf and fruit, the formal but luxurious rendering of the bulls' tuft of hair; and in the upper moulding, the frequent use of the rosette and double-lotus fascia, present only on the one Rhodian altar which also has the double cornucopiae (above, p. 26). All these features are to be found on the altars represented in figs. 78, *a–d*, 79, *a–d*, 80, *a–e*.[155] Most of them, already present on the few altars of hellenistic date, and still more pronounced on the pieces of Roman date,[156] Cos has in common with very similar altars from Cnidos, and, still more, Halicarnassos, where the workmanship and style of some surviving pieces, though not of such high quality, is akin to that of Coan altars.[157] Looked at from the Rhodian point of view, the distinction may be expressed in general terms thus: the Rhodian stone itself is almost invariably of the usual grey or grey-fawn 'Lartian', a hard and unyielding material, which allowed little scope for elaborate chiselling; the stones tend to be shorter than the Coan pieces of corresponding diameter; the mouldings are (except for the few elaborate pieces noted above) simple, without fasciae, and the bucrania, with one or two exceptions, both rigid and more rough and plain, while the garlands lack the naturalistic detail of the Coan, Cnidian, and Halicarnassian pieces. Though an attempt was evidently made to enliven the grey monotony of the Rhodian monument by the use of colour, the over-all impression of austerity and provincialism is in marked contrast to the rich decorative effects of the best pieces from the other centres. These three Dorian cities seem then to have formed the main centres of production of the finest monuments of this type, while the very much larger Rhodian group, though it adopted the same style, either from these centres or as part of the general fashion of the age, was stylistically inferior to them, and on that account not likely to have acted itself as a centre of dissemination of the style; if a single centre be sought for that, then it will be wiser to seek it in one of the other three cities named, and particularly Cos. It is probably significant in this connection that, unlike Rhodes, and (so far as I am aware) the Rhodian world as a whole, the bucrania and garland motif was not, at Cos, confined to the funerary altar. It occurs also on a large number of low oblong blocks, possibly used as public benches, which have been found all over Cos, not least in the Agora. These are without exception decorated with bucrania and garlands on the front and short sides. I illustrate some examples in figs. 89, *c–d*; 90, *a–d*. Save one, they are uninscribed, but the workmanship of the decoration closely resembles that of the altars, and they may probably be assigned to the later hellenistic and Roman periods.[158] These benches (or 'bench'-altars) show the popularity of the decoration at Cos, as contrasted with its restricted funerary use in the Rhodian world.

One major functional feature distinguishes the use of this type of monument in the Dorian cities in question from its use elsewhere in the Greek world. It appears that, almost without exception, in those cities the circular monuments with bucrania and garlands are used as tombstones, and rarely, or never, as votive monuments.[159] Elsewhere they fulfil both functions: at Athens and on Thera[160] and Delos[161] they are also votive. On the other hand, funerary examples of a rather special kind are known from Mytilene.[162] Correspondingly, as already noted, on Rhodes the circular votive altars are almost invariably undecorated (see above, pp. 25–6). One particular class of the Dorian altar calls for attention in this respect. These are the circular altars with richly decorated upper and lower Ionic mouldings of the type already described (meander, cyma reversa, astragal, etc.: see above, p. 26), the cylinder of which is filled by ornately carved figures of three or more winged Victories or Maenads in a dancing movement; their wings are outspread and touching, and in some examples the figures are linked by garlands of ivy, laurel, and pine-cone, which either grow from the wings, or are supported by the figures, in the manner of bucrania. One excellently preserved piece, and three damaged examples, in Rhodes (figs. 84, *a–d*; 85, *a*),[163] and one or two further specimens from Cos[164] (fig. 85, *b–c*) reveal the local popularity of the style; almost alone among the circular monuments, they bring before us some reminiscence, however faint, of major glyptic work of the area. They bear a close similarity to the cylindrical votive 'Dionysiac' altars on which groups of Maenads execute dances. One fine example of this class with the same general style of mouldings, etc., comes from Rhodes (fig. 85, *f*).[165] Another example is from Pergamon (fig. 85, *g*), and it is not improbable that the style of figured altar (found also in neo-Attic sculpture) owes its origin to fashions originating in Pergamon.[166] The employment of the Nikai as holders of the garlands perhaps supports this, for they are close to the winged figures of the Pergamene Altar, but

the altars themselves are not particularly distinguished and are, unmistakably, Rhodian work. There is no doubt that these altars which,
in their present state, are all without inscriptions, are funerary, for two at
least of them were found in the Cova necropolis.[167]

Apart from the Nikai, and from snake motifs (see below pp. 38–40), no
decoration other than the garlands and bucrania (or (rarely) stags'
skulls) occurs on the Rhodian cylindrical altars as a main feature, but, as
with the rectangular altars, there is sometimes a rectangular sunk panel
below the garlands, for a 'Totenmahl' or other funerary relief. On one
particularly elaborate altar of white marble (fig. 86, *a*),[168] on which the
bull-head supporters have been replaced by the naturalistic head of a
stag,[169] the raised frame of the relief, formed of laurel leaves, passes
beneath the muzzle of the stag; the lower ledge consists of an undecorated
curved ledge. In the relief itself, the dead woman lies on a couch, holding
a phiale from which a serpent is drinking; beside her sits another woman,
probably her mother, while at the foot of the couch a servant girl stands
holding a casket. The inscription is divided between altar and supporting
base, which in this instance unquestionably belongs to the altar; that on
the altar, placed (exceptionally) above, and not below, the garland,
reads, in letters of the second century B.C., Ἀρχεστράτηι | Στρατοκ⟨λ⟩εῦς
Φαγαία, while the base has Ἀγησάνδρου | Σωσιγένους | Βρασίου. Here the
relief is clearly an integral part of the original design, for, had it not been,
the first inscription would have been inscribed in the usual way below
the garlands.[170] On another altar, of 'Lartian' stone, a normal 'Totenmahl'
is represented within a regular rectangular frame, without ledges.[171] On
three uninscribed altars the rectangular reserved space has been prepared,
but no relief has been carved (fig. 87, *a, b*);[172] we have already encountered an instance of this on a rectangular altar (above, p. 17, fig. 32, *b*).
In these cases it is evident that the relief plaque was part of the original
design, for it is difficult to imagine that it would have been conceived as
a second thought and then left blank. Similarly, on the altar from the
Peraea (fig. 44, *a*) the bucrania and garland which flank the upper part
of the relief field are placed abnormally high, and were evidently so
placed as a part of the over-all design including the relief-field.[173]

Other decorative features are rare on the altars, but one other remarkable piece deserves mention. The (uninscribed) altar is itself of the usual
type, decorated simply with bucrania and a narrow tubular garland of
laurel leaves, but on top of the altar there is carved, in one piece with it,
part of the outboard hull of a ship; the monument evidently commemorates a sea-captain or mariner (fig. 87, *c, d*).[174] On another, of very much
later date, the deceased, a θρεπτός, crudely carved, stands in a curved
niche, below which is the inscription.[175]

Such variations of the regular decoration are rare, and one may suppose that for the most part the monuments, both circular and rectangular, were prepared *en masse*, with garland and bucrania, in the mason's yard, and that a suitable inscription was added on the client's instruction. The extent to which mass-production, and consequent lowering of standards, might go is indicated by a curious double monument consisting of two circular altars, with the usual mouldings, bucrania, and garlands, and their bases, all in one piece; a time-saving device of the simplest sort (fig. 91, *a*).[176]

The distribution of this class of circular altar with bucrania and garlands within the Rhodian state, was, as might be expected, pretty well universal. They were the most common type of funerary monument on Chalke[177] and Karpathos,[178] and numerous examples are known from Syme,[179] Telos,[180] and Nisyros,[181] both of the altars themselves and of the familiar rectangular bases already discussed, on which they invariably stood. Examples also occur on Kasos, though the normal Kasian tombstone in the pre-Rhodian period was of a type all its own: a small, cylindrical disc, or flattish stone, of which many examples have recently been published.[182] Curiously, from the Peraea no examples are available for illustration.[183]

Thus, to summarize briefly the foregoing analysis, we may say with confidence that the rectangular altar with margins, with or without bosses, and the cylindrical altar on a rectangular base were the typical funerary monuments, not only of Rhodes itself, but also of the whole Rhodian state, at least in the later hellenistic period, though the cylindrical altar, unlike its rectangular counterpart, was not exclusively Rhodian.[184] However, the traditional type of vertical, frequently plain stele, which we have seen to have been in fashion in the later fourth and the third century, before the two types of altars predominated, also continued in use into the Roman period, and may be briefly characterized here.

4. LATER HELLENISTIC STELAI AND OTHER MONUMENTS

The stelai are, for the most part, marked by two characteristics: (*a*) though some are of the regular dimensions, the feature already noticeable in the classical reliefs of Krito and Timarista,[185] and of Kalliarista,[186] and in the plain stelai of the early hellenistic period (see above, pp. 9–10), their shortness in comparison with other contemporary reliefs, continues to be conspicuous in the later reliefs, whether they bear only an inscription, or also carry a relief; and (*b*) the relief, if there is one, usually a scene of parting or a domestic scene, is frequently inset in a small rectangular field (fig. 92, *a–e*),[187] while on some stones the sunk field occupies more of the surface of the stele, with figures in varying relief (fig. 93, *a*).[188] There is only one surviving instance of an 'Ionian'-style naiskos-tombstone surmounted by triglyphs, of the second century (fig. 93, *b*).[189] Occasionally the relief is carved not within a sunk field, but on a ledge (fig. 93, *c*).[190] On one small pedimental stele of white marble from Karakonero, of excellent workmanship, a young warrior leans against an unfluted Doric column and gazes at his plumed 'Corinthian' helmet held in his outstretched right hand, while his circular shield occupies the centre of the pediment; the whole composition rests on a ledge (fig. 93, *d*).[191] On another the figure of the deceased, a youth wearing a himation in the Attic style, holding in one hand an apple and in the other a hare (?), accompanied by a small, fawning dog, stands in a deeply recessed field (fig. 95);[192] on another very small piece (0·4 m high), with a similar theme—a youth facing right, holding an apple in his right hand, with a begging dog in front of his left foot—the relief itself occupies most of the surface (fig. 96, *a*).[193] The inscriptions on the plain stelai tend to be written, as earlier, towards the bottom,[194] but on the relief stelai they are sometimes both above and below the relief (fig. 96, *b*).[195] As regards the stone, there is perhaps for the first time a preponderance of white marble over grey 'Lartian' stone; this probably reflects the growing preference for figure reliefs, for which 'Lartian' stone was unsuitable, since figures were hard to carve in that material, and, when carved, were hardly visible in relief.

Small stelai of this type, and others of the classicizing type on which the persons are represented in a parting embrace,[196] were, if we are to judge by their surviving numbers, far less popular than the rectangular and circular altars, and, though numerous, are scarcely sufficiently homogeneous to be regarded as representative of a Rhodian school.

One piece stands, in theme and style, apart from this largely undistinguished collection: the funerary relief of Hieronymos, the son of Simylinos, of the Tloian deme, signed by a sculptor named Demetrios.[197] This remarkable relief (fig. 97) occupies a section of a horizontal block *c.* 1 m long, and 0·3 m high. Along the upper part, in a sunk field flanked by horizontal palmettes, is inscribed Ἱερωνύμου / τοῦ Σιμυλίνου / Τλωίου; below this, in a sunk field occupying the entire surviving width of the stone, is a series of figures which seem to fall into three groups, and below that again, the sculptor's signature in letters of the late third or early second century B.C.: Δημήτριος ἐποίησε.[198] In spite of the apparently symmetrical form of the relief, it is evident that both to left and to right blocks are missing, and it appears probable that in its complete form, with side blocks and pediment, it formed the central member of the entrance porch of a funerary heroon.[199] It is regrettable that the provenance of the relief is not known in detail. It was acquired in Alexandria for Hiller von Gaertringen by A. Schiff, a member of the 'Expedition von Sieglin', and there seems no reason to doubt the accuracy of the statement of Hiller, that it was found in or near Trianda (Ialysos), and then shipped to Alexandria.[200] It was probably inserted in the superstructure of an isolated funerary monument, rather than in that of a tomb in a necropolis; such single monuments, or even groups of monuments, are, as already noted, features of the high land south of Rhodes, and are also found at and near Lindos (see above, p. 5 and note 1(c)). Little though we know of burials in the Rhodian countryside, such individual funerary monuments were once to be seen all over the island. Another block probably to be assigned to another isolated tomb is discussed below, p. 36.

The nature of the scene and the identity of the figures represented have been much debated, and remain uncertain. The relief in the central field, as it survives, is divided into two sections of unequal size. On the left, a small scene, now incomplete to the left, is separated by a horizontally jointed door-post from the remainder. It portrays a group of five persons—three seated, two standing—of which the main figure is clearly the complete figure seated to the left, facing outwards and reading from a scroll; opposite him, a second figure sitting on a stool is listening to him intently, clearly as an equal, while two standing figures have been interpreted as youthful disciples. As the original editors pointed out, the scene closely resembles that of the representations of the seven philosophers in the mosaics of Torre Annunziata and of Umbra Sarsina,[201] and there can be little doubt that the scene is one of philosophical instruction or debate, though the relationship of our scene to the later mosaics can hardly be determined. To the right of this terrestrial scene, and separated from it by a vertical pillar probably representing the door separating the living world from the Underworld,[201a] is placed a scene which has been interpreted as portraying the gods and powers of the Underworld: first Hermes, in his role as psychopompos, then a veiled Persephone and a seated Pluton, behind whose throne stands a man leaning on a stick, who, to judge from his position in the centre of the composition, may be the dead man, Hieronymos, envisaged this time as having passed through the portals of Hades (guarded by Hermes), and perhaps continuing his instruction among the departed, next to Pluton himself. To the right of Hieronymos (if it be he) is a third group of figures facing to the right: first a young man and a woman sitting on blocks of natural rock beneath a tree, looking at the scene before them; they, it is suggested, are the spirits of the dead, recalling the figures of Polygnotos' *Nekyia*. Beyond them stands a female figure with the wings of a butterfly, wearing a chiton and holding in her right hand a staff; and beyond her again a shrouded figure seated on a rock, bent forward, her back to the winged figure, and facing a third female figure whose face is lost, represented as rising out of, or sinking into, the earth or lower regions, as far as the knee, and holding a mantle around and above her head in 'velificatio'. The exact interpretation of these figures in an Underworld setting remains conjectural, but the original supposition of Hiller von Gaertringen and C. Robert, that the scene is the Meadows of the Departed, with the judgement described by Plato in the Myth of Er, and that the figure to the right is sinking to the lower depths of Tartarus, remains the most plausible. If it is correct, the winged figure is to be interpreted as a judge of the Underworld, and may be Nemesis herself, Νέμεσις πτερόεσσα, who condemns the figure on the extreme right to due punishment; the seated figure between them perhaps representing a further Infernal deity. Whatever may be the correct detailed interpretation of this relief, it stands alone, not only in Rhodian, but in Greek art before the Roman period, as a highly imaginative and symbolic treatment of a funerary theme. The occasion appears at first sight to be that of the death of a teacher, and Hiller originally associated it with an epigram he had previously published commemorating the death of an otherwise unknown, and unnamed, schoolteacher,[202] but it is at least possible, as Hiller later thought, that Hieronymos is in fact the notable Peripatetic philosopher from Rhodes, who died *c.* 220 B.C.[203]

A further monument which probably came from a similar separate funerary monument with an architecturally designed entrance may also be noted (fig. 98). This is an oblong block of white marble, complete on all sides and with anathyrosis on three sides for union with surrounding blocks; the cuttings at the back, clearly ancient, evidently fitted into projecting bosses of the parent structure prepared to receive the block.[204] The front face is decorated with three skeletal bucrania, that on the left encircled with an olive wreath, that in the centre with a wreath of ivy and ivy blossom, and that on the right with another olive wreath. The inscription, of the later hellenistic age, carved symmetrically beneath the first and the third wreaths, commemorates a citizen of Termessus and his Ephesian wife, who are both described as 'Benefactors', no doubt of a koinon, under whose auspices they were buried. The block was seen by Newton on Monte Smith in 1853, and probably came originally from the western Necropolis area, or Rhodini, where other isolated tombs, such as the Ptolemaion, are attested. It is clear that it formed part of a free-standing monument, and is not, for example, a loculus-cover.

The existence of isolated tombs such as these is also indicated by the last group of funerary monuments we have to consider: individual pieces of sculpture, some of which at least once formed part of large tombs and monuments. Of these the most notable are perhaps the statues in panoply, mostly of Roman date, several of which have been found on the island;

these have nothing specifically Rhodian about them, and we need not consider them further.[205] One or two other subjects with undoubted funerary significance may, however, be noted. Of these, representations of lions and snakes take pride of place.

Lions. Lions are common features of funerary monuments in the fourth century throughout the Greek world, and they are certainly very frequent in and around Caria and the Rhodian area. This may be due in part to the influence of the lions of the Mausoleum, though the prominent Lion Monument on the promontory at Cnidos (fig. 99),[206] be it earlier or later than the Mausoleum, may have been no less influential in determining subsequent development. It is probable at all events that, at least as sepulchral decoration, the lion was a popular subject in the area from the Archaic age onwards. In its portrayal, naturalistic observation was largely or completely lacking, and the body usually has few of the muscular peculiarities of the lion, while the stance, usually seated, is canine and rigid rather than leonine, and the execution of the mane over-elaborate and over-formalized. This type of stone lion is represented on Rhodes from the late Classical period by two standing lions found in the late Classical necropolis of Ialysos (Marmaro) in 1934 (fig. 100, *a, b*);[207] the faces of both are severely damaged, but the whole treatment is more rigid, and, in particular, the exaggerated treatment of the mane less realistic, than that of the Cnidian lion. The most familiar of all Rhodian lions, that set up, after a varied history, in the main courtyard of the Museum (fig. 101, *a*),[208] is probably of hellenistic date, if not of the fourth century, for the round face and symmetrical mane recall markedly the fourth-century Cnidian piece; the head of the heifer or bullock between his paws closely resembles that of the lion from Kaunos described below. Among isolated fragments of lions we may call particular attention to a noble but fragmentary head, preserved only to the eyes (fig. 101, *c, d*);[209] the brushed-back style of the mane and the very human brow reveal the technical influence of the sculptors of the Mausoleum, though the features have a more romantic cast than those of the lions which were once part of the ornament of that structure.[210] On one lion, of which only the trunk survives (fig. 101, *e*), an attempt has been made to render the loose, tufty hair of the flanks in an impressionistic manner.[210a]

That these lions once formed parts of various funerary monuments is not open to doubt, and it is of some interest that in an epitaph inscribed on the lintel of the door of a pyramidal tomb in the Peraea the dead man, Diagoras, states that his statue stood on the summit of the pyramid, and that the doorway or façade of the tomb was guarded by a pair of lions; in the neighbourhood of the structure itself are the remains of a lion, probably one of the two in question, which, though now sadly defaced, reveals some elements of grace and muscular flexibility (fig. 101, *b*).[211]

A singularly realistic lion recently found at Kaunos may close this survey of Rhodian lions, for Kaunos was itself subject to Rhodes inter- mittently from the early second century B.C. until the Imperial period (fig. 101, *f*).[212] The lion sits *gardant* on his haunches, the body upright and tense, the head turned to the left; the left leg is stretched vertically to its full height, while the right rests in a lifelike manner on the finely ren- dered head of a bull. Workmanship and style are alike of a high order.

Snakes, symbols of the soul of the dead and of the Underworld, are perhaps the creatures most frequently encountered in funerary art and symbolism, and their appearance on Rhodian monuments is only natural.

We may first consider those circular altars, otherwise plain, and of the normal type discussed above, in which a snake is twined round the cylinder. Examples of this type of 'snake-altar' are known from Rhodes, Nisyros, and Cnidos (figs. 102, *a*, *b*; 103; 104), and no doubt there are examples from elsewhere in the area.[213] Evidently the snake was not only decorative and by its form suitable for representation on a cylindrical monument; it naturally also has reference in some way to the Under- world. However, the similarity, in all other respects, of these few altars to the main group of cylindrical altars decorated with bucrania and garlands should warn us against interpreting the motif as an indication of a 'Hero-cult' or of an identification of the dead man with the snake; the dead person was not regarded, in these few instances alone, as a semi-divine 'Hero'. The role of the snake is rather that of apotropaic guardian of the tomb, like the lions in the epitaph noted above. This interpretation is borne out by another epitaph, also from the Peraea (Buzburun, Tymnos), set upon the grave of an old warrior, in which the snake, which stood on the monument, either free-standing or in relief, calls attention to itself specifically as 'the guardian of the tomb'; in life the dead man has carried the same creature as a blazon on his shield.[214] There is no reference to cult or 'Heroization', and the snake here fulfils precisely the same protective function as did the two lions on the nearby tomb at Turgut.

Three elaborate pieces, in which the snake formed the main element in a larger composition, are worthy of notice. The first (fig. 105, *a*, *b*),[215] which probably stood on a base on the top of a hypogaeum, consist of a representation, in white marble, of a bell-kantharos with decoration of six acanthus and lotus leaves, round which is entwined, in very high relief, the scaly body of a snake, the bearded head of which (now lost, save for the beard) rested on a vertical rim or lip set on the edge of the upper surface of the kantharos; on it are carved two wreaths of olive with suspended garlands. There is no sign of an inscription, and the date of the monument cannot be closely determined. The snake-coils are,

however, close to those of the various serpentine monsters of the Great
Frieze of the Pergamene altar,[216] and the group, kantharos and snake
together, bears all the signs of elaborate Rhodian work of the late
hellenistic period. The central theme itself, the association of the funerary
vase and the chthonic snake, is not unexampled, and may be paralleled
in the same area by a group of monuments of which there are three in
Halicarnassos and one on Cos. On these, a snake issues from, or encircles,
a skyphos decorated with ivy leaves, which is itself represented as carved
in relief on a rectangular altar, below a shield, on the main body of the
monument (fig. 106, *a–c*).[217] The subject is not particularly Rhodian, and
may be regarded as one of several local versions of the basic association.

No less striking is the second piece (fig. 108, *a*, *b*).[218] This consists of a
cubic block of 'Lartian' stone, the upper surface of which is carved in the
form of a ram's head, with elaborately carved horns; round the head,
and round the entire block, is entwined a plastically modelled snake, its
head (now severely damaged) surmounting the head of the ram like a
uraeus, its body terminating in a pendent coil on the front of the block.
Below the snake, and suspended from it by a fillet, is a sheathed sword,
lying obliquely across the face of the block, with apparently a sash folded
over the coil of the snake. This monument also bears no inscription, but
the slack, loose rendering of the snake resembles, on a small scale, like
the previous piece, the creatures of the Pergamene altar, and it is probably to be assigned to approximately the same date. The scabbarded
sword terminating in a curved hilt (in the form of a bird-head) closely
resembles that of the sword represented behind the helmet on the Rhodian
relief in Copenhagen (fig. 94), and also that on a funerary relief from the
neighbourhood of Byzantion (fig. 109, *a*),[219] as well as those represented
on the balustrade of the precinct of Athena at Pergamon[220] and on the
façade of the Bouleuterion at Miletus.[221] These analogies also serve to
date the monument with sufficient precision for our purpose. The ram's
head, a common feature of Imperial altars and sarcophagi, is rarely
found on earlier monuments, but I hesitate on that account to date the
Rhodian piece to the Roman period.[222] Rams already play a part in
funerary sacrifices in the hellenistic age, and indeed earlier, and it is to
these practices that the representation may indirectly refer.[223]

The third piece (fig. 105, *c*) consists of a shallow, roughly circular base,
diameter 0·70 m, height 0·24 m, formed of snake-coils, the coils rising in
circles and terminating in the head (now lost) which projected above the
coils. The coils are heavy (height 0·1 m), and very much in the Pergamene style. The monument was probably complete in itself.[223a]

A fourth piece[224] may also be noted. This is a circular epithema, or lid,
on which a snake is curled, wreathed over three rolls of papyri (fig.
109, *b*). Here too we may regard the snake, in part at least, as guarding

and protecting the written word of the dead man, perhaps his testament,[225] rather than as symbolizing his 'Heroization'.[226]

Among other pieces of which a snake is the main feature we may notice a small altar which combines several of the features which we have discussed individually (fig. 110, *a*).[227] It consists of a small base surmounted by a cylindrical altar, with bucrania and garlands, without upper mouldings, surmounted in turn by a conical omphalos surrounded by a snake, the three elements all made in one piece. On the base is the inscription ʽΙέρων / Δεισιθέμιος / κατὰ τὸ ὅραμ[α] / Ἥρωι, in letters of the second century B.C. This is evidently not a tombstone, but a dedication to a chthonic Hero, no doubt the familiar Rider-God of that name; in any case he is regarded as a personified chthonic entity, who appeared in a dream to Hieron. The inscription is thus probably not testimony to the existence of a 'human' Hero-cult in Rhodes.[228] The monument is small and insignificant, but the survival of a similar omphaloid cone with an encircling snake as a separate unit (fig. 110, *b*), which evidently once surmounted a similar altar, attests to the existence of larger monuments of this type, which stand on the narrow margin between chthonic and funerary cult. A number of reticulate omphaloi with encircling snakes found in the eastern Necropolis (fig. 110, *c*) clearly formed part of funerary monuments.[229]

Finally I may call attention to representations of the *dolphin*, the sea-creature loved by all Greeks, of which some fine stone specimens may be seen in Rhodes Museum.[230] Like the lion, the dolphin is not exclusively connected with funerary beliefs and funerary art, indeed it occurs but rarely in funerary art, and then in a stylized manner suggesting usually a purely decorative function, in opposed pairs, in the same way as rosettes, as on a fragment from Tanagra (fig. 111, *a*).[231] Whether or not their appearance in such cases is symbolic, and connected in some way with the supposed role of the dolphin as conveyor of the dead, is an open question.[232] In any case, while there is no surviving representation of the dolphin on Rhodian funerary stelai or altars, there are nevertheless several life-size representations of them which must have formed part of larger monuments. The most natural context for the dolphin is certainly either as a support for, or as a feature of, an ornamental fountain, as on the fountain of Cn. Babbius Philinus in the Lower Agora at Corinth (where the dolphin had a particular association both with Poseidon, the god of the Isthmus, and with Palaemon, who was brought to shore at Lechaeon on a dolphin's back (fig. 111, *b*)[233]). However, the kindly creature was deeply embedded in the affections of the seafaring communities of the ancient Greek world, and it became a symbol of the sea and of seafaring activities, and it is as such that it appears frequently on the stamps of amphorae of Thasos and Rhodes (fig. 111, *c*).[234] Artemidoros of Perge, when he dedicated his rock-cut altars of the gods on Thera, included a metrical dedication to Poseidon Pelagios, and below it his mason carved a realistic pair of dolphins, whom Artemidoros in his simple verses describes as εὔνουν ἀνθρώποις νενομισμένον (fig. 111, *d*).[235] Whatever the exact significance of such representations, or the variations of intention behind them, there can be no doubt that ultimately and invariably they reflect the affection of an individual or of a community for this creature. At Rhodes, which lived by its overseas commerce and transport, and which made the ways of seafarers safe by her firm suppression of piracy throughout Aegean waters, it does not surprise us to find splendid life-size examples of dolphins, which may well have stood on, or as, funerary monuments. First and foremost is an imposing creature in grey stone, which formed the upper element of some monument (fig. 112, *a–b*).[236] The surface is roughly worked and entirely unornamented, and there is no concession to decorative requirements; it is an unadorned, authentic dolphin, seen at first hand by a perceptive artist. A very similar piece, both in style and in treatment of the stone, is a representation of a young dolphin, it too represented in the act of swimming (fig. 112, *a*).[237] A different treatment is found in the figure, in white marble, of a foreshortened dolphin, plunging vertically, a captured fish held in its mouth (fig. 112, *c*). It is supported on a cone resting on a base, and probably acted as a support for a larger monument, funerary or otherwise.[238]

This may conclude our survey of those monuments which fall outside the two main classes of rectangular and circular altars, and also of the few isolated objects treated above. By way of summary, we may emphasize the main features, positive and negative, of the Rhodian funerary monuments which we have surveyed.

For the period from before the synoecism (408/7) we have very little monumental material, but what there is indicates a dependence on Attic and Ionic models, and the same is true of the best fourth-century figured stele, that of Kalliarista. These figured stelai are few in number, and it seems improbable that they were in frequent demand. At the end of the fourth century, and in the early part of the third, the plain, narrow stele, with or without pediment, and frequently with a roughly cut inscription, seems to have been in use, but the total number of tombstones of early hellenistic date, as of the fourth century, is remarkably few. This may reflect in part the smaller population of the city at that time, as compared with the later hellenistic period, from about 175 B.C. onwards, for which period tombstones abound, particularly those of the two classes here considered in detail, the rectangular and the cylindrical altar; but it has been suggested above that there may also have been considerable reuse of tombstones for building purposes after the various disasters which struck the city in the period between 323 and 220 B.C. The discussion has shown that the style and shape of the rectangular funerary altar with margins is a peculiarly Rhodian monument (whether with or without the 'collar-bosses' on the upper surface) which has a non-funerary parallel, if not model, in the epistatai-altars at Lindos. On the other hand the circular funerary altars standing on a trochilus on a square base, though far more numerous at Rhodos than elsewhere, cannot be assigned to a Rhodian origin; Rhodos was far the largest city in the area in the late hellenistic age, and their numbers may merely reflect that fact. They occur also frequently as funerary monuments at Cos, Cnidos, and Halicarnassos, and those of Cos are of outstanding quality. It is wisest therefore to regard such altars as a common product of the Dorian hexapolis area. Cylindrical monuments with the same decorative style occur elsewhere, notably at Delos, with varied uses, and there is no doubt that the style as a whole, together with the decoration of bucrania and garlands, was fashionable in the later hellenistic age, and it would be unreasonable to regard the monuments of this class as deriving directly from a single source. The same is true of the decoration itself, which is found on so many of both the rectangular and the cylindrical altars; it conforms in the beginning to the type of bucranion and garland decoration found on Pergamene architecture; and it may possibly owe its origin to Pergamene models; but the style became universally popular and soon lost any immediate link with a single source. It may be emphasized again that the Rhodian decoration is far less elaborate and evolved than, and also structurally far inferior to, that found on the altars from the other cities mentioned, especially Cos. That was probably partly the result of the very unmalleable stone available on the island, though the effects of mass-production in a large mercantile city must also be taken into account.

Also to the later hellenistic and Roman periods belong the plain rectangular cinerary caskets, in the shape of small sarcophagi. Not one of these very numerous objects, which, in this precise style, seem to be exclusively Rhodian, has any decoration of any sort, and although the workmanship shows some variations, it is impossible to date most of them even approximately, unless they are inscribed. Those that are, are rarely datable earlier than the second century B.C. The funerary stelai of the same period, and of the Roman period, are mostly small; there is a tendency (noticeable on the rectangular altars) for the uniform surface of the stelai to be broken by reliefs, either inset or free-standing; no instance of this survives from the earlier period, in which the normal stelai are plain.

Such are the monuments, very 'minor monuments' for the most part, by which the Rhodians commemorated their dead. Collectively they are of interest in several ways. First, in the field of sculptural history, they provide us with some indication of the humbler products of Rhodian sculptors contemporary with the portentous sculptural works such as the Laocoon and the Sperlonga group. The style is the product of currents of the time, but nevertheless develops along its own lines, particularly with the rectangular altars. Secondly, more generally we are able to see by study of the monuments of this class in the Rhodian islands and the Peraea that Rhodian customs spread, in one way or another, to these Rhodian dependencies of the hellenistic age, and that 'Rhodianization' involved all aspects of life, religious and social and artistic as well as merely political. Finally, in the wider context of Greek funerary art, the Rhodian monuments provide a coherent body of stylistically distinct monuments of the hellenistic age, at a time when Athenian funerary art had ceased to exist, to be placed alongside the numerous other distinct regional groups, the painted stelai of Demetrias, Alexandria, and Sidon, the oblong monuments of Boeotia, the figured stelai of Byzantion, and others, as well as, in a wider context, the East Greek 'Ionian' stelai. This is one way, and a very significant one (for it reflects the innermost beliefs of communities and individuals) in which the variety of the hellenistic world is brought home to us. The primacy of Athens in almost every field having passed by the end of the fourth century B.C., the traditions of individual communities all over the Greek world were able to reassert themselves.

We shall consider in Part II what we may learn from these monuments of the domestic, social, and religious customs reflected in the inscriptions. There is a great deal of relevant material, and its interpretation is not easy.

5. APPENDIX

Unpublished Cylindrical Altars at Arundel House

I owe to the generosity of Mr. B. F. Cook the opportunity to publish here a group of hitherto unpublished altars at Arundel, which he had previously intended to publish himself. I am also much indebted to Mr. Francis Steer, F.S.A., Archivist to His Grace the Duke of Norfolk, who obtained permission from the Dowager Duchess of Norfolk for me to study the altars, and gave me every facility for doing so. Fig. 117, *a, b* shows the stones in their present location.

The first five altars published here—four from Rhodes and one from Cos— have been at Arundel for many years, and their earlier history cannot be determined. They were presumably brought at some time from Arundel House in the Strand, where the Arundel Marbles were originally exhibited (see most recently the excellent account by D. E. L. Haynes, *The Arundel Marbles* (Oxford, printed for the Visitors of the Ashmolean Museum, 1975), *passim*); but no record of their move survives. The sixth altar—of Cycladic origin—was among those discovered in debris when Norfolk and Howard Streets were recently demolished (cf. B. F. Cook, *Trans. Lond. and Middlesex Arch. Soc.* xxvi (1975), pp. 247–8; cf. Haynes, op. cit., p. 14). The Rhodian and Coan altars have a particular interest since they are, unless I am mistaken, the only pieces in the Arundel Collection that can be identified as coming from those islands.

A. RHODIAN

(i) 'Lartian' stone, height 0·50 m, diam. 0·35 m; fig. 118, *a* and *c*.
Inscribed below bucrania and garland:

$$\Xi\epsilon\nu o\kappa\lambda\hat\eta s$$
$$\dot\epsilon\gamma\gamma\epsilon\nu\acute\eta s$$

The altar and decoration are alike of the commonest type, and closely resemble, e.g., figs. 58, *d*, 68, *a*, and they call for no particular comment.

(ii) 'Lartian' stone, height 0·68 m, diameter 0·50 m; fig. 118, *b*.
Inscribed below bucrania and garland:

$$\mathcal{A}\lambda\kappa\iota\kappa\rho\acute\alpha\tau\eta$$
$$T\iota\mu\alpha\chi\acute\iota\delta\alpha$$
$$\Phi\acute\upsilon\sigma\kappa\iota\epsilon$$

Letters of the mid-hellenistic period. The inscription is among the very few examples from Rhodes of the use of the vocative case without the addition of χρηστ- χαῖρε, and the only instance of a demotic in the vocative case.

The decoration of heavy garlands with fillets and the large pendent pearl necklace closely resembles that of fig. 67, *b*.

(iii) 'Lartian' stone, height 0·45 m, diameter 0·33 m; fig. 118, *d*.
Uninscribed.

The decoration closely resembles that of no. ii.

(iv) 'Lartian' stone with prominent broad pink veins on surface, height 0·65 m, diameter 0·54 m; fig. 118, *e*.
Uninscribed.

The decoration consists of a garland of fruits and ivy and olive leaves with pendent bunches of grapes; compare figs. 59, *c*, 60, *b*, etc. The upper cavetto moulding is more elaborate than those on nos. i and iii.

B. COAN (?)

(v) Grey marble, height 0·63 m, diameter 0·44 m; fig. 118, *f* and *g*.
Inscribed:

(i) $B\rho\acute\iota\theta\iota o\nu\ M\epsilon\nu\epsilon\sigma\theta\acute\epsilon\omega s$
$\chi\rho\eta\sigma\tau\grave\eta\ \chi\alpha\hat\iota\rho\epsilon$

(ii) $\underset{.}{M}\eta\nu\acute o\delta o\tau\epsilon\ \Pi\iota\kappa\alpha\nu\theta\iota o s\ \kappa\alpha\grave\iota$
$T\epsilon\beta\acute\epsilon\rho\iota\epsilon\ '\!E\gamma\nu\acute\alpha\tau(\iota\epsilon)\ \underset{.}{\Theta}\alpha\eta\iota s\ (?)$
$\chi\rho\eta\sigma\tau o\grave\iota\ \chi\alpha\acute\iota\rho\epsilon\tau\epsilon$

Lettering of (i) late hellenistic/early Imperial, of (ii), in a different hand, slightly later.

The marble itself, its dimensions and decorative elements are all paralleled at Cos, though the upper moulding lacks the usual dentil-frieze. For the fascia with central phiale cf. figs. 78, *d*, 79, *d* and for the rich and heavy garland of fruit and flowers ibid. 79, *a*–80, *b*. For the thick fleshy bucrania see p. 27.

The inscription in lines 3–5 is by a different hand from that of lines 1–2, and clearly belongs to a second use, though not necessarily of much later date. As in some Coan inscriptions (see above, pp. 29–30) the reuse seems to have occurred in the early Imperial period (i–ii A.D.), after a primary use in the late hellenistic/ early Roman period.

In (i) the name *Βρίθιον* is a diminutive of which the full name *Βριθώ* is more commonly attested. It occurs as the name of a 'Melian' nymph* and it also occurs as a personal name, but seems rare.† The masculine form *Βρίθων* is also attested in one or two instances.‡

In (ii) the patronymic and cognomen in lines 3–4 respectively are difficult to read, and my readings are tentative and not very satisfactory. In line 3 *Πικανθιος* seems probable (the cross-stroke across the vertical bar of the *pi*, which might point to an *epsilon*, is not, in my opinion, the stroke of a letter; the *theta* has a small central dot, and could be an *omicron*). I cannot parallel the name *Πίκανθις* (masc.) and see no evident etymology for it. In line 4 ’*Εγνατ* is clear, followed by a group of five letters, of which the last three are unmistakably *ΗΙΣ*. The first two could be either *ΘΑ* or *ΟΛ*. Since a single compound name is not possible, and the praenomen stands in the vocative, I see no alternative to an expansion, e.g. ’*Εγνάτ(ιε) Θαης*. For the gens Ignatia on Cos see Paton and Hicks, 361, ’*Εγνατία Σεκόνδα*, and Herzog, *Koische Forschungen* 61, *Μάρκου ’Εγνατίου Πρόκλου, ζῆ. Θαης*, if correct, recalls the familiar Egyptian *Θαῆς, Θαῆσις*, etc., but it is not easy to imagine an Egyptian name here, and in any case most of this plentiful group of names are feminine.

C. CYCLADIC

(vi) Island marble, probably Parian, height 0·66 m, diameter 0·55 m (rectangular cutting in upper surface, 0·16 m × 0·23 m); fig. 118, *h*.

Uninscribed.

Publ.: B. F. Cook, *op. cit.*, p. 247, no. 2, and pl. 8.

The rich full garlands with pendent bunches of grapes and fillets are typical of Delian (figs. 72, *d*, 73, *c–d*) and Parian (fig. 74, *g–h*) altars. There is no indication whether the altar is funerary or votive, but the cutting in the upper surface, if original, presumably held the base of a small statue, and points to a votive use.

It may be noted that the smooth weathering of the decoration of this altar, as to a lesser extent that of no. v, suggests that it may have been submerged in the sea.

---

* See Tzetz. on Hes. *Op.* 144 (Gaisford, *Poet. Gr. Min.* iii, p. 110).

† Thera: *IG*, xii. 3, 490; 493; Amorgos, ibid. 7, 491 (*Βριθ[ώ]*); *ILind.* 51 b 1, l. 11; cf. also *Βριθαγόρη, Inscr. Bulg.* i², 413 (*SGDI* 5536).

‡ *PPetr.* iii. 39, col. ii, line 11; col. iii, line 1; *JHS* xlviii (1928), p. 179, no. 2 (*SEG* ix, 890), of unknown origin, in the collection of Lord Mersey, Bignor Park, Pulborough, Sussex.

PART II

SEPULCHRAL INSCRIPTIONS
AND BURIAL PRACTICES

I. INFORMATION REGARDING IDENTITY, ETC.

I T will be convenient first of all to analyse briefly the information normally recorded on Rhodian tombstones. This, in Rhodes as elsewhere, should enable us to determine the status of the deceased, and on the basis of such determination we might hope (ideally) to arrive at some correlation between the tombstones themselves and the cemeteries to which they belong, at least where we have precise information as to where the inscriptions were found—the extent to which the necropoleis were restricted in usage to certain classes of the population, and so on. I may emphasize here that it is no part of my purpose to discuss the ideas, and particularly the ideas concerning the afterlife, to be found in metrical epitaphs, for these fall outside my scope in so far as they do not supply information regarding the status of the deceased; a few marginal formulae are discussed below, in section 3.

The inscriptions on Rhodian tombstones of the hellenistic and Roman periods, among the largest series known from any Greek city other than Athens, fall into the following categories.

(*a*) One large group is formed by those on which the name of the dead person is followed by the patronymic (and possibly the name of earlier ancestors as far as the fourth generation),[239] and by the demotic. This was clearly the full form of description of a citizen on his tombstone, and it is not likely, save in exceptional circumstances, that a citizen would ever be represented in any other way. This practice is standard in Athens at least from the earlier fourth century onwards,[240] and it is likely that the Rhodian usage, established soon after the new city was founded, was based on the Athenian model. At that time it is doubtful if the formula existed elsewhere in precisely the same terms. We may call it, then, as others have done,[241] the 'Attic' formula, without however implying that it was rigidly followed at either Athens or Rhodes: see (*e*) below.

(*b*) The second and, as it were, corresponding, group is that of foreigners who appear with their city-ethnic, thus indicating full citizenship of a foreign state. The foreign citizen normally does not have the patronymic on his tombstone at Rhodes, by contrast with Attic practice in this respect, but sometimes he has[242] (as in Athens sometimes he has not), without any discernible difference in status.

(*c*) Another group, the interpretation of which in general is not open to doubt, is that of the single name, commonly taken to indicate persons of a humble station in life, not falling into other known categories. No doubt they included many Greek slaves, identifiable at times by their names, though foreign slaves, as long as their racial origin remained identifiable, were probably usually denoted by their foreign ethnic.

(*d*) Single names, with either a foreign ethnic, or with some other descriptive mark, were probably often those of slaves, or their descendants called ἐγγενής on their tombstones, but also no doubt of members of the free population as well, including metics, a shadowy class at Rhodes, where the foreign population was probably considerably in excess of the citizen body.

(*e*) One other class creates a considerable difficulty: those whose names are followed by the patronymic but no further indication of civil status.[243] In some communities, in which further differentiation was not necessary, this was a sufficient record of the citizen, and it may be maintained that these persons were in fact citizens of Rhodes whose surviving relatives did not bother to record their demotics, which were not, it would then follow, obligatory. This is possible, not only for Rhodes but also for the corresponding large group at Athens.[244] Unfortunately we cannot reach a decision on this point since although the demotic along with the patronymic was recognized in many Greek communities as the hallmark of the citizen, in Rhodian documents the demotic is not regularly used even where it might be expected, for instance in inscriptions recording honours for Rhodian citizens and in lists of Rhodian civic magistrates and priests, where the patronymic sufficed.[245] It is therefore not possible to establish precise rules for the presence and omission of the demotic, and unless we are prepared to accept the view that the sepulchral inscription recorded obligatorily in every instance the full civil status of an individual—just because it was his tombstone—we must admit that the distinction between the two groups is difficult to establish, and perhaps does not exist. However, one argument of considerable force stands on the other side. At Rhodes there existed one class of persons which needs to be accounted for in funerary inscriptions, namely the very large class of persons who lived in the city of Rhodes, Rhodos, and were not hereditary members of the demes into which the territory of the old cities was divided after the synoecism; persons, that is to say, who had themselves migrated or whose ancestors had migrated to Rhodos and, while possessing full rights of citizenship at Rhodos—including the right to hold public office—were outside the hereditary deme-framework of the old cities; Rhodos itself possessed no deme-organization independently of the old cities.[246] Possibly, then, in spite of the difficulty of reconciling this with practice at Athens, where no secondary class of citizenship existed, these funerary inscriptions of persons with patronymics denote non-demesmen citizens. It is a further question whether the persons so named are of the same class as the Ῥόδιοι, who, though seldom described as such on tombstones,[247] seem to have constituted a separate class from the demesmen. The civil title Ῥόδιος is largely, but not exclusively, confined to the sons of foreigners to whom ἁ ἐπιδαμία, the right of residence, had been granted by the state, and represents a form of naturalization. It seems to have been bestowed largely on sculptors, and they use it regularly in their signatures on the bases of their works;[248] it is otherwise rarely attested. This question can hardly be answered at present; if it was not obligatory to record the bestowal of the status indicated by Ῥόδιος on the tombstone, then all those whose tombstones record name and patronymic only discussed above may have been Ῥόδιοι. This is certainly an economical hypothesis, since, while there are adequate parallels elsewhere for the existence of a larger and smaller citizen body (as at Cyrene between the Μύριοι and the πολῖται, and at Alexandria, where the Ἀλεξανδρεῖς, who are distinct from the demesmen, seem to be close parallels to the Ῥόδιοι[249]), the existence of yet further distinctions seems *a priori* unlikely. The persons with name and patronymic only may then be identical with the Ῥόδιοι, of whom, in the second century B.C., when sculpture was especially in vogue in Rhodes, the numerous foreign sculptors, resident over a number of years, formed one group.[250] They cannot be identical with the logically prior group of those ὧι ἁ ἐπιδαμία δέδοται, identifiable as the fathers of Ῥόδιοι, since those always appear with their foreign ethnics. Unfortunately the fluctuation of usage in non-funerary documents prevents us from reaching any firm conclusion on this point at present. As usual, as material accumulates, the answer appears increasingly uncertain. One point remains true: there is hardly a single instance in which the demotic is used without the patronymic,[251] and consequently it is the patronymic and not the demotic which constituted the indispensable means of public identification for the Rhodian citizen.

The same problem arises in respect of the class represented by single names only, which occur largely, but not entirely, on the cinerary caskets. It may be maintained in such cases also that usage was elastic even to the extent of the single name being used for citizens, full or partial, patronymic and demotic being omitted; that this is so in many cases on cinerary caskets, which were not themselves actually funerary monuments but were placed in the loculus or grave, while the tombstone itself stood above the hypogaeum, with full details of the deceased, seems very likely, though there are numerous caskets on which full details are recorded—they are indeed as numerous as those which carry only the single name.[252] While it cannot be assumed that the single name represents in all cases an individual without defined civil status, nevertheless some must be of that class of persons, numerous in all large mercantile cities of the ancient world, who lacked any form of citizen rights, but were nevertheless resident permanently in the city. The caskets apart, such persons are represented on true funerary monuments, stelai, etc.,[253] on which the single name evidently represents the full credentials of the individual, and they may be assigned without hesitation to this humble class of residents, or to the servile population. Here too, however, a word of warning must be given. There are instances in which the base of an altar or stele, the only surviving member, carries an incomplete inscription, mostly the patronymic preceded by the article, or by the copula, without the deceased's own name;[254] in such cases there can be no doubt that the deceased's name stood alone on the main monument, and we must beware of regarding such inscriptions, particularly those on circular monuments, as complete.

2. THE 'SEPULCHRAL GENITIVE'

The funerary inscriptions themselves, whatever the information they record, are, except for a very few instances in which they are in the dative case, in either the nominative or the genitive case, the former being more common. Not unnaturally there is no distinction between the use of the two cases in respect of the category of the deceased—demesmen, foreigners, and humble non-citizens all appear indifferently in either case, so far as can be determined. On the other hand there appears to be a distinction, if only slight, in the type of monument on which the cases occur; on round and rectangular monuments which form the main object of study of Part I above, the names are almost equally in the nominative or in the genitive, but on the simple funerary stelai the names are almost always in the nominative (or, in the Roman period, the (quasi-)vocative, with $\chi\rho\eta\sigma\tau\grave{\epsilon}(\grave{o}s)$ $\chi\alpha\hat{\imath}\rho\epsilon$), while on the caskets the genitive case is normal, the nominative rare. It is natural to ask both how this case-usage corresponds to practice elsewhere, and what its significance may be.

Practice elsewhere is clearly defined. In Athens of the post-Euclidean period, out of the many thousands of tombstones, there is no unequivocal use of a simple genitive standing by itself, and its occurrence has been denied.[255] Similarly, in the very different environment of Boeotia, whence large collections of tombstones have been published, though peculiarities of usage and formula do exist,[256] the genitive seems not to be used,[257] and in those of Chalkis, Eretria, and Demetrias in Thessaly the genitive is

2. The 'Sepulchral Genitive'

equally unknown.[258] On the other hand there are regions where the genitive is more frequent than the nominative. This is particularly so in some cities of Akarnania—though not in all—and the practice varies curiously between almost adjacent cities.[259] The genitive is indeed found spasmodically in some Aegean communities—on Thera, Paros, and Amorgos,[260] for example, to consider those cities where enough tomb-stones exist to give weight to such figures—but it is only common in two areas, the Dorian communities we are concerned with, Rhodes, and the Rhodian Islands and Peraea,[261] Cos,[262] Cnidos,[263] and, to a lesser degree, Halicarnassos,[264] and also in Lycia, notably at Telmessos.[265] The examples from Telmessos are all from rock-cut tombs, and most of them are of the fourth century, and thus considerably earlier than the examples from Rhodes and the Dorian regions. In the Imperial period Telmessos, like the other cities of southern Asia Minor, uses almost invariably the 'construction-formula', both for rock-cut tombs and for sarcophagi: ὁ δεῖνα κατεσκεύασεν μνημεῖον (or σωματοθήκην, or σορόν or ἡρῶιον, etc.),[266] followed by the name of the deceased (if he is not himself the constructor of the tomb) in the dative. It is natural to suppose that the genitive of the tombstones depends on an (unexpressed) substantive (e.g. τὸ μνημεῖον, ὁ τάφος), and is not a genitive indicating dedication. The expressed usage is found in Archaic metrical, and some prose, epitaphs, τοῦ δεῖνος τόδε σῆμα, τοῦ δεῖνος τόδε μνῆμα, etc., and the simple genitive is also found in the Archaic period.[267] It seems evident, then, that the usage is a survival such as might be expected in relatively undeveloped regions like Akar-nania, but it is surprising that it was prevalent in advanced societies such as Rhodes and Cos in the late hellenistic and Roman periods. It is un-fortunate in this connection that almost no early epitaphs survive from the area of the Dorian hexapolis, to enable us to determine regular Archaic practice in the region.[268] One point is to be noted: the significance of the distinction between the use of the nominative, by which the deceased was identified, and the genitive by which (in a loose sense) his ownership of the tomb was expressed, was not felt at the date with which we are concerned. This is shown by one or two joint tombstones in which the name of one party is given in the nominative, that of the other in the genitive, as e.g. Φερενίκα Φερενίκου / γυνὰ δὲ Ἀριστοκράτευς, || Ἀριστο-κράτευς / Ἀριστοξένου.[269] Clearly no difference was conceived in the posthumous status of the husband and wife. The occurrence of the accusative case on a casket is unexpected.[269a]

3. THE 'SEPULCHRAL DATIVE'

There are a few Rhodian epitaphs in which the name of the deceased is expressed in the dative case. The use of the dative with the preposition ἐπί is of course normal practice in Boeotia (often with ἥρωι),[270] and means '(This gravestone is) *on* x'; the same usage is found in Thessaly, where it occurs in the form of a dedication in the dative to the dead person, described as ἥρως, while the rest of the epitaph gives the true name of the deceased in the nominative.[271] In general, however, the unaccompanied dative, which seems to imply a direct dedication to the deceased, is rare before the Roman period, when it becomes particularly common in epitaphs involving, as is so frequent, the 'construction-formula', in which case the dative is simply that of the party for whom the tomb is built,[272] and when it also occurs frequently under the influence of the datival use found in Roman epitaphs.[273] At Rhodes it seems to occur unequivocally only in three cases. The first reads Ἀπολλόδωρος / Ἀγησάνδρωι τῶι πατρὶ καὶ Καλλίσται τᾶι ματρί,[274] the second[275] Μένιππος Καρ(πασιώτας?) Ἀρίσται τᾶι γυναικὶ / χρηστὰ χαῖρε, and the third Αἰλίᾳ Μενεσθείᾳ τῇ καὶ Καλλικλείᾳ Φλάουιος Δράκων ὁ ἀνήρ.[276] The last is of the Roman period, and probably reflects the influence of the Latin dedicatory formula, *Dis Manibus*, to which the dative case of the name of the deceased may stand in apposition,[277] or a suppressed 'construction-formula'; it is in any case of no significance for the pre-Roman period. The first example, inscribed on a circular monument, is, however, relatively early, probably of the late third century B.C. (and, if so, perhaps among the earliest surviving monuments from the eastern necropolis). The most probable explanation of the dative in this instance is indicated by an inscription on a circular altar on Cos, probably of the first century B.C.[278]: Γαΐου Ἐλουΐου Γαΐου / Ῥωμαῖος (sic) vac. ⟨Γ⟩άϊος / ἐξελεύθερος τῷ αὐτοῦ / πάτρωνι ἐπέθηκε τὸν / βωμόν, i.e. the *libertus* 'set up the altar on' his *patronus*. It is true that in a similar case,[279] Φιλομάθης Σελεύκου· / Ἐπίνοια τροφὸς Ἡροδότ[ου?(ος?)]/ Τρύφων, Φιλομάθει, Herzog understood τὸν βωμὸν ἀνέθηκαν[280], but there seems no reason to prefer the notion of *dedicating* (ἀνέθηκ-) the altar to the familiar *setting it on* (ἐπέθηκ-) the deceased, though the distinction may be slight.[281] It is in this latter sense, and not that of a dedication, that I understand the dative of the Rhodian inscriptions.

More obviously dedicatory in intent are those few epitaphs in which the normal nominative or genitive funerary formula is followed by the word θεοῖς or by the name of a specified deity in the dative. These need individual explanation. Two are from the eastern necropolis, and certainly have a funerary context. The first,[282] Ῥοδοφῶντος / Ἀπολλωνίου / καὶ τᾶς γυναικὸς / αὐτοῦ / Σωτοῦς Ναυτέλευς, / θεοῖς, is a perfectly normal epitaph except for the addition of the word θεοῖς, and it may be accepted as such, though the inscription itself is not reliably recorded, and was also said to have been, for an unexplained reason, written on both sides of the stone. Hiller commented 'Propter θεοῖς—nisi de catachthoniis deis agitur—fortasse melius inter bases honorarias collocandus fuisset titulus, quamvis in media necropoli inventus', but the correct formula for the man and his wife also argues for a funerary origin. The second piece from the eastern necropolis is a circular monument of the usual type with bucrania, but is clearly dedicatory and not funerary:[283] Ἀπολλώνιος / Ἑρμᾶι Ἁγεμόνι καὶ Ἥρωι δαίμονι, in letters of the Roman period. The dedication was presumably erected in a funerary precinct, like the dedication to Hero discussed above (p. 40); there is nothing to suggest that it is a tombstone, though the dedication to the ἥρως δαίμων may refer to the *Manes* of a dead person.[284] Another inscription[285] bearing the θεοῖς formula is a funerary stele of the Roman period, and clearly reflects Roman formulae, for the dedication is made μνείας χάριν, *memoriae causa*, by a father for his daughter, θεοῖς: Νείκ[ω]ν Παλεοπολίτ[ας] / Εὐκαρπίαν Παλε(οπολίτιδα) τὰν θυ/γατέραν μνείας χάριν. Here we are in the world of Roman funerary concepts. Finally, an epitaph from Nisyros,[286] also of late date, combines the dedicatory and the funerary formulae. The stone is a small funerary stele, with a representation of the deceased woman, and the inscription Φαρνάκης Ἀν/τιφάνου Μύν/διος Ἡρὼ 'Επαφρίωνος Μυν/δίαν τὴν ἑ/αυτοῦ γυναῖκα / θεοῖς, φιλοστόργιστα ε/ἰς αὐτάν. It may then be said that in the hellenistic and Roman periods the use of the dedicatory formula θεοῖς in a funerary context is very exceptional, and that where it is certain it can usually be explained by the influence of Roman practice and Roman concepts.

4. SINGLE AND MULTIPLE PRIVATE GRAVES

Private graves of more than one person, mostly family graves, were a regular feature of Greek necropoleis at all times, and at Rhodes evidence for them is plentiful in two ways. In the first place, important family and group burial complexes were excavated in a largely undamaged condition in the Necropolis areas, particularly in the Ai Yanni neighbourhood, and secondly, the sepulchral inscriptions themselves very often record the names of more than one member of a family, and especially of man and wife. These two types of evidence, the excavated tombs and the tombstones, very rarely coincide, and it is necessary to consider them both in relation to one another and separately.

The best-preserved examples of family grave complexes are those excavated by the Italian Archaeological Service after the First World War in the Makry Steno area, at the point where the present Themistokli Sophouli Street turns west. On either side of the road at this point large burial complexes of the later hellenistic and Roman periods were found. These are still standing and, as already described (see above, p. 3), they are open hypogaea with courtyards approached by steps, consisting for the most part of a façade with a lower arched or rectangular series of cells containing the ashes or bones of the deceased, along with the funerary vases and other gifts, and, above them, the rock-cut or (in this particular case) stone-constructed terracing on which stood the funerary monuments. In some cases a row of loculi intervened between the *cellae* and the terrace above (see fig. 5). The normal, if not invariable, practice, was for the ashes of the deceased to be placed in a casket (osteotheke) against the side of the *cella*, and for the inhumed person to be placed on the floor in a wooden coffin, traces of which sometimes remain.[287] The *cellae* contain anything up to twelve caskets, of the exactly uniform pattern already described (pp. 12–13), the majority inscribed, and a few uninscribed. The loculi above the *cellae* each contained a single casket.[288] The caskets are themselves not funerary monuments, but simply ash-containers, and the true funerary monument stood on the terrace above, as may be seen at Cova. The unusual inscription on a circular altar from Makry Steno, Ῥηγείνου Διοδότου· ὅπου ἐκάη, seems to indicate a direct connection between the monument and the ashes in the casket below.[288a] It is regrettable that there survive, out of well over a thousand Rhodian tombstones and caskets, almost no complements between a casket and a funerary monument, but at least one pair does exist, consisting of a casket with the names of two men, and a rectangular base of a circular funerary altar with an almost identical inscription.[289] (It may be noted that while the base was found in the eastern necropolis area the casket was found in a house near the Street of the Knights.) There can be no doubt that these two objects represent the casket and the funerary monument of the same pair of men, and they provide the pattern for what was, no doubt, a uniform practice. The two inscriptions are not identical, that on the casket being shorter. As we have already commented, in many cases, as here, the version on the casket was shorter by the omission of some detail of civil status, but it is not possible to assume that that was always so, since in some instances the casket carries a full statement of the civil status.[290]

The family graves with inscribed caskets discovered *in situ* in the Ai Yanni necropolis are often of considerable extent, and contain the remains of kin embracing three or four degrees of propinquity. Normally the ashes contained in the caskets and the corresponding inscription are of one person only, and the relationship to each other of the individuals buried is not stated, as it quite often is on the tombstones, and consequently it has to be inferred from the names. This in turn is only possible when the patronymic, and in some cases the demotic or ethnic, is given; in instances where the caskets are all inscribed with only a single name the relationship remains conjectural. One example of a family burial group is provided by one of the main hypogaea at Ai Yanni (that with the

Doric frieze) consisting of five *cellae* and nine loculi.[291] The *cellae* contained (from the left) (*a*) a large plain marble sarcophagus inscribed Ἐπικράτευς (*NS* 362), with skeleton, originally lying within a wooden coffin, and some insignificant gifts, (*b*) an uninscribed casket, (*c*) three caskets, of which two are inscribed, viz. Ἐπιτυνχα/νούσας (363) and Καλλιόπης (364), and one uninscribed, containing a long hairpin, an ear-pick, and three trinkets, (*d*) an uninscribed casket, two cinerary urns, and the remains of an inhumation burial, and (*e*) eight inscribed caskets and three cinerary urns. The inscribed caskets clearly belong to one family of Rhodian demesmen of the Lindian Peraean deme of Amos, for the inscriptions read (365) Νουμηνίου / Νουμηνίου / Ἀμίου, (366) Μέδοντος / Νουμηνίου / Ἀμίου, (367) Τιμοθέου / Νουμηνίου / Ἀμίου, (368) Εὐαγόρα / Εὐνίκου / Ἀμίου, (369) Ἀρτεμεισίας, (370) Ἐπαφροδίτου, (371) Ἀριστοβουλίδος, and (372) Πλούτου. The names are those of the father (365) and two sons (366 and 367), or else of three sons of a father buried elsewhere, and, perhaps, a cousin of the sons (368), together with four persons of humbler rank, who may have been servants or manumitted slaves. The grave is that of a well-to-do family (less the mother) from the Peraea, which, like many others, had settled in the capital and prospered there in the second century B.C. The loculi above contain caskets with the ashes of Rhodian demesmen of Camiran demes of about the same date—seemingly unrelated to the Amians. They are, from left to right, (*a*) (373) Θευδώρου Μενάνδρου, (*b*) (374) Μενάνδρου Θευδώρου Πλαρίου, (*c*) (375) Σωσικράτευς Καλλικράτευς Τλωίου, (*d*) (376) Θευδώρου Θευδώρου Λελίου, (*e*), containing two osteothekai, (377) Ῥοδοκλεῦς Ἀρχιπόλιος Νισυρίου, and (378) Θευδώρου Λέοντος Πλαρίου, (*f*), containing three caskets, two uninscribed and one with the inscription (379) Λέοντος, (*g*), containing two caskets, (380) Χαιρέα Θευδώρου Πλαρίου and (381) Χαιρέα Χαιρέα Πλαρίου, and (*h*), containing two caskets, (382) Μιννίδος, and (383) Ξενοχάριος. The Tloioi were certainly located in the Peraea,[292] and the Lelioi inhabited the centre of the island, south of Profiti Elia,[293] while the location of the Plarioi is still unknown.[294] The Nisyrioi also belonged to the Camiran deme system.[295] Evidently this was a large family grave with the remains of members of different Camiran demes who intermarried—their exact relationship is not as clear as in the preceding group—together, once more, with their servants Minnis and Xenochares. Although intermarriage between demesmen of different cities was naturally frequent,[296] and it may be that these Lindian and Camiran families were related by marriage, there is no sign that this is so, and it is perhaps more probable that the two groups of burials, those in the *cellae* and those in the loculi, were not connected in spite of the proximity of their burial-places.

A final example is provided by a hypogaeum immediately adjacent to the preceding. It consists of three rectangular *cellae* and, on one side, two loculi apparently added later.[297] The first two *cellae* (A and B) contained burials, and the third (C) contained eleven caskets, one of which was uninscribed, and a funerary urn. The loculi were empty. The inscriptions on the caskets are: (385) Τιμακράτευς Διοτίμου Ἀμνιστίου, (386) Ἀριστοτέλευς Τιμακράτευς Ἀμνιστίου, (387) Διοτίμου Τιμακράτευς Ἀμνιστίου, (388) Ἀριστοτέλευς Φιλογένευς Ἀμνιστίου, (389) Φιλωνίδα Αἴσχρωνος, (390) Αἴσχρωνος Αἴσχρωνος Καρπαθιοπολίτα, (391) [Αἴσ]χρωνο[ς] Γ Καρπαθιοπολίτα, (392) Λυσά[νδρας] Θευφάντου Πεδιάδος, (393) Εὐφρανορίδος Θευφάντου Πεδιάδος, (394) Εὐφράνακτος Ἀνδροτίμου, and (395) Εὐφράνασσα Δεξιναύτα Ἱστανία. Here again we encounter a family group of mixed Rhodian descent: the Amnistioi, a group of two or three generations, are Camirans, the Carpathiopolites are Lindians, the Pedieis are probably Lindian, and the Histanians are Camiran. Once more, there is no explicit relationship between the Lindian and Camiran elements. In addition we notice here that there are two persons with patronymics but no demotics, and one of these, Philonides (389), seems to be the son and brother of a Carpathiopolite. Here it is likely that the demotic has simply been omitted. On the other hand, in yet another adjacent hypogaeum[298] the persons recorded on four out of the five caskets have only name and patronymic, and the fifth has no patronymic and the foreign city ethnic Βαργυλιῆτις. Here too at least two, and perhaps three, generations are represented, this time of a 'Rhodian' family (cf. above, pp. 47–8).

Examples of such family or group graves could be multiplied,[298a] but these suffice to show the general nature of such multiple burials at Rhodes, as represented by the surviving remains. The purely epigraphical evidence for multiple burials consists of tombstones on which more than one dead person is named. We have already noticed that the family relationship is not recorded on the caskets of multiple burials, and that the actual funerary monument, stele or altar, corresponding to the casket or coffin of the hypogaeum, hardly ever survives. Thus there is little or no link between the archaeological and the epigraphical evidence, and we are left in doubt as to the type of burial which the tombstones marked: were they simple joint tombs of husband and wife and children, buried separately and apart from their relatives, or do the tombstones on which the names are recorded constitute the monumental expression of the multiple graves, or at least of part of them? We cannot answer these questions, but we can at least notice the main characteristics of these joint or family tombstones.

They are, of course, not an exclusively Rhodian phenomenon. They are equally common at Athens in the fourth century,[299] before the sumptuary legislation of Demetrius of Phaleron, which seems to have resulted in the reduction of the number of such joint tombstones. Whereas, however, in Rhodes the use of the joint inscription recording the names of husband and wife, and perhaps children, seems common in all sections of the population—demesmen, 'Rhodians', and foreigners—in Athens they are almost confined to citizens, perhaps because the foreign population of Athens increased significantly after the fourth century, and the post-Demetrian period was not favourable to such inscriptions. Rhodes and Athens apart, there is little evidence of joint funerary inscriptions, and in some places, notably Boeotia, the practice seems scarcely to have existed; for instance at Tanagra out of 1,100 funerary inscriptions there are only three joint inscriptions,[300] and at Thespiai out of 330 under ten are double.[301] In all cases (and particularly in Boeotia) we must exclude from reckoning those instances in which the tombstone has been reused (perhaps upside down) at a later, perhaps a much later, date.[302] On the other hand, at Rhodes in the later hellenistic and Roman periods the ratio is 1 : 10, slightly lower than at Athens (1 : 7).

The main features of the Rhodian joint inscriptions may be briefly noted. First, such inscriptions are confined to the two main types of funerary monument, the circular monument (being sometimes inscribed on the base on which the monument stood, and sometimes on the monument, and sometimes on both) and the rectangular, which seems normally to have stood directly on the terrace or similar paving, and not on a separate base.[303] On stelai and on caskets they are much less common.[304] Second, by far the greatest number of such inscriptions record the name of husband and wife, normally either in the full formula (nominative or genitive), ὁ δεῖνα τοῦ δεῖνος + demotic, καὶ ἁ γυνὰ ἁ δεῖνα τοῦ δεῖνος + demotic, or the shorter version ὁ δεῖνα τοῦ δεῖνος + demotic, καὶ ἁ γυνὰ ἁ δεῖνα. Very occasionally, the wife is named first, and the name of the husband follows, καὶ τοῦ ἀνδρὸς (τοῦ δεῖνος),[305] no doubt because the wife died first. Third, there is a further class of monument in which persons, a man and woman normally, are buried together without any indication of their relationship, but usually with an indication of their racial or city ethnics, these being different.[306] Such inscriptions clearly denote relationships determined by individual circumstances and cannot be associated with any specific category of persons. Thus those in which a man and a woman of different origins are recorded no doubt reflect an irregular union. Some clearly indicate a humble social status, for the persons commemorated are in several cases described as ἐγγενεῖς, persons born in slavery;[307] it was natural for slaves to cohabit. Sometimes two male, or two female, persons who were probably slaves, or at least of humble origin, seem to have been buried together,[308] as, for example, Λυσίμαχος καὶ Σαπὶς Μαιῶται χρηστοὶ χαίρετε[309] and Βίθυος καὶ Εὐετηρίας,[310] Φιλουμένα καὶ Ὀπώρα χρηστοὶ χαίρετε,[311] Πλούτου καὶ Προπόσιος,[312]

Μύρτιδος καὶ Μυρτοῦς.[313] On the other hand, an inscription recording the names of two women,[314] *Εὐφροσύνα Ἐφεσία χρηστὰ χαῖρε καὶ Ἰσιγόνη Φα-σηλῖτις* (where the formulation indicates that the second name was added later, though the hand seems to be the same) can hardly be indicative of a servile status, and the nature of their relationship is not clear. No less uncertain is the epitaph[315] *Ἀρτεμοῦς Φασηλείτιδος καὶ Δαμονίκου Φασηλείτα καὶ Ὀλυμπιάδος Λυκαονίσσας*, and further variation is provided by an epitaph in which the names of father and daughter, members of the Physcian deme, are separated by that of a metic from Myndos: *Ἀλέξανδρος Φιλτάτου Φύσκιος, | Διονυσάριν (sic) Μυνδία μέτοικος, Ὀλυνπιὰς Ἀλεξάνδρα Φυσκία.*[315a] Such inscriptions elude exact analysis.

One particular feature of the joint inscription remains to be noted. In an overwhelming majority of cases the names—husband, wife; husband, wife, and children—are inscribed in one hand, i.e. presumably at one and the same time. Particularly in west Greece there are many instances in which names of the members of one family (presumably) have been added in the course of time to a single tombstone,[316] and there are numerous examples at Athens and elsewhere,[317] but at Rhodes this does not seem to have been the case. Normally the names of all the deceased appear to have been inscribed at one time, and I know of only one example in which the names on one stone, belonging to the members of one family, are said to have been inscribed in different hands, and that stone, of Imperial date, is unfortunately lost.[318] How are we to imagine the process of the erection of the tombstone? Did the parents undertake the entire operation in their lifetime, as was so frequent in Asia Minor at a later date, or did the survivors—the children, normally, or the koinon—erect a provisional memorial (or perhaps simply provide for the casket or sarcophagus in the loculus) for the first parent deceased, and, when the other died, replace it by a joint tombstone? That, a practice frequent in the modern world, seems the most natural explanation. Sometimes, however, the children's names are also recorded in the same hand (with, occasionally, in the Roman period, the word *ζώντων*, 'in their lifetime', added, a formula which is universally used in Asia Minor during this period, when the monument has been erected in the lifetime of the *paterfamilias*),[319] and it seems natural to suppose that, not only when the parents' names stand alone, but also when the children's names are recorded in the same hand, the inscription was carved on the instructions of the children in their own lifetime (*ζώντων*), or on those of another survivor.[320] In the case of an inscription of Roman date the intervention of a third party is explicit: *τούτου προνοεῖ Φλάουιος.*[321] The practice, especially common in Roman Asia Minor in the later Imperial period, by which it was customary for the parent to erect in his own lifetime a funerary heroon for his parents, his children, his descendants, and his dependents, with a formula such as ζῶν ἑαυτῷ καὶ τοῖς γονεῦσι καὶ τῇ γυναικὶ καὶ τοῖς τέκνοις, certainly did not yet exist in the later hellenistic period.[322] Simultaneous or contemporary deaths of two or more members of a family, all commemorated posthumously, must have been very rare, even if mass disasters were not unknown in ancient Rhodes. This problem is potentially not without significance when we are assessing the career of an individual named in a joint epitaph. If he or she was the first of a family to die, there may well have been a lapse of twenty years or more between that death and the erection of the monument, and allowance must be made for his or her lifespan being correspondingly earlier than the date suggested by the lettering of the tombstone.

It is clear from this analysis both of the group-burials in hypogaea and of the tombstones recording joint burials that the family link was in this respect strongly felt and sustained. The same feeling is very clearly attested at Rhodes by the numerous statues erected by members of one family to one member of it; the recorded relatives regularly include children, grandchildren, uncles, and aunts, and may even stretch as far afield as collaterals of the third generation.[323] Such dedicatory monuments have no real parallel in Athens, where they are few in number and are limited to dedications by fathers, brothers, etc.,[324] while on the other hand the Rhodian pattern is repeated at both Telos and Nisyros in the Rhodian period and is also found at Cos.[325] Those group graves which contain the remains both of related family groups of citizens and of persons of humbler status side by side, may in addition indicate that the Rhodians of the later hellenistic age, like the Romans, associated slaves, and freedmen,[326] with the members of the family in burial. We are not on the whole well informed as to the disposal of the bodies of slaves in the Greek world before the Roman period,[327] and it would be unwise to assign a distinctive practice to Rhodes in this matter, but it may at least be said that the hypogaea of Ai Yanni, with their inscribed caskets, provide a clear example of household graves extending beyond the recognized kinship groups.

5. BURIAL AND COMMEMORATION OF MEMBERS OF KOINA

One category of multiple burial stands apart, that of koinon burials, in which the members of a koinon were buried together, regardless, it appears, of family relationships. There are various aspects of this practice to be considered.

First we may note that the practice of burying members of social, religious, and gentilicial groups in a common grave was of long standing in the Greek world. The earliest example is provided by the notice found at Campanian Cyme, of the first half of the fifth century, οὐ θέμις ἐν/τοῦθα κεῖσθ/αι ἰ μὲ τὸν βεβαχχευμένον, 'None has the right to be buried here save the initiated' i.e. of Dionysus.[328] The practice seems to have been a feature of the cult of the chthonic Dionysus, whose initiates were Βάκχοι, and it continued in Athens and in Boeotia until a late date. The last lines of a decree of the Athenian Iobacchi, of the later second century A.D.,[329] although it does not explicitly state that the Ἰόβακχοι were buried in a cemetery belonging to the koinon, certainly suggest that only the members of the society were concerned in the burial:[330] ἐὰν δέ τις τελευτή/ση ἰόβακχος, γεινέσθω στέφανος αὐ/τῷ μέχ(ρ)ι * ε′, καὶ τοῖς ἐπι-ταφήσασι τι/θέσθω οἴνου κεράμιον ἕν, ὁ δὲ μὴ / ἐπιταφήσας εἰργέσθω τοῦ οἴνου. The verb ἐπιταφέω, 'to be present at the burial', otherwise un-attested,[331] probably refers to formal participation of the members of the koinon in the funeral. Recognition of the duty of members of a thiasos to give due burial to their 'brother' is clearly attested in another law of Attic thiasotai, of the third century B.C., from the Peiraeus, in which the coherence and solidarity of members is stressed;[332] it states [εἰὰν δέ τι]ς αὐτῶν ἀπογίνητ[αι φρά]σει ἢ υὸς [ἢ ἀδελφὸς ἢ] πατὴρ ἢ ὃς ἂν οἰκειότατος εἶ τοῦ θιασοῦ, τοῦ δ’ ἀπογινομένο[υ] ἰέναι ἐπ’ ἐχφορὰν καὶ αὐτοὺς καὶ τοὺς φίλους ἅπαντας. However, as in the law of the Iobacchi, it does not follow from this that the burial took place in a cemetery belonging to the thiasos. The 'friends' may have accompanied the body to the family grave. In Boeotia, at and near Tanagra, on the other hand, burial in a koinon-grave is clearly indicated by a number of burials carried out by named koina, expressed in characteristically brief epitaphs, of which the earliest is Γαλάτας· οὗτον ἔθαψαν τὺ / Διωνιουσιαστή, of the third century B.C.;[333] a similar practice obtained at Chalkis across the Euripos.[334] Though the practice of collective burial of members of societies may have originated in the cult of Dionysus,[335] it certainly soon spread to other cult koina, and also to the various types of secular koina which soon pro-liferated throughout the Greek world. In the strictly cult-koina we find the practice once more at Tanagra in the thiasos of the Athenaistai, τὺ Ἀθηναϊστή, the burial of one of whose members is recorded in identical terms to those employed by the Διωνιουσιαστή:[336] Ἐπὶ Λυκάονι· οὗτοι ἔθαψαν τὺ Ἀθηναϊστή, and again, Ἐλπίς· ταύτην ἔθαψεν ἡ σύνοδος τῶν Ἀθηναϊστῶν;[337] in less specific terms, we find [τοῦτ]ον ἔθα[ψαν οἱ σ]υν-θύται.[338] The practice of common burial spread to the other secular, professional, and gentilicial koina, which, while preserving a religious basis, embraced many other aspects of life, and is attested from numerous cities and regions—notably Attica, Rhodes, and in the Roman period, south Russia and Asia Minor.[339] It is to be emphasized that the practice we are here considering, the acceptance of responsibility by a koinon for the burial of its members, must be distinguished from the Roman practice of forming *collegia* expressly for the purposes of burial, the *collegia funeraticia*, as they are called.[340] To these there seem to be few parallels in the Greek world, and they need not be further considered here.

Nowhere is the practice better attested in the pre-Roman period than at Rhodes, where we are able to see the whole process, from the purchase of land by the koinon for a burial-ground to the burial of the individual member and the funerary ceremonies which accompanied and commemorated it. It is only natural that in hellenistic Rhodes, where the social koina were so numerous, and played so vital a part in the life of the foreign population, they should have a highly developed system of benefits for their members; with their grandiloquent titles, their own magistrates, priesthoods, assemblies, cults, and social services, they provided foreign residents in Rhodes and Rhodian territory with the same type of social environment, the same modes of advancement, and the same opportunities for lavish benefactions, as were provided by the civic organization for Rhodian demesmen, who themselves rarely, if ever, belonged to them. They were, so to speak, a microcosm of the state, and the loyalty that they evoked in their members was rewarded with honours similar to those awarded by the state. That the feeling of belonging to a society was an active element in the communal life of koina, and extended to the practice of common burial, is explicit in the decree of the thiasotai of the Peiraeus quoted above.[341] That such cultivation of social life in all its aspects, and especially its emphasis on common banquets, etc., might have an adverse effect on family coherence, was stressed by Polybius in his account of the moral decline of Boeotia,[342] but this does not seem to have been so at Rhodes.

The main interest of the Rhodian material lies not in the evidence it provides for burial by koina, a widely attested practice, but in the light it throws on the general question of the ownership and development of burial-grounds by koina. We are also able to see in some detail the form of commemoration provided by the koinon, in terms both of the actual ceremonies performed at the grave, and also of the honorific inscriptions and particular forms of decoration carved on the tombstones. The evidence belongs almost entirely to the last two centuries before Christ, though a little of it is of Imperial date.

First, the ownership of burial-grounds. This is dealt with in detail in two documents emanating from the koinon of the Aphrodisiastai Hermogeneioi, of the second century B.C.[343] They are inscribed on the front and back of a block which was evidently erected within the burial precinct. The first document consists of a decree of the koinon introduced by a Benefactor, εὐεργέτας, named Zenon, of Selge, in the eponymous year of the Priest of Helios, Aratophanes, on the seventeenth day of Panamos.

The preamble reads 'In order that the documents relating to the survey of the land (or, the title-deeds: ἀμφουριασμοί) of the real estate belonging to the koinon, and of the burial-plots (ταφίαι), may be accessible, as far as is possible, to all members of the koinon (ἐρανισταί) for ever, and that no injustice may be done to any member, it has been decreed by the koinon . . .'[344] Provisions follow for the election of an individual who is to prepare a stele of Lartian stone and, having acquired from the magistrates of the koinon the texts of the deeds, to inscribe them on the stone and erect the stele in the area of the graves of the koinon, at whatever point he judges most conspicuous and secure. The magistrates are to make copies of the deeds available to him, and to repay his expenses.[345] A second decree, also proposed by Zenon, of a later, no doubt the subsequent, year, that of the priest Agoranax, ordains that since the man chosen had died before he could carry out his task, the koinon should elect two men to put into effect the same provisions within the space of sixty days from their election. And the chief magistrate (ἀρχερανιστάς) shall . . .[346] The inscription breaks off here, and was apparently continued on another block, for the stone itself is complete.[347]

The second document, on the back of the stele, contains the copies of the deeds of ownership and of the conveyances referred to in the decree, and is headed ἀπὸ τοῦ χρηματισμ[οῦ . . .], i.e. 'from the archive'; the deeds are dated by yet a third Priest of Helios, Archinos, but, for a reason that is not clear, only one conveyance is recorded—of a very complex nature—relating to the purchase of a plot of land in the city by the koinon, and it does not cover the sepulchral land referred to in the decree; in other words, it carries one deed of the ἔγγαια, real estate belonging to the koinon.[348] Nevertheless it seems clear from the first decree that ταφίαι—apparently an exclusively Rhodian word, found at Kamiros in the neuter plural form τάφια or ταφῖα[349]—formed one of the main categories of land owned by koina, and they were no doubt extensive. The use of the plural, ταφίαι, indicates, strictly speaking, that there was more than one such burial-plot belonging to each koinon, and this should probably be accepted literally, for it does not seem likely that the word refers to individual graves. It is possible that such plots were all in one area, as they certainly were at Cos,[350] and contiguous, but had been bequeathed or bought up separately, as need arose. A gift of land to a koinon for this purpose is attested, among a series of benefactions, in an inscription from Kamiros.[351] Each no doubt had its own title-deed or survey document, which, in the case of the koinon of the Aphrodisiastai Hermogeneioi at least, was duly registered, and inscribed on the surviving stele which was set up in the burial-place, like the boundary stones at Cos.[352]

Another document, probably of a slightly later date—perhaps of the early first century B.C.—records the various ceremonies and honours connected with the burial of a distinguished member and Benefactor of a koinon. A large block of 'Lartian' stone now in Venice (fig. 113, *a–d*)[353] carries on its four faces decrees and honorific inscriptions in honour of, and dedications by, Dionysodoros of Alexandria, a lifelong resident in Rhodes, and member of τὸ κοινὸν τὸ Ἀλιαδᾶν καὶ Ἀλιαστᾶν (or Ἀλιαστᾶν καὶ Ἀλιαδᾶν). The texts are inscribed in a perplexing sequence which seems to reflect the order in which Dionysodoros himself had them inscribed. This order has been much debated,[354] but it is sufficient for our purpose to observe that the main text is a decree of the koinon in honour of Dionysodoros (who had been a paying member of the koinon, ἐρανίζων, for thirty-five years) in which the tributes to be paid to him both during his lifetime and after his death are recorded. They include crowning with the largest golden crown permissible by law, and a consequential sum of three obols (presumably contributed by each member) εἰς στέφανον is to be set aside for him at each session of the synod of the koinon; and the same honours are to be continued for him after death.[355] These honours are to be proclaimed at each session of the synod, when, presumably, the crown was awarded to, and duly returned to the koinon by, Dionysodoros.[356] And after his death, the decree continues, the officials of the koinon are to purchase with the sum accumulated a crown and double fillet and to proclaim them at the synodos, and the crown is then to be sold, and the epistatas of the koinon is to deposit the purchase-price with the koinon at the meeting in the following month, and the secretary is to enter in the accountant's records, 'To the account of Dionysodoros, the Benefactor, who was crowned with a golden crown for ever, (the cost of) the crown that was bought';[357] by this means Dionysodoros would remain a Benefactor in perpetuity. There follow the specifically funerary honours: the proclamation and the ritual of coronation are to be carried out every year in the month of Hyakinthios 'among the burial-plots as well' (καὶ ἐπὶ τᾶν ταφιᾶν); and the money collected in that month for this purpose is to be used every year by the magistrates in perpetuity for the crown to be proclaimed ἐπὶ τάφοις, and his monument (that which survives) is also to be crowned (καὶ στεφανούντω αὐτοῦ τὸ μνημεῖον). Any attempt to annul these honours is subject to severe penalties.[358] A record added subsequently to the decree states that among the honours decreed to him in perpetuity is that of libations ἐπὶ τῶν τόπων, i.e. ἐπὶ τῶν ταφιᾶν, on the burial-ground(s).[359]

The second part of the decree reveals that at Rhodes, as elsewhere, a considerable commemorative ritual might be attached to the tombs of members of koina. Much the same sort of practice was no doubt current at other places where koinon-burials are attested, at Athens, at Tanagra, at Cos, at Chios, and in the Bosporan area,[360] but the Rhodian evidence is the only detailed statement we have. Particularly worthy of note is the annual coronation of the funerary monument, and the annual performance of libation, presumably on the funerary altar, on the terrace above the hypogaeum. These commemorative reunions at the tomb were certainly not only calculated to keep alive the memory of the departed 'friend' or 'brother', but also in general to cement the bonds which linked the members of the koinon to each other.

It is unfortunate that we have no means of identifying any koinon burial-plot. There is indeed much that remains uncertain in the whole procedure: whether there was one burial area for all koina (as seems to have been the case at Cos),[361] whether burial within the plot was open to all members, or only to Benefactors, or to members selected by the koinon, or also to members who had expressed a wish to that effect. The tombstones of Benefactors are easily identified since they carry the title εὐεργέτας, but we have no means of telling who else may have been buried in the plot. In some places, notably Tanagra, and Phanagoria, as we have seen (p. 59), the epitaph states plainly that the deceased had been buried by the koinon, but this does not seem to have been explicitly recorded at Rhodes.

We may now turn to consider the other side of the evidence for burial by koina, that provided by the tombstones. A few of the large number of Rhodian tombstones carry an indication of one sort or another that the individual had been honoured by a koinon. These may probably be regarded as tombstones which had been set up in a koinon-plot. It could be maintained, indeed, that an individual bearing an honorific title bestowed on him by a koinon need not necessarily be a member of the koinon, but might be a member of the general public, and also that even if he was a member of a koinon, the fact that his tombstone carries his honorific title is not in itself proof that he was buried in a koinon-plot. These are certainly valid considerations, but I do not think that they compel us to alter the view that members of koina, particularly those who had been honoured by them, were buried in koina-plots. For this there are two especial reasons: (*a*) we know from the dossier of Dionysodoros that the commemorative ceremonies of koina were held in the grave precincts belonging to the koina, and we know that Dionysodoros himself was a member of the koinon which decreed the honours, as well as being a Benefactor of it; there can then be no doubt that Benefactors might be buried and commemorated in the grave precincts of the koina, and not in private graves; and (*b*) the εὐεργέται attested on tombstones are called mostly simply εὐεργέτας, and very occasionally εὐεργέτας τοῦ κοινοῦ, but never εὐεργέτας of this or that particular koinon.[362] From this it follows most naturally that they were buried within the precinct of the, or a, koinon of which they had been proclaimed Benefactors, and not in a private grave, where further specification of the koinon could hardly have been omitted. Therefore we need have little hesitation in supposing that the tombstones of Benefactors come from koina-cemeteries. On the other hand some tombstones indicate that the deceased was honoured by a number of different koina, without being said to be a member of any, and it obviously cannot be inferred that the individual was a member of all of them (though for all we know he could have been),[363] or that he was buried in a koinon-plot. Nevertheless, as far as we can tell, almost all persons honoured by koina were foreigners, and therefore likely to be members of them. An exception to foreign nationality is provided by a tombstone of the rectangular type, of white marble,[364] which commemorates two Lindian demesmen, one a Λαδάρμιος, the other a Καρπαθιοπολίτας, of whom the former is described as a εὐεργέτας τοῦ κοινοῦ, while the other has no additional title. The Ladarmian had evidently been a Benefactor of the κοινόν (perhaps without being a member of it), and it is clear from the formula εὐεργ. τοῦ κοιν. that the koinon had been responsible for his burial, and therefore, in all probability, since only one koinon is mentioned, that he was buried within its burial-plot. The common burial of, or (at least) common monument to, the two men, who were evidently not directly related by blood, is in keeping with the practice within koina, of which other examples are given below (p. 67).

  This matter might be settled decisively if the provenance of the tombstones relating to members of koina could be assigned to a particular cemetery. Unfortunately, however, they seem all to have been discovered casually, and their provenance is vague. Where it is ascertainable, they seem, as might be expected in view of their general dates, to come from the eastern Necropolis area, where no doubt private and koina burial areas existed side by side.

  One further point requires clarification: does the word εὐεργέτας, Benefactor, refer to the benefactor of a koinon, or to the benefactor of e.g. the state as a whole? The fact that the persons so described on their tombstones are almost entirely foreigners, and that virtually no demesman or citizen of Rhodos is so described, is not in itself sufficient indication that the title is used with reference to a body other than the citizen body.[365] However, honorific documents bestowing εὐεργεσία issued by koina show clearly that εὐεργέτας, *tout simple*, was a frequent honorific title in Rhodian koina.[366] Dionysodoros carries the title εὐεργέτας in first place, immediately after his ethnic, in such a way as to form an honorific 'cognomen': [ἀ]ρχερανιστὰς Ἁλιαστᾶν καὶ Ἁλιαδᾶν | [Δ]ιονυσόδωρος Ἀλεξανδρεὺς εὐεργέ/τας ἐπαινεθείς, κ.τ.λ.; ἀρχερανιστὰς | Διονυσόδωρος Ἀλεξανδρεὺς εὐεργέτας; Δ. Ἀ. εὐεργέτας τοῦ κοινοῦ,[367] and there are numerous other examples of this usage. Certainty is not possible, but one or two inscriptions, discussed below, with the full title, εὐεργέτας τοῦ κοινοῦ confirm that usually the benefactor is benefactor of a koinon.

In one group of epitaphs of members of koina, the distinction between funerary and honorific inscriptions is often blurred in a way that is unfamiliar elsewhere. These tombstones may carry a full list of the honours bestowed on the deceased in a way that is hardly distinguishable from an honorific dedication inscribed on a statue base.[368] There are, however, usually indications in the text—by the use of the nominative or genitive case, not found in honorific inscriptions in which the accusative is invariably used, by the addition of an acclamation in some funerary inscriptions, or by the addition of θεοῖς in the honorific dedications, or by the addition in the funerary inscription of the wife's name—that the monument is a funerary monument. Sometimes, nevertheless, the issue remains uncertain, and the occasional difficulty of distinguishing between the honorific and the funerary may be illustrated by the fact that, as stated, Hiller von Gaertringen originally regarded the honorific dossier of Dionysodoros as funerary, even though its form—a large rectangular slab—is not paralleled among the funerary monuments of Rhodes. In general, however, the distinction can be made on the basis of one of the criteria noted above, especially by the use of the case. It is also safe in fact, even if the method is unsound, to distinguish by the type of monument, for the honorific inscriptions occur on plain cylindrical or rectangular bases, and not on the rectangular monuments, and only once on the cylindrical ones decorated with bucrania and garlands. Other texts consist of a summary statement with a finite verb, that an individual has been honoured by a koinon;[369] none of these embodies an explicit funerary formula, but some of them are inscribed on bases worked to receive a stele, and can hardly be statue bases. In any case, the recording of the honours bestowed by the koina on the deceased, and the consequent approximation between the two types of monument, reflect plainly the prestige attaching to such honours in the mind of the foreign population of Rhodes. Such grandiloquent details are never recorded on the tombstones of Rhodian demesmen.

One circular funerary monument (fig. 114, *a, b*) with bucrania and garland—the only one of its type to carry an honorific decree of a koinon, in this case the koinon of the Athenastai—is of exceptional interest,[370] both because the benefactions conferred on the koinon by the deceased are recorded in precise terms, and also because below the decree stands a summary funerary formulation of the honours bestowed by another koinon, that of the Artemisiastai. The decree itself, which is unfortunately badly phrased and obscure, as well as partly illegible, records that Chrysippos, described as ἐγγενής, son of Merops,[371] in addition to various unspecified εὐεργεσίαι, had acted with courage 'when an obstacle arose on the occasion of the carrying out to burial of the doctor, Menophilos, enduring every danger; he entered the house with the bearers and carried out the corpse (κᾶδος), and taking in his hands the sarcophagus (ἀγγεῖον) set it on the tomb.'[372] The nature of the 'obstacle' (κώλυμα) can only be conjectured—the original editor suggested that it reflected the unpopularity of the doctor, which manifested itself in demonstrations; while it has also been proposed to see in it the result of an epidemic of plague which rendered contact with the body dangerous.[373] The latter conjecture is supported to some extent by the reference to personal danger, but the absence of any explicit reference to λοιμός or to λοιμικὴ διάθεσις or περίστασις, such as one encounters in texts relating to epidemics, makes it uncertain.[374] The decree then apparently states that the koinon is in the habit of recording the names of Benefactors, and that it 'bestows freedom of action (?) on other koina'.[375] It then returns to the record of Chrysippos' virtues and benefactions, and ends with the decision to erect a statue of him and to crown him (or it) with a gold crown from funds provided by the treasurer, and to inscribe his name on a roll of honour of some sort.[376] The honours recorded below the decree and the funerary formula are those bestowed, also during the lifetime of Chrysippos, by the koinon of the Artemisiastai: Χρύσιππε | χρηστὲ χαῖρε· | τιμαθεὶς ὑπὸ τοῦ κοινοῦ | τῶν Ἀρτεμεισιαστᾶν χρυσέωι στεφάνωι καὶ εὐεργεσίαι. The fact that honours here recorded were bestowed by a different koinon from that which passed the decree may perhaps explain the otherwise most obscure reference to the 'freedom of action' bestowed on other koina: they were free, in spite of the prior claim of the Athenastai as being, no doubt, the koinon to which Chrysippos originally belonged,[377] or with which he was in some other way especially associated, to record their honours on the tombstone of the member of another koinon, whether he was a member of the second koinon or not. The second, abbreviated record thus associates the altar with those 'honorific' tombstones already discussed which carry the summary statement of honours bestowed in life by more than one koinon.[378]

Pride of place among the funerary monuments of Benefactors and members of koina belongs to the funerary monument of the same Dionyso-doros, whose honours we have already examined.[379] His tombstone (fig. 113, e, f) is conspicuous as one of the finest examples of the rectangular altars. Unfortunately, owing to damage to the upper surface it is impossible to determine whether it had a central boss; it certainly did not have more than one. The front face has the usual upper and lower mouldings, while the main surface (A) is occupied by four sunk panels each containing a wreath, namely (from left to right) three of olive or laurel and one of poplar (as on the honorific monument), and, below them, on the fascia of the lower moulding, the sepulchral inscription,

Διονυσοδώρου Ἀλεξανδρέως εὐεργέτα καὶ ἀρχερανιστᾶ, thus conforming to the titles of Dionysodoros in the 'dossier' compiled by him. Contrary to normal practice on such altars, the back (B) has also been inscribed. Here too the upper part carries four wreaths in sunk panels, the first, second, and fourth of olive or laurel, the third of poplar (once more as on the honorific monument), and below this an inscription of twelve lines recording the honours of one Iacchos and of Dionysodoros, both Alexandrians, the former possibly the brother of the latter.[380] The last line contains the additional names καὶ Διονυσίου Ἀλεξανδρέως καὶ Ἰθάκης Σολίδος, perhaps the son and wife, or more probably (since the relationship is not specified) another brother, and the sister-in-law, of Dionysodoros. On it are recorded the honours bestowed on Dionysodoros by the various koina mentioned in the honorific texts of the 'dossier', including in particular the proclamation by the koinon of the Haliastai of honours in the necropolis, ἀναγόρευσις τᾶν τιμᾶν ἐπὶ τῶν τόπων. Dionysodoros was probably not a member of all these koina,[381] but the funerary monument, extended to include his brother, also a Benefactor, was probably erected by common agreement or enterprise of the koina involved, possibly in line with the interpretation suggested above for the decree referring to 'freedom of action for other koina'. It was evidently erected some time before his death, since not all the honours bestowed on him by the koinon of the Haliadai in the main dossier are mentioned, and it was set up in the cemetery of the koinon of the Paniastai, which is mentioned first, and without name, and at it and on it were performed the ceremonies described in the dossier.[382] The inclusion on the same stone of his next-of-kin shows that family-ties were fostered within the koina (in spite of Polybius' doubts, mentioned above). In this connection another funerary monument, more precisely two funerary monuments, erected by a koinon are of interest. The two monuments provide, as already mentioned, the sole example of the survival of both the cinerary casket and the monument which stood on the terrace. The casket,[383] which was found in a Turkish house in the City of the Knights, is inscribed on two sides; (a) has the names of both deceased (who can hardly have been related by blood), Δώρου Μήδου | καὶ | Προτίμου Σιδωνίου, while (b) has simply εὐεργετᾶν. The rectangular base, supporting a circular monument, which was found in the eastern necropolis area and stood on the terrace above the hypogaeum, is inscribed towards the left end, Προτίμου Σιδωνίου | εὐεργέτα τοῦ κοινοῦ, and towards the right, Δώρου Μήδου.[384] It will be observed that Doros is not called a εὐεργέτας on the base, but his name is inscribed in far larger letters. Here, then, two unrelated foreigners of very different stock, united by the bond of membership of the koinon, were buried or commemorated together, just as the two Lindian demesmen, one of whom was a εὐεργέτας τοῦ κοινοῦ, were.

Other tombstones of Benefactors of koina are either of single individuals, or of single individuals to whose names those of their wives have
been appended. Some, as already explained, contain the full statement of
honours which had accrued to the individual, others simply record the
title εὐεργέτας or εὐεργετίς.[385] In one way or another, they all attest the
importance of the koina in the life of the foreigner, and the satisfaction
felt in membership. The evident encouragement given to them by the
state no doubt paid a rich dividend in terms of social harmony, εὐνομία,
of which in the later hellenistic age Rhodes, as Strabo tells us (652), was
the outstanding example.

Formally the funerary monuments of members of koina show a
significant variation in one respect from those of demesmen, in that they
frequently carry a relief representation of one or more crowns, as lavishly
indicated on the tombstone of Dionysodoros. The award of crowns after
death was, as we have seen, a feature of the rituals of the koina, and
the crowns so represented correspond to those awarded in this way.
Posthumous crowns were not infrequently awarded to meritorious
citizens elsewhere, and might be referred to in an epigram or epitaph,[386] or, alternatively or in addition, be represented on the stone,[387]
but at Rhodes this practice once again seems to have been confined
to koina, and to have been eschewed by demesmen and their
families. The representations of crowns are found placed in various
positions on the stone—at the top in a panel, or panels, at the bottom,
separating the two halves of an inscription horizontally, or even, in at
least one instance, in panels on the rectangular base supporting a circular (fig. 113, *h*) altar.[388] To return to an earlier phase of our discussion, we have already seen (pp. 22–4) that the conical bosses on the
rectangular funerary altars are probably best explained as supports for
wreaths and crowns placed on the altars at commemorative festivals;
though these bosses are not confined to the monuments erected for
foreigners.

Citizens and foreigners of all degrees, from rich merchants and men of
letters to slaves, do not, however, exhaust the full range of those for whom
provision was made in the cemeteries of Rhodes. There is in the British
Museum a remarkable solid stone skyphos round the body of which is
a decoration in relief of ivy leaves terminating in stylized blossoms;
below the decoration, in letters of the later hellenistic period, are the
words ἀποταφων ταφων (fig. 115, *a–c*).[389] Across the solid top of the vase
are vine leaves in low relief. The object, some 0·14 m high, which
has a broken under-surface, evidently surmounted a small column or
base, and formed a ὅρος-stone, marking the limits of a cemetery, of the
type referred to in the list of donations to the Kamiran koinon of
eranistai; the land there given by the Benefactor ἐς τάφια was defined

within expressed limits, ὡς ὅροι κεῖνται.³⁹⁰ The skyphos with ivy round it is frequently found in a sepulchral context, represented on tombstones, etc.,³⁹¹ and is very suitable as a marker delineating a sepulchral area.

The phrase inscribed on the vase, ἀποταφων ταφων, is capable of more than one interpretation. Newton, when publishing the inscription, pointed out that the lexicographical tradition for the word ἀπόταφοι is twofold, Hesychius s.v. defining it as meaning οἱ συνηριστευκότες τοῖς ἐλευθέροις δοῦλοι, καὶ μὴ συνταφέντες αὐτοῖς,³⁹² whereas the Suda s.v. quotes Deinarchus for the definition ὁ ἀπεστερημένος τῶν προγονικῶν τάφων.³⁹³ He therefore concluded, by combining the two passages, 'that the word ἀπόταφος was in the time of Deinarchos applied to those who were deprived of the right of burial in the tomb of their forefathers, and that slaves who had earned their liberty were also called ἀπόταφοι because they had the privilege of a separate place of burial'. He went on, 'In our dedication [?] ταφών must be understood as the Doric contracted form of ταφεών, "a burying ground", which occurs in two Palmyrene inscriptions, C.I. 4507, Waddington–Lebas, Pt. vi, § 8, nos. 2619, 2621; in another Palmyrene inscription, No. 2625, ibid., we have ταφαίων.' He concluded that the skyphos was 'broken off from a small pillar which marked the boundary of such a burial ground, or surmounted a large tomb; see C.I. 534, 535', these latter being the Attic horoi of sepulchral periboloi, ὅρος μνήματος and ὅρος σήματος 'Ονησίμου. This interpretation is quoted by Hiller von Gaertringen in his re-publication of the stone, and there the matter has rested. If, however, we are to accept in full Hesychius' definition, which, unlike that of the Suda and the other lexicographers, is not necessarily confined to Attic usage, and may therefore be a better guide to the Rhodian use of the word, the ἀπόταφοι are slaves who had fallen in battle alongside their masters (συνηριστευκότες), and who, though not buried with them, were nevertheless given a special burial-place, as were the foreigners who aided in the return from Phyle in 403 B.C.³⁹³ᵃ On the other hand, the meaning given by Deinarchus to the word, which seems to imply that all burials were normally or frequently family graves, does not seem applicable to Rhodes (or to Athens), where the basis of common burial is normally the individual, or the individual and his wife; it is difficult to believe that all those buried singly, or as husband and wife, were ἀπόταφοι, as contrasted with those accommodated in the larger family graves we have considered above. I therefore prefer to accept the definition of Hesychius, while admitting that it is certainly curious for an honour such as this form of burial seems to have been, to be denoted by an adjective compounded with ἀπό, for such compounds normally have a privative or adversative sense, as in ἀπότιμος, and in lyric compounds such as ἀποχρήματος, ἀπόφονος, etc.³⁹⁴

This may be explained by the circumstances surrounding such a burial. The citizens, the masters of the slaves, who fell in battle in defence of the city, in a siege, for example, would naturally receive an honourable public collective burial in a polyandrion, and it was in contrast with such a public burial and an honoured public grave that a slave buried separately could be called ἀπόταφος, in the first sense given to the word in the *Etymologicum Magnum*, s.v., τὸν χωρὶς ταφέντα καὶ ἀλλαχῇ τοῦ τῶν ἄλλων νεκρῶν τάφου· ἢ τὸν ἀπεστερημένον προγονικῶν τάφων. He was not subject to the casual, even nameless, burial of other slaves.

Even if we accept this special meaning—which would explain the rarity of the word, for which the inscription on the stone skyphos is the only documentary evidence—there remains the question whether we are to accept the grammatical interpretation given by Newton, and accepted by Hiller, and regard ταφων as a nominative singular, ταφών, on which ἀποτάφων, genitive plural, depends: 'the burial ground of the ἀπόταφοι'. This seems very uncertain. ταφαιών is found only in the inscriptions of Palmyra, in the second and third centuries A.D.,[395] and the form ταφών, supposedly a Doric contraction of that, is found only here; the only securely established Doric forms of the root ταφ- are formed in τοφ-: τοφιών, ἐντόφια, etc.[396] At the same time we know that the Rhodians regularly used other words for grave-plots and cemeteries, ταφῖα, ταφίαι, and even τόποι.[397] I prefer therefore to regard the word as a normal genitive plural of τάφος, with a quasi-possessive or 'thematic' sense, or as dependent on the substantive ὅρος, understood,[398] ἀποτάφων remaining substantival. On this interpretation the two words mean '(The boundary) of graves of those buried separately', i.e. the slaves who fell in battle. It is worth noting in this connection that Diodorus, in his account of the siege of Rhodes in 305/4, states that after it was over the Rhodians honoured those who had acquitted themselves valiantly with suitable rewards, καὶ τῶν δούλων τοὺς ἀνδραγαθήσαντας ἐλευθερίας καὶ πολιτείας ἠξίωσαν.[399] It may well be that in addition those who fell were honoured by public burial in the manner suggested. The skyphos itself is probably of late hellenistic date, and if it does commemorate such a burial it may be of the time of the siege of the city by Mithradates in 88, the Rhodian resistance to which is described by Appian.[400]

This specialized category of burials brings to a close our study of Rhodian sepulchral practices, save for an examination of the various invocations and acclamations found on Rhodian tombstones. Such formulae, from the simple χαῖρε to more complicated expressions involving notions of the afterlife, differ from region to region, and no general analysis is wholly valid, but it is worth examining Rhodian practice in this respect.

6. INVOCATIONS, ETC., IN RHODIAN SEPULCHRAL INSCRIPTIONS

Χρηστέ (-τός) (etc.) χαῖρε. The use of the most common form of invocation, that of χρηστ(ός/έ/οί) χαῖρε(τε), is in general a feature of the fourth century and later, but in some regions its usage is more restricted than in others. As has been pointed out,[401] while in Athens its use is never common, and is restricted to foreigners, in other regions the formula is found on the tombstones of citizens as well. In the course of time the usage spread considerably, and a complete chronological and sociological study of the term would fail through lack of precisely datable evidence, and uncertainty regarding the categories of the population to which individuals belonged. At Rhodes the evidence is relatively abundant, and its interpretation, with a few exceptions, free from uncertainty, and the general validity of the statistics not open to doubt. While the chronology of the stones cannot be determined with precision, it is clear that almost all those which carry this formula belong to the period of approximately 300 years between, say, 200 B.C. and the end of the first century A.D. For a later date the evidence fails, and in any case the formula seems largely to have died out, while no tombstones of the earlier hellenistic age seem to have the formula.

In general it may be stated without hesitation that the Rhodian usage appears to have been essentially the same as the Athenian. In both cities χαῖρε is mostly accompanied by the adjective χρηστ-. More important, as at Athens, the formula is virtually never used on the tombstones of demesmen—there are only five instances out of approximately 250 tombstones of this class, a ratio of about 1:50[402]—whereas in all other categories the differential is far less. On the tombstones of those designated by name and patronymic only—partial citizens (see above, pp. 47–8)—the ratio is about 1:14, and for those designated by their name and a racial ethnic (e.g. Λυδός) and those designated by name and city ethnic (e.g. Κυρηναῖος) it is respectively just under 1:3 (out of a total of about 120), and just over 1:4 (out of a total of about 240), while among those who have only a single name on their tombstone the formula is even more frequent, forming a half (66 out of a total of 135).[403] We may say then, that, as at Athens, the usage is almost confined to foreigners and persons of humble status. It is worthy of note that at Rhodes, as elsewhere, foreigners, who were not familiar with the χαῖρε formula in their homelands, adopted it. The usage evidently spread widely in the foreign population of the mercantile city.[404] The evidence from the Rhodian Islands and Peraea for the use of the formula is slighter, but the practice there was clearly the same.[405]

Associated formulae, also based on the notion of a dialogue, as in metrical epitaphs, also occur. There are several instances of χαῖρε· καὶ σύ (γε) (πολλά),[406] and one instance of a longer formula involving a dialogue: Δαματρία Σύρα / χρηστὰ χαῖρε. / "χαίρειν", προσεῖπας, "εὐτυχῶν ἀπότρεχε".[407] In the former instances the χαῖρε is most commonly linked with the preceding name: the passer-by says 'X, farewell', and the dead person replies '(Greetings) to you too'; but there are other instances in which the whole phrase is clearly spoken by the deceased,[408] and in others there is inevitable ambiguity. It has also been maintained that the χαῖρε should be assigned to the deceased and the καὶ σύ γε to the living, and this may exceptionally be the case. In the second formula, the living person repeats in direct speech the reply of the deceased.

A few other formulae occur on Rhodian inscriptions, and require individual consideration since they imply a more precise conception of the status of the dead than the banal χρηστός. Two epithets which seem to be almost unexampled elsewhere, at least before a later period, are ἐλεήμων and εὐδαίμων. ἐλεήμων[409] is certainly surprising, for it is in any case rare except in a cult context, where it is found applied to Aphrodite and, through her, to Arsinoe Philadelphus.[410] The notion of compassion or mercy probably refers less to the human compassion of the deceased when alive than to the compassion exercised by him as a kindly spirit, but it is not possible to be certain of such a delicate nuance when the use of the word, and even the concept of 'mercy' as an acclamation on a tombstone, is so rare. The notion of εὐδαίμων, combined with χρηστὸς χαῖρε in one epitaph,[411] refers more unequivocally to the state of well-being enjoyed by the deceased; it is thus closely related to the more common ὄλβιος. Εὐσεβής is of course among the most frequent words found in metrical epitaphs, and poetical phraseology generally, to express the dwelling-place of the dead, in such phrases as δόμοι εὐσεβέων and χῶρος εὐσεβέων.[412] In one Rhodian inscription, which reads Ἀράχθεως καὶ Νύσας, Αἰγυπτίων εὐσεβῶν,[413] a particular significance is perhaps to be attached to the nationality of the two deceased. εὐσεβής is rarely found on tombstones by itself,[414] and native Egyptians are not often found abroad, though they occur as ministrants of the Egyptian cults.[415] It is thus possible that the two persons here described as εὐσεβεῖς, who are not necessarily man and wife, may have been ministrants of the worship of the Egyptian cults in Rhodes.[415a] The state priests of Sarapis and Isis were Rhodians,[416] but in some cities some humbler ministrants were native Egyptians. The name of the man, Ἀράχθης, is a common Egyptian name;[417] Νῦσα has no especial links, but can hardly be the original name of an Egyptian. Another formula is καὶ κατὰ πᾶν ὅσιος, which occurs in one inscription only, following χρηστὸς χαῖρε.[418] This raises the same question as that raised by the καὶ σύ γε formula: who is speaking? The formula is, so far as I know, unique, and there are no parallel texts to solve the problem, while ὅσιος rarely stands as a laudatory epithet in the conventional manner.[419] It is certainly possible that καὶ κατὰ πᾶν ὅσιος is spoken by the survivor—who says χρηστὸς χαῖρε, and adds, as it were as an afterthought, 'and in every way pious'. Alternatively the dead man may be envisaged as speaking, σύ after καί being omitted, perhaps accidentally, the point being that the survivor is ὅσιος because he has carried out the duties of burial, etc., as a man may be ἱερῶν πατρωίων ὅσιος.[420] On the whole I prefer to regard the phrase as referring to the dead man, who is ὅσιος as he might be εὐσεβής, and to suppose that the χαῖρε has been added in its conventional position out of habit.

A more directly religious conception lies behind the attribution to the dead of specific divine or Heroic status. Thus, in two tombstones the dead are referred to as δαίμονες ἀγαθοί. The first of these is a large rectangular altar with two bosses—among the finest examples of the type—and commemorates a metic from Apamea and his wife:[421] Μητροδώρου Ἀπαμέως μετοίκου / καὶ / τᾶς γυναικὸς Εὐταξίας / Ἀπαμείτιδος, δαιμόνων ἀγαθῶν, in lettering of the second century B.C. The second,[422] said to be part of the base 'of a funerary column' (a stele or a circular column?), carries in letters also of the second century B.C. the inscription Θευδότου καὶ Ἰά[δος?], δαιμόνων ἀγαθῶν. The use of the term δαίμονες of the dead is paralleled elsewhere, particularly in Caria (at Mylasa),[423] and is not surprising in view of the chthonic nature of the later Agathos Daimon, from which it can hardly be dissociated. In Rhodes the cult of that deity certainly flourished at least among the foreign population, for there existed in the late hellenistic period a koinon of Ἀγαθοδαιμονιασταί at Lindos[424] and also one of Διοσαταβυριασταὶ Ἀγαθοδαιμονιασταὶ Φιλώνειοι at Rhodos.[425] In addition, a small altar of about the same date carries a dedication to Ἀγαθὸς δαίμων and Ἀγαθὰ Τύχα.[426] The two tombstones show that the notion of the dead as δαίμονες ἀγαθοί already existed as early as the second century B.C. among the foreign population of Rhodes. There are also other signs that the concept of the ἀγαθοὶ δαίμονες was recognized in the area, for the living no less than for the dead: in the will of Posidonios of Halicarnassos there is provision for sacrifices of a goat to the combined Agathos Daimon of Posidonios and his wife Gorgis, Δαίμονι ἀγαθῶι Ποσειδωνίου καὶ [Γ]οργίδος.[427] Granted the relatively early date of the tombstones, it seems very unlikely that the term is, as Hiller thought,[428] a translation of the Latin *Dis Manibus*, which is itself largely an Augustan, or post-Augustan, formula.[429]

From the δαίμονες ἀγαθοί we may pass to the Heroes, ἥρωες, a term very frequently found on hellenistic and later tombstones, in Boeotia and Thessaly, regions in which it must be regarded as normal practice, reflecting originally at least the conception of the dead as Heroized, if not deified, though already by the fifth century the religious content was no doubt much diluted by familiarity. In other parts of the Greek world it is rare, and particularly so before the Roman period, and in the Rhodian area there are only a few examples of it. These are considered in detail in an appendix, below, pp. 76 ff. Two tombstones, however, one from Rhodes and one from Karpathos, stand apart from the main group, and are of considerable interest. That from Rhodes reads:[430] Ἀναξίδος Κωΐας καὶ Τίμωνος / Αἰγιν[άτα] / ἀδελφῶν ἡρώων. The meaning of the term ἀδελφοί here is not immediately clear. It obviously cannot bear its basic meaning of 'brothers by blood', as it probably does on another tombstone recording two ἐγγενεῖς,[431] and since the dead persons are man and woman, and possibly man and wife, it is possible to see here the usage familiar from the Septuagint and from Egyptian papyri, according to which the term is used between husband and wife.[432] It seems, however, more plausible to regard both parties, male and female, who are foreigners, as 'brothers' in the sense of fellow members of a koinon, as is found at Halicarnassos[433] and later very frequently in the Bosporan koina,[434] in the koinon of the Athenian Iobacchoi, and elsewhere.[435] There are, however, no instances of this use of the word in the abundant documentation for Rhodian koina, so the matter is best left open. The inscription from Karpathos is more ambiguous. It reads:[436] [Ἀ]γαθίππου τοῦ Φιλοκράτευς Ἀθηνα[ί]ου κ]α(ὶ) Δαμοῦς τᾶς ἀδελφᾶς αὐτοῦ καὶ τῶν / . . . . ἡρώων. Here a genuine blood relationship is possible, for the ethnic of the woman is not given and she may have been an Athenian, but so also is the relationship of husband and wife, and yet again the 'brotherhood' may be that of membership of a koinon.[437]

These isolated expressions, so few in number, serve to emphasize that Rhodes was largely uninfluenced by the funerary practices and sepulchral epigraphical usages of Asia Minor and, in the Roman period, of Rome itself. At the same time the number of Roman citizens, mainly Greeks of local origin, is very small compared with the figures at Cos; at Rhodes 1:50, at Cos 1:3, on their tombstones. At Cos, where Romans settled in large numbers in the early Imperial period, the tombstones are inscribed, either in first or second usage, with the names of Roman citizens, and Roman sepulchral formulae, though not common, are far more frequent than on Rhodes. Although these bearers of Roman names at Cos are of all conditions, from those possessed of the *tria nomina* to freedmen and even humbler persons denoted by a single name, they all collectively attest considerable Romanization in Cos,[438] while on the other hand it seems fair to conclude that few Romans settled permanently on Rhodes, though many studied there, and that Roman influence on the social life of the city was very slight in the period under consideration. At the same time it had a large population of foreign Greeks and non-Greeks, whose life we see reflected in the documents, not least the tombstones, relating to the koina. This noticeable lack of penetration of Roman civilization in depth into Rhodes must be considered under many aspects and cannot be pursued further here.

APPENDIX

'Hero' or Mortal?

There remains for consideration one question of fundamental significance, which concerns especially the cylindrical monuments. Are we to consider such monuments by reason of their altar-like form indicative of a 'Hero-cult', or not? The problems connected with Hero-cult are innumerable and often insoluble, and have ramifications into the related fields of chthonic worship, belief in immortality, and so on, and here we shall confine ourselves to a consideration of the problem only as it affects our understanding of Rhodian funerary practice. Numerous studies of the topic provide an accepted background for the discussion.[439]

It has recently been stated that 'the clearest indication of a claim to Hero-cult was an altar either at the tomb or as a tomb monument . . . In the late Hellenistic period there are a number from Rhodes and the islands, usually cylindrical with relief swags and bucrania.'[440] Are there grounds for supposing that at Rhodes (and indeed elsewhere) in the late hellenistic period there was a correspondence between the two factors, belief as to the status of the dead, with corresponding ritual, and the type of funerary monument? And more especially, can we establish that the cylindrical monument indicated the 'Heroization' of the person commemorated on it? The problem may be considered in its barest form, in terms of the strictly relevant evidence and without conjectural interpretation.

1. Obviously, the only certain means of determining whether a dead person is regarded as a 'Hero' is either when provisions are recorded in a decree or other document for ceremonies to be held at his tomb of a 'Heroic' nature, and are expressly so described, or by the sepulchral inscription on his tomb—in other words, when he is called ἥρως. As an example of the first type of document we may cite a civic decree of Aigiale (Amorgos), in which provision is made for the ἀφηροϊσμός of Aleximachos, involving public celebrations of great magnificence including a public banquet (δαμοθοίνια), sacrifices, and various gymnastic competitions, all to be held in perpetuity.[441] There are numerous other examples of such 'Heroization', though on a less lavish scale. An instance of private provision for such 'Heroization' is provided by the Testament of Epicteta of Thera, in which the entire cult-foundation is formulated in terms of worship of her descendants as Heroes.[442]

2. On some tombstones the act of 'Heroization' of the deceased, either publicly or privately, is expressly stated in a verbal clause. In some places this process was regular. At Thera in the Roman period the process is recorded briefly as a public act, e.g. *IG* xii. 3, 865, ἁ βουλὰ καὶ ὁ δᾶμος / ἱερέα Ἀσκλαπιοῦ / διὰ γένους Μᾶρκον / Οὔλπιον Κλαυδιανὸν / Ἀγλαοφάνη τὸν εὐ/εργέταν τᾶς πατρίδος ἀφηρώιξε (cf. also 864–87), and as a private one, e.g. ibid. 919, Εἰρηναῖος καὶ Ἐπίκτησι[ς] / Εἰρηναῖον τὸν υἱὸν ἀφηρώιξεν (cf. 891–932). In such cases there can be no doubt that as a result of the act of 'Heroization' the deceased has become a ἥρως.

3. The use of the single word ἥρως (ἡρώϊσσα) with a dedicatory formula expressed or understood, representing an act of dedication in honour of the dead 'Hero', also occurs at Thera, ibid., nos. 878–85 (e.g. 882: ὁ δᾶμος / Πα⟨ι⟩σιφάνεια[ν] Χαι/ρεδάμου ἡρῶσσαν; 883: ὁ δᾶμος / Πολυάνορα / Πολυκράτου (?) / ἥρω), and we have already seen the same formula on the Hero-altars at Mytilene and, on stelai, at Cnidos (note 162).

4. In some regions the word ἥρως is used regularly or frequently on tombstones without any notion of public or private dedication, as a simple addition to the name. Thera once more has examples of this, ibid. 887 ff.,[443] there are a few from Mytilene (see above, note 162), and it is frequent in Boeotia (see *IG* vii, Index, p. 760, s.v. ἥρως), and Thessaly (see *IG* ix. 2, Index, pp. 328–9, s.v. ἥρως, etc.) and at various locations in Lycia.[443a] On the other hand at Athens the formula is rare,[444] and again occurs only in the Roman period, and seemingly with persons of humble status.

5. Thus, leaving on one side those so-called 'Hero-reliefs', which belong rather to the realm of the votive than of the funerary monument,[445] we may say that in some regions a dead man, however humble his status, was in one way or another designated as a Hero on his tombstone, while in others it was very rare. What the use of the word means in terms of belief and of ritual is not easily determined. At one end of the scale it is clear that the youth Aleximachos at Aigiale was publicly 'Heroized' in such a way as to be virtually a god, ἰσόθεος. But at the other extreme, at Thera and in Boeotia and Lycia, to take the regions offering most examples, the humble persons denominated as 'heroes' certainly did not receive elaborate public festivals. In these cases the word evidently had lost much of its original meaning and force, and become a general term for a dead person, like ὁ μακαρίτης, 'the happy, or blessed one', which, though of ancient origin, is used today in colloquial language of any deceased person held in affectionate memory (ὁ μακαρίτης ὁ μπάρμπας μου, ὁ μακαρίτης ὁ Βενιζέλος). There is no likelihood that a specifically 'Heroic' ritual was associated with the burial of these 'Heroes', and in general it seems likely that in cases where private epitaphs simply carry the denomination ἥρως, without reference to any particular act of

'Heroization' or ritual provisions, such as we have seen for Aleximachos, such ritual, and even the accompanying notion of increased 'worth', cannot be assumed. The matter was stated very clearly à propos of Boeotia by the comedian Plato, one of whose characters says τί οὐκ ἀπ-ήγξω, ἵνα Θήβησιν ἥρως γένηι;: 'Why don't you go and hang yourself—and become a Hero at Thebes?'[446] It indicates a further reduction of status that ἥρως was also used as a hyperbolical form of praise awarded to a living benefactor, from the fourth century onwards.[446a]

6. At Rhodes itself, the use of ἥρως is rare. It occurs on only two un-doubted tombstones. The first is a circular altar with bucrania and narrow garlands (fig. 116, *a*), on which are inscribed, in letters probably of the second century B.C., the words Κάλλωνος ἥρωος.[447] The natural explanation of this inscription is that it refers to the 'Heroic' status of Kallon, and is thus an example of the notion of 'Heroization'. It is not possible to regard "Ηρωος as a patronymic, for "Ηρως (unlike "Ηρων and 'Ηρώ) if it occurs at all, is extremely rare as a personal name. Granted, however, that this is an instance of explicit 'Heroization' it is to be em-phasized that the individual is not identified as a Rhodian demesman, but appears to belong to that large, unidentifiable class indicated by the use of the name by itself, without patronymic or other distinguishing mark. The second is the circular altar from Makry Steno, noted above, p. 74 and note 430, in which it is associated with the word ἀδελφός, ἀδελφῶν ἡρώων, one a Coan woman, the other an Aeginetan man; on this Maiuri commented rightly, 'Il culto eroico delle tombe non appare quasi affatto nell'epigrafia sepocrale di Rodi; in questa iscrizione trattasi di due stranieri, come di stranieri trattasi anche nelle iscrizioni della vicina Carpathos (IG xii. 1, 986–7).' Of the inscriptions from Karpathos, IG 986 discussed above, commemorates one or more Athenians, 987 an Ephesian woman and a man of Kidramos.[448] Another tombstone from Rhodos naming heroes is a pedimental stele inscribed in letters of the first or second century A.D. :[449] ὁ δᾶμος. / Ἀσκληπιοδώ/ρου / Ἀριστοκλεῦς / ἥρωος / καὶ τᾶς γυναι/κὸς αὐτοῦ / Κλυμένης· / ὁ δᾶμος. / Ἱεροκλίωνος / τοῦ Ποροσ/δέκτου / ἥρωος. However, the epigraphical formula of the funerary dedication, and the notion of civic 'Heroization' implied by ὁ δᾶμος, are both un-Rhodian, and it is doubtful whether the stone is to be regarded as of Rhodian origin. Two other examples from the Peraea, to which Maiuri should have referred, do not seriously invalidate this largely negative picture: Ἐφ. Ἀρχ., 1907, p. 218, no. 15 (Losta), a large block, inscribed Δεινοκλεῦς / ἥρωος,[450] and ibid. 1911, p. 67, no. 68 (Bozburun), a base inscribed [Θ]αρσύν[ο]ντι ἥρωι. Of these, the first may be votive, and the second certainly is, and both may refer to Hero-cults, which may have originated at one time in funerary cult, but neither is a normal tombstone. It is also possible that the two persons may be local

'civic heroes' (living or dead), like Nikias of Cos or perhaps Marcus of Side.[451] One other piece to which Maiuri might have called attention was found in the area of Ialysos (Kremaste). This is apparently an undecorated circular altar, inscribed with the one word ἡρώιων ('in ara rotunda marmoris caerulei maculati').[452] It is probably not funerary for, as we have seen (above, p. 26), the plain monument, unlike the decorated one, is normally votive and not funerary. If it is votive, there is more than one possibility as to its purpose. It evidently must refer to a shrine of Heroes. As such it may be civic, as at Rhodos and other cities, where 'the Heroes' are included in the formal oaths of the city.[453] At Lindos in the late hellenistic period an especial cult of the Hero Lindos and the ἄλλοι ἥρωες—i.e. the legendary heroes of the city—was inaugurated, no doubt as an act of religious antiquarianism.[454] A similar cult may have existed at Ialysos (though the full epigraphic record of Kamiros is silent as to any such cult of heroes there); in that case the altar may simply have stood in the temenos of the cult. It may, however, equally well be the altar of a funerary shrine of the deceased 'heroes' of a family or phratry. What it can hardly be is an ordinary tombstone, of the type under discussion, for the word ἡρώων has no proper names in apposition to it.

7. Two dedications in the dative from the eastern necropolis must be considered along with the two pieces from the Peraea noted above. The first is the dedication Ἱέρων Δεισιθέμιος / κατὰ τὸ ὅραμ[α] Ἥρωι,[455] carved on a small but complex base, described above (p. 40), terminating in an omphalos encircled by a snake (fig. 110, *a*). It is evident that this is a dedication to a chthonic Hero, who has appeared in a dream to the dedicant, and not a tombstone. The 'Hero' is not an identifiable, dead mortal, but most probably the god Hero(n) often anguiform or associated with snakes,[456] whose cult is attested at Kedreai in the Peraea by a koinon of Ἡροεῖσταὶ Σαμοθραικιασταί.[457] This is not, of course, to deny the chthonic nature of the dedication. It no doubt stood in a funerary peribolos, as did many other similar objects, including the second piece now to be considered. This is a circular altar with bucrania etc. and reads Ἀπολλώνιος / Ἑρμᾶι Ἀγεμόνι καὶ Ἥρωι δαίμονι.[458] It is less easily interpreted than the previous piece. It is clearly a dedication, in the first place, to Hermes in his role as Leader, or Conveyor, Psychopompos, of the Dead; the same cult-title, Ἀγέμων, is known from a rock-cut dedication on the slopes of the acropolis at Lindos[459] and from elsewhere.[460] The Heros Daimon, however, is not likely to be the god Heros, for if he was he would hardly be called δαίμων. We must conclude rather that the Ἥρως is a 'Heroized' dead person, who, however, has lost his individuality, and may be an 'ancestor-Hero', whose 'Heroization' need not have been a direct consequence of his death. This is borne out by the fact, discussed above, that on two tombstones the dead persons are referred to

as δαίμονες ἀγαθοί (above, p. 73), for though the evolution of the two notions is not clear, one can hardly doubt that the ἥρως δαίμων embodied the notion of the dead as δαίμονες ἀγαθοί. The form of dedication to Hermes and the Hero indicates clearly the almost divine status of the latter—he is not only a δαίμων, he is in a literal sense, ἰσόθεος. Neither of these two dedications has any immediate connection with the direct 'Heroization' of the dead.

8. Evidence for the 'Heroization' of the dead is clearly very slight at Rhodes, and it behoves us to reconsider the view that the circular monuments so common there reflect funerary Hero-cult. As we have seen, the only unequivocal use of the term ἥρως of a Rhodian is on the circular altar inscribed Κάλλωνος ἥρωος, and on the late stele with some un-Rhodian features; the other three references to ἥρωες are all explicitly to non-Rhodians. Moreover, the stele apart, these monuments are like all the other funerary altars with bucrania and garlands, and it is quite clear that the use of the term ἥρως cannot constitute the norm; on the contrary, these altars are exceptional in this respect. In addition, the general circumstances are equally against the hypothesis that the circular altar itself indicates 'Heroization'. While it is true that more stelai, and fewer cylindrical altars, come from Makry Steno than from Cova, that is because the earlier graves were at Makry Steno and Kizil Tepé; and the stelai, unlike the cylindrical monuments, are frequent in the third century; but in the later hellenistic period the various different types of monument, stelai, rectangular and cylindrical monuments, with their caskets, all come without distinction from the main eastern necropolis, and the only difference in the formulation of the epitaphs seems to lie in the predominant use of the nominative on the stelai, which were regarded simply as grave-markers, whereas the monuments were regarded as altars for funerary libation—but not Hero-altars. Thus we cannot claim a different, 'Heroic', status for those commemorated on the cylindrical monuments from those on the rectangular monuments or the stelai. It is noteworthy in this connection that one of the few epitaphs at Cos to name the deceased as ἥρως, the family tombstone of the Paconii, is, like the curious Rhodian example, inscribed not on a circular monument, but on a stele.[461] At Nisyros and Cnidos too Heroes are named on late stelai.[462]

9. There is undoubtedly a gradual, although never complete change in burial practices in Rhodes in the later hellenistic period; the rock-cut hypogaea, which the soft rock invited, replaced to a considerable extent —but never altogether—the pit-graves surmounted by stelai; and the change led to a very considerable elaboration of funerary and commemorative rituals, and the development of funerary periboloi and terraces, but the rituals are those accorded the dead, regarded as dead mortals—οἱ μεταλλαχότες, as they are called in more than one Rhodian inscription.

The rites, etc., ordained in the one instance of which we have details, that of Dionysodoros (above, pp. 61 ff.), are not those of, for instance, the ἀφηροϊσμός of Aleximachos of Aigiale. There is clearly no warrant or reason to call the rites 'heroic', in the absence of any link between the monuments themselves or the epitaphs on the one hand, and the established cult of Heroes on the other. The funerary cult of Heroes is, on the present evidence, largely foreign to Rhodes and the Rhodian world (as to many other places, including Athens); and it is therefore desirable to avoid the use of the term 'Heroization'. Some compensation for its absence was provided perhaps by the lavish posthumous honours bestowed on benefactors of koina, but it is significant that such honours affected only members of the foreign population who belonged to the koina.

NOTES

Abbreviations used frequently in the Notes are as follows:

1. *Epigraphical publications*

(a) *IG* xii. 1, containing the inscriptions of Rhodes and the neighbouring islands, edited by Hiller von Gaertringen (1895), is referred to simply as *IG*, followed by the number of the inscription. Other fascicules of *IG* are given their full numeration. '(*IG*, sq.)', after a reference to an inscription, indicates that I have studied the squeeze of the inscription in the Berlin collection.

(b) Further inscriptions published by Hiller (as I refer to Hiller von Gaertringen) in *Athenische Mittheilungen* are indicated as *AM* followed by volume number and serial year.

(c) *NS* = A. Maiuri, *Nuova silloge epigrafica di Rodi e Cos* (Florence, 1925).

(d) *Ann.* = *Annuario della (Regia) Scuola Archeologica di Atene.* Most of the relevant inscriptions occur in vol. 2 (pp. 125–31, ed. G. G. Porro; pp. 150–79, ed. A. Maiuri).

(e) *Cl. Rh.* = *Clara Rhodos* (Istituto Storico-Archeologico di Rodi, 10 vols.), esp. vol. 2, pp. 219–35, nos. 60–142, ed. G. Jacopi.

(f) *Tit. Cam.* = *Tituli Camirenses* in *Ann.* (as (d) above), 27–9 (N.S. 11–13), 1953, pp. 142–318, ed. M. Segre and I. (i.e. G.) Pugliese Carratelli.

(g) *Tit. Cam. Supp.* = *Tituli Camirenses, Supplementum,* in *Ann.* (as (d) above), 30–2 (N.S. 14–16), 1952–4 (1955), pp. 211–46, ed. I. Pugliese Carratelli.

(h) *Supp. Rod.* = *Supplemento epigrafico rodio,* in *Ann.* (as (d) above), 30–2 (N.S. 14–16), pp. 247–316, ed. G. Pugliese Carratelli.

(i) *Nuov. Supp. Rod.* = *Nuovo Supplemento epigrafico rodio,* in *Ann.* (as (d) above), 33–4 (N.S. 17–18), 1955–6 (1957), pp. 157–81, ed. G. Pugliese Carratelli.

(j) *ILind.* = K. F. Kinch and Chr. Blinkenberg, *Fouilles de Lindos,* Pt. II, *Les Inscriptions,* 2 vols. (Berlin and Copenhagen, 1941).

(k) Peek, *Inschr. dor. Ins.* = W. Peek, *Abhand. sächs. Akad. der Wiss. in Leipzig,* Phil.-hist. Klasse, 62. 1 (1969), 'Inschriften von den dorischen Inseln'.

(l) Peek, *Inschr. Nis.* = id., *Wissenschaftl. Zeitschrift der Univ. Halle,* 16, 1967 (6), pp. 369–89, 'Epigramme und andere Inschriften von Nisyros'.

(m) Susini, *Supp. epigr.* = G. Susini, *Ann.* (as (d) above), 41–2 (N.S. 25–6), 1963–4 (1965), pp. 203–92, 'Supplemento epigrafico di Caso, Scarpanto, Saro, Calchi, Alinnia e Tilo'.

(n) Carratelli, *Assoc.* = G. Pugliese Carratelli, *Ann.* (as (d) above), 22 (N.S. 1–2), 1939/40 (1942), pp. 147–200, 'Per la storia delle associazioni in Rodi antica'.

2. *Other works relating to Rhodes*

(o) Van Gelder = H. van Gelder, *Geschichte der alten Rhodier* (The Hague, 1900).

(*p*) Jac., *Sped. dei Cav.* = G. Jacopi, *Lo Spedale dei Cavalieri e il Museo Archeo-logico di Rodi* (Le Guide dei Musei Italiani, Rome, 1932).

(*q*) Inglieri = R. U. Inglieri, *Carta archeologica dell'isola di Rodi* (Florence, 1936).

(*r*) Fraser and Bean = P. M. Fraser and G. E. Bean, *The Rhodian Peraea and Islands* (Oxford University Press, London, 1954).

3. *Other works*

(*s*) *KF* = R. Herzog, *Koische Forschungen und Funde* (Leipzig, 1899).

(*t*) *PH* = W. R. Paton and E. L. Hicks, *The Inscriptions of Cos* (Oxford, Clarendon Press, 1891).

(*u*) *B & WG* = P. M. Fraser and T. Rönne, *Boeotian and West Greek Tomb-stones* (Skrifter utgivna av Svenska Institutet i Athen, 4°, **VI**, Lund, 1957).

Other abbreviations are those commonly employed, or are self-explanatory.

Location of stones, etc.

(1) The present location of stones in Rhodes Museum is indicated as follows:

Ct. = Central Courtyard
UG = Upper Gallery
LG = Lower Gallery
IGard. = Inner Garden (around sunken court)
OGard. = Outer Garden (with portico)
Tr. = Trench below steps separating IGard. and OGard.
Cast. = Castello and its grounds
Eph. = Area behind the Department of Antiquities (Ephoreia), in which recent and current excavated material is placed

(2) Monuments which are unpublished, and which I have been enabled to discuss and reproduce here through the kindness of Dr. Konstantinopoulos, are indicated by the letters UP. There are a few instances in which I have been unable to read very worn inscriptions satisfactorily, and which I have regarded as unpublished since I have been unable to find corresponding inscriptions among published pieces, but it is possible (though not, I think, likely) that they have been read differently by others, and have in fact been published. *Ex abundanti cautela* I have indicated these by UP (?).

NOTES

1. Necropoleis of a date later than the mid fourth century have not been found in the areas of the 'old cities', and mostly not later than the early part of the century. This raises a question of some interest—where were the later inhabitants buried? I cannot go into this problem here, though certain aspects of it will be encountered when discussing individual tombs of the old cities. It must suffice here to note the following points:

(*a*) The Archaic and Classical necropoleis of *Ialysos*, in the area north and west of the main road between Trianda and Kremaste, below Phileremo (and some distance from the Mycenaean necropoleis at Makry Vounara and Moschou Vounara, which are on the lower north-west slopes of the mountain), continue, at Ambelia, close to Kremaste, into the fourth century, but not beyond the middle of it: see Jacopi, *Cl. Rh.* 3, pp. 153 ff., esp. tombs 153–60 (Campanian and late r.f. vases); Laurenzi, *Cl. Rh.* 8, pp. 1 ff.; Inglieri, Fogl. Nord, no. 22; Konstantinopoulos, *Ialysos–Kamiros* (Aths., 1971), pl. 16.

(*b*) At *Kamiros* the late Classical graves at Kalathomilo, south of Kalavarda, also seem to go down to about the middle of the century: see Jacopi, *Cl. Rh.* 6–7(1), pp. 157–78. Whether, as R. A. Higgins, *BM Cat. Terracottas* (1954), p. 10, maintains, the production of terracottas—the principal grave furniture—at Kamiros stopped, gradually or at once, after the synoecism or not, is uncertain. There were no figurines in the graves at Kalathomilo, but on the other hand, at Lindos, local terracotta production may have continued into the hellenistic age (see *Lindos*, I, pp. 7–8, 38–41; see, however, D. B. Thompson, *Hesperia* 21, 1952, p. 119 n. 13 (c): 'all the figures are pre-Tanagraean in character'), and the town of Kamiros was inhabited for centuries after the synoecism, and coroplastic production, so plentiful in the Classical period, is not likely to have died out completely. Until the main hellenistic cemeteries have been found this question can hardly be answered decisively.

(*c*) At *Lindos* there are numerous tombs of the Graeco-Roman period cut in the rocks around the town, notably the splendid rock-cut tombs of Kambana (Frangoekklesia), the subject of the engraving by L. Mayer, *Views in the Ottoman Empire*, pl. 16, cut in the face of the plateau above the modern village, facing the Acropolis; see Dyggve in *Lindos*, III. 2, pp. 491–504 (cf. also *ILind.* 623, 'L'Archokrateion'; H. Lauter, *Antike Kunst*, 15, 1972, pp. 51–2; Konstantinopoulos, *Lindos* (Aths., 1971 (?)), pp. 38–40). Others lie on the road north of the village, while a substantial heroon at Atsinganovounaro, south-west of the village, was tentatively reconstructed by Blinkenberg, *ILind.* 659; it had a façade decorated with armour. However, none of these monuments could be described as necropoleis, and the Classical and post-Classical necropoleis are no doubt to be sought beneath the modern village.

2. For Ross's account of the environs of the city see *Reisen auf den gr. Inseln*, iii (1845), pp. 70–113 (visit of 1834); iv (1852), pp. 54–80 (visit of 1844). For that of Newton see *Travels and Discoveries*, i (1865), pp. 137 ff. (visit of 1853). The accounts of Italian archaeologists are mainly to be found in scattered notices, principally by Maiuri and Jacopi, in *Boll. d'arte, Ann.*, and *Cl. Rh.*, and there is no single complete work containing the results of their topographical researches. There are, however, brief accounts of the necropoleis in Maiuri's *Rodi* ('Il piccolo cicerone moderno', no. 21, Rome and Naples, 1922), pp. 37–40, and in Jacopi's text to the *Guida d'Italia* (*Possedimenti e colonie*) *del Touring Club Italiano* (Milan, 1929), pp. 106 ff.; also in *Encicl. Ital.* s.v. Rodi, p. 557.

The annual reports of the Greek Archaeological Service in *Arch. Delt.*, since its recommencement with vol. 16 in 1960, contain a great deal of material relevant to the necropoleis, and vol. 24 (1969), 1970, Chr. 2, pp. 467 ff., has extremely useful plans of the main necropoleis. The excavations of the late J. Kontis under the auspices of the Archaeological Society of Athens appeared in the Πρακτικὰ Ἀρχ. Ἑτ. between 1951 and 1960. These are mainly, but not entirely, concerned with excavation in the modern city, conducted with the aim of determining the street plan of the Classical city (cf. Kontis, Συμβολή εἰς τήν μελέτην τῆς ῥυμοτομίας τῆς ʽΡόδου (Rhodes, 1954); id., *Ath. Mitt.* 73, 1958, pp. 146 ff.). For an up-to-date plan of the ancient city grid see the plan prepared by G. Konstantinopoulos with the assistance of Frau Christa Grossmann, *AAA* 3, 1970, p. 55. The work of J. Bradford, *Ancient Landscapes* (London, 1957; reprint, 1974), contains, pp. 277–86, a summary of his important article in *Antiq. Journ.* 36, 1956, pp. 57–69, with some additional photographs of ancient roads.

3. The sketch-maps in *Arch. Delt.* 24 indicate the localities in more detail. My own plan, based on the Greek Ministry of Communications and Public Works map of 1 : 5,000, kindly made available to me by Dr. Konstantinopoulos, is intended principally to show the general layout of the cemeteries and their relation to the circuit of the city wall, where this is known. Inglieri's sheet, *Rodi e Dintorni* (1 : 50,000), includes most of the necropolis area, but the layout of the modern town on the south has changed very considerably since the last war and, in addition, the physical features are almost unidentifiable on the map.

4. See further, pp. 4–5.

5. For the rock-cut pit-graves immediately south of the city wall on the Acropolis, adjacent to the modern wireless station, see Newton, op. cit., pp. 165–6 (apparently referring to these); Jacopi, *Cl. Rh.* 6–7(2), pp. 445 ff.; and the tombs recently excavated by Miss Fatourou, *Arch. Delt.* 18, 1963, pp. 324–5 (*Chronique des fouilles 1964*, p. 876 and figs. 1–2), which are just across the road from those by the wireless station. In the latter sector the city wall runs both beside and above the tombs (see figs. 1–3), and is clearly later than they are. The wall seems to have curved at just this point, however, and the precise relationship of wall to graves is not clear. The finds from the new tombs include an r.f. pelike, and a Corinthian-style black-glaze skyphos of the late fifth/early fourth century; those of Jacopi included a Kertch Vase.

6. See Maiuri, *Ann.* 2, pp. 168–9; id., *Rodi*, p. 39. It appears from Maiuri's first account that the great underground cavern, through which there is now access to the hypogaeum proper, was found first, and was regarded by him simply, and perhaps rightly, as a medieval quarry into which some ancient tombstones had found their way. In 1917 the hypogaeum itself was found, and in his account in *Rodi*, published in 1922, the true nature of the whole complex is correctly described: 'risalendo la Macrí-stenó oltre il quartiere di S. Giovanni, sul lato sinistro, fu messo in luce nel 1917 un grande monumento sepolcrale costituito da un grande basamento con sottostante ipogeo composto d'una serie di camere sepolcrali e di piccoli loculi per il deposito delle urne e dei vasi cine-

rari.' The complex is not, I think, described elsewhere. There is a photograph of the façade, *Cl. Rh.* 1, p. 51, fig. 34.

6a. The tombs in Hodos Lindou are published in *Arch. Delt.* 24 (1969), 1970, Chr. 2, pp. 453 ff., esp. pp. 455 and 467 ff., with Σχεδ. 2, 9, and 10 (Hodos Vasilissis Annis Marias); these lay immediately outside the line of the wall. Those on the west side of Hodos Grigoriou E′ are in *Arch. Delt.* 25 (1970), 1973, Chr. 2, pp. 500 ff.; these tombs, which are of the first half of the fourth century, lie beneath a stretch—the lowest stratum—of road P40, and inside the line of the hellenistic wall: see the plan, ibid. Σχεδ. 1. The stratum of P40 investigated at this point contained a Rhodian bronze coin of the fourth century, while the well-constructed tomb below yielded material of the earlier fourth century (p. 503). As Miss Zervoudaki says, ibid., it appears probable that the original wall lay east of its hellenistic successor at this point.

7. For the Cova or Acandia necropolis see Maiuri, *Ann.* 2, p. 171; id., *Rodi*, p. 39; Inglieri, p. 21, no. 34; Jacopi(ch), *Boll. d'arte*, 6(2), 1927, p. 332; id., ibid. 7(2), 1928, p. 514; Laurenzi, ibid. 30, 1936, p. 132. For emergency excavations carried out in 1969, on the slightly higher ground behind the British War Cemetery, which brought to light a large number of pit-graves, see below, note 39. For a fuller plan of the area see now *Arch. Delt.* 25, 1970, Chr. 2, p. 516, Σχεδ. 8.

8. This monument is very briefly described by Inglieri, loc. cit., but has never been published; cf., however, now the remarks of Lauter, op. cit., p. 52.

9. The figures are regarded by Inglieri as representing 'Dioniso, Satiri e Menadi', but I am very doubtful of these identifications. It is natural to suppose that the central figure is the dead person (compare the 'Tomb of Alketas' at Termessos, G. Kleiner, *Diadochen-Gräber* (*SB* Wiss. Ges. Goethe-Univers., Frankfurt/Main, i(3), 1962), pp. 71 ff. and pls. i–v; G. E. Bean, *Turkey's Southern Shore* (London, 1968), fig. 60); and other figures in relief are, from the left of the horseman outwards, a figure pouring a libation into, or on to, a kantharos, a figure standing frontally in a garment with deep vertical folds, a sitting lion (?) facing right, and a large kantharos, to the left of which are some draperies. On the left wall are running, or mourning, female figures, like the Nikai or Maenads on the circular altars discussed below, pp. 31–2, and, on the right wall, a tent-like structure with, at the far end (nearest the road), a female head facing inwards (??).

10. The terrace has now (since 1970) been incorporated in an enlarged restaurant which has been opened on the site. The altars were still there when I last visited the establishment.

11. For the Ptolemaion see Ross, *Reisen*, iii, p. 91, and iv, p. 78; Newton, op. cit., pp. 179–80; Lauter, op. cit., pp. 54 ff., pl. 16, 1–4. Both Ross (who says that the local inhabitants in his day called it τό κουφόν βουνίν) and Newton say that it derived its name from the supposed discovery there of a Ptolemaic coin. Loyalty to the popular belief that a Ptolemy was buried there dies hard, and

is generally accepted by the κοσμάκης. For its restoration see Maiuri's note in *Boll. d'arte*, 4(2), 1924–5, p. 336; Jacopi(ch), ibid. 6(2), 1927, p. 328.

12. For this period see my remarks in *BSA* 67, 1972, pp. 122–3.

12a. The adaptation of the monuments to the landscape in the Rhodini 'Park' area has now been well discussed by H. Lauter, *Antike Kunst*, 15, 1972, pp. 49–59, 'Kunst u. Landschaft—Ein Beitrag zum rhodischen Hellenismus', with whose general observations I fully agree. Ael. Arist., *Or.* xliii, 540, speaks of the acropolis, i.e. the Monte Smith area in general, as πεδίων καὶ ἀλσῶν μεστή.

13. See especially the remarks of Maiuri, *NS*, p. 59, explaining the principle on which he worked in publishing the tombstones there: 'Quanto alla indicazione della provenienza, mancano talvolta precise notizie sul luogo del rinvenimento e per l'ambiguità stessa dell'odierna toponomastica locale, generalmente con duplice e diversa denominazione di luoghi in greco ed in turco, ho preferito attenermi ad una più generale divisione della necropoli rodia in necropoli della regione occidentale e della regione orientale; intendendo con la prima tutta la parte collinosa a monte della città, racchiudente le pendici di M. Smith, la regione del *Dokuz-soqáq* (= nove strade), dell'antica via *Macrí-stenó*, del *Kizíl-tepé* ricche di monumenti funerari, del *Bibér-dagh* fino alla valle di *Sandurlí*; e con la seconda, in particolar modo, la vasta necropoli che dal torrente *Deirmen-deré* si estende fin verso Asgúru e Coschinu, in parte sul terreno sabbioso della baia di Coschinu ed in parte sulle colline e sull'altipiano circostante.' The location of Deirmen-dere (Deressi), the Valley of Windmills, is not wholly certain. Hiller, on *IG* 197 and Tab. I, and Inglieri, text to Foglio Nord, no. 7, assign it to the ravine which descends from Koskinou to the sea (see Inglieri's and Hiller's maps, where the ravine is marked), while Maiuri, as quoted above, and in *Ann.* 3, p. 260, calls the ravine of Rhodini, 'che scende per una profunda incassatura dell'altopiano di Asgúru al mare', by this name. I suspect that we should accept Maiuri's view, for it seems unlikely that many tombstones have come to light in the more remote ravine of Koskinou. In *Cl. Rh.* 2, p. 73, however, he extends the term to cover the whole area from the walls to the Koskinou ravine.

14. See *Rodi*, p. 40: 'Della necropoli del IV. sec. non sono venute finora alla luce che pochissime tracce.'

15. See *IG* ii². 10136–42, seven Ῥόδιοι, and *SEG* xxii, 895. Several of these are of the fourth century. Note also the bestowal of Athenian citizenship on Ainetos the Rhodian, who resided in Athens and served in Alexander's campaign, *SEG* xxi, 310. For Alexandria see Fraser, *Ptol. Alex.* ii, p. 149, note 209.

16. See Dunant, *Arch. Delt.* 23, 1968 (1969), Chr. 1, pp. 237 f.

17. See the account by Arvanitopoullos, Γραπταί Στῆλαι Δημητριάδος, pp. 16 ff.; id., Θεσσαλικὰ Μνημεῖα (Athens, 1909), pp. 63–93. Note also the reuse of Classical stelai as covering for later tombs at Pyri (Thebes, *Arch. Delt.* 20, Chr. 1, p. 239 and pl. 84); and in Potidaea (*AAA*, 7, 1974, pp. 190–1).

18. See Diod. xix, 45, a graphic description of the inundation of the lower part of the city: . . . ὥστε πολλὰς μὲν τῶν οἰκιῶν συμπίπτειν διὰ τὸ βάρος, οὐκ ὀλίγους δὲ καὶ τῶν ἀνθρώπων ἀπόλλυσθαι· (3) θεατροειδοῦς δ᾽ οὔσης τῆς ῾Ρόδου καὶ τὰς ἐγκλίσεις τῶν ὑδάτων κατὰ τὸ πλεῖστον εἰς ἕνα τόπον ποιουμένης εὐθὺς τὰ ταπεινὰ τῆς πόλεως ἐπληροῦτο . . . (8) ὅμως δὲ τηλικούτων ἀτυχημάτων γενομένων σώματα μὲν διεφθάρη πλείω πεντακοσίων, οἰκίαι δὲ αἱ μὲν τελέως ἔπεσον, αἱ δὲ διεσείσθησαν.

19. Polyb. v, 88–90, with the commentaries of Holleaux, *Études*, i, pp. 445–62, and Walbank, ad loc. Polybius is concerned not with the earthquake itself, but with its consequences in the form of international aid for the Rhodians, but he says (88, 1), ἐν ὧι συνέβη τόν τε κολοσσὸν τὸν μέγαν πεσεῖν καὶ τὰ πλεῖστα τῶν τειχῶν καὶ τῶν νεωρίων.

20. *Ann.* 2, p. 150, no. 27. This is dated by L. H. Jeffery, *Local Scripts*, pp. 349–50, with caution, to 'not later than the sixth century'; by Maiuri, *Ann.* loc. cit. to not later than the first half of the fifth century. As Maiuri said, its discovery might point to the existence of a small community in the neighbourhood, or it may have been moved from elsewhere. According to Maiuri it was found, 'sulla terrazza superiore della collina di M. Smith in una delle zone più ricche di tombe greche del secolo III–II a. C.', and from this it must be supposed, I think, that it was found somewhere in the Ai Yanni–Makry Steno area, for this description hardly fits the few pit-graves found on the Acropolis itself, close to the city wall (see above, p. 3 and note 5); cf. Guarducci, *Epigr. gr.* I, p. 333.

21. Cf. below, p. 9, with note 24.

22. Mendel, *Catalogue*, i, no. 2; Schede, *Meisterwerke der türk. Museen*, i, pl. 10, left; Pfuhl, *Jahrb.* 50, 1935, p. 25, Abb. 12. According to Mendel's catalogue, 'La stèle provient de Rhodes; elle avait détaché du mur d'une église située au bord de la mer, près de la mosquée du quartier franc, quand R. von Schneider la vit en 1882.' The mosque was presumably in the Neochori area, but I do not think its location can be determined more closely.

23. This famous stele was first published in *Cl. Rh.* 4, p. 35, figs. 10–11, and pl. 1; also ibid. 5(1), p. 31 and pls. iv–vii (cf. also Jac., *Sped. dei Cav.*, pp. 40–1 and frontispiece; for subsequent bibliography see Lippold, *Das gr. Plastik*, p. 206, note 16; cf. also Lullies and Hirmer, *Greek Sculpture* (London, 1960), pl. 185; Kurtz and Boardman, *Greek Burial Customs* (London, 1971), pl. 59; cf. also Frel, *AAA* 5, 1972(1), p. 75, 4, and p. 77, fig. 5 (remodelling of head of Krito). The inscription is republished in *Tit. Cam.* 162. The stele is usually dated to the late fifth century (see Pfuhl, op. cit., p. 24; Lippold, op. cit., p. 206). The inscription looks to me to be of the fourth rather than the fifth century, and I am glad to see that Hiller suspected the same: a note of his in *Tit. Cam.* loc. cit. reads 'litterae bonae saec. iv?'. Professor C. M. Robertson writes (2 Oct. 1970): 'I would find this kind of drapery treatment [i.e. that of Krito and Timarista, and of the Attic stele of Mnasagora and Nikochares, Diepolder, *Att. Grabrel.* pl. 5] very surprising more than a decade or two after the end of the Peloponnesian War.' My view that the inscription should be dated *c.* 390–365 remains, and if we are to seek a mean between the two views we should assign

the stele to a date not later than 380. If that is correct it must belong to a grave later than the synoecism of Rhodes, at which date the whole cemetery was supposed to have been closed. The archaeological context, as described by Jacopi, *Cl. Rh.* 4, p. 37, is indeed vague: 'Alla profundità di circa un metro e mezzo sporadicamente in prossimità delle tombe L e XCV del sepolcreto di Macri Langoni, si ritrovava, meravigliosamente intatta, la più bella stele funeraria che ci abbia tramandato il V secolo.' [See ADD.]

24. See Laurenzi, *Boll. d'Arte*, 30, 1936, p. 132, speaking of the area of the 'Polveriera' (Arsenal) on Monte Smith: 'ivi si è ritrovato infatti un tratto assai notevole, particolarmente importante perchè appare impostato su una necropoli antecedente alla fondazione della città, continente materiale anteriori al 408 a. C.' Inglieri, Foglio Città, text, no. 32 (Qïzïl Tepe): 'Saggi compiuti nel 1934 hanno dimostrato, per il materiale ceramico ritrovato, che la necropoli è, in parte, precedente alla fondazione di Rodi.' There is some mystery about this material and, though I cannot go fully into the matter here, it seems possible that Laurenzi and Inglieri have given a confused account of the excavation of Jacopi at the south end of M. Smith, discussed above, note 5, in which material of the early fourth century was discovered. The Polveriera seems to have stood in this area. I am grateful to Dr. Konstantinopoulos for giving me his views on this important and difficult matter. We would, I think, agree that apart from the stele of Charonidas (above, note 20) there is at present no evidence for material dating from before the synoecism in the city area.

25. See V. Poulsen, *Catal. Anc. Sculpt. Ny Carlsberg Glyptothek* (1951), p. 31, no. 13 (inv. 1996) (*Billedtavler* (1907), pl. II, no. 13); Arndt–Amelung, *Einzelauf.* 3765.

26. In *Billedtavler* the figure is regarded as that of the deceased, but in the Catalogue Poulsen describes the stone as either funerary or votive. Lippold, *Gr. Plast.*, p. 67, plausibly regards the figure as Dionysus.

27. See *Cl. Rh.* 9, pp. 81 ff. (Peek, *GVI* 893), there dated by Laurenzi to the mid fourth century (cf. already id., *Boll. d'arte*, 30, pp. 132–3); cf. Clairmont, *Gravestone and Epigram* (Mainz, 1970), no. 32, and pl. 16. Dimensions: H. 1·30 m, W. 0·84 m.

28.   "Οστις ἄριστος ἔπαινος ἐν ἀνθρώποισι γυναικός
         Καλλιαρίστα Φιληράτο τοῦτον ἔχουσα ἔθανεν,
         Σωφροσύνας ἀρετᾶ[ς] / τε· ἀλόχωι πόσις ὄν⟨ε⟩κα τόνδε
         Δαμοκλῆς ἔστασεν, μνημόσυνον φιλίας·
         Ἀνθ' ὧν οἱ δαίμων ἐσθλὸς ἔποιτο βίωι.

29. See *Cl. Rh.* 9, p. 91, a fragment with figures of two warriors, dated by Laurenzi to the Classical period. He published, ibid., one or two fragments of the fourth century whose precise provenance is unknown.

30. (17, *b*) Mendel, iii, 878. The relief is considerably larger than the stele of Kalliarista: H. 1·42 m, PW. 0·95 m. (17, *c*) Unpublished, Copenhagen, Nat. Mus. Inv. 5622, found south of the city, 'on the beach'; dimensions, PH. 0·385 m, W. 0·312 m, Th. 0·08 m.

31. (18, *a*) *NS* 113 (Tr.), Τίμαρχος Δαμομένευς, H. 1·19 m, W. 0·345/380 m, Th. 0·095/115 m, letters, 0·028 m, of which Maiuri says 'Il tipo e le proporzioni dell'iscrizione rispetto alla grandezza della stele, mostrano che la stele non era originariamente destinata a contenere questa umile iscrizione funeraria, ma o un testo di diversa natura o un'epigrafe sepolcrale di maggior rilievo.' As I indicate below, I regard this type of unsymmetrical, almost casual, inscription as characteristic of the period. (18, *b*) *NS* 103 (UG), Ἀριστομένης Μενεδάμου, H. 0·56 m, W. 0·25/26 m, Th. 0·70/075 m, letters 0·010 m, a more regularly, stiffly carved inscription. A similar fashion of inscribing names in an irregular style seems to have prevailed at Chios on the rectangular tombstones of the 4th cent.: see Forrest, *BSA* 58, 1963, pp. 63–4; it is noteworthy that in the earlier third century 'the stone is usually much smaller than in fifth century examples'.

32. (19, *a*) UP (OGard.), Μναοὶς Μνάσιος Ἐρινα̂ις, H. 1·14 m, W. 0·35/38 m, Th. 0·080/10 m, in very fine sharp lettering between ruled lines, of the late fourth/early third century, on white marble, very un-Rhodian in style and substance, but certainly Rhodian, since Ἐριναεύς is a Rhodian demotic. (19, *b*) UP (Tr.), Ῥοδόκλεια Δαμαγήτου, γυνὰ δὲ Ἀγέλα, H. 1·30 m, W. 0·35/39 m, Th. 0·105/110 m, letters 0·020, omicron 0·010.

33. There are very many examples of such stele-bases in Rhodes Museum, some inscribed, some uninscribed, some belonging to the stele inserted into them, some not (as may be seen most obviously by the fact that stele and base in some instances bear different names). The bases supporting the stelai illustrated in figs. 18 and 19 may serve as examples; of these 18, *a* seems to belong to the stele, but *b* does not, while 19, *a* belongs, and *b* may do.

34. The measurements and tapering of the monuments are clear from the dimensions given above, notes 31 and 32, for figs. 18, *a*, *b* and 19, *a*, *b*. Some stelai are a great deal less even than 0·50 m: e.g. *NS* 108 (IGard.) Ἡρακλείδα χρηστὲ χαῖρε, H. 0·38 m, W. 0·14/18 m, Th. 0·068/078 m (fig. 20, *a*), and *NS* 102 (IGard.) Ἀριστόβιος Ἀρισταίου, H. 0·60 m, W. 0·22 m, Th. 0·05 m (fig. 20, *b*). These very small stelai (of which there are a considerable number in IGard. round the parapet of the sunken courtyard) are not all late; that of Aristobios is undoubtedly of the third century.

35. 21, *a*, UP (OGard.) Στρατωνίδας Ἀλεξικράτευς; *b*, UP (UG), Πραξίων / Φιλίωνος / κατὰ γένεσιν, / [καθ' ὑοθ]εσίαν δὲ Καλλία / Νισύριος; *c*, IG 1448, now in Hanover, Ἐράτων / Ἐράσιος / Κεδρεάτας; *d*, IG 1459, also in Hanover, Ἴλαρον / χρηστὰ χαῖρε. Others are, e.g., *Cl. Rh.* 2, p. 228, no. 102: ——ου / [καθ' ὑοθ]εσίαν δὲ Ἀρχιπόλιος / Φύσκιος; ibid., p. 234, no. 136: [—— καὶ] / Ἀρτεμι-δ[ώρας] / Ξενοβούλου Ποντωρέων (this presumably originally carried two full names and patronymics corresponding to the plural demotic Ποντωρέων. Jacopi's restoration as simply two names in the genitive offends Rhodian usage for demotic and patronymic: see below, p. 47); *NS* 104, and 105–6, a pair of stelai of father and son (105), Γόργων / Καλλιξείνου, and (106), Καλλίξεινος / Γόργωνος, the first pedimental, the second with a plain horizontal moulding: see *NS*, p. 76, where the two stelai are reproduced side by side; *Arch. Delt.* 20

(1965), 1968, p. 597 and fig. 753 (*Chron. d. fouill. 1967*, p. 979, fig. 17), Πολύευ-κτος / Σιδάτας; ibid. 24 (1969), 1970, p. 480 n. 1, Σωσὶς / 'Ονασιφῶντος / Νισυρία.

36. *NS* 108 (fig. 20, *a*; cf. above, note 34) and 109. An instance of the continuation of the inscription from stele to base, such as occurs between altar and base (see below, pp. 25–6), and is established by the fact that the inscription on the base begins with the word καί or, e.g., γυνὰ δέ (see below, p. 25, and note 122), is found on the stele and base of Nikaineta in the Makry Steno catacomb (UP); the stele has Νικαινέτας τᾶς 'Εργοίτα Κυμισαλίδος, and the base γυναικὸς δὲ Ἀγεστράτου Φιλίσκου Κυμισαλέως.

37. *IG* 331, now in Vienna, of which the original editor, Benndorf, *Reisen*, i (1884), p. 25 (fig. 20), says, 'Der eine (Fig. 20) ist eine o.m.56 hohe Giebelstele von guten Verhältnissen mit erhaltenen Einsatzzapfen, welche über den unten angebrachten Inschrift: 'Ονασιφάνεια / Νικαγόρα in deutlichen Spuren den Umriss einer Malerei, und zwar augenscheinlich einen Sitzfigur, erkennen lässt.' Hiller, *IG*, says ' in superiore stelae parte figurae sedentis pictae vestigia apparent'. Dr. R. Noll, to whose kindness I owe the photograph reproduced here (fig. 22), tells me that there is now no trace of the colour (cf. Noll. *Gr. u. röm. Inschr. der Wiener Antikensamml.* (1962), p. 25, no. 22, 'einst mit Spuren eines gemalten Bildes (Sitzfigur?)'). Conze, publishing summarily the two stelai reproduced here as fig. 21, *c* and *d*, *AZ* 1866, Anz. cols. 246–7, suggested that they too may have carried a painted representation above the inscriptions: 'Die Inschriften, namentlich die erstere, sind so auffallend tief herabgerückt, dass mir sehr wahrscheinlich ist, es sei die oben jetzt glatt und leer bleibende Fläche des Steines ursprünglich bemalt gewesen', but that is an inference, not an observation. It may be noted that M. Chaviaras, in publishing a funerary stele with the inscription towards the bottom, Ἀρχ. 'Εφ., 1913, p. 15, no. 43, wrote ἐκ τούτου εἰκάζω ὅτι ἐπὶ τῆς στήλης ὑπῆρχε ζωγραφία, ἧς ὅμως οὐδὲν ἴχνος διασώζεται. An example of a painted stele with incised (not painted) inscription is the stele from Cyme in Istanbul, Mendel, iii, p. 324, no. 1086; the inscription is immediately below the upper moulding.

38. These two stelai are both standing in the sunken open passage leading to the inner chamber of the main Makry Steno hypogaeum. *a*, H. 1·25 m, W. 0·43/5 m, Th. 0·18 m; dim. of base, H. 0·51 m, W. 0·63 m; *b*, H. 0·99 m, W. 0·40/42 m, Th. 0·17 m; base, H. 0·51 m, W. 0·64 m. In the same passage there are also two very worn fragments of red stucco bases. The stelai, to judge by their mouldings as compared with those of other stelai and bases assigned on their letter forms to the early third century, are of the middle or later hellenistic period.

39. There are other examples of tufa bases in Tr. The recent excavation of ninety-one pit-graves cut in the rock on the site of the Anamorphoterion, on the high ground immediately above the British War Cemetery, brought to light a certain amount of third-century material (black ribbed-pelikae, Hadra-type hydriae), but the inscriptions all seem to be of the second century: see *Arch. Delt.* 24 (1969), 1970, Chr. 2, pp. 476–80; cf. above, note 7.

40. See briefly Fraser, *Ptol. Alex.* I, pp. 164 ff., with the notes.

41. See below, pp. 74–5.

41a. A recently published cylindrical altar of late date, from Karakonero, *AAA*, 8, 1975(1), p. 37, no. 1 and fig. 1 reads ἡ σορὸς Αἰλίου / Ζωσίμου καὶ / τοῦ υἱοῦ αὐτοῦ / Οἰνοφόρου καὶ / τοῦ θρεπτοῦ αὐ/τοῦ Αἰλίου 'Επι/κτήτου καὶ τέκν/ων αὐτῶν, but the σορός presumably refers not to the altar but to the associated sarcophagus or casket.

42. Described as 'cista' by Hiller in *IG*, as 'urna cineraria' by Italian archaeologists, and by Greek archaeologists as τεφροδόχος, τεφροδόχη, and ὀστεοθήκη.

43. For a published collection of inscribed caskets see *NS* 80, 94, 131–3, 138, 140–1, 157, 162, 169–71, 177, 180, 188, 193, 200, 202, 210, 212, 216, 218, 240, 241, 297–333, 335–6, 338, 346, 348–58, 363–83, 385–401, 405–20.

44. In fig. 27, *a* all the caskets visible are inscribed on the lid; they are *NS* 405–8, and 27, *b* is *NS* 407.

45. See, e.g., *Ann.* 2, p. 175, no. 162ª (fig. 26, *a*).

46. *NS* 405–8 (407 = fig. 27, *b*) are probably all of the third century; 407 certainly is. *Ann.* 2, p. 178, no. 181, is also early, if the copy is to be trusted; I have not seen it. An early and very large pair of caskets are *Ann.* 2, p. 175, nos. 162ª and ᵇ, (*a*), fig. 26, *a*, H. 0·42 m, W. 0·51 m, Th. 0·42 m, 'Ιεροκλεῦς τοῦ Φιλιστίδα Βρυγινδαρίου, and (*h*), fig. 26, *b*, H. 0·41 m, W. 0·52 m, Th. 0·54 m, Φιλιστίδα Φιλίνου Βρυγινδαρίου, from the eastern necropolis. The hands of each are different, but no doubt the Philistidas of both is the same person. The hand of (*b*) is plainer than that of (*a*), and is perhaps likely to be the earlier.

47. *NS* 346, Πώλλας 'Ρωμαίας Τρυφαίνας; *Cl. Rh.* 2, p. 224, no. 85, Μάρ(κου) Αὐρ(ηλίου) / 'Ερμοκράτου / 'Επαφρίωνος / καὶ Αὐρ(ηλίας) Ζωσίμης / καὶ τῶν τέκνων / αὐτῶν, probably the latest surviving casket.

48. For the Peraea see Fraser and Bean, p. 42, nos. 30–1 (Bozburun), 35 (Selimye); Roos, *Opusc. Ath.* 9, 1969, p. 61, fig. 1, from Büyükkaraağaç (Pyrnos(?)), near Marmaris (Physkos) (here fig. 28); for the islands see *IG* xii. 3, nos. 11, 15, 22, 23 (Syme); 50 (Telos); xii. 1, 968 (Chalke). They seem to be less frequent than the typical Rhodian funerary monuments, the altars, perhaps because cremation was not as frequent as inhumation, or because, in these small communities, the practice of burying in loculi had not developed.

49. The Sardian group, including some published earlier, is published in Buckler and Robinson, *Inscr. Sardis*, 105, 109, 112 (here fig. 29, *a*; *Beschr. ant. Skulpt.* no. 1123), 113–15, 117 (*BM* 1031, here fig. 30), 118–24, 129–33. The cistae are of about the same dimensions as the Rhodian. They are without exception inscribed on the slope of the lid (which is often all that is preserved), which is a less frequent practice in Rhodes than that of placing the inscription on the short face. The main difference stylistically seems to be that the Sardian

cistae are normally (but not always) decorated with palmette-acroteria at the four corners and that, as in both examples reproduced, the key and the lock of the chest are carved in relief on the long side. These Sardian examples seem, like the Rhodian, to date from the second century B.C. onwards (dating by stephanephoros, and then by priest of Rome). One or two from Ephesus (*BMI* 639–41), of the Roman period, are almost identical with the Sardian. For an example from Thyateira see Keil and von Premerstein, *Zweite Reise*, p. 44, no. 77 (i a.C.). There are one or two examples from Pergamon, now in the Museum at Pergamon; they slightly resemble the Rhodian, as the examples given here (fig. 29, *b*, *c*) show, but the acroteria on 29, *b*, do not occur at Rhodes, while the dimensions of 29, *c*, are unparalleled at Rhodes. On 29, *b*, there is a crown in relief on the short side; cf. below, p. 68.

50. I would for this reason assign to Rhodes the uninscribed casket of unrecorded provenance (here fig. 25, *a*, *b*) in Istanbul Museum, Fıratlı, *Les Stèles funéraires de Byzance gr. rom.* (Bibl. archéol. et hist. de l'Inst. franç. d'Arch. 15, Paris, 1964), pl. 66, bottom, reproduced here, with Dr. Fıratlı's kind permission, from a photograph taken by Mr. M. Lowe. I also reproduce here (figs. 29, *d*, *e*) examples of Carthaginian ash-caskets (now in the Parc archéologique), whose remarkable similarity to the Rhodian caskets is undoubtedly due to chance.

51. For these see especially W. Altmann, *Die römische Grabaltäre der Kaiserzeit* (Berlin, 1905), *passim*; J. M. C. Toynbee, *Death and Burial in the Roman World* (London, 1971), pp. 253 ff.; M. Honroth, *Stadtrömische Girlanden* (Vienna, 1971), *passim*.

52. Called by Hiller 'ara rectangula', by the Italian archaeologists 'ara quadrangulare', and in Greek commonly described as παραλληλεπίπεδος βωμός. Once again, these monuments are very numerous, and I have not thought it necessary to give a full list of them. I have myself studied most of the available monuments of this class, but owing to the illegibility of some of the stones and the margin that must consequently be allowed for discrepancy in readings I have in some cases been unable to determine whether a stone, and the inscription on it, are published or not. I have therefore in each case given the inscription as a means of identification, and I am especially grateful to Dr. Konstantinopoulos for allowing me to include these uncertain items in the publication.

53. There are several large upper members, discovered in recent years, in the garden of the Department of Antiquities, and I have come across others at times. I reproduce here (fig. 31, *a*) an example (Eph.) carved in the red stone called σωμακί; see next note.

54. I owe to a local mason the information that the stone is still quarried on Profiti Elia, but my informant did not know the word σωμακί, given to this stone in Hiller's day; see his lemma to *IG* 486: 'in ara rotunda lapidis rubri (σωμακί)'; see also Merker, *Hellenistic Sculpture of Rhodes*, p. 6, with note 15 on p. 21. Circular altars of this stone, such as *IG* 486, or fragments of them,

seem very rare (there is one in LG), and only fragments of rectangular altars survive (mostly of the large upper members; see note 53). [See Add.]

55. The two pieces are: fig. 32, *a*, *NS* 219 (OGard.), Ἑρμαῖος Καππάδοξ / χρηστὸς χαῖρε, H. 0·45 m (base, 0·12 m), W. 0·45 m, Th. 0·26 m; fig. 32, *b*, UP (OGard., under palm-tree), no inscription, remains of two bosses, H. 0·82 m (base 0·26 m), W. 0·67 m, Th. 0·46 m; the front of the base, on which the inscription was probably carved, is damaged.

56. The full series consists of the following items: *ILind.* 149 (*c.* 198 B.C.; fig. 34, *a*), 154 (*c.* 196 B.C.), 195 (*c.* 169 B.C.; fig. 34, *b*), 202 (*c.* 163 B.C.), 209 (*c.* 160 B.C.; fig. 33, *a*), 230 (*c.* 134 B.C.; fig. 33, *b*), 253 (*c.* 114/13 B.C.), 258 (107 B.C.), 290 (88 B.C.; not by epistatas), 306 (67 B.C.; not by epistatas).

57. See, e.g., *ILind.* 140 (*c.* 202 B.C.; rectangular), 193 (170 B.C.; cylindrical), 200 (164 B.C.; cylindrical), 195 (has mouldings on the sides, not pediments; it seems unfinished, for Blinkenberg records that the central section of the upper surface had been left rough, and it may have been intended to smooth off this part), 212 (150 B.C.; cylindrical), 215 (rock-cut; on Acropolis).

58. *ILind.* 306 (67 B.C.), a dedication by Αἰσχίνας καὶ Κτήσων νακορήσαντες; ibid. 290 (88 B.C.), a dedication by Ἄττας ὁ ἐπὶ τοῦ δοχείου καὶ Ἀλέξανδρος ὁ ἐπὶ τοῦ ἀνδρῶνος; ibid. 289 (89 B.C.), inscribed on a small slab, is a dedication by Ἐπίγονος, ὁ ἐπὶ τῶι δοχείωι. Blinkenberg understood the δοχεῖον to be the large series of cisterns built in front of the stoa, probably as a precaution at the time of Mithradates' operations, and the ἀνδρών as a lodging-house for the labourers, and some such meaning is perhaps more likely than the usual one of a refectory or banqueting-place (cf. Nock, *HTR* 29, 1936, p. 46; Crampa, *Labraunda*, III, 2, *Greek Inscr.* II (Act. Inst. Ath. Suec. 4°, V, III, 2), p. 10); of the duties of the two men he says, on no. 289, 'Epigonos a probablement été contremaître pendant la construction . . .', and, on 290, 'Les deux hommes, Ἄττας et Ἀλέξανδρος, étaient sans doute des fonctionnaires appointés et ont probablement eu à faire avec la construction des rangées des citernes.' The infrequent use of ἐπί+the dative, for the usual genitive, meaning 'in charge of' is unexpected in such a set formula.

59. See, e.g., the description of *ILind.* 195, 'Autel d'épistate rectangulaire'; cf. on 149, 'Forme analogue aux autres autels dédiés par les épistates; les imitations de frontons de temple, qui se trouvent souvent sur les petits côtes, font ici défaut.'

60. On 195 see note 57.

61. *Tit. Cam.* 119.

62. Another possible instance of a rectangular altar, of the type now under consideration, at Kamiros (fig. 35, *c*) is an uninscribed block of veined brown marble—a very unusual type of stone on Rhodes, perhaps 'σωμακί' (see above, note 54)—with a (later?) circular depression in the upper surface. Enough, however, remains to show that the stone had a raised margin to left and right,

and that the sides had mouldings only, and no pediments; but it is not certain that it had a margin at the back. The piece, whatever its precise purpose, was clearly votive, and not funerary; it is uninscribed, and was apparently found in the centre of the city, where it now stands against a wall of the lower sanctuary.

63. For rectangular altars at Kamiros see *Tit. Cam.* 84–5, and 135–43, the series of nine altars forming part of one monument, each carrying a dedication in the genitive to a different deity or hero, in letters of the early hellenistic age.

64. See *Tit. Cam.* 66, 70, 72–78c, all very much of the same age, to judge by the lettering—the middle or later second century B.C. I illustrate here (fig. 36) no. 76, in the Louvre (Froehner, *Catal.* no. 27). Such diskoi were the subject of a study by Jacobsthal, *Diskoi* (93 Winckelmannsprogr., Berlin, 1933). The earliest example from Kamiros is the classical painted diskos with the figure of a youth, *Cl. Rh.* 3, p. 251, fig. 248, Jacobsthal, p. 13, fig. 7, and p. 17. He discusses the Rhodian dedicatory shields in detail on pp. 23 ff. Jameson, *Hesp.* 27, 1958, pp. 122–3, no. 1, published a shield-dedication from Karpathos, as he thought, but in fact this is from the neighbouring Kasos: see Susini, *Supp. Epigr.*, pp. 217–18 and fig. 12.

65. See *ILind.* 160, 171, 180, 187, 218, 226, 439, 451 (515, 516). Both at Kamiros and at Lindos almost all the surviving shields are of white marble, and not of 'Lartian'. The Lindian examples cover a wider span of time than the Kamiran—from the early second century B.C. to at least c. A.D. 100, without any difference in the style of the shields.

66. Only the upper member of this monument survives (cf. above, pp. 13–14). It is (or was until 1971, but I did not notice it in 1972 or 1974) sitting on the ledge of the terrace of an abandoned taverna on the road between the village of Lindos and the beach. It is of a sparkling white marble, and not, like the epistatai-altars, of 'Lartian'. Its measurements are, H. 0·16 m, W. 0·67 m, Th. 0·40 m, diam. of boss, 0·18 m.

66a. UP.

67. Nat. Mus. 1791, of unknown provenance, reproduced by Altmann, op. cit., p. 7, fig. 3. Fig. 41, *b* shows clearly the careful anathyrosis of the circular epithema. The monument is uninscribed. The piece from Thera (fig. 40, *d*), on which, below a neatly executed triglyph-frieze, bucrania and a pendent garland surround the body of the altar, carries the inscription, *IG* xii. 3, 469, a dedication in honour of Augustus, of the period after Actium. There is one, and only one, Rhodian altar which has a similar low, round cushion on its upper surface, and it differs fundamentally from all the other Rhodian rectangular altars in that it has no margins or pedimental sides; it is in fact a plain, rectangular block with a cushion on its upper surface. It is inscribed Ἀσία Σελευκὶς / χρηστὰ χαῖρε (*Arch. Delt.* 25 (1970), 1973, Chr. 2, p. 515, and pl. 438b; Eph.), here fig. 41, *c*. It differs from the Athenian piece (and resembles the Rhodian bosses) in that its upper surface is smooth, and not rough-picked. It is therefore not a base for an epithema. For a rectangular Telian altar with

a rudimentary rectangular boss see below, note 87, and fig. 49, *b–c*. Another Theraean monument, *IG* xii. 3, 882 (here fig. 56, *b*) has a curious conical apex which resembles that represented in the last row of the 'Apotheosis of Homer' (*BMSculpt.* iii, 2191; *BMI* 1098; and many subsequent publications, especially D. Pinkwart, *Das Relief des Archelaos von Priene* (Kallmünz, 1965), and in *Antike Plastik*, iv(7), 1965, pp. 55 ff.). It seems probable that on the 'Apotheosis' this represents the sacrificial fire burning on the altar; such fires are represented, more or less schematically, on altars on Pergamene Hero-reliefs (*AvonPerg.* 7, nos. 311–12, 314 (?), 317; Pfuhl, op. cit., p. 65), and also on that on the Coan tombstone, *Ann.* 33–4, N.S. 17–18, 1955–6, pp. 150–2, nos. 230 *a–d* (cf. below, note 217) and one may be seen burning vigorously, with a pyramidal type of flame, on the painted stele from Demetrias, Arvanitopoullos, *Γραπταὶ Στῆλαι Δημητριάδος*, pl. 5 (and pp. 154–5), and on the circular altar represented on the circular altar with a sacrificial scene, of unknown origin, Mendel, ii, no. 564 (here fig. 85, *h–j*), and on a rectangular altar with garland of oak and olive-leaves, represented on a relief of Roman date, now in the Museum at Pergamon (*AvonPerg.* 7, p. 339, no. 422). A sestertius of 46 B.C. (*BMCat. Rom. Rep.* i, p. 522, no. 4034, and iii, pl. li, no. 9) has obv. a garlanded bucranion, and rev. a circular altar with garland and a fire burning on the top; cf. Grueber's note 1 on pp. 521–2 (at end of p. 521). For another sestertius and a denarius of the same date with a crested Corinthian-style helmet akin to that on fig. 93, *d*, see note 191. [See ADD.]

68. *NS* 163 (UG); for the inscriptions on this monument see below, p. 73.

69. UP (OGard.). The last word is written ζωνν. Dim.: H. 0·485 m, W. 0·53 m, Th. 0·25 m, bosses diam. 0·11 m, letters 0·040–60 m, omicron 0·025 m. My date for this example is based on the general style of the lettering, and must be regarded only as an approximation.

70. (45, *a*), *Cl. Rh.* 9, p. 100, fig. 66 (IGard.), no visible trace of inscription; (*b*), UP (IGard.), no visible trace of inscription, H. 0·53 m, W. 0·51 m, Th. 0·375 m; relief H. 0·26 m, W. 0·28 m; (*c*), UP (Tr.), is in a battered condition, but the relief itself is only slightly damaged. The place on the upper surface originally occupied by the boss has (as in some other examples) been excavated subsequently: diam. of hole, 0·10 m. A similar piece from the Rhodian Peraea (Karaça), *BSA* 52, 1957, pl. 16 (c), is reproduced here, fig. 44, *a*. Note the bucrania flanking the upper part of the relief panel, under the moulding. For an example in the British Museum, probably from the Peraea, see below, note 117.

71. *Cl. Rh.* 5(1), p. 96, no. 26 (IGard.; inv. 13659), Ἰσιδώρα Μυρὶς γυνὰ δὲ [Φ]ιλοκράτευς καὶ Μαδουσι. (on lower moulding) χρηστὰ χαιρε[τε?], H. 0·46 m, W. 0·61 m, Th. 0·29 m, letters 0·02 m (inscribed below relief); relief, H. 0·23 m, W. 0·42 m. γυνὰ δέ, without a preceding patronymic, is anomalous.

72. UP (UG), uninscribed.

73. One well-executed example of the 'Totenmahl' relief of the votive class is *Chr. des fouilles 1960*, p. 860, fig. 3. Another, much inferior and of later date, is

Cl. Rh. 2, p. 50, no. 20. The first is certainly votive, and the second may well be, but only the lower half survives, and one cannot be certain. There is a very late example in the Nat. Mus. in Copenhagen (Inv. 8630), bought by Kinch in Rhodes, here fig. 47, *b*. Measurements, H. 0·39 m, W. 0·71 m, Th. 0·10 m. It is uninscribed, and I hesitate to date it more precisely than to the Imperial period. In any case, it represents the nadir of Rhodian art.

74. (a), UP (described above, note 55, and fig. 32, *b*). The circular monuments of this group are: (b), UP (UG), H. 0·45 m, diam. 0·35 m, rectang. space 0·15 m×0·175 m, below, fig. 87, *a*; (c), UP (Cast. grounds), H. 0·50 m, diam. 0·35 m, rectang. space 0·14 m×0·185 m, below, fig. 87, *b*; (d), UP (Eph.).

75. Benndorf, *Reisen*, i, pp. 26 f., fig. 22; *IG* 441, now in Vienna, Κώμου Λαοδικέως.

76. Κῶμος is otherwise attested as a name (e.g. *IG* 1028, K. of Phaselis; 1340, K. as potter's name on amphora-stamp; *BMI* 898, line 7, Halicarnassos; *Inschr. Priene* 53, line 74; *SGDI* 1909 (*DGE* 338), manumitted slave, Delphi), and the relationship of name to theme may be fortuitous. Such plays upon names are nevertheless familiar from tombstones and from the *Anthology*.

77. *Cl. Rh.* 2, no. 32 and figs. 37, 38 (now on exhibition in Museum, in innermost corner of room next to Infirmary), already described, Jacopi, *Sped. dei Cav.*, p. 46, no. 638; Laurenzi, *Röm. Mitt.* 54, 1939, p. 43, fig. 1; uninscribed, H. 0·60 m, W. 0·59 m, Th. 0·42 m.

78. 'Εφ. Ἀρχ., 1913, p. 11, no. 22, *Arch. Delt.* 20 (1965), Chr. 2, p. 602 and pl. 768, a. H. 0·62 m, W. 0·62 m, Th. 0·32 m, diam. of boss 0·12 m (M. Chaviaras, loc. cit., wrongly describes the altar as having *two* bosses: ἐπὶ τῆς ἄνω ἐπιφανείας σώζονται αἱ βάσεις δύο μικρῶν κιονίσκων). For other examples of this type of altar from Nisyros see below, note 109.

79. Previous editors do not comment on this object, the identification of which is indeed far from certain.

80. UP (OGard.), inscribed Παρνασσοῦ Γαλάτα, H. 0·485 m, W. 0·62 m, Th. 0·31 m, letters 0·015 m. The altar is referred to by Laurenzi, *Boll. d'arte*, 30, 1936, p. 132: 'un'ara con i segni monetari di Rodi, cioè la rosa e il volto d'Elios'.

81. For the representations of the rose and the radiate head of the Sun on Rhodian amphora-stamps see V. Grace, *Amphoras* (Agora Picture Book, no. 6), figs. 23–5, and, for some recent examples, *Explor. de Délos*, 27 (1970), Index, p. 380, s.v. Helios and Rose. The Helios-head is always radiate, and bears no resemblance to our piece. The rose is more similar. A phiale dedicated by a Rhodian architheoros, Philodamos, at Delos, in or before 279, carried an embossed representation of Helios, presumably as a mesomphalic decoration: *IG* xi. 2, 161B, line 16, φιάλη ἔκτυπον ἔχουσα Ἡλίου πρόσωπον, ἀνάθημα Δηλιάδων χορεία ἐπ' ἀρχεθεώρου Πολυχάρμου (*per err.* for Φιλοδάμου: see Durrbach, ad loc. and ibid. 162B, line 13). I may call attention here to the representation

of Helios as the parasemon of an Olbian decree for a Rhodian, Ἀγησ—, the son of Hagesandros, *Nadp. Olb.* (1968), no. 24 and pl. xiii, here fig. 57. The head is much more like the coin-heads, from which it was probably taken, than is our piece. On representations of Helios see the iconographical study of H. Hoffmann, *Journ. Amer. Res. Cent. in Egypt*, 2, 1963, pp. 117–23.

82. See *BMCCaria*, pls. xxxvi–xliii. It is worth remarking that the face of the Helios-head on the heavy Rhodian bronze coins assigned by Head to 88–44 B.C. is noticeably rounder and fatter than on earlier issues, and to that extent at least corresponds to the plump face on the tombstone, which is of about the same date: see on these coins Head, p. cxiii and p. 261, nos. 342–5, with pl. xli, nos. 3–4. But the style of the two representations is very different. On Rhodian coins the 'rose' is always open, and not closed as on the stone. I may call attention in this connection to the upper member of an aediculate tombstone in Cos (Castello), which has a Rhodian rose, also of the closed variety, in the centre of the pediment (fig. 44, *d*); the stone does not appear to be of Rhodian origin.

83. *IG* 546 and 549.

84. *IG* 909, from Gennadi, in Lindian territory. Most of the altars published by Hiller have now disappeared, and I have been able to identify only the two mentioned in the previous note, which are both in Rhodes Museum (546, LG; 549, UG (inv. 105)); how many with bosses he actually published must therefore remain uncertain.

85. *NS* 98 (UG), 148 (LG), 163 (UG), 175 (UG), 198 (UG), 243 (LG), 342 (UG); *Cl. Rh.* 2, p. 216, no. 56 (LG), all of which have been identified by me as having bosses and pedimental sides. For *NS* 46 (IGard.), 219 (OGard.), 230 (LG), 243 (LG), 342 (UG), he refers to the 'cornici', but not, in the case of 342, to the boss.

86. *Cl. Rh.* 2, no. 32. In his original description of the altar in *Sped. dei Cav.*, pp. 46–7, Jacopi was cautious, but had, I think, seen the possibly correct solution: 'Sul significato delle due prominenze a tronco di cono sulla faccia superiore di questo altare e di altri simili si discute ancora. Forse servivano all'incastro d'un plinto statuario, per il caso che la famiglia dell'estinto l'avesse commesso, scegliendo l'altare, decorato in modo convenzionale, già pronto nella bottega del marmorario. O forse le prominenze potevano servire a reggere corone o altri ornamenti della tomba, secondo un rituale che ci sfugge.' For the interpretation that the bosses formed supports for crowns see below, p. 22.

87. *Röm. Mitt.* 54, 1939, pl. 43. Laurenzi claimed that the votive altar represented on the votive relief in Munich (Gl. 203), Furtwängler, *Illustr. Kat. Glypt. München* (1907), pl. 22, Lawrence, *Later Greek Sculpture*, p. 24, fig. 41, a (further bibliography in W. Hornbostel, *Sarapis* (Leiden, 1973), p. 356, note 1), here fig. 50, *a*, was of the Rhodian type, and that the projection on the upper surface was of a boss of the type now under discussion: 'Le ricerche piu minute attraverso le relazioni di scavo e le pubblicazioni di materiali ellenistici . . . mi consentono di affermare senza riserve che l'altare rappresentato sul rilievo

monacense è un'ara funeraria rodia, tipica nel senso più limitato della parola, vale a dire conosciuta solo nell'isola di Rodi, a partire dal secondo secolo avanti Cristo. — Infatti mentre a Rodi si sono trovate centinaia di esemplari di queste are, caratterizzate dal timpano decorante i lati corti e dall'incavo rettangolare sul piano superiore, dove sono risparmiate delle zone più alte, non si può ricordare un solo altare di questo tipo, che sia stato trovato non soltanto nella Grecia continentale o asiatica, ma neppure nelle isole dipendenti politicamente da Rodi.' This view is untenable for numerous reasons, each sufficient to refute the hypothesis regarding the altar on the relief: (i) as Konstantinopoulos has already pointed out, *Arch. Delt.* 18, 1963, p. 26, note 89, the altar on the relief is not funerary; (ii) as is clear on inspection (I have to thank Dr. D. Ahrens, Keeper of the Staatliche Antikensammlungen in Munich, for enabling me to study the piece itself), the stone itself is not Rhodian—it is a faintly yellow marble to which there is no precise parallel on Rhodes—and the subject, sacrifice before a deity, has nothing to connect it especially with Rhodes. I subscribe to the view of Furtwängler that the relief is probably of Attic or Boeotian origin. In any case (iii) the 'cushion' on top of the altar is clearly not circular, like the Rhodian bosses, but flat and rectangular, and has a cavity at the front left corner, probably for pouring libations: see fig. 50, *a* and the enlarged detail in U. Hausmann, *Griech. Weihreliefs* (1960), Abb. 56; and (iv) in other respects— general shape and proportions, number and type of mouldings, etc.—the stone differs considerably from the Rhodian funerary altars. Bieber, *Hellenistic Sculpture*[2], p. 126, says that Laurenzi has 'rightly proved it' to be a local product of Rhodes. For the error regarding the restriction of this type of altar to Rhodes itself see below, p. 24. Miss Richter, *Portraits of the Greeks*, iii, p. 278, suggested that the seated figure in the relief 'bears a marked resemblance to the portraits of Euthydemos (of Bactria)'; the resemblance, if it exists, must surely be fortuitous.

I may refer here to, and illustrate (fig. 49, *b–c*), a rectangular white marble uninscribed altar lying in a farmyard below the village of Megalochorio on Telos. This has a rectangular flat elevation in the centre of the upper surface, which resembles that on the Munich relief. But it is, I think, evident from the rough state of the stone and the lack of pronounced mouldings on the side pediment that the altar was left in an unfinished state.

I may note here that the presence of pedimental sides on a rectangular structure, as on the altar on the Munich relief, is not in itself a sign of Rhodian origin: see, for example, the Delian incense-burner, *Expl. de Délos*, xviii, pl. xc, no. 970, and, for an earlier period, the altars represented on the Attic vases noted below, note 91.

88. *Supp. Epigr.* p. 284, no. 12, and p. 286, no. 15. The two stones are republished below, p. 24 and note 108, with figs. 53, *a* and *b*. The passage quoted occurs on p. 269 of Susini's article.

89. e.g. (a) *NS* 384 (UG), with two bosses (fig. 39, *a*), commemorates five persons whose relationship to each other is obscure: 'Ἰσίωνος Χαλκιδέως / καὶ τᾶς γυναικὸς / 'Ηκατέας Βηρυτίας / καὶ Ἀριστοβουλίδος Βηρυτίας (sister of Hecatea?) / καὶ τοῦ υἱοῦ αὐτᾶς / Ἀσκλαπιάδα Φασηλείτα (his father was presumably a Phase-

lite) / καὶ Ἀρέτης Λύδας (servant of one or all members of the family group?);
(b) *NS* 342 (UG), a family monument, one boss (fig. 38, *b*): Ἀγαθοστράτου
Ἀστυ/μήδου Βρασίου Φλα/υίας Νεικασῶ Ἑρμη⟨ι̂?⟩/δος καὶ τῶν παιδί/ων αὐτῶν;
here it might be argued that the monument was erected when only the first-
named had died, and that the other names were added in advance of death;
but, if so, one would expect the bosses to correspond to the eventual number
of persons commemorated; (c) *IG* 549 (UG), a monument of husband and wife,
one boss (fig. 38, *a*): Ὠφελίωνος Σύρου / καὶ τᾶς γυναικὸς / Μενεστράτης [Κ]ραγίας;
(d) UP (Eph.), monument of husband and wife, one boss: Ἀγορακλεῦς / Ἀπολλο-
δότου / Καρπαθιοπολίτα καὶ / τᾶς γυναικὸς Συρία[ς] . . . . . κῶνος / Βρυκουντίσσας.

90. This was suggested by M. and N. Chaviaras, Ἀρχ. Ἐφ., 1911, p. 64: 'Η
ἄνω πλευρά (of the altar reproduced below, fig. 54, *c*) διασώζει διαιρέσεις, ἐξ ὧν
διακρίνονται ὅτι ὑπῆρχον δύο κιόνια διαμέτρου 0·10, ἐφ᾽ ὧν πιθανῶς ἐφηρμόζοντο
ἀγάλματα. That is unacceptable for physical reasons: the bosses have no central
holes for a statue—at the most they have a very small compass-hole (see fig.
40, *a*), and though there would be room between two of them for a terracotta or
bronze collar of a hollow bust or protome to have fitted over them, the busts
themselves would have been too close. Physical reasons apart, it is also unacceptable, as stated in the text, because of the discrepancy at times between
the number of bosses and the number of persons commemorated on the monument.

A similar view was expressed by A. H. Smith, in describing the BM example
discussed below, note 117, in *BMSculpt.* i (1892), p. 339, no. 724: 'Above it is
roughly worked to fit the plinth of a statue.' Smith presumably thought of
a single plinth (of what material?) supported by both bosses, but it is useless
to ask exactly what he envisaged (he seems to have been followed by Pfuhl,
JDAI 20, 1905, p. 91). Newton, in publishing the inscription of the same altar,
BMI 445 (cf. below, note 117), said, 'The upper surface of the marble above the
panel is cut away so as to form an oblong sinking, in which are reserved two
circular spaces; on these may have rested some object which fitted into the
sinking.'

91. For braziers on altars see the Nikias-crater, Beazley, *ARV*², p. 847, no. 1,
illustrated, Rumpf, *Religion der Griechen* (*Bilderatlas z. Religionsgesch.* 13/14,
1928), fig. 43; and the BM sherd, E 494, *BMCat. Vases*, iii, pl. 16, Rumpf,
ibid. 31. The superficial resemblance of the outline of the two-layered brazier
with draught-holes to our bosses is evident, but the brazier is of course standing
wholly on top of the altar. The fragmentary bell-crater from Al Mina in the
Ashmolean Museum, *JHS* 59, 1939, p. 21, fig. 54, shows the whole structure:
first, the top of the altar with volutes, then the insulating layer of wood and
mortar, represented by a speckled surface, then the fire-brick resting on that,
and, on top of the fire-brick, the altar with four layers of draught-holes.
Beazley discusses, loc. cit., the construction of the insulating layer of the fire-brick
(ἐπίπυρον?). An excellent example is also provided by the vase in Bonn, *CV*
Bonn (1), pl. 19, 1–2, and pl. 20, 1–2 (*ARV*², p. 1171, no. 4); see also that in
Ferrara, *CV* Ferrara (1), pl. 12, no. 5 (brick, but no underlayer). The Douris
vase in Boston, Beazley, *Boston Vases*, iii (1963), pl. lxxiii (*ARV*², p. 435, no.

89), shows a more evolved form of the brick, which has been fashioned to fit the somewhat exaggerated volutes of the altar (cf. also ibid., pl. xcix (*ARV*², p. 1142, no. 1), which resembles the Al Mina vase, with Beazley's comments, Text, iii, p. 71). A fragment of an Attic cantharos from Lindos, *Lindos*, I, no. 2722, provides a good representation of an altar with a fire burning, in which the fire is placed straight on the altar; cf. above, note 67.

92. Yavis, op. cit., pp. 160 ff., has a class of 'altars with barriers' which, he says, served 'to retain the coal and ashes'. He includes (p. 164, no. 92) in this category the example of the Rhodian altars discussed above, p. 18, describing it as having 'a rectangular barrier on three sides with two low bosses on the upper surface in the shape of truncated cones'; but he makes no attempt to explain how the bosses can be accommodated to his interpretation of the barriers.

93. *Assoc.* p. 153, no. 12 and pl. xi, 1, H. 0·08 m, W. 0·28 m. The inscription (i a.C.)reads τὸ κοινὸν τὸ 'Ιατροκλείων | ἐπᾳιͅνεῖ καὶ στεφανοῖ | 'Ιε . . . . τίμου.

94. See below, note 117, and fig. 56, *a*.

95. In Greece funerary cones are particularly common at Thespiae: see Wilhelm, *Beiträge*, pp. 72–4; *B & WG*, p. 37, note 15; Plassart, *BCH* 82, 1958, pp. 147 ff., nos. 241 ff. (and p. 147, note 1). I illustrate here (fig. 51, *a*, *b*) Plassart, no. 258, Μᾶρκε Καστρίκιε Εἴκαρε, and Wilhelm, op. cit., pp. 72–3 and fig. 36, Λύσων, both from Thespiae. For such cones in general see in addition to Wilhelm, Pfuhl, *JDAI*, 20, 1905, pp. 88–91; Kurtz and Boardman, op. cit., pp. 242–4 (phalloid markers). In Italy the cone occurs not infrequently as a complete funerary monument, or as an element of one in Etruria: see Altmann, op. cit., p. 30, and the illustration in Scullard, *The Etruscan Cities and Rome* (London, 1971), pl. 54; Nogara, *Gli Etruschi e la loro civiltà*, p. 261, fig. 143; Giglioli, *L'Arte Etrusca*, pl. 77, 1; 144; 150.

96. For such cakes see in general Stengel, *Opferbräuche der Griechen* (1910), pp. 66 ff., 126 ff., and Eitrem, *Opferritus und Voropfer* (Christiania, 1915), pp. 272 ff., and the studies mentioned in the following notes.

97. See Ziehen, *RE*, s.v. Πελανός, cols. 246–50, and G. Herzog-Hauser, s.v. Popanon (1), cols. 49–50.

98. See below, note 100.

99. See Rohde, *Psyche*³, pp. 231 ff. (E.T., pp. 166 ff.); Farnell, *Greek Hero Cults*, pp. 352–4; Stengel, op. cit., pp. 126 ff.; R. Thönges-Stringaris, *Ath. Mitt.* 80, 1964, pp. 62 ff.

100. See, for example, the πυραμίδες (pyramidal cakes) on, e.g., the 'Totenmahl' relief published by Furtwängler, *Collection Sabouroff*, pl. xxx. Furtwängler points out that pyramides are also particularly associated with the cult of the dead. See further Thönges-Stringaris, op. cit., a detailed study, with an excellent series of photographs, Beil. 1–30, which shows clearly the many varieties of cakes, etc., represented on the reliefs; πυραμίδες are conspicuous.

See further below, note 103. For πυραμίδες on a Rhodian 'Totenmahl' table see fig. 86, *c*. The representation of actual objects connected with funerary cult on tombstones is, of course, frequent from Classical times onwards: see in general Johansen, *Attic Grave Stelai* (Copenhagen, 1951), pp. 157–8.

101. *BCH* 36, 1912, pp. 230 ff., whence Hiller, *Hist. gr. Epigr.* 102, and Peek, *GVI* 1451; cf. below, note 203. The inscription, the present location of which is unknown to me, reads:

> Οὔ τί σε νώνυμνον κρύπτει τόδε Δωρίδος αἴης
> σῆμα περὶ τραφερὴν θηκάμενον σπιλάδα,
> Εὐμοιρέω Ἀρίδεικες· ἀποφθιμένοιο δὲ σεῖο
> μείλια καὶ πελανοὺς ἔμ πυρὶ βαλλόμεθα
> ἁζόμενοι Μούσαις, τὸν ἀοίδιμον αἴ σε τιθηνοῖς
> χερσὶ Πλατωνείους θρέψαν ὑπ' ἀτραπιτούς.

Cf. further on this epigram the discussion by P. Boyancé, *Le Culte des Muses chez les philosophes grecs* (Paris, 1937), pp. 278 ff. Boyancé regards the poem as commemorating a funerary foundation of a shrine of the Muses.

102. Note also Sokolowski, *Lois sacr. cit. gr.*, Suppl. (1962), no. 109, from Loryma (late hell./early Imperial), a very fragmentary text of a *lex sacra* relating to the cult of Zeus Atabyrios, in which provision is made for certain sacrifices; in line 4 the word [-π]έμματ[α-] stands in isolation (Sokolowski misunderstands the relationship of the Peraea to the Rhodian state when he says 'L'inscription a été trouvée à Loryma, mais le culte est Rhodien, transporté, semble-t-il, par des mercenaires de Rhodes'; so again in his comment on no. 110).

103. See Thönges-Stringaris, op. cit., p. 91, no. 155, and Beil. 23, 2; Mendel, iii, no. 1025.

104. I have noted this slope particularly in *NS* 163 (fig. 37, *b*) and 384 (fig. 37, *d*), but it is also noticeable on other pieces. On the other hand, in most instances the upper surface is level, and in a few cases it even slopes away from the edge, which must have caused liquid to collect in the gutters. It would therefore be unwise to lay much emphasis on so variable a feature.

105. It may be put on record here that the first known reference to the bosses occurred as long ago as 1851, when Samuel Birch described briefly the stone discussed below, note 117. In a note on recent BM acquisitions which appeared in German in the *Arch. Anzeig.* of that year, p. 128, he says, 'Noch sind ober-wärts an der altarähnlich ausgeschnittenen Bedeckung zwei runde Gegen-stände, *wie Küchen* [my italics], wahrzunehmen . . .'

106. So Laurenzi, quoted above, note 87. Even when Laurenzi wrote, such altars had been published and described from both the Rhodian Peraea and the Islands.

107. See Benndorf–Niemann, *Reisen im SW. Kleinas.*, I, p. 22, fig. 17 (here fig. 52, *b*), from Loryma (Yavis, op. cit., p. 175, no. 105); Chaviaras, Ἀρχ. Ἐφ., 1911, p. 64, no. 58, from island off Buzburun (here fig. 54, *c*); p. 69, no. 77,

from Selimye; id., ibid. 1913, p. 3, no. 87, from Pirnarı (?); Bean and Cook, *BSA* 52, 1957, p. 62, with note 10, and pl. 16c (here fig. 44, *a*) from Karaca, with reference also to a second 'smaller one lying buried'. It is often not easy to determine the form of the monuments from the descriptions in *Ἀρχ. Ἐφ.* (the altar, p. 64, no. 58, is described as a stele), and there may be more rectangular altars than I have recorded.

108. *Telos*: Susini, *Supp. Epigr.* p. 284, no. 12 (two bosses; here fig. 53, *a*): Κλήνωνος | Ἀριστοκλείδα | Τηλίου || καὶ τᾶς γυναικὸς Ἀλκινόης, and p. 286, no. 15: Χλόη Εὐοδίωνος | χαῖρε (here fig. 53, *b*). The former, which Susini does not illustrate, is set high in the arch above the entrance to a derelict windmill by the bay of Ayios Antonios, and the inscription is not visible on my photograph. In addition to these two pieces there is also the unfinished piece, discussed above, note 87, para. 2, and fig. 49, *b*, *c*.

109. *Nisyros*: (a) Ἀρχ. Ἐφ., 1913, p. 11, no. 22, one boss (cf. above, note 78, and figs. 48, *a*, *b*, 49, *a*); (b) Peek, *Inschr. Nis.* 386, no. 34 (two bosses), here fig. 54, *a*: [Ἀπολ]λώνιος Ἀστυπαλαιεὺς | χρηστὸς χαῖρε. The third piece (c) illustrated here, fig. 53, *c*, *d*, is apparently uninscribed, but it cannot be examined since, as the photograph shows, a more than life-size marble statue has been laid down immediately in front of it, so as to conceal the lower half, and there was, on the occasion of my stay on Nisyros in 1971, no available means of moving either monument.

110. *Chalke*: described by Ross as 'ara quadrata albi marmoris, cuius pars adversa et duo latera sertis floridis ornata sunt. Subter his sertis fuit nomen eius in cuius honorem positus est titulus, quod nomen legi nequit; deinde exsculptae sunt duae coronae.' The altar was thus of the same type as those on which are represented crowns awarded by koina (see below, p. 68), but it is unexpected to find the crowns associated on a rectangular monument with garlands but not bucrania. The stone is now apparently lost.

111. *Syme*: there are two altars of this type in the Chaviaras Collection in Syme, here figs. 54, *b* and *c*, but of these the second is certainly from the Peraea (above, note 107), and the first, which seems to be unpublished (inscr. —ώνακτος —αίου | Ἀγεμάχου Ἀπολλωνίου) is of a dark grey colour which might also be from there.

112. See Fraser and Bean, pp. 145–7. The alliance between Telos and Rhodes there referred to, and dated to the middle or late third century, was published by Ser. Charitonides in *Arch. Delt.* 16, 1960, pp. 94 ff. (cf. *Bull. Épigr.* 1964, p. 202, no. 332), and there dated by him to the earlier third century. To judge by the photograph of all the fragments in *Arch. Delt.* this may be correct, but it makes little difference to the present argument.

113. See Fraser and Bean, pp. 147–52.

114. For the early links of Telos with Cos see Robert, *Rev. Phil.* 1934, pp. 46–7; Fraser and Bean, p. 146. For those of Nisyros see Herzog, *Heil. Ges.*, p. 45, and Fraser and Bean, p. 147.

115. But not to all of them. None is reported (to the best of my knowledge: see Susini, *Supp. Epigr.*, p. 234) from Karpathos, while Kasos, lying between Karpathos and Crete, preserved its own type of flat circular tombstone throughout antiquity, and was unaffected by Rhodian usage, though it too was incorporated in Rhodian territory (see Fraser and Bean, pp. 152–3): see the illustrations in Susini, op. cit., pp. 219 ff., figs. 14–27. Pfuhl, *JDAI*, 20, 1905, pp. 88–9, drew attention to this unusual type of tombstone.

116. It is now in the store-room of the Castello, where I have examined it. There are clear, but illegible, traces of an inscription on it. An indication of how stones have been moved in these closely linked islands is provided by the following examples: (a) *IG* xii. 3, 67, was seen by Bent on Telos and by Hiller about ten years later on Nisyros; (b) ibid., Supp. 1282, was seen by Herzog on Cos ('sub platano famosa'), but he was told it had come from Nisyros; (c) *IG* xii. 3, 261, 268, and 269, and *CIL* iii, 459, were all transported from Anaphe to Thera.

It is of course perfectly possible, indeed I believe likely, that this particularly Rhodian type of tombstone may have been made solely in Rhodes, and exported thence according to demand, to customers in the islands. It is always difficult to distinguish stones satisfactorily, but, for what my observations are worth on this technical matter, I may state my opinion that the Telian altars may quite well be of Rhodian stone, i.e. the grey 'Lartian', and that the decorated Nisyrian piece (note 109, (a)) is of a white marble which could be Rhodian, while the other two Nisyrian pieces (ibid. (b) and (c)) are of a stone indistinguishable from Rhodian 'Lartian'. Nisyros is perhaps a special case for, as M. Chaviaras pointed out, ᾿Εφ. Ἀρχ., 1913, pp. 6–7, the volcanic stone of the island, especially the lava, is unsuitable for working.

Reference should be made here to the small group of Coan altars published as *PH* 192–7 and 351, 354, described by Paton as 'tetragonal altars ornamented with *bucrania* and garlands' (Yavis, p. 159, nos. 58–62). As far as I know, these altars are now lost (I am grateful to Miss S. Sherwin-White for informing me that she too has not identified any of them), and the possibility exists that they may have been of the Rhodian type. However, if they were, it is strange that Paton did not refer to their salient features, the bosses (if present) and the reserved upper surface, etc. I have therefore left them out of account.

117. *BMSculpt.* i (1892), no. 724, H. 0·62 m, W. 0·78 m, Th. 0·375 m, with two bosses, diam. 0·13 m, inscription (*BMI* 445), Ἑλλανίων Ταρσεύς. As fig. 55 shows, the right anta carries a wreath (as on the piece illustrated in fig. 47, *a*), the left is plain, and the inscription is inscribed at the right end (lettering of ii a.C.) beneath the figure reclining on the couch, to whom the inscription and the wreath both refer. The whole stone bears considerable traces of a white stucco, with which it was evidently once covered, perhaps in modern reuse—no other altar retains any trace of stucco. There is one other feature which sets this stone apart from the others: the clearly marked working of the bosses. As figs. 55 and 56, *a*, show, the upper part of each boss has been cut back very slightly, but unmistakably, and worked smooth, leaving the lower section as a sort of collar. This suggests, as already pointed out above, p. 22, that some object was

placed over the bosses, as Smith conjectured (see above, note 90), when he described them as supporting the plinth of a statue. I have already indicated that I consider that this collar may have been provided to support the wreaths, natural or artificial, which were placed over the bosses. The collar is much clearer on this than on any other piece.

There is some doubt as to the provenance of this piece. Birch, in publishing a note of its acquisition in *Arch. Anz.* 1851, p. 128 (cf. above, note 105), said of it, and of another piece acquired with it, 'Beide gedachte Marmorwerke waren früher von Kapitän Graves R.N. aus Lykien fortgeschafft worden', while Smith, loc. cit., gives its provenance as 'Xanthos? Presented by J. Scott Tucker, Esq. R.N.'. On the other hand, the label on the object itself reads 'Pedestal with a banquet scene from the tomb of Hellanion of Tarsus. 2nd century B.C. From Iasos. Given by J. Scott Tucker, 1851.' Dr. B. F. Cook of the Department of Greek and Roman Antiquities of the B. F. Museum, who has kindly examined the references to this stone in the various editions of the *Synopsis of the Contents of the British Museum*, which preceded the publication of Smith's *Catalogue*, pointed out to me that Smith had probably realized that the stone was not of Xanthian origin, but did not investigate its history more fully. The inscription is published in *BMI* (as no. 445) as the last item in the collection of the inscriptions of Iasos, but on p. 54, in the short introductory note to the section, Newton writes: 'The following inscriptions, Nos. ccccxl–ccccliv, were taken from the ruins of Iasos during a visit made by the Duke of St. Albans to that site in 1872, and were shipped on board his Grace's yacht "Xantha" under my supervision.' This seems to exclude the possibility that no. 445 was part of that collection of inscriptions from Iasos, though it would of course be possible that it came independently from there, other things being equal. The only reliable surviving evidence we have for its origin seems to be the original statement of Birch that the stone was acquired by Graves in Lycia. However, Graves himself spent much of his time in Rhodes preparing the Admiralty Charts of 1837–44 of Rhodes and the Dodecanese, and he may have acquired it there or in the Peraea. *Non liquet.*

118. See below, pp. 66 ff.

119. There are very many such bases in Rhodes Museum. The circular altars I illustrate below are mostly standing on such bases (59, *c*, 60, *a–c*, etc.).

120. 58, *a* (Ct.), inscription of altar defaced (traces of $E\Gamma\Gamma ENH\Sigma$ (?) in large letters); base, not belonging, uninscribed; *b* (LG), inscription not identified; *c*, *Arch. Delt.* 20, 1965, p. 598 and pl. 759; *d* (Ct.), *NS* 69 (*BCH* 34, 1910, p. 245, no. 26), Μικίων Ἀλεξιδάμου / καθ᾽ ὑοθεσίαν δὲ / Ἀλεξιδάμου Βρυκούντιος. Hiller discussed this type of double base with recessed mouldings apropos of the base of Nikagoras, *IG* 202, in *AEMÖ* 16, 1893, pp. 248–50; this base consisted of two separate rectangular blocks. Such bases, single and double, are naturally also found in the Rhodian islands; for *Syme* see *IG* xii. 3. 10, 14, Supp. 1274, now all apparently lost. A large group comes from Brykous on Karpathos (cf. Hiller, loc. cit.): see *IG* 1003–5, 1012, 1016, for double bases, and for single ones 1006, 1008, 1014, 1015, etc.; cf. Susini, op. cit., p. 234. In publishing some from

Telos, ibid., Susini did not apparently perceive that they supported ordinary circular altars, of which he publishes several without their bases. He writes, p. 269, that among the most common monuments on Telos is 'la base parallelepipeda sormontata da un pulvino circolare di forma svasata, decorato da un collarino di raccordo con la base e che sembrerebbe destinata a sorregere una colonna od un altro fastigio: ma la mancanza assoluta di segni di grappe o di altri incavi e la ruvidezza del piano superiore del pulvino fanno ritenere che esso non fosse sormontato da nessun altro elemento monumentale'. The rough-picked surface with smooth margin is of course the normal means of effecting the join between the two elements. Peek, *Inschr. dor. Ins.*, publishes other examples from the islands, but since he does not publish photographs it is not always clear what type of monument he is describing. See, however, nos. 55, 58 (Telos), 64, 68, 77 (double), 80 (Nisyros). In his *Inschr. Nis.* there are more, e.g. nos. 2, 4 (*IG* xii. 3, 131), with sketch of double base; for two more see *Cl. Rh.* 6–7, pp. 549–50, nos. 8–9.

121. *a*, UG, uninscribed; *b* (Ct.), more elaborate, *Cl. Rh.* 2, p. 200, no. 32, with base below. In neither case is it certain that the two elements belong together. The simple circular lower member of this type is far less common than the rectangular. For the very elaborate types of large altars with Ionic mouldings see below, pp. 26, 31.

122. *NS* 89, *b* (the stone is not reproduced in *NS*, though the text is printed underneath the photograph of its twin, 89, *a*). The base of the altar, below, fig. 86, *a*, also belongs to the altar, for the inscription begins on the altar and continues on the base; cf. below, note 168.

123. See already the comments of Hiller, *AEMÖ* 16, 1893, p. 249: 'Dieser Zusammenhang der einzelnen Elemente ist nothwendig gegeben, wenn wir auch, soweit mir bekannt, in keinen Falle Basis und Grabaltar *desselben* [Hiller's 'Sperrung'] Grabdenkmals besitzen.'

124. 59, *a*, uninscribed (see note 121); 59, *c*, *NS* 89, *b* (see note 122); 60, *b*, *BCH* 34, 1910, p. 246, no. 33; 60, *c*, ibid., no. 40 (*Ann.* 2, p. 171, no. 138); all UG.

125. See, e.g., *NS* 20; *Cl. Rh.* 2, p. 200, no. 32 (fig. 59, *b*; Ct.); *Supp. Rod.*, p. 281, no. 51, a (fig. 61, *a*).

126. *Tit. Cam.* 16 (fig. 61, *b*), one of a long series (*Tit. Cam.* 9–53) of such dedications, sometimes on rectangular blocks (fig. 62, *a, b*), often with separate mouldings, sometimes (in the third century) on circular bases with mouldings; ibid. 101 (fig. 61, *c*), a dedication to Trajan, among the latest of Kamiran documents.

127. *ILind.* 89, 91 (fig. 62, *c*), 96, 105 (fig. 62, *d*), 118, 125, 136, 137, 162–3, 193, 200, 212, 217, 219, 229, 243, 246, 248, 251, 260, 268, 282–3, 292, 302, 322, 330, 345, 353, 395, 469, 472, 473, 486. Many of these were made with separate upper and lower members, now lost. At Lindos the large rectangular monument, common at Kamiros along with the dedicatory shields (for which see above, p. 15), seems to be much less frequent, just as the epistatai-altars are not

found at Kamiros. For similar plain cylindrical bases at Athens see Travlos, *Pictorial Dictionary*, fig. 135.

128. There are occasional instances of undecorated cylindrical funerary altars (sometimes called 'cippi'), but they are rare, and seem to occur mainly when the honours paid to the deceased by a koinon are recorded—i.e. the honorific notion is still present. See fig. 63, *a*, *b*, *c*, *d*: *a*, *Supp. Rod.*, p. 266, no. 17 (OGard.) (iii/ii a.C.): Κορίνθου Σαμίου / τιμαθέντος ὑπὸ Διοσαταβυριαστᾶν / Ἀγαθοδαι-μονιαστᾶν / Φιλωνείων τῶν σὺν / Φίλωνι κοινοῦ θαλλοῦ στεφάνωι; *b*, *IG* 157 (Ct.): Φιλοκράτευς Ἰλιέως / ὧι ἁ ἐπιδαμία δέδοται, τετιμαμένου ὑπὸ Ἰσιαστᾶν ἐρανιστᾶν; *c*, *IG* 541 (Ct.), possibly the tombstone of Philocrates' brother and his wife: Φίλωνος / Ἰλιέως / καὶ τᾶς γυναικὸς / Εὐφροσύνας / Σολίδος; *d*, UP (Eph.): Τιβερίου Κλαυδίου / Πετρωνίου / τριετεῦς, / ἀπολομένου κατὰ / θάλασσαν, / Ἐπα-φρίωνος Μυ(ν)δίου / καὶ Εἰσιδώρου Ἐφεσίου / καὶ Κατάπλοος Ἐφεσίου.

129. *a*, upper moulding (IGard.), hollowed out above; *b*, reversed lower moulding hollowed out, serving as basin of fountain (see p. 26, below); *c*, reversed upper moulding (Eph.) hollowed out below. For such Ionic mouldings see the study by Miss Lucy Shoe, *Hesp.* 19, 1950, pp. 338–69 (and pls. 108–9), 'Greek Mouldings of Cos and Rhodes', which contains a detailed analysis of architectural mouldings, with occasional reference to circular altars. I do not think that she refers to any of the altars under discussion, but it has not proved possible to identify all the pieces listed by her on pp. 349 ff. of her article.

130. At the corner of Navarinou and Rhiga Pherraiou Streets.

131. *IG* 658 = *NS* 119 (IGard.). The correct reading is Ἀρτεμεισία / Ἀθηναίου, / Ἀφφάριον / χρηστὴ χαῖρε. See also below, note 139, for the decoration on this stone.

132. See above, note 124, *c*, inscribed Ἀπολλώνιε Ἀρκάς. My photograph, taken to show the clearest part of the painted decoration, does not show the inscription. Apart from the square meander visible on the lower part of the cylinder, the cyma reversa in very low relief is also painted in the cavetto moulding at the bottom. There are also clear traces of a leaf-design attached to the garlands, which was also painted white: see the line-drawing of the stone given by Konstantinopoulos, *Arch. Delt.* 18 (1963), 1964, pl. 11, γ (upside down). Another recently found uninscribed circular altar (Eph., from οἰκ. Χρυσόχου) has a pattern of white circular blobs connected by stalks on the lower cornice: fig. 60, *d*.

133. See in general for such decoration M. Stephan, *Die griechische Guirlande* (diss. Berlin, 1931), and A. E. Napp, *Bukranion u. Guirlande* (diss. Heidelberg, 1933), *passim*, both useful typological works which, however, lack direct contact with the monuments, and fail to consider any of the Rhodian, and most of the Coan, material; Altmann, op. cit., pp. 1 ff. Beazley pointed out, *JHS* 59, 1939, pp. 35–6, that bucrania linked by garlands already occur on some late r.f. Attic vases: see the photographs on p. 37. He says, 'The use of the bucrane in fourth-century vases may point to a similar use in contemporary architecture,

but this is not certain. What is certain is that both uses were derived from the practice of decorating sanctuaries and other buildings with the actual skulls of slaughtered animals, alternating with other real objects. Single ox-skulls, or a couple of them, very often appear in the pictures on fifth- and fourth-century vases: what is represented is a real ox-skull, which we are to think of as fixed to a wall . . . But what we want is an *alternation* of real ox-skulls and other objects: and this we find in the picture on an Apulian Greek calyx-crater in the British Museum (F. 249 . . .); while an alternation of real bucranes and shields is almost certainly represented, as Loewy pointed out (*Jb. der kunsthist. Samm-lungen in Wien*, N.S. 2, p. 8) on a fourth-century marble relief in Athens (Svoro-nos, pl. 156, 2465).' It seems clear that a new impetus was for some reason given to the motif in the early third century, for it was certainly not frequent in the fourth century; cf. also Stephan, p. 54.

134. The description in Diod. xviii, 26, 5 of the θρόνος (?) with relief heads of τραγέλαφοι with garlands on the hearse of Alexander, ἔχων τραγελάφων προτομὰς ἐκτύπους ἐξ ὧν ἤρτηντο κρίκοι χρυσοῖ διπάλαιστοι, δι' ὧν κατεκεκρέ-μαστο στέμμα πομπικόν, κ.τ.λ., is obscure by reason of the uncertainty as to the object in question (θρόνος MS.; θριγκός Wachsmuth, Fischer (BT), Kurt Müller, *Der Leichenwagen Alexanders* (Leipzig, 1905), pp. 56 ff., Geer (Loeb); θρᾶνος Ussing, Bulle (*JDAI* 21, 1906, pp. 58–61)), but the use of τραγέλαφοι with linked pendent garlands closely resembles the hellenistic architectural use. For the frieze of the 'Arsinoeion' at Samothrace (Conze, etc., *Archäol. Untersuch. auf Samothrake*, pl. 62; cf. *B & WG*, p. 192, note 11), now in Vienna, see fig. 65, *a*. For the bucrania and rosettes on the various friezes of the 'Ptole-maion' see *Arch. Untersuch. auf Samothrake*, II, pls. 38–47, esp. 39–40 (photo-graphs).

135. Dörpfeld, *Ath. Mitt.* 35, 1910, p. 382, and pl. 20; cf. Hansen, *Attalids of Pergamon²*, p. 222 (3rd edn., p. 237); Napp, op. cit., p. 4.

136. *AvonPerg.* 2, p. 53, pl. 30 (cf. Napp, loc. cit.; *B & WG*, p. 195), and the Pergamon Museum reconstruction, von Massow, *Führer²* (1936), p. 34 and Abb. 26; Rohde, *Pergamon*, p. 17, fig. 8; id., *Griech. u. röm. Kunst in den Staatl. Museen zu Berlin* (1968), Abb. 36. Napp discusses also the frieze of the Ionic temple on the Theatre terrace, *AvonPerg.* 4, p. 41 and pl. 38, here fig. 71, *b* (isolated block), which, although of Imperial date, is probably based on the decoration of the propylon of the stoa of the Athena sanctuary, at least in the alternation of bucrania and eagles. Stephan, op. cit., pp. 22–4, argues that the decoration of leaf garlands is of Alexandrian origin, or strongly influenced by Alexandrian practice. (cf. Honroth, op. cit. (note 51), pp. 7–8). There are numerous examples in the third century from Alexandria, but it is clear (see Beazley quoted above, note 133) that the union of bucrania and garlands had already occurred before this date. Zahn, *Priene*, p. 411 (cf. Stephan, p. 32), already pointed to the specifically Pergamene elements in this decoration on vases.

137. For bucrania in isolation, forming part of a Doric architrave, see also the examples at Delos, from (a) the proskenion of the theatre, *Explor. de Délos*

xviii, pl. cviii, no. 949; *Guide de Délos* (1965), pl. 9, 1, where bucrania and tripods occupy alternate metopes; (b) the Portico of Antigonos, where bucrania are carved on the triglyphs (here fig. 65, *b*); cf. *Guide*, pp. 92–3, no. 29; and (c) the unidentified base, ibid., no. 14 (here fig. 65, *c*) close to the Base of Philetairos, with alternating bucrania and phialai.

138. For 60, *b–c*, see above, note 124; 67, *a*, *IG* 644; 67, *b*, *NS* 431, for which cf. next note.

139. *NS* 431 (IGard.). Note that the central point of the swags on the altar illustrated in fig. 64, *d* (note 131) is decorated by double cornucopiae reminiscent of those found on Ptolemaic coins. This decoration is to the best of my knowledge unparalleled in Rhodian sculpture, save for the 'throne' published by Picard, *BCH* 83, 1959, pp. 409 ff., though single cornucopiae occur on Rhodian coins of the fourth century, as emblems (*BMCCaria*, pl. xxxvi, 12). It is, however, frequent on Coan altars: see, for example, the great altar which now carries the Greek flag in the Nomarcheion at Rhodes, *Cl. Rh.* 2, p. 224, no. 86 (here fig. 79, *c*), also *Cl. Rh.* 1, p. 96, no. 78B (here fig. 78, *b*); cf. below, note 155, and others illustrated below, figs. 78, *c*, 79, *a–b*. In spite of the fact that typologically the decoration of the Rhodian piece is wholly Coan—in addition to the cornucopiae, the upper dentils and the fascia with rosettes are purely Coan in the context of circular altars—it is of 'Lartian' stone, and not likely to be Coan. In any case it lacks the very characteristic luxuriance of its Coan counterparts, and the fascia is narrow as compared with the Coan ones. Whether the Coan double cornucopia is in any way due to the island's Ptolemaic links (see Fraser, *Ptol. Alex.* i, pp. 232–3) I would not venture to say. The presence of the same feature on east Greek stelai from Smyrna, on which a pillar in the background is surmounted by linked cornucopiae (Pfuhl, *JDAI* 20, 1905, p. 56, Abb. 12, and p. 63, nos. 32–6, esp. 36; *BMSculpt.* 704 (*CIG* 3232)) raises doubts about this.

On an otherwise uninscribed altar in the Makry Steno catacomb the space above the wreaths is occupied by the monogram ⊖, which I am unable to parallel or explain. It could be an abbreviation of the demotic Θυσσανούντιος, but, in the absence of a personal name, this seems pointless.

140. Note the variety presented by fig. 66, *b* (*AvonPerg.* (7)2, pp. 313–14, no. 403, pl. xli; Mendel, iii, p. 430, no. 1184), from an unidentified Pergamene building, in which lions' heads occupy the intervals between the curly bucrania, and the garlands are replaced by strings of pearls (as, e.g., in the gymnasion at Olympia: see below, note 181, and fig. 91, *d*). The architrave may well belong to the Roman period, though Willemsen (op. cit., below, note 206), p. 68, dates it on general grounds to the Regal period.

141. 68, *a*, *IG* 231 (OGard.); *b*, above, *NS* 237, below, *Ann.* 2, p. 159, no. 70; base *IG* 156 (UG).

142. See Napp, pp. 11 ff., who rightly compares the Magnesian altar, *Inschr. Magn.* 220 (photograph), dated by Kern from the letter forms to the late

second or early first century B.C. This has paterae in the spaces above the garlands; cf. the Mytilenaean altar below, note 162, and fig. 83, *a–b*.

143. Cf. above, note 135.

144. Of about the same date as these two pieces, or even earlier, is, I think, *IG* 243, an altar now in the café at Karakonero (fig. 64, *e*; originally published, *BCH* 5, 1881, p. 334, no. 8, where it is described as 'cippe conservé dans le Konak du gouverneur'). This is the monument of a Nisyrian, Νίκων Φιλομβρό-του, καθ' ὑοθεσίαν δὲ Ἀγαθάνδρου Νισύριος. Nisyros was not incorporated in the Rhodian state until 200 B.C. (see Fraser and Bean, pp. 147 ff.), and the use of the name with patronymic and demotic (ethnic) should indicate that the island was already incorporated. A date after 200 is, on this premiss, necessary.

145. For the general development of the cylindrical altar see Pfuhl, *JDAI* 20, 1905, pp. 84 ff., and the excellent work of W. Altmann, *Die römische Grabaltäre der Kaiserzeit* (Berlin, 1905), to which I have already frequently referred: see also the lists of such altars given by Yavis, pp. 136 ff., 142 ff., which contain many of the items discussed here. The earliest example of an altar with sculptured decoration is probably the fifth-century piece from Mycenae, *IG* iv. 496 (here fig. 69), Athens, Epigr. Mus., 221, with decoration consisting of a snake-like taenia ending in a ram's head, the taenia and the body of the altar both being inscribed with a type of 'Ephesian' incantation, discussed at length by L. H. Jeffery, *BSA* 50, 1955, pp. 69–72, 75–6, who dates it to 'the second half of the [fifth] century or later'. The Altar of the Twelve Gods in Athens, Travlos, *Pictorial Dict.*, figs. 579–80 (*NM* 1731), is of the first half of the fourth century. In general, circular altars are rare before the hellenistic age but note the Archaic series from Didyma, *AJA* 77, 1973, p. 185 and pl. 35, fig. 23 (plain cylinders with Ionic mouldings); cf. also Yavis, p. 137, nos. 1–2; the piece from Delphi, *FdD* iv, pl. 77 (here fig. 70), with frieze of women attaching fillets to a garland, dated by Napp, p. 3, to *c.* 300 B.C., is now generally regarded as hellenistic. The Ionic frieze at the bottom (the top is missing) associates the piece with the large Rhodian examples described above.

146. I would therefore disagree with Altmann, op. cit., p. 4, who regards the decoration of bucrania as basically funerary, and representative of the flowers used in funerary garlands which were placed on the tombs: 'Wie man die Grabmäler mit Myrthen bepflanzte, so bekränzte man nun auch die Gräber mit Eppich, behing die Altäre mit frischen Blumen und Blattgewinden. Was lag näher, als diesen beweglichen Schmuck in Stein zu übersetzen? Der Guirlandenschmuck, mit dem der eigentliche Zylinder geschmückt ward, ist eine Überträgung der Wirklichkeit in die Kunst.' Undoubtedly, in due course, the use of the decoration became very largely (but not wholly) funerary, but it was not originally so, and irrespective of the origin of the motif itself—probably, as Napp, p. 1, says, it derives from observation of garlands (and, we may add with Beazley quoted above, note 133, the skulls of slaughtered oxen) hung in temples, etc.—in the present context the question is simply whence came the artistic impetus. For other aspects of Pergamene influence—on the Nike-altars —see below, p. 31.

147. See next note, *init.*

148. (i) For *Pergamon* see (a) *AvonPerg.* 7(2), p. 337, no. 418, and pl. 41 (here pl. 71, *a*), the altar dedicated by Eumenes II θεοῖς πᾶσι καὶ πάσαις, which has very naturalistic bucrania and deeply carved garlands of various fruits with ears of corn (also found on Delian altars, see below, note 151, and figs. 73, *d*, 74, *a*), and flowers of the finest quality, described by Winter as 'ein Glanzstück dekorativer Naturschilderung ohnegleiches'; I do not find it markedly superior to the best Coan pieces, to which it is certainly closely akin (cf. Stephan, op. cit., pp. 38 ff.); (b) *AvonPerg.* 7(2), p. 338, no. 419 (here fig. 71, *c*), with Ionic upper moulding, plain multiple moulding below, and stags' heads (see note 169) supporting a naturalistic laurel wreath; (c) for ibid., p. 340, no. 425, see note 162 below. None of these is funerary, and the rareness of cylindrical altars at Pergamon may partly reflect the fact that the hellenistic necropoleis there have not yet been excavated.) The most frequent type of votive monument at Pergamon is the rectangular altar, with various minor differences. The small limestone altars, of which I here illustrate one (fig. 71, *d*; *AvonPerg.* 7(2), no. 436, dimensions H. 0·175 m, W. 0·22 m, Th. 0·16 m) are all uninscribed, but are evidently votive.) A further, very worn example in the Louvre, *Cat. Somm.*, p. 163, no. 2904, with phialai above the garlands (here fig. 73, *b*), is from the Expédition Téxier, and is said to be from 'Asia Minor'; it is probably from Halicarnassos or Cnidos. For a cylindrical altar of Imperial date from Side (now in Side Museum) see Bean in A. M. Mansel, *Side Agorasi ve Civarındaki Binalar 1948* (Ankara, 1956), p. 96, no. 73, and pl. xxx (here pl. 82, *c*), which has, in addition to bucrania with fillets, and rosette on the brow, and garlands, a relief bust of the deceased and standing figures of his parents in relief; inscribed Αὖλος Σεπόννιος / Αὔλου υἱός. Cf. also fig. 116 *d* from Perge (Antalya Mus.). [See ADD.]

(ii) For *Thera* see above, note 67, and figs. 40, *d*, 56, *b*, and the dedication by Ptolemaic troops, *IG* xii. 3, 466 (with good drawing of the stone, which is damaged) (*OGIS* 102). Also from Thera in the Louvre, *Cat. Somm.*, p. 14, no. 2329 (cf. Stephan, p. 25), is the Ptolemaic dedication, *IG* xii. 3, 468 (*OGIS* 112).

(iii) For *Delos* see below, note 151.

(iv) For *Paros* see the two examples published by Orlandos, *Ἔργον 1962*, p. 190, fig. 223 (*Chron. des fouilles 1962*, p. 825, fig. 16), here fig. 74, *h*, apparently uninscribed (see Orlandos, p. 192), and *IG* xii. 5, 351; 373 (fig. 74, *g*); 422. A piece in the Louvre, inscribed Χαρίτιον χρηστή, taken as Parian by Napp, p. 11, is of uncertain origin. It is cited by him as Clarac, *Musée*, Text, vol. II, 2, p. 850, no. 446, but Clarac says only that it is of 'marbre de Paros', a very vague description of any white marble. It was assigned by Boeckh, *CIG* 2311, to Delos, on the strength of Muratori's statement, iii, p. mdclv, 10, 'lapis ex Insula Delo, atque ex Templo Apollinis advectus'. However, although funerary altars of this type are attested from Delos (see below, note 151), the provenance is best left open. The recent catalogue of Cycladic funerary monuments by M.-T. Couilloud, *BCH* 98, 1974, pp. 398–408, includes only *IG* xii. 5, 373 and 422, and omits 351. *CIG* 2311 is republished by her, *BCH* 99, 1975, p. 322, no. 5 (and fig. 7, p. 321).

The cylindrical and rectangular altars (all votive), apparently of the first century B.C. or A.D., recently published from Samos, *Samos*, xii (1972), nos. 179, 179, *a* (cylindrical), 178, 180 (rectangular), are quite unlike both the Cycladic and the Dodecanesian types; the circular altars are narrow and tapering, and the rectangular are close to the Roman type. No. 173, and pls. 80–2, a large votive altar with figures of the 'Egyptian Gods' in relief, is similar to the votive pieces from Halicarnassos, for which see note 157 (Altar of the Muses, etc.). For No. 180, the rectangular altar with dedication to Gaius Vibius Postumus, see below, note 449.

(v) On the *Mainland* the most notable example in Athens is the familiar altar in the precinct of the Theatre of Dionysos, on which the bucrania are replaced by Silenus-masks: Schöne, *Griech. Reliefs*, Taf. 5/6, Rodenwaldt, *Kunst der Antike²*, pl. 504, Tavis, *Greek Altars*, fig. 75, Travlos, *Pictorial Dictionary*, fig. 690, here fig. 75, *a* (cf. Napp, pp. 6–7), *IG* ii². 2949. A large circular altar was discovered recently in the excavation of the Athenian Agora (S 2525), and I am grateful to Mr. Leslie Shear, Jr., for permission to reproduce it here in advance of publication, fig. 75, *b*. The triglyphs evidently occupied the whole height of the cylinder between mouldings; the metopes contain single bucrania, in the architectural style. The monument is not in its original position, and now has no inscription, so its function is not immediately clear. It is natural that cylindrical funerary altars should be rare in hellenistic Athens, for their period of production falls within the period of post-Demetrian austerity. From the Roman period two inelegant and over-decorated altars, (a), from the neighbourhood of Plato's Academy, here fig. 75, *d* (*Ἔργον 1963*, p. 12, fig. 12), inscribed Ὀλυμπιόδωρος Στειριεύς, and (b), *IG* ii². 7796, Πό(πλιος) / Δημήτριος / Χολλείδης, now in Venice, here fig. 75, *c*, form a pair as regards decoration: on (a) the upper moulding consists of a cyma recta with palmettes and running tendrils, and astragal below, and the lower moulding of a cyma recta with palmettes and reversed lotus motif, and astragal above, while on (b) the palmettes of the upper moulding alternate with a looped lotus-pattern, and the lower moulding is virtually as in (a); the skeletal bucrania, the garlands, and rosettes in the interstices are in general similar, but not identical, on the two altars. Two other examples of the regular type, in the Louvre, said to be Athenian in the *Cat. Somm.*, p. 14, no. 2327, and p. 16, no. 2270, are probably not originally from there: see Dain, *Inscr. grec. du Louvre*, nos. 9–10, with his comments (Stephan, pp. 35–8, regards them both as Attic, and consequently regarded Attica as the 'Herstellungszentrum' of the type of circular altar with garlands, bucrania, and fasciae, of which she also gives one or two Coan examples; but it is abundantly clear that such pieces are rare in Attica). A badly damaged circular altar or base in the Agora, Inv. S 714, carries standing figures in relief in the Imperial style, and the bucrania with pendent necklaces and fillets seem to be a subsidiary element in the decoration. The lower moulding (the only one preserved) is Ionic.

There are two altars of the same general type in Thebes Museum, found locally; both are unusually slender with pronounced tapering upwards (figs. 76, *a*, *b*). Fig. 76, *b*, of white marble and almost columnar in shape, is of late date. On both the Athenian Mask-altar and the second Theban piece the swags are very thick and ponderous, and the style is very different from that of the Aegean altars. On both there are rosettes in the spaces above the garlands. An altar at Corinth is very similar both in dimensions and in the execution of the decoration (fig. 76, *c*); the altar was reversed and reused in the Byzantine period, and carries a dedication of the reign of Constans II (A.D. 641); *Corinth* VIII, iii. 510. Fig. 76, *f*, is of a conventional altar in Chaeronea Museum.

(vi) *Cyprus*. For an example from Salamis see the dedicatory altar, I. Nicolaou, *Cypriot Inscribed Stones* (Republic of Cyprus, Ministry of Commun. and Works, Dept. of Antiq., Picture Book no. 6, Nicosia, 1971), p. 27 and pl. xxxii (*AA* 1963, p. 582, fig. 53; *SEG* xxiii, 611; Mitford and Nicolaou, *Inscriptions from Salamis* (Nicosia, 1974), no. 2 and pl. I. 3), here fig. 76, *d*, inscribed Ἑρμεῖ Ἐπηκόωι / Διαγόρας Τεύκρου / ὁ εἰς αἰῶνα γυμνασίαρχος, of late hellenistic or early Roman date. The altar is slender, and the decoration consists of a garland of grapes and other fruit, supported by lions' heads, with rosettes in the spaces between the loops of the garland; fillets are suspended from the lions' heads. It has simple upper and lower multiple mouldings. A circular funerary monument, a cippus in general shape, in Nicosia Museum (*BCH* 3, 1879, p. 174, no. 39), inscribed Ἡγησιανέ, χρηστὲ χαῖρε, here fig. 76, *e*, carries multiple convex and concave mouldings and a horizontal garland of ivy-leaves and fruit; the workmanship is stiff. Similar, undecorated, cippi are common in Cyprus: see *Cesnola Collection*, pp. 552–3.

(vii) Finally, one remote example of a circular altar, from Nehavend, here fig. 76, *g*. This was discovered by Professor Roman Ghirshman during the exploratory excavations there, and was, he tells me, subsequently destroyed by the local inhabitants. Ghirshman published this photograph (which I am indebted to him for permission to reproduce) in his *L'Iran, Parthes et Sassanides* (*L'Univers des Formes*, Paris, 1961; Eng. trans., *Iran, Parthians and Sassanids*, London, 1962), fig. 24. The garlands carved immediately below the upper moulding are wholly formalized, and lack all traces of naturalism.

149. See Altmann, op. cit., pp. 5–6. He reproduces, fig. 2, a cylindrical altar from Tibur, in the Vatican (Lippold, iii, 2, p. 365, no. 110, and Taf. 157) carrying a dedication in Greek and Latin to Agathos Daimon (*IG* xiv. 1123). Others in the Vatican are Lippold, op. cit., p. 276, no. 6(113B) and Taf. 124; p. 289, no. 25, with skeletal bucrania and Medusa heads above bucrania; p. 396, no. 34 (Taf. 167; *CIL* vi .245); p. 406, no. 50 (Taf. 170; *CIL* vi. 32452). Most of these cylindrical altars are of the Imperial type which developed from the time of Augustus onwards, with florid decoration in which figures such as Erotes frequently form part of the composition. See further Honroth, op. cit. *passim*, and the description of the individual monuments described in Lippold's *Katal. Vatik. Skulpt.* iii, 2. They are in any case very few in number as compared with the normal rectangular altars and cinerary urns which form the main theme of Altmann's book, and which are now well described by J. M. C. Toynbee, *Death and Burial in the Roman World* (London, 1971), pp. 253–68.

150. Bondelmonte, p. 72 (ed. de Sinner, 1824), already commented on the 'innumerable' altars lying about on the island during his residence there in

c. 1420: 'insuper et innumerabilium opus columnarum insignitum capitibus *Cerbiae* et, per omnes partes, hinc inde Caesaris signo reperimus, una cum urceis cadaverum combustorum infinitis, quorum vestigia usque in hodiernum diem perhibent testimonium'; cf. Ross, *Reisen*, iii, p. 90, note 26. My own count of about 200 makes no pretence at completeness.

151. The circular altars on and from Delos raise problems concerning their original purpose and use. Roussel called attention to this in *Délos, Col. Ath.*, p. 27, note 0; 'Quelques autels, ornés de bucranes et de guirlandes et portant un nom, peuvent avoir été conservés dans les maisons pour commémorer le souvenir d'un mort; ainsi celui qui a été publié [*BCH*] xxix, p. 244, n. 114; on en a retrouvé la base moulurée qui était travaillée séparément et il me paraît improbable qu'on a pris soin d'en transporter simultanément de Rhénée les deux parties. Il faut attendre qu'une étude speciale et attentive ait été consacrée a cet ordre de documents: Ch. Picard en a le soin (cf. [*BCH*] xxxvi, p. 119, note 3).' A number of such altars are briefly discussed and illustrated by W. Déonna in *Expl. de Délos* (*ED*), xviii, esp. pls. cvi–cix, and his discussion, pp. 380–3. On plates 72–4 (cf. also Yavis, op. cit. p. 149, who gives further instances), I give a selection, perhaps the majority, of such altars, figs. 72, *a*, *b*, and 73, *a*, being from the British Museum, the remainder photographed on Delos. Some of these are shown to be dedicatory by their inscriptions (see list (a), below), others funerary (see list (b)), while one or two are, or appear to be, uninscribed. [See ADD.]

(a) Dedicatory

    (i) *IDélos*, 2152, here fig. 72, *c* (*ED*, xviii, p. cix, no. 957, and p. 383)
    (ii) *IDélos*, 2153, here fig. 73, *d* (*ED*, xviii, p. cvi, no. 938, and p. 382)
    (iii) *IDélos*, 1746, here fig. 72, *d*
    (iv) *IDélos*, 1747, here fig. 73, *c*
    (v) *IDélos*, 1791, which is markedly taller than other Delian altars (0·82 m ×0·60 m), here fig. 82, *e*.

(b) Funerary

    (i) *BCH* 34, 1910, p. 416, no. 76, here fig. 74, *a* (*ED*, pl. cvi, no. 939)
    (ii) *BCH* 29, 1905, p. 244, no. 114, here fig. 74, *b*
    (iii) *IDélos*, 2480, here fig. 74, *e*
    (iv) Michaelis, *Ancient Marbles*, p. 589, no. 209 (*CIG* 6894)
    (v) Michaelis, ibid., no. 210

For further examples of either category see *ED*.

(c) Uninscribed

    (i) *BMSculpt.* iii, nos. 2480, 2482, 2484, here figs. 72, *a*, *b*, 73, *a*
    (ii) *ED*, pl. cvi, 940 (stags' heads; cf. below, note 169); cix, no. 952
    (iii) Some very worn examples said to be from Rheneia in the Ashmolean Museum, Michaelis, p. 564, nos. 96–104 (of which he says 'there is no doubt of their being connected with sepulchres'); for no. 96 see note 148 (i), ADD.
    (iv) Michon, *BCH* 35, 1911, pp. 308–22

Hollow cylinders of the same type (some perhaps adapted from altars) were used on Delos, as at Pompeii, for well-curbs: see *ED*, pp. 94–6, and pls. xxxvii–xxxviii, here figs. 74, *c, d*; for the very similar stone-and-terracotta well-curbs at Pompeii see Pernice, *Hellenistische Kunst in Pompeii*, V, pp. 12 ff. and pls. 8 ff., here pl. 116, *c* (fluted). With the triglyph-friezes on these pieces we may compare those on the circular altars found at Akrai, Bernabò Brea, *Akrai* (Catania, 1956), p. 140, no. 22 (Tav. xxvii, no. 7), p. 141, no. 27.

The decoration of the Delian altars covers a wider range than the funerary series from Rhodes, Cos, etc. In general (though there are exceptions) the bucrania are fleshy and naturalistic, and the garlands richly and carefully carved, equalling in one or two instances the best work from Pergamon or Cos: see especially the opulent and naturalistic rendering in all aspects of nos. 73, *c, d*, 74, *a, b*; also fig. 72, *d*, with its excellently executed ears of corn, and its Ionic moulding, and 73, *a*, now much worn, with metopal decoration of alternate bucrania and rosettes. The skeletal bucranion is not on the whole popular at Delos, though there are one or two instances on circular altars. The best example is, however, on the rectangular altar, here fig. 74, *f*, of which I have not discovered the place of publication, if any. Déonna, op. cit., p. 383, drew attention to the similar bucrania on the short side of the rectangular altar represented on the bronze relief, *BCH* 45, 1921, pp. 242 ff., and fig. 2 (further bibliography in *ED*, p. 383, note 5); cf. also Pernice, op. cit., pl. 41, 1; 40, 4.

152. This is argued by Marcadé, *Au Musée de Délos* (Bibl. éc. fr. d'Ath. et de Rome, 215, 1969), pp. 469 ff., 486, who attributes a considerable role to Rhodian influence on decorative elements on Delian minor monuments. The Delian decoration is, however, as I have shown, clearly not of the dry Rhodian style: see previous note.

153. For the terraced necropoleis in the eastern Necropolis zone see p. 5. For similar necropoleis at Cnidos see, for early descriptions, Texier, *Description de l'Asie Mineure*, ii, pp. 314–15, and pl. 134; iii, pl. 164; *Antiquities of Ionia*, iii, p. 21; Newton, *Halicarnassus*, ii, pp. 471 ff., 480 ff. (Lion-tomb); Hamilton, *Researches in Asia Minor*, ii (1842), p. 43 (quoted by Smith, *BMSculpt.* ii, p. 203), 'A cippus or stele, with an inscription, appears to have been placed upon the terrace, and perhaps served to conceal the entrances into the vaults beneath, which in some cases must have been entered through the roof. We found several of these cippi lying about; they are generally circular, and ornamented either with festoons, and the caput bovis, or with a serpent entwined round them twice. The inscription is placed either round the circular part of the stone or on the flat base or pedestal in which it stands, for we found instances of both.' For recent excavations see Love, *Arkeol. Derg.* 16(2), 1967, pp. 137 ff., who describes the typical structure of the tombs, and (fig. 38) publishes a photograph of a circular altar with bucrania and garlands, with a funerary inscription; ibid. 17(2), pp. 126 ff. (and fig. 24); *Arch. Rep. 1970–71*, p. 53; *Arkeol. Derg.* 20(2), 1973, pp. 140–1, terracing of Sanctuary of Aphrodite; ibid. 21(2), 1974, pp. 85 ff.

154. These stones come largely, if not entirely, from the main hellenistic

necropolis of Cos, on the site of the Turkish village of Kermeti (Tourkochori, Ghermè), on the western edge of the modern city (see Paton and Hicks, p. 165). The necropolis has disappeared in modern building development and there appears to be no indication of the structure of the tombs, and especially whether they resembled the Rhodian terraced hypogaea (the main surviving Coan tomb is the vaulted heroon of Charmylus, the Χαρμύλειον, at Pyli, for which see the study by Schatzmann, *JDAI* 49, 1934, pp. 110 ff., and, for the inscription, *PH* 349 (cf. Herzog, *KF*, p. 139, and p. 165, note 1)). [See ADD.]

155. These altars are all in the Castello at Cos, either in the M(oat), or in the St(oreroom) in the Keep, or on the terrace (T) above the moat. Fig. 78: *a*, *NS* 450 (M), Παρμενίσκου | τοῦ Φιλίππου | ἱερατεύσαντος | ʽPέας; *b*, uninscribed (M); *c*, *Cl. Rh.* 2, p. 225, no. 89 (St) (also *Cl. Rh.* 1, p. 96, fig. 78B), G. Iuli G. l. Dionis, | Γαΐου ʾΙουλίου Γαΐου | Δίωνος; Γαΐου ʾΙουλίου Γαΐου υἱοῦ ʽΡούφου; *d*, ibid., p. 233, no. 126 (St) (inscription visible on left part of cylinder), ʽΟρδιωνία Διονυσία |, Hordionia | Dionysia | vivet. The last two stones illustrate well the natural bilinguality of the Roman settlers on Cos. By contrast, *a* and *b* are simpler than most Coan altars, the garlands being of the plain laurel-wreath type, and the lettering of *a* is among the earliest that I have seen on Coan altars. Fig. 79, *a–c*, all have the double cornucopia and rosette and lotus-fascia, *a*, *NS* 564 (M), Μάρκου Σενπρων(ί)ου Γράκου; *b*, uninscribed (T); *c*, *Cl. Rh.* 2, p. 224, no. 86, at Nomarcheion in Rhodes, supporting flagstaff, inscription erased, Σεραπιάδος | Ἀντιγόνου ζῆι; *d*, uninscribed (T), has a triglyph-frieze with metopes containing alternate rosettes, phialai, and single cornucopiae. Fig. 80, *a*, *Cl. Rh.* 2, p. 226, nos. 90–3 (St), with four approximately contemporary inscriptions, of which two are partly visible on the photograph, no. 90, *a*, above garland, Ἀριστόφως | Σήστας | Ἀναξίλα, and *c*, below garland, Καφισοκλέους | τοῦ Πραξιτέλους; the fascia contains, in addition to the rosettes, single lotus-flowers (?); 80, *b*, uninscribed (M); note the small blossoms, probably of ivy; 80, *c* (Rhodes, Cast. grounds), a large altar (H. 1·12 m, diam. 0·75 m) standing on a base with the inscription *IG* 291, Εὐφάνης Εὐφάνευς | Τύμνιος, but altar and base do not seem to belong together, and the altar appears to be Coan, though the absence of a dentil-moulding at the top is noteworthy; the altar itself is inscribed twice, (*a*) erased, beneath the bucranium, (*b*) on the lower part of the cylinder, largely illegible, Πτολεμαι . . . ρ.κλου (?) Χρ(?)—; 80, *d*, uninscribed (M); 80, *e*, a Coan altar now in Istanbul, inscribed Ἀπολλωνίου | τοῦ Ἀπολλωνίου | Μάγνητος (*PH* 190; Mendel, iii, no. 1151; cf. Kern, *Inschr. v. Magnesia*, p. xix, s.v.). For an altar in Istanbul with many Coan features, but apparently not Coan, see below, note 184 (c).

156. Thus the decoration of the upper moulding and the rich garlands of the stylized variety are already present in fig. 78, *a* and *b*, though they have not the sumptuousness of 78, *c* and *d*, of the first century B.C. Nevertheless, the finest example of all, fig. 79, *c*, is itself probably of late hellenistic date, for the surviving, but largely erased inscription, visible on the photograph below the garland, has none of the characteristic features of the Coan script of the early Imperial period, as shown in the other examples illustrated; this altar is also

the largest surviving circular altar from the whole region, being 1·40 m high and 1 m in diameter.

157. For Halicarnassian altars with bucrania see Texier, op. cit. ii, pl. 134, below, left, two, one of which, Μνασέα Δ / Εὔνικε (?Εὐνίκου) / χρηστὲ χαῖρε, is *CIG* 2666, from a copy of Beaufort's. Newton, *Halicarnassus*, etc., II, i, p. 270 n. *e*, says, of the garden of Salik Bey's harem, that it contained, *inter alia*, 'several altars with festoons and bulls' heads on one of which is a sepulchral inscription to a certain Diodotos, son of Dionysios'. He publishes another, p. 341, and ii, p. 708, no. 75, Ἑκατέα / Θευδά[μου] / χρηστὴ χαῖρε. There are about ten such altars in the Museum and the courtyard of the castle at Budrum, of which I reproduce here eight (fig. 81, *a–h*) from photographs kindly provided by Professor K. Jeppesen of Aarhus University. 81, *a*, is inscribed (a) Μᾶρκε Αὔδιε, / Λευκίου υἱέ, / χρηστὲ χαῖρε, (b) Μᾶρκε Αὔδιε, / Μάρκου υἱέ, / χρηστὲ χαῖρε, the second presumably son of the first. Professor Jeppesen informs me that all the other altars are uninscribed. The pieces cover a fairly wide spectrum of decoration and style; only three (*e, g, h*) have the dentilled upper moulding with frieze, and (like the Coan) none has an Ionic lower moulding (though there is a fragment of one such moulding in the Museum); the filleted bucrania seem to be mostly of the full, fleshy type (*e, h*; those of *f* and *g*, though damaged, appear to be of a less luxuriant type); one, *b*, has the stags' heads in place of the bucrania; the garlands are mostly of the full type with abundant fruit, especially pendent grapes (*a, b, d, f*), but *c*, the slender altar with a more restrained type of garland of fruits, has no bucrania. In general the pieces, even at their most elaborate, as *e, g, h*, are inferior in style and workmanship to their Coan counterparts; the reappearance of the Coan double-cornucopia motif in *h* is worthy of note. Bean has provided me with a photograph (fig. 80, *f*) of the altar with bucrania and garlands of the Roman period from Fenerburnu (Akyerler), east of Halicarnassos, published in *BSA* 50, 1955, p. 137, no. 47: τὸ μνημεῖ[ον Φιλοστόργου α' καὶ Γ(αίου) Ἰ(ουλίου) / Φλώρου καὶ τῶν γυ/ναικῶν αὐτῶν καὶ / τῶν ἐκ τούτων ἐσομένων· / ζῶσιν.

The two best-known circular altars from Halicarnassos are, however, not funerary but votive, (a) *BMSculpt.* ii, 1106 (here fig. 81, *j*), representing the Nine Muses, recently studied in detail by D. Pinkwart, *Antike Plastik*, Lief. vi, pp. 89 ff., to which I may refer for details; mouldings and fascia are precisely the same as those on the Coan altars; and (b) ibid. 1107, now worn and damaged, representing five male and five female figures, perhaps deities.

For Cnidos the evidence so far published (for recent excavations see above, note 153) is no less abundant. I illustrate here (fig. 82, *a, b*) two with bucrania and garlands in the B.M. (*a*), the better piece, *BMSculpt.* ii, 1357, uninscribed, has a fully developed bucrania-and-garland decoration which is close to that of the Coan pieces in execution, but the garlands lack the outstanding naturalistic quality, and (as usual at Cnidos) the upper moulding is simple, multiple, or cavetto, as at Rhodes, not dentilled as at Cos and Halicarnassos (occasionally). The second piece, (*b*), *BMInv.* 1955-2-18, is less Coan and more Rhodian in some respects. It carries two inscriptions of, I would suppose, the first century A.D. (Le Bas 513; *SGDI* 3535), (*a*), across the centre of the fillets of one bucranion, $Δαμὼ χρη/στὰ χαῖρε$, and (b), lower down on the same segment of the cylinder, and probably earlier than (a), $Διονυσᾶ Διονυ/σᾶδος, Κνίδιε ἀπὸ$ / $'Ρόδου, χρηστὲ χαῖρε$. The formula $Κνίδιος ἀπὸ 'Ρόδου$ is, to the best of my knowledge, unique. There was natural and frequent intercourse between the two cities, but presumably we are to understand that Dionysas had settled in Rhodes, and had been brought back for burial in his native land; cf. Teles, p. 29, Hense (cf. Rohde, *Psyche*, i³, p. 218, note 1): $ὅμως δὲ τὸ ἐπὶ ξένης ταφῆναι$ $ὄνειδος$. (Naturally in most cases this did not happen: see the explicit wording of a tombstone of late Imperial date from Intercisa: $Πιστόνας ἀπὸ Κυ/[π]ροβήλων$ $ἀποδημῶ[ν / ἐτε]λεύτησεν ἐνταῦ/θα$ (*SEG* xv, 630); cf. also *SEG* xviii, 595; *SB* 6124: *IG* xiv, 2026; cf. Lattimore, *Themes in Greek and Latin Epitaphs*, pp. 199 ff. See also the unusual epitaph of Imperial date, *IG* xiv, 1976 (Peek, *GVI* 1169), of one Rufinus Aterius, a resident of Rome who migrated to Egypt and died there, and whose body was brought back to Rome and re-interred there by his wife Damostrata (l. 16: $Δαμοστρατείας ταῦτα τῆς φιλανδρίας$); and the case of the merchant of Myra in Lycia, who travelled to Canosa to bury his brother who had died there (Moretti, *Riv. Fil.* 100, 1972, pp. 180 ff.).) As already noted above (note 153) early travellers saw numerous altars of this type in the terraced Cnidian necropolis. For circular 'snake-altars' from Cnidos see p. 38, and note 213.

158. These 'benches' are largely unpublished, but the most elaborate (not reproduced here) is to be found in *Cl. Rh.* 5(2), pp. 20–1, and fig. 10. There are several in Cos Museum, more in the moat and the storeroom of the Keep, more outside the *Casa Romana*, others outside the Museum at the Asclepieion, and two built into the wall of the Old Metropolis in the city, whitewashed over. There are two (unmistakably Coan) in Rhodes Museum (IGard. and OGard.). No doubt there are more. The only variation in shape is that the best pieces have 'sofa-volutes' at the extremities of the upper surface, whereas the smaller ones finish rectangularly. As figs. 89, *c*, *d*, 90, *a–d* show, the bucrania and garlands of these pieces are all slightly different, within a narrow range, and some are of good workmanship, and resemble the altar-garlands, while others are much cruder. On the upper surface of many, but not of all, are two small rectangular dowel-holes, sometimes symmetrically, sometimes unsymmetrically placed, with pouring-channels leading to them. The function of these escapes me. Since they are not always present they cannot have been an essential part of the finished monument. If they had supported an upper member of some sort, one would expect all the pieces to be furnished with them. The rear surfaces are also rather puzzling; some are totally plain, having simply been worked smooth, and on none, I think, is the palmette-and-tendril frieze above the main decoration continued on to the back. In several pieces, however, and not only the best, the bucrania and garlands are continued on the rear, but the garlands are left unworked, only the outline being carved. It looks then as if the 'benches' had a natural front and back, but that they were not necessarily standing against a back wall which would make their decoration at the back unnecessary. We may compare the Rhodian rectangular altars, only one of which (that of Dionysodoros of Alexandria; see pp. 66–7) is decorated on the back, and

which stood on the terraces above the graves, and were certainly not meant to be viewed from the rear, though they did not necessarily stand against a rear wall.

Only one inscribed piece of this class is known to me, *NS* 571 (M) (fig. 90, *a*), which, for good measure, is inscribed on both faces, (*a*), the front face (as in fig. 90, *a*), Ἐπικήτου τοῦ Δημη/τρίου κονχυλιαβάφου, and (b), the back, [*M*]άρκου Πομπηίου Ἐφηβικοῦ ζῆ. These are both funerary inscriptions, and it may be that the stone is in fact a tombstone. Before, however, assuming that all the pieces of this class were tombstones (as Jacopi, who describes the piece published by him as 'altare funerario a rilievo') we should note that this piece alone has no decoration in the upper fascia, only the inscription, and that therefore an incompletely executed bench may have been utilized (twice) as a tombstone, or alternatively that the bench style may have been utilized for a monument of a different category. The fact that such pieces have been found at the Asclepieion and in the agora argues strongly against their being tombstones and in favour of their being a type of altar; but in any case the usual absence of an inscription is puzzling. The nearest parallels in both shape and decoration are the rectangular funerary altars from Rheneia, published by M.-T. Couilloud, *BCH* 99, 1975, pp. 322 ff., and figs. 8–10 (*ED*, xxx, p. 222, no. 500) with rudimentary bucrania and garlands; cf. also the Pergamene altar, *AvonPerg.* 7(2), p. 344, no. 436 (here fig. 71, *d*).

I may also mention here the very fine architrave of garlands, with masks, from the proskenion of the theatre at Cos, which is placed above the outer entrance of the Castello: see Benndorf, *Reisen in südwestl. Kleinasien*, i, p. 5; Napp, op. cit., p. 7, who assigns it, on partially false premisses (the date of the round altar at Delphi, above, note 145) to the first quarter of the third century. It might well be substantially later, like the bulk of the material with garlands from Cos.

159. An exception is perhaps *NS* 276, discussed below, p. 79, where, however, the distinction between funerary and votive is considerably blurred. From this point of view an interesting altar (which, however, does not provide an exception to the rule) has been published by Peek, *Inschr. dor. Ins.* 2 (Rhodos), here fig. 114, *a–b*. It is a normal cylindrical altar with bucrania (skeletal) and laurel garland, but above and below the garland is inscribed the text of an honorific decree of a koinon of the later hellenistic period, in honour of a Chrysippos, ἐγγενὴς Μέροπος. The altar, however, is in fact his funerary monument, and the epitaph stands below the decree: see below, pp. 65–6 and notes 370 ff. The whole inscription is thus only an elaborated form of the frequent funerary monument (discussed ibid.) in which the dead man is said to have been honoured by a koinon; in this instance, exceptionally, the honorific decree itself is recorded.

160. See above, note 148, (ii) and (v).

161. Smith, *BMSculpt.* iii, nos. 2480–4, treats the Delian altars in the B.M. (see above, note 151) as votive, but we have seen, note 151, that there are also

Delian altars with funerary inscriptions on them. Yavis, op. cit., p. 149, in his analysis of the Delian altars, does not refer to their funerary use.

162. The Mytilenaean circular funerary altars are a separate class, and I am particularly indebted to Miss Chatzi, epimeletria of the antiquities of Chios and Lesbos, for providing me with photographs of them. I reproduce here (fig. 83, *a, b*) *IG* xii. 2, 286, the best representative of this group of funerary monuments, all of which carry the formula indicating public burial, ὁ δᾶμος, followed by the name (and title, e.g. τὸν εὐεργέταν, if any) of the deceased in either the accusative or dative case, with or without the word ἥρωα, ἥρωι. The ὁ δᾶμος formula is found at Cnidus at a late date (*BMI* 833–47), as well as at some other places including Halicarnassus; there is an excellent discussion of it by G. Hirschfeld, *BMI* 833–47, introductory note, p. 34. It is worth noting that all the examples from Cnidus are on marble slabs, which may have formed the revetment of a public mausoleum. The provision of such public burial at Cnidus is explicit in the decree in honour of Artemidoros, of i a.C., *BMI* 787, which includes, lines 8–11, honours in life, [ἕω]ς κα ζώηι, καὶ ἐπεί κα μεταλλάξηι / [τ]ὸν βίον ταφᾶι δαμοσίαι καὶ ἐνταφᾶι / [κατ]ὰ πόλιν ἐν τῶι ἐπισαμοτάτωι / [τ]οῦ γυμνασίου τόπωι. The practice is then considerably older than the date indicated by the plaques. The same formula occurs in Lycia and elsewhere (inscribed within a wreath at Cyme, fig. 83, *e*; also from Cyme, Peek, *GVI* 1917, *B & WG*, Suppl. (*Op. Ath.* 10, 1971), p. 79, and fig. 41, which is not, as stated there, from Erythrai, but from Cyme; cf. Robb., *Bull. 1973*, p. 451, no. 378) on stelai with normal funerary reliefs of ii a.C.: see Robert, *Rev. Phil.* 1944, pp. 44 ff.; Pleket, *Greek Inscrs. Leyden*, p. 40, nos. 35 ff.; cf. *SEG* xvii, 534; cf. also p. 78, and note 386. To return to the Mytilenaean pieces, the altar of 286 consists of a normal cylinder with plain upper and lower mouldings, surrounded by a stylized, plain, deeply curving garland of laurel leaves, which passes over alternate bucrania and paterae; in the field above, at the highest points of the garland, are rosettes. The inscription, of the early Imperial period to judge by the lettering, is engraved partly on the upper moulding (line 1), and partly in the small space between it and the top of one curve of the garland. The most remarkable feature is, however, the representation, in low relief, on the upper surface (fig. 83, *c*; good line-drawing in *IG* xii. 2, 286, whence J. Harrison, *Prolegomena*, p. 330, fig. 98) of a patera similar to that on the body of the cylinder, and of two snakes drinking from it, a motif customarily associated with 'Hero-cult' (cf. Pfuhl, *JDAI* 20, 1905, p. 85); compare *IG* xii. 5, 325, from Paros, 'Basis cylindricata . . . in parte adversa duo serpentes exsculptae sunt, qui ex patera in columna posita bibunt', inscribed Εὐφροσύνη ἡ μαῖα / Μελίσσηι / ἡρωίσσηι; cf. also the rectangular altar in Herakleion Museum, Yavis, op. cit., p. 173, § 65, no. 2. The other cylindrical altars of this group have the same type of garland–bucrania–paterae decoration, but not the snake motif on the top, while the snake is also represented on another stone, *IG* xii. 2, 287, which, however, is not a cylindrical altar, but one of a series of rectangular funerary monuments for Heroes. The same deeply curving decoration of laurel wreath and paterae is found on a Coan altar which is very much *sui generis* at Cos, *PH* 165 (T), on which the main funerary inscription is in

the dative (fig. 83, *d*) (Paton does not mention the paterae). The conical altar from Cyme already referred to above (this note), now in Istanbul (Pfuhl, op. cit., p. 88, fig. 18; Mendel, iii, p. 322, no. 1084; Yavis, p. 149, fig. 40), inscribed ὁ δῆμος, has, in addition to its unusual fir-cone epithema, very similar decoration to the Mytilenaean pieces—garland–bucrania–paterae—though the garland is composed of fruits, etc., in this instance. A parallel for the motif of snakes drinking from a patera is provided by a Pergamene cylindrical altar of white marble from the Asclepieion, *AvonPerg.* 7(2), p. 340, no. 425, on which the snakes drinking from the patera are carved on the cylinder and not on the upper surface (fig. 83, *f*); they are entwined with garlands of olive branches. This is said by Winter to be 'wohl aus frührömischer Zeit'; cf. Herrmann, *Omphalos* (see note 229), p. 44, note 119. Note also the circular casket-lids, with snakes in relief, *AvonPerg.* 7(2), nos. 426–32, here fig. 83, *g*, in the Asclepieion, one of several examples; a further analogue is provided by a Delian offertory-altar, here fig. 83, *h*, *ED*, xviii, pl. 102, fig. 899 (cf. p. 369), *IDélos* 1898, found in the Kabirion, with which the snakes were naturally associated. S. Wide, *Archiv f. Religionswiss.* 12, 1909, pp. 221–3, apropos of the altar in Herakleion Museum with a snake climbing to drink from a phiale (Yavis, *Altars,* loc. cit. above), identifies the snake with the dead man: 'Der Tote ist in Schlangengestalt aus der Erde gekrochen und hat sich dem Altar genähert, den er geschickt erklimmt. Schon scheint er mit dem Munde die Schale erreicht zu haben und schickt sich an, die dort eingegossene Spende zu geniessen.'

Quite distinct from this special category of funerary altars at Mytilene is a pair of altars now in private possession in Scotland (here fig. 83, *j–k*), *JHS* 79, 1959, p. 159, and pl. V, below, identified as Mytilenaean by L. Robert, *RÉA* 62, 1960, pp. 276 ff., no. IV (cf. *SEG* xviii, 433–4), one containing a bilingual (funerary?) dedication by the Decurions and the family of Theopompos to their *nutrix,* Iulia Musa, and the other a simple inscription, presumably funerary, Εὐτυχίας / θυγατρὸς / Σωτῆρος. The first altar is broken above, but the second has a well-preserved 'Coan' rosette-fascia surrounded by a dentil-moulding. On the first piece is a bucranion (skeletal) and garlands with fillets, which have been completely hacked away on the second piece, though the outline is still visible.

163. (a) UP (Eph.) (fig. 84, *a–b*) with five Nikai, uninscribed. The upper moulding and fascia has linked rosettes and bucrania (for which compare the rectangular altar from Nisyros, pp. 18–19 and fig. 48, *a*, *b*, 49, *a*); (b) *Cl. Rh.* 5(1), pp. 36 ff., no. 6, and plates 18–21 (Jacopi, *Sped. dei Cav.,* p. 46, no. 13639, and fig. 23) from Cova (Eph.) (fig. 84, *c*); (c) ibid., p. 41, fig. 22 (IGard.) (fig. 84, *d*); (d) UP (Eph.), fig. 85, *a*. The dimensions of (a), the largest, are H. 1 m, diam. 0·85 m. The provenance of (a) is not known to me, that of (b) is 'Cova', that of (c) the Piazza dell'Arsenale (Plateia Symes). In addition to (b) and (c) Jacopi, *Cl. Rh.* 5(1), pp. 40–1, speaks of a further example from Cova, and one from Trianda, one of which is probably (d) here. Ross, *Reisen,* iii, pp. 91, 99, saw an altar of the same type at Rhodini, and another near Trianda, and it is likely that the latter is also (d). A further small fragment consisting of a head and torso of a Nike and part of a garland is published in *Cl. Rh.* 2, no.

22; this is E601 on the wall of the room with funerary reliefs in the Museum. The mouldings of (b) have been separated from the cylinder, as in other instances referred to above, p. 26. (a) has, above the Ionic moulding, a cavetto decorated with tendrils and acanthi which can just be made out on the photograph. Note also the way in which the extremities of the figures trespass on the meander. A variant is provided by the modest cylindrical altar from Rhodes, *Beschr. ant. Skulpt. Berlin*, no. 1153 (now in Marburg), in which the garlands are supported by Erotes; the roughly carved inscription, Ἀγήσαρχο(ς) / Κνίδι(ο)ς, Ἐλ/πὶς Κνιδί/α, was omitted by Hiller from *IG*, and does not seem to have been republished: here fig. 85, *d–e*.

164. Mendel, *Catal.* iii, no. 1150 (cf. Pfuhl, op. cit., p. 85, and note 143). The same altar is given in Texier, op. cit. ii, pl. 134, below, left, who says, 'Cet autel, qui est sur une des places de Cos, a été creusé pour faire un mortier à piler le grain. La sculpture qui le décore rappelle la plus belle époque de l'art. Trois génies ailés soutiennent des guirlandes; ils portent à la main des bandelettes et paraissent s'acheminer vers un sacrifice', and quotes apropos, *et tenues Coa veste movere sinus*; 'ce vers ne peint-il pas d'une manière exacte cette délicieuse composition?' The garlands are in fact supported by winged Nikai, just as in the Rhodian pieces. Also reproduced in A. N. Modona, *L'isola di Co* (1933), pl. xiii.

165. *Annuario*, 4/5, 1921–2, pp. 237 ff. (fig. 85, *f*; in Castello), from Trianda. The altar has a full Ionic moulding with dentils above and below, and is surmounted by a cavetto cornice with acanthi and tendrils, as is the Nike altar in fig. 84, *a–b*, and the unattached upper moulding, given in fig. 64, *a*, which may well have belonged to just such a Nike altar. Like them it also has a fascia of linked bucrania and rosettes, while the lowest part of the cylinder has another tendril frieze and, below that, another Ionic moulding.

166. *Ant. Denkm.* ii, pl. 35, and pp. 15–16 (Conze); Lawrence, *Later Greek Sculpture*, pl. 45, now in Istanbul (Mendel, ii, no. 575; here fig. 85, *g*), a convex slab with a figure of a maenad, once part of a circular altar. For a similar altar made of seven slabs, each with a figure of a maenad, found in Rome, see Loewy, *Not. Scav.* 1908, pp. 445 ff. The circular altar in Istanbul, reproduced here as fig. 85, *h–j*, Mendel, ii, n. 564, is of uncertain provenance. It portrays Erotes and other figures and animals carrying sacrificial objects, accompanied by a musician playing a pipe, while one figure is carrying a double cornucopia, suggestive of Cos. Another figure is making a sacrifice on a circular altar on which a fire is burning (cf. above, note 67).

For the question of the stylistic relationship between the Pergamene Gigantomachy and the later large-scale Rhodian works, notably the Laocoön, see the discussion by D. Thimme, *AJA* 50, 1946, pp. 354 ff. More immediately relevant to the monuments under discussion is the close similarity between the winged Nikai of the Rhodian altars and the various winged figures of the Altar: see, e.g., Kähler, *Der grosse Fries von Pergamon*, pls. 3, 25, etc.; wings, drapery, and movement closely resemble one another, in both style and technique.

167. See *Cl. Rh.* 5(1), pp. 36 ff.

168. *Cl. Rh.* 5(2), pp. 9 ff., no. 27 (IGard.).

169. The distinction between stag's head and bull's head is most clearly marked by the antlers, even though those may be, as in the present instance, formalized. There is an altar with stags' heads on the terrace of the Castello at Cos, and another, of rather different style, with five-tined exaggerated antlers, from *AvonPerg.* 7(2), no. 419 and pl. 41 (here pl. 71, *c*; cf. note 148 (i)).

170. On a much inferior piece, *IG* 574 (fig. 86, *b*), now in Vienna, where Ἱεροῦς is squeezed in just under the moulding above the bucranion, it is possible that the inscription and the relief are not part of the original design of the stone; but they probably are.

171. UP (OGard.) (fig. 86, *c*), inscribed Ζήνων / [Σ]ελγεύς, a homonym of the proposer of the decree of the koinon of the Aphrodisiastai Hermogeneioi concerning the ownership of burial-plots, discussed below, pp. 61–2. For a similar type of relief field on a cylindrical altar at Cos see fig. 86, *d*, with a recessed frame with woman and child in relief.

172. See note 74. There is no trace of paint in any of the reserved spaces.

173. On the altar illustrated on fig. 32, *b*, they are also carved above centre as part of the integral design.

174. Uninscribed (UG; fig. 87, *c–d*). Dimensions H. 0·48 m, diam. 0·42 m, Ht. of prow 0·16 m. Mentioned by Laurenzi, *Boll. d'arte*, 1936, p. 132: 'Gli scavi [at Cova] appena iniziati hanno reso già alcune are cilindriche a festoni e teste di torello, fra cui una molto importante per la sua rarità, poichè appare sormontata da una prora di nave.' The structure of the hull occupies the diameter of the upper surface. On the upper surface of the ship there are two holes, probably for attaching a metal superstructure of some sort, and another small hole, perhaps for an aphlaston, in the prow. Although the left side (as in fig. 87, *d*) of the hull is broken, the complete construction presumably did not extend beyond the circumference of the altar on that side any more than it did on the right. The hull is identical on its two sides. I am not able to elucidate further the type of ship represented.

175. *Cl. Rh.* 5(1), pp. 94 f., no. 25, from Makry Steno.

176. IGard. The piece, H. (with base), 0·62 m, W. 0·65 m, Th. 0·40 m, roughly worked behind, is probably that referred to in *Cl. Rh.* 1, p. 21 ('fra gli altri anche un esemplare gemino'). There is a double inscription on the base, difficult to read (*SGDI* 3858). [See ADD.] I read, (a) — / —μανευς / Τύμνιος (b) — / Θευδότου Ἀργεία. The relationship between the two deceased does not appear to have been stated: l. 1 of (b) must have contained the woman's name; cf. below, pp. 56–7. Compare the rectangular altars with bases in one piece, fig. 32, *a–b*. A close parallel to the double altars is provided by the two stelai in one block at Tanagra, *IG* vii. 1577–8 (here fig. 91, *b*); oddly, ibid. 1599 consists of two stelai carved in one block with *one* inscription carved across them both;

ἐπὶ Ζω|σαρίωι (fig. 91, *c*). Martial, i, 93, refers to a double funerary altar, under which two *primipilarii* were buried:

> Fabricio iunctus fido requiescit Aquinus,
> qui prior Elysias gaudet adisse domos.
> Ara duplex primi testatur munera pili;
> plus tamen est, titulo quod breviore legis:
> 'Iunctus uterque sacro laudatae foedere vitae,
> famaque quod raro novit, amicus erat.'   [See ADD.]

177. For *Chalke* see *IG* 971, Susini, *Supp. epigr.*, p. 259, nos. 1 and 2 (undecorated?); Susini says of the funerary monuments of Chalke (p. 253): 'Il tipo monumentale comunemente diffuso nell'isola è l'ara cilindrica, talvolta decorata da festoni e bucrani.'

178. For *Karpathos* see *IG* 1023, 1029. Susini, p. 234, says 'Per quanto concerne i tipi monumentali, i non molti esemplari tuttora disponibili consentono solo di dedurre che la struttura prediletta dalle officine dell'isola era quella dell'ara cilindrica, decorata con festoni e talvolta con bucrani, talvolta sovrapposta ad una base parallelepipeda che reca superiormente il segno d'incavo per l'infissione dell'ara.' At Karpathos there are also a large number of single and double bases for such altars: see above, note 120.

179. For *Syme* see *IG* xii. 3, Supp. 1275. Such altars are rare on Syme now. There is one in the Chaviaras Collection (fig. 88, *a*), H. 0·50 m, inscr. Τιβερίου Κλαυδίου Ἀφροδᾶ, but it seems likely from its style to be Coan, as are many of the stones both in the Chaviaras Collection and in the public one (see the notes in Peek, *Inschr. dor. Ins.*, p. 13).

180. *Telos*: *IG* xii. 3, 78. Susini, p. 269, writes 'Il tipo più comune tra i monumenti sepolcrali di Tilo è l'ara cilindrica, di piccola o media grandezza, provvista di cornice nella parte superiore e talvolta anche in basso, decorata sul suo stesso fusto da festoni in rilievo, sovente retti da bucrani, con bandelle e pendenti disegnati, sempre in rilievo, tra i festoni'; cf. ibid., nos. 8, 21, 28. I illustrate here, fig. 88, *b* (the same altars as in Susini, fig. 53, but taken from another angle), the group of three altars superimposed one on the other, built into the wall of the cemetery below Megalochorio; the lower two altars have evidently lost their upper and lower mouldings. The centre piece, of white marble, is in a curious low relief found also on a Rhodian piece (IGard.; fig. 88, *d*) which has lost its mouldings. The three pieces are uninscribed; cf. Susini, p. 269, fig. 53, who wrongly states that the altars are 'nel monastero della Panaghia'; they are in fact in the adjacent cemetery wall. Fig. 88, *c*, is a plain altar of Rhodian type built into the same wall (cf. above, pp. 25–6, with note 128, and fig. 63, *a–d*).

181. For *Nisyros* see *IG* xii. 3, 127, 149, 165, and Peek, *Inschr. Nis.*, pp. 372–3, no. 2 ('Rundbasis in Form der für Rhodos und ziemlich alle dorischen Inseln typischen Rundaltäre'), id., *Inschr. dor. Ins.*, p. 30, no. 69. For the bases see above, note 120. I illustrate here two altars, fig. 89, *a–b*, and, for a third,

a 'snake-altar', see below, p. 38, and fig. 102, *b*. Fig. 89, *a*, H. 0·40 m, diam.
0·30 m, uninscribed, is conspicuous for having the garlands and bucrania
immediately below the upper moulding (cf. above, p. 32 and note 173).
Fig. 89, *b*, H. 0·78 m, diam. 0·50 m, of very provincial workmanship, is peculiar
in that the skeletal bucrania are linked only by a pearl necklace. This is rare as
the main feature on the cylinder (cf. pl. 76, *f*), but occurs when bucrania are
linked with rosettes, etc., in the fasciae of the upper mouldings of a few richly
decorated pieces: see above, note 165, and the fascia of the side of the rectangular Nisyrian altar, above, pp. 18–19, and fig. 48, *a*, *b*. In an architectural
context it occurs on the architrave of the gate of the gymnasion at Olympia,
Olympia, ii, pl. 176, here fig. 91, *d* (cf. Gardiner, *Olympia*, p. 292 (reconstruction)), and on the Pergamene block, fig. 66, *b*; cf. Napp, op. cit., pp. 14–15.

182. See Susini, p. 212; ibid., pp. 219 ff., fifteen examples of disc-tombstones.

183. I know of no published example, and Bean confirms that he has no record
of any from his travels in the area, though he points out that he might not have
heeded them if they were uninscribed.

184. I may take this opportunity of illustrating three uninscribed altars of
unknown provenance, which are certainly not Rhodian: (a) in Venice, inv.
no. 2, Dütschke, *Antike Bildwerke in Oberitalien*, V, p. 139, no. 365, H. 0·70 m,
diam. 0·65 m, here fig. 91, *e*; (b) in Venice, inv. no. 275, Dütschke, ibid.,
p. 106, no. 281, here fig. 91, *f*; (c) in Istanbul, no. 6275, here fig. 91, *g*. Both
(a) and (b) have the heavy, naturalistic fruit-garlands with pendent grapes,
characteristic of Delos and Paros (see above, figs. 72–4, *passim*), and could be
Cycladic in origin. (c) might be Coan, as are many other altars in Istanbul, but
it lacks the characteristics of the style, especially the mouldings, fasciae, etc.,
and its origin must remain open.

The unpublished altar in Istanbul reproduced here as fig. 91, *h* (published
here through the kindness of Dr. Fıratlı) is of some interest. It was found recently
on the site of the ancient Nicomedia, and there is therefore no doubt as to its provenance. The colour and density of the pale fawn limestone, and the general style
of the cylinder, no less than the laurel-garland of the bucranion, resemble the
Rhodian series to a degree that I have not noticed in any other non-Rhodian
altar. For the λιθοξόοι of Nicomedia see Robert, *Hellen.* 11–12, pp. 35–6.

185. See above, p. 9. Merker, *Hellenistic Sculpture of Rhodes*, p. 7, calls attention
to the fact that the free-standing sculpture of the period at Rhodes is also
markedly on the small side.

186. See p. 9.

187. 92, *a*, *Cl. Rh.* 5(2), pp. 28 ff., no. 37 (UG); *b*, ibid. 5(1), p. 90, no. 23 (UG).
In neither case does the base belong to the stele; *c*, *SGDI* 3988, now in Vienna;
the reading ΘΑΙΗΤΑ questioned by van Gelder in *SGDI*, is clear on the photograph and on the squeeze (IG), but it is not impossible that the iota was
inserted after the other letters had been engraved; *d*, UP, in Copenhagen, Nat.
Mus. Inv. 8629, of white marble, PH. 0·72 m, W. 0·37 m, broken below,

inscription missing; *e, IG* 481 (Berlin, Pergamon Museum), is an example of very inferior workmanship, of a single figure in a small field. With the almost rectangular fields of 92, *a, b,* we may compare the similar reserved fields on a few rectangular and circular altars, noted above, p. 17, with note 74, and figs. 44, *a,* 45, *a–d,* 86, *a, b, d,* 87, *a, b.*

188. UP, Copenhagen, Nat. Mus., 2620, found in the city of Rhodes (1903), PH. 0·385 m, W. 0·312 m, Th. 0·088 m. The figure and lyre are of very inferior workmanship, but the palmette-acroterion is less crude, and inhibits me from dating the piece later than the early Imperial period: it might be considerably earlier.

189. Konstantinopoulos, *AAA* 6, 1973(1), p. 117, fig. 5. Note the funerary urns placed symmetrically along the top of the triglyph-frieze. Inscription: Χαριτίμου / τοῦ Τιμαγόρα / Φαγαίου.

190. *Cl. Rh.* 5(1), p. 92, fig. 61 (UG).

191. Dontas, Πρακτ. Ἀρχ. Ἑτ., 1954, pp. 357 ff., and fig. 9; Konstantino-poulos, *Rhodos* (Athens, 1970), pl. 20. The stele, H. 0·92, W. 0·42, is studied by A. Borbein, *Marburger Winckelmann-Programm 1968*, pp. 74–101, who dates it to the second half of the second century B.C. Borbein sees in the stele, which he subjects to a minute stylistic analysis, a reflection of the close cultural links between Rome and Rhodes in the later hellenistic period, but I find this very fanciful. It is based to a large extent on his interpretation of the column against which the youth is leaning as a specifically 'Tuscan' column, on account of the neck-band below the capital. However, the notion of the strictly Tuscan order of the Vitruvian system (for which see A. K. Lake, *Mem. Amer. Acad. Rome* 12, 1935, pp. 89–149) seems unduly rigid (see Plummer, *Simpson's History of Architectural Devel.* i (N.Y. 1966), p. 306), and in any case it seems impossible to determine whether the column represents this supposed Tuscan capital; it seems closely to resemble, e.g., the columns on the Tanagra reliefs, *B & WG,* p. 8, nos. 11–12, p. 9, no. 17 (and pls. 3, 4).

I take this opportunity to publish here a fragmentary marble stele from Rhodes in Copenhagen, Nat. Mus. 5619, fig. 94, with a representation of a plumed Corinthian-style helmet and sword, PH. 0·41 m, W. 0·44/6 m, Th. 0·080/100 m; at top, horizontal cornice with dentils. The helmet seems to be identical with that represented on the stele discussed above, though the divided brim is not visible there. The plume on fig. 94 is fuller but similar. Compare also the helmet and plume on the Side weapon frieze (below, note 220) and on the denarius of 46 B.C. discussed above, note 67.

192. *Cat. Ancient Sculpt., Ny Carlsberg Glyptotek* (1951), p. 165, no. 229, a (Billedtavler (1907), pl. lxxiii, 230a), inscribed Δαμοκλεῦς / Τιμασαγόρα / Φυσκίου, unhappily translated by Poulsen as 'the young man is called Damo-cleus and he is the son of Timasagorus [*sic*], grandson of Physcius'; a hat-trick. The letters are of the second century B.C. The object in the left hand appears to be a hare, held by the ears. The motif of ephebe with dog, and sometimes with a hare, is not uncommon on Attic reliefs of the fourth century (see Conze, *Att.*

Grabrel., pls. 185 ff., esp., for the hare, pl. 208 (*IG* ii². 12765); and the fourth-century relief in Brauron Museum, from Porto Rafti, inv. E.B. 6; for examples from Thessaly see *AAA* 6, 1973(1), pp. 130 ff.; also the relief in Berlin (inv. 1871), of *c.* 460, reproduced, Boardman, *Greek Art²* (London, 1973), fig. 115), but in view of the similarity of the animal's posture, one may wonder whether the sculptor had not seen the fine early hellenistic mosaic from Rhodes (now exhibited in the portico of OG) in which a centaur holds a hare in an identical position (*Arch. Rep.* 1968–9, frontispiece). The hare is the natural catch of the hunt, and Poulsen's reference to the hare as 'an erotic symbol possessing many of the gifts of Aphrodite (Philostr. I 6, 6) and therefore a plaything of the young ephebe' is out of place here. (Neither explanation fits the scene on the w.f. lekythos found at Anavysso, in which a woman standing beside a tumulus is holding a hare, apparently by its haunches (*Arch. Rep.* 1962–3, p. 8, fig. 8). The position here suggests that the creature is a pet nestling in the crook of its mistress's arm.) The hare held by the centaur on the mosaic, by the youth on this stele, and on the r.f. kylix, Beazley, *ARV²*, p. 322, no. 37, Mus. of Fine Arts, Boston, *The Museum Year 1971–2*, p. 42, is clearly booty; so also is that held by the youth on the Gorgos cup, Beazley, *ARV²*, p. 213, no. 242 (D. B. Thompson, *An Ancient Shopping Centre* [*Agora Picture Books*, 12, 1971], fig. 67). For another relief of similar subject, representing a naked youth carrying a spear, also carved in a large sunk field, from the area of Rhodini, see *Chron. des fouilles, 1958*, p. 730, fig. 14; the elongated, tapering limbs suggest a late hellenistic date.

193. *Cl. Rh.* 2, p. 66, no. 29, and fig. 34. A lifeless stele in low relief, from Rhodes, now in Naples, was published by De Franciscis, *Rend. Linc.* 1946, pp. 432–43 (cf. Guarducci, *PP* 8, 1952, pp. 211–14), here fig. 96, *c*. The figures, a girl holding a bird and a child facing her, are also standing on a ledge, which forms the lowest section of the stele, and is inscribed with two penta-meters. This is, of course, a very common treatment, much more so than the use of the narrow ledge in the centre of the stele; cf. Borbein, op. cit. (above, note 191), pp. 87 ff., who also emphasizes that such ledges seem particularly (though not exclusively) Rhodian. In the pediment is a Siren. [See ADD.]

194. See (a) fig. 20*a*, *NS* 108 (IGard.), Ἡρακλείδα | χρηστὲ χαῖρε, H. 0·38 m, W. 0·15/18 m, base (which seems to belong), H. 0·17 m, W. 0·36 m, Th. 0·26 m; (b) fig. 22, *IG* 331, Ὀνασιφάνεια | Νικαγόρα.

195. *NS* 48, *Cl. Rh.* 2, no. 30 and fig. 35 (Jacopi, *Sped. dei Cav.*, p. 45, fig. 22) (from Soroni, N. of Kamiros), (UG). The inscription has been republished by Peek, *GVI* 1625 (*Gr. Gr.* 217).

196. Published by G. Dontas, Ἀρχ. Ἐφ., 1958, pp. 208–16 (two examples from Rhodes, one from Telos); a further example in *Chron. des fouilles 1961*, p. 887, fig. 17. Dontas regards these as representative of a local tradition, and compares the stele of Krito and Timarista (fig. 16). The two Rhodian pieces are H. 0·88 m, W. 0·42 m, and H. 0·30 m, W. 0·28 m, and the Telian piece H. 0·96 m, W. 0·49 m.

197. First published by Hiller von Gaertringen and C. Robert, *Hermes*, 37, 1902, pp. 121–46, 'Relief von dem Grabmal eines rhodischen Schulmeister', and reproduced and discussed many times since, especially in Brunn–Bruckmann, *Ant. Skulpt.* (1906), no. 579 (B. Sauer), and most recently by Nilsson, *Gesch. Gr. Rel.* ii² (1961), pp. 234–5 and pl. 4, 1, with p. 234, note 4, a bibliography to which should be added the article of G. Arrighetti, *Stud. Class. e Orient.* 3, 1955, pp. 123–8 (see below, note 203), and the remarks of G. Dontas, Εἰκόνες καθημένων πνευματικῶν ἀνθρώπων εἰς τὴν ἀρχαίαν Ἑλληνικὴν τέχνην (Βιβλ. τῆς ἐν Ἀθην. Ἀρχ. Ἑτ. 46, 1960), p. 70. Curtius, *Mitt. deut. arch. Inst.* 4, 1951, pp. 20–32, identifies the group on the left as the remaining portion of a group of the Seven Wise Men, and maintains that the figure usually regarded as the deceased is an initiate, that the winged figure is Pysche-Tyche, and that the figure rising at the right end is Nyx.

198. Damatrios is no. 49 in Blinkenberg's list of sculptors, *ILind.* i, pp. 52 ff. He is approximately contemporary both with the Demetrios (Δημήτριος Δημητρίου Ῥόδιος) who collaborated with Theon of Antioch (for bases signed jointly by them see Blinkenberg, ibid., no. 63; to the list there given add the base found in Alexandria, *CIG* 4684 *e* (*SB* 8549)), and also with Δημήτριος Διομέδοντος Ῥόδιος, ibid., no. 62, but there is no reason to suppose identity.

199. See the detailed argument of Hiller and Robert. It is immediately evident that only half the figure on the extreme left is preserved on the block; there are in fact dowel-holes in both ends of the block, where it joined other blocks.

200. Op. cit., p. 121.

201. For these see *Röm. Mitt.* 12, 1897, pp. 328 ff.; cf. Hiller, *BCH* 36, 1912, p. 237; Curtius, loc. cit.; Picard, *Les Statues ptolémaïques du Sarapieion de Memphis* (1955), p. 45, note (2), and pp. 157–8. The Sarsina mosaic is now Helbig, *Führer⁴*, IV, p. 327, no. 3350 (Parlasca), with further bibliography of both mosaics.

201a. For the wall of Hades see Curtius, op. cit., p. 22. For the 'Portal of Death' see also the remarks of Ashmole, *JHS* 87, 1967, p. 5, regarding the porch or entrance represented on the Portland Vase.

202. *Hermes*, 37, 1902, pp. 140 ff. The iambic epigram is *IG* 141 (Peek, *GVI* 1916).

203. See Hiller, *BCH*, 36, 1912, pp. 230–9, where he suggested that the epitaph of Arideikes, who is described as a follower of Plato (lines 5–6: τὸν ἀοίδιμον αἴ σε τιθηνοῖς / χερσὶ Πλατωνείους θρέψαν [sc. αἱ Μοῦσαι] ὑπ' ἀτραπιτούς; cf. above, note 101), there published (Peek, *GVI* 1451, *Gr. Gr.* 189), and the Hieronymos relief were closely associated, and that the two monuments, one of the Aristotelian, and the other of the Platonist, could have been executed by the same sculptor. In *Hermes*, 54, 1919, pp. 105–7, he maintained that the Physkian Δαμάτριος Ἀριδείκευς, ματρὸς δὲ ξένας, of the Lindian list, *IG* 766, line 14 (*ILind.* 88, line 288), was the son of the Platonic philosopher, who had thus carved the relief for his father's philosophical colleague and opponent.

130 Rhodian Funerary Monuments

Difficulties and doubts about this chain of arguments were clearly felt by Wilamowitz, *AA* 1913, p. 43, and later by Hiller himself, *GGA* 1942, p. 163; the whole series of arguments are examined by Arrighetti, op. cit., pp. 124 ff., and I need not go into the details here. It suffices to say that both the Arideikes hypothesis and the epitaph, *IG* 141, can be regarded as irrelevant to our relief, and that if the Hieronymus of the frieze is to be identified with any known person, the only one at all plausible is the Peripatetic philosopher. The Platonic element in the representation is not decisively against this (*contra*, Arrighetti), at least as far as the first scene is concerned, for, as Hiller pointed out, the description of the relief on the grave of Isocrates, given in the *Vit. X Orat.* 838b, foreshadows the same scene, with a group of students seated round a table: ἦν δὲ καὶ αὐτοῦ τράπεζα πλησίον ἔχουσα ποιητάς τε καὶ τοὺς διδασκάλους αὐτοῦ, ἐν οἷς καὶ Γοργίαν εἰς σφαῖραν ἀστρολογικὴν βλέποντα αὐτόν τε τὸν Ἰσοκράτην παρεστῶτα; cf. Brendel, *Röm. Mitt.* 51, 1936, p. 8.

204. *IG* 385, inscribed Ἀριστοβούλου / Τερμεσσέως / εὐεργέτα / χοραγήσαντος τρίς // καὶ τᾶς γυναικὸς Ἰσιγόνης / Ἐφεσίας / εὐεργετίδος. Dimensions, H. 0·48 m, W. 1·07 m, Th. 0·28 m; cutting at sides W. 0·09 m, depth 0·06 m.

205. *Cl. Rh.* 2, pp. 57 ff., nos. 25–6, of which the first (also in *Cl. Rh.* 1, p. 23, fig. 4) is particularly fine (IGard.); *Ann.* 4–5, pp. 245 ff. (*Cl. Rh.* 1, p. 54, fig. 37) (IGard.), torso surrounded by a snake within naiskos on raised podium (cf. below, pp. 38–9); *BMSculpt.* iii, no. 2252. The first three are from Makry Steno, and the B.M. piece was found 'near the city of Rhodes'. For this type of monument as a whole see C. Vermeule, *Berytus*, 13, 1959/60, pp. 1 ff., esp. pp. 32 ff., where there is a full list, including the two Rhodian pieces, nos. 25–6 (p. 33, no. 3, and p. 15, B7). In this connection I may call attention to the now destroyed monument at Atsinganovounaro near Lindos consisting of a heroon with a relief of armour: see above, note 1, c.

206. *BMSculpt.* ii, no. 1350, with the excellent discussion. The lion has been frequently republished, e.g. Richter, *Animals in Greek Sculpture* (N.Y., 1930), fig. 27. Newton's opinion that it is the monument which surmounted the grave of the Athenians who fell at the Battle of Cnidus in 394 has now been superseded by the view that the lion shows the influence of its kinsmen of the Mausoleum: see Krischen, *Röm. Mitt.* 59, 1944, pp. 172–81; W. L. Brown, *The Etruscan Lion* (Oxford, 1960), p. 151, note. For the Mausoleum lions see below, note 210. For lions, funerary and decorative, in general see F. Willemsen, *Die Löwen-Kopf Wasserspeier vom Dach des Zeustempels* (*Olympische Forschungen*, iv (1959)), which contains a valuable discussion of the chronology of lions in Greek art, with excellent photographic documentation; cf. also H. Gabelmann, *Studien zum frühgriechischen Löwenbild* (Berlin, 1965), and, more briefly, C. Vermeule, *AJA* 76, 1972, pp. 49–52, 'Greek Funerary Animals, 450–300 B.C.'. For the funerary lion in Roman Anatolia, where the word λέων frequently occurs in epitaphs, see Robert, *Étud. Anat.*, pp. 394–7; Kubińska, pp. 61–3, who gives a full list of epigraphical and monumental references, e.g. *SEG* vi, 431: Αἴλιος Ἀγχαρηνὸς Χρήσιμος ἐποίησα τὴν λάρνακα σὺν τῷ βωμῷ κὲ τῷ λ[έ]οντι ἑαυτῷ κὲ γυνεκὶ κὲ τῇ ἀδελφῇ αὐτοῦ.

207. *Cl. Rh.* 8, p. 19, fig. 6, and pp. 203–5, and figs. 206–7. Vermeule, op. cit., p. 56, says that the lions 'had been moved in antiquity', but they were found in a trench close to a grave in the necropolis, so the distance of removal is likely to have been insignificant.

208. In the later Turkish period this monument, *Cl. Rh.* 1, p. 75 and fig. 40 (Jacopi, *Sped. dei Cav.*, p. 26, no. 221), was in the Turkish governor's Konak at Mandraki : see Belabre, *Rhodes of the Knights* (Oxford, 1908), p. 165, fig. 168. In *Cl. Rh.* 1, p. 75, it is dated to the Roman period. Willemsen, op. cit., pp. 65, 69, assigns it to the early hellenistic period.

209. IGard. The provenance of this piece is not known to me.

210. See *BMSculpt.* ii, pp. 129 ff., nos. 1075 ff., and the photographs in Brunn–Bruckmann, nos. 72–3.

210a. This lion is in IGard. against the outer wall of the Museum building.

211. Fraser and Bean, p. 44, no. 41 (*SEG* xiv, 718, Peek, *GVI* 1178) :

. . . . . ἀργιόδοντες ἐπ᾿ εὐξέστοιο μένοντες
τοῦ[δ]ε τόπ[ο]υ . . *EPE.ΘΕ*, αὐτὰρ ἐγὼ κορυφᾶι
ἀκροτάται β[εβαὼς] ἐπιόσσομαι, ὄφρα ἑ μῆτις
πημήνηι δειλὸς φὼς ἐπινισόμενος·
ἦ γὰρ δὴ τόδε γε ἀνδρὸς ἀρειφάτου ἔπλετο σᾶμα
Διαγόρα κεδνᾶς τε ἀντιθέοιο ἀλόχου,
ἅν τε πατὴρ κίκλησκεν Ἀριστομάχαν, περὶ πασᾶν
ἔξοχον εὐτεκνίαι σωφροσύναι τε φ[ρε]νῶν.

For the tomb, ibid., see pl. 41. On line 2 we commented, 'We understand that a pair of lions stood beside the door, and a statue of Diagoras on the summit of the pyramid. In the yard of the house nearest [*sic*; not 'next'] to the tomb is, or was, a damaged marble lion'; see fig. 101, *b*. The tomb is referred to by Kurtz and Boardman, p. 286.

212. See Roos, *Opusc. Athen.* 8, 1969, p. 157, fig. 12, *a* and *b* (cf. p. 154). For the relations of Kaunos with Rhodes see Fraser and Bean, pp. 106–7. Fig. 101, *g*, shows a lion couchant with a calf's head between its paws, now in the forecourt of the Museum at Pergamon. Similar but stylistically inferior 'Phrygian' funerary lions from heroa at Iconion are reproduced by Kubińska, op. cit., on dust-wrapper, and pls. iv–vi; cf. Buckler and Calder, *JRS* 14, 1924, pp. 32–3 and pls. iii, iv, xiv. Willemsen, op. cit., pp. 54–5, assigns the introduction of the motif of the prey between the paws to the late fourth century B.C.

213. *Rhodes*: (a) *IG* 317 (lost?), of which Hiller says 'ara rotunda marmoris caerulei, quam anguis circumdat, herois quasi symbolum'; (b) UG (fig. 102, *a*), H. 0·57 m, inscribed below coils, —— / —απτόλιος / Ἁλικαρνασσέ[ως]; (c) LG, *Supp. Rod.*, p. 298, no. 77; *Nisyros*: fig. 102, *b*, H. 0·41 m, diam. 0·28 m, inscribed above and below coils, Ἀριστο/κλῆς τοῦ ἀγαθοῦ / Ἀριστοκλεῦς; the sigmas are square (Ϲ). Note the clearly visible beard, a frequent feature of representations of snakes. *Cnidos*: (a) fig. 103, *BMSculpt.* ii, 1355, H. 0·77 m,

132   *Rhodian Funerary Monuments*

uninscribed; (b) fig. 104, ibid. 1356, with base inscribed twice (*BMI* 852), (i) on the front (?), Ἀφθονήτου γυναικὸς / Τιβερίου Ἰουλίου / Τροφίμου; (ii) on the back (?), in a different and later hand (Ζ=Ξ; Υ=Υ), Εὐπορίας μνείας / χάριν· / Γλαυκίας Διονυσίου / μνείας χάριν· Τύχη Προσδέξι⟨ο⟩ς τοῦ ἰδί/ου τέκνου / μνείας χά/ριν. These two altars from Cnidos are noted by Küster, *Die Schlange in der griech. Kunst u. Relig.* (*RVV* 13(2), 1913), p. 66, note 6; he explains the motif as representing the snake climbing the altar to reach for food on the top, as on the circular altars noted above, note 162, fig. 83, *a–d*, and *f–h*, on which snakes are represented as drinking. I prefer to regard the position as indicating defence of the tomb, as stated in the epitaph quoted in the next note. Küster, pp. 68–70, gives much evidence for the snake as protector of graves. Kurtz and Boardman, op. cit., p. 239, say 'We might have expected snakes to appear as tomb monuments, but . . . they were clearly not considered appropriate in individual monuments.' This is not true of the Rhodian area.

214. Ἀρχ. Ἐφ., 1911, p. 65, no. 63 and fig. 13, whence Peek, *GVI* 1260, *Gr. Gr.* 173, from Bozburun (seen smashed in fragments by Bean in 1948; see Fraser and Bean, p. 41, no. 27, a; cf. *SEG* xiv. 704):

> Ὦ ξένε, θάησαι, παριὼν ἰδὲ τόνδε δράκοντα,
> ἀνδρὸς ἐπὶ κρατερο[ῦ] σάματι φαινόμενον·
> ὃς ποκα ναυσὶ θοαῖς πάτρας ὕπερ ἄλκιμον ἦτορ
> δεικνύμενος, πολλοὺς ὤλεσε δυσμενέων.
5   πολλὰ δ' ὅ γ' ἐν χέρσωι κατενήρατο φοίνια δοῦρα
> ἀνδρῶν ἀντιπάλων σάρκας ἐρειδόμενος.
> νῦν δὲ θανὼν γηραιός, ἐπ' αὐτῶι τόνδε δράκοντα
> εἵσατο τοῦδε τάφου [θ]οῦρον ἔμεν φύλακα,
> ὃν καὶ ἐπ' ἀσπίδος εἶχεν, ὅτ' Ἄρεος ἔργα ἐπονεῖτο,
10   πολλὰ ἐπὶ δυσμενέσιν πήματα μαιόμενος.
> τοὔνομα δ' εἴ κ' ἐθέληις αὐτοῦ καὶ πατρὸς ἀκοῦσαι,
> εἰδήσεις ἐτύμως τὰ κατώτατα γράμματ' ἀναγνούς.
>
> Ἀπολλώ[νι]ος . . . . . . ωνος (*litt. grand.*; [Ἀθηνί]ωνος
> suppl. Peek)

The letters are dated to the first half of the second century B.C. by the editors, but I think a date in the middle of the third century, or even earlier, is possible. Kurtz and Boardman, op. cit., p. 239, say of this poem that it 'reveals that the snake monument—"fierce guardian of the tomb"—is there because a snake was the dead warrior's blazon', but in view of the ascertained use of the snake as defender of the tomb it may be that this was only a coincidence.

215. *Cl. Rh.* 1, p. 21, fig. 2; ibid. 2, pp. 23–4, fig. 39 (Jacopi, *Sped. dei Cav.*, p. 61, fig. 32). It was found above a hypogaeum at 'Deirmen-dere' (cf. n. 13) of which it clearly formed the external monument: H. 0·82 m, diam. max. 0·56 m.

216. See, e.g., the coiled giants on the north frieze of the Great Altar, the so-called 'Beissergruppe', well reproduced in Kähler, *Der grosse Fries von Pergamon* (Berlin, 1948), pls. 12–13, 16, and the creature twined round Alkyoneus on the east frieze, ibid., pl. 33. There are numerous others on the altar.

217. I know of three such monuments. Two are built into a farmhouse on the platform once called Agia Marina, and are mentioned by Newton, *Halicarnassus*, II, i, pp. 324–5, and pl. 48 (here fig. 106, *b–c*). The other, fig. 106, *a*, is in the courtyard of the castle. A fourth example is recorded by Newton, ibid., p. 270, note *e* (cf. Bean and Cook, *BSA* 50, 1955, p. 92, note 41), as having supported an arcade of a *konak* on the front: 'In front of this Konak is an arcade, in one of the piers of which is a block of grey marble, on which is sculptured in relief a shield. This block measures 3′ 8½″ by 2′ 4″ in depth. The diameter of the shield, now broken, has measured about 1′ 9″. Traces of a triglyph appear on the opposite edge of the stone.' This cannot be the block in the castle, the shield of which is complete. If, as seems most likely, this latter block (fig. 106, *a*) was uniform with the other two, the upper frieze must have been attached to the upper surface by means of the holes in it: see the detailed publication of these by R. E. Allen, *BSA* 71, 1976, pp. 1 ff. There is another example of the same type on Cos, lying upside down in the ditch beside the road on the way from Cos to Pyli, of which unfortunately I have no photograph (perhaps the same, or part of the same, monument as that described by Benndorf–Niemann, *Reisen im SW Kleinasien*, 1, p. 15; note also the shields in the pediments of the Coan tombstone, Laurenzi, *Ann.* N.S. 17–18, 1955–6, pp. 150–2, nos. 230, *a–d*; Allen, op. cit., pl. 1 (*c*). A Rhodian parallel to the shield on a funerary monument is a shield depicted on an otherwise bare wall of a large ruined funerary precinct in Dokuz Sokak (see plan, opp. p. 1), *Ἔργον 1959*, p. 131, fig. 143 (*Chron. des fouilles, 1959*, p. 816, fig. 6; *AAA* 6 1973, p. 116 fig. 3), here fig. 107, *a*, already mentioned by Newton, *Trav. and Discov.* i, p. 170. (Excavation of the area within the precinct facing the shield has now (1974) begun, and undisturbed graves have been discovered: see fig. 107, *b*.) For shields on tombs and tombstones see in general Pfuhl, *JDAI* 20, 1905, pp. 148–9. Note also, though it did not belong to a funerary monument, Newton, *Halic.* II, ii, p. 698, no. 6a, with the dedication of ὁ δῆμος to Claudius and the Delian Artemis: 'On a round buckler with a sword under it, sculptured in relief on an oblong slab of white marble.'

218. UP (?) (OGard.).

219. Fıratlı, *Les Stèles funér. de Byzance*, p. 128, no. 218, and pl. lxvii (Mendel, ii, 1080).

220. *AvonPerg.* 2, pls. 43, 1; 44, 1 and 2; 45, 1 and 2 (esp.), with sashes; von Massow, *Führer durch das Perg. Mus.*² (1936), p. 37, fig. 28. The frieze from the south-eastern gate of Side, uncovered in 1965, Mansel, *AA*, 1968, pp. 239–79, esp. pp. 262 ff., probably of the second century B.C., consists of finely executed representations of pendent (Pergamene?) armour (cf. id. pl. 37; Bean, *Turkey's Southern Shore* (London, 1968), pp. 84–5, and pl. 30), including swords and scabbards.

221. *Milet*, 1, 2, pp. 80 ff. and pl. xv. A further, very similar sword is represented in the still unpublished frescoes of the painted hypogaeum of Lyson and Kallikleia, near Verria: see Makaronas, *Μακεδονικά*, 2, 1941–52, p. 634 and

pl. xviii; the bird-head of the hilt of the sword seems closely to resemble that on the Rhodian block. Another representation occurs in the chamber-tomb on the hill behind Eretria, *AM* 26, 1901, pp. 333 ff., esp. p. 343, and the drawing in Kurtz and Boardman, op. cit., p. 280, fig. 64 (cf. Auberson and Schefold, *Führer durch Eretria* (Bern, 1972), pp. 149–50 (and p. 200, note 111)). The hilt of the sword carried by the seated German (?) beneath Augustus' left breast on the Prima Porta statue has the same head: see, e.g., H. Kähler, *Die Augustusstatue von Prima Porta* (Cologne, 1959), pl. 18. An early example of the bird-head may be seen on the fine fourth-century Attic relief of the tribal victory of Leontis, recently found in the Agora, I 7167, knowledge of which I owe to Professor Homer Thompson.

222. See Altmann, op. cit., pp. 49 ff., the altars of the Volusii (second half of first century A.D.), and, in general, his chapter on such decoration, pp. 68 ff., 'Verzierung mit Widderköpfen'. He adduces (pp. 9–10), as an instance of early Greek usage, the triangular base at Delos (ibid., fig. 4; *IDélos* 1), but he does not refer to the best examples on stone, that of the altar from Mycenae, above, fig. 69 and note 145, and the archaic architectural block from Eleusis, Richardson, *AJA*, 2, 1898, pl. viii; Kabbadias, Γλυπτὰ ’Εθν. Μουσ. 58. He also reproduces a Pergamene ram's head (his fig. 61), which seems close to the Rhodian one. On the whole he assigns the regular use of the ram's head at the angle of rectangular altars to the influence of Etruria, where it is common from an early date (pp. 11, 70–1). For the ram in Greek funerary cult cf. Kurtz and Boardman, op. cit., p. 282.

223. See particularly the provision of rams in the commemorative festivals for the Heroized Aleximachos, son of Kritolaos, at Aigiale (*IG* xii. 7, 515; Laum, *Stiftungen*, ii, 50; Sokolowski, *Lois sacrées des cités gr.* (1962), no. 61, lines 39–86, only), lines 74 ff.: ὅπως δὲ καὶ ὁ ἀγὼν γίνηται, οἱ ἐπιμελη/[τ]αὶ τῇ νουμηνίᾳ σφαξάτωσαν ἅμα τῇ ἡμέραι κριὸν ὡς βέλτιστον πρὸς | [τ]ῷ ἀγάλματι ὧι ἂν στήσῃ Κριτόλαος τοῦ υἱοῦ Ἀλεξιμάχου, κ.τ.λ.; cf. below, pp. 76 ff. The sacrificial ram also figures in Kamiran *leges sacrae*, Sokolowski, ibid., nos. 94, line 11, and 104, line 5, with the specifically Kamiran terms πρατήνιος = πρήτην = 'yearling', used of the ram in 94, and in 104 of the he-goat; cf. Phot. *Lex.* s.v. πρατήνιος· ἡλικία τις αἰγός. ἐν Καμιρέων ἱεροποίαι τράγον πρατήνιον θύειν νόμος (i.e. as in 104). The word is already in Hesych., s.v. πρατήνιον and s.v. πρητῆνας, from Ar. Byz., but without the Kamiran reference; cf. also LS⁹, s.v.

223a. (Tr.) On one smooth vertical surface of the block there is a small hole, just over 1 cm in diam., which may have been used for joining another piece; but there is no anathyrosis.

224. *Cl. Rh.* 5(2), p. 23, no. 34, H. 0·18 m, from Makry Steno now apparently lost. Note also the snake around the cuirassed statue above, note 205.

225. It is worth recalling in this connection that we know of two instances in which papyri were buried in the grave, in the manner of the Egyptian *Book of the Dead*; in the tomb at Derveni, which yielded the papyrus with the commentary on an Orphic text (*Arch. Delt.* 18 (1963), 1964, pp. 193 ff.; *Chron. des* *fouilles 1961*, p. 794, figs. 4 and 5; Kapsomenos, *Arch. Delt.* 19 (1964), 1965, pp. 17 ff., and pls. 12 ff.); and in the circular tomb at Callatis, *Dacia*, 5, 1961, pp. 295 ff., which has not yet been published. It is thus possible that the papyrus on the lid represents a religious or funerary text, or a testamentary or funerary 'Stiftung'.

226. See Appendix, pp. 76 ff.

227. UP (Eph.), H. 0·65 m, W. and Th. of base, 0·325 m, letters 0·020 m.

228. See Appendix.

229. Fig. 110, *b* (Eph.), UP; 110, *c*, in open peribolos of Cova necropolis. Another similar piece is lying beneath the stairs by the mosaic in the inner courtyard of the Museum. Such conical pieces presumably stood on inscribed rectangular bases. Another cone, *Cl. Rh.* 5(2), p. 21, fig. 11, noted by Herrmann, op. cit. below, p. 44, encircled by an olive-wreath (fig. 110, *d*), is obviously an epithema (anathyrosis beneath), but the form of the lower member is unknown. It can hardly be described as an omphalos. For the omphalos in funerary art see the old but detailed study of Br. Schröder, *Stud. z. d. Grabdenkm. der röm. Kaiserz.* (1902), pp. 25 ff.; Pfuhl, op. cit., pp. 88 ff.; Roscher, *Omphalos (Sächs. Abh.* 31(1), 1915), esp. pp. 60 ff., 'Grabmonument in Omphalosform'; K. V. Herrmann, *Omphalos* (Orbis Romanus, 13, 1959), who, though mainly concerned with early representations, has much to say of the close relationship between βωμός and ὀμφαλός, typified, *inter alia*, by the inscription βωμός beside the Delphic omphalos on a b.f. neck-amphora in Munich (his pl. 1; Beazley, *ABV*, p. 95, no. 5; cf. id., *Paralipomena*, p. 36), and of sacrifices to Heroes. Roscher illustrates numerous monuments (some of which, however, are simply conical tumuli), of which two votive pieces from Delos are particularly akin to the Rhodian piece: (a) the relief of an omphalos encircled by a snake, Taf. III, 3 (Bulard, *Mon. Piot*, 14, 1907, pp. 62 f., fig. 20), which is typologically almost identical with our piece and, though it is not a tombstone, it probably has a chthonic significance; (b) Taf. V, 2 (Bulard, op. cit., p. 62, fig. 19), a cone or omphalos very similar to our fig. 110, *b*, with the addition of a snake. The thin tapering shaft standing on a rectangular base with trochilus, 'dalla necropoli di Rodi', published *Cl. Rh.* 5(2), no. 33, and figs. 12 and 13, is presumably a tombstone, and as such unique; its decoration in low relief is on three levels, at the bottom four wreaths (one of laurel, one of olive, and two of ivy), in the middle two skeletal bucrania, and at the top a single wreath of ivy. The base, like the monument, is uninscribed, but there is said to be a hole in the upper surface (the column is now built in as part of the window-frame of a window in the Castello, and has lost its base), which carried an epithema.

230. See S. Stubbing, *The Dolphin in the Literature and Art of Greece and Rome* (Menasha, 1929), *passim*; and, above all, Rumpf, *Meerwesen (Ant. Sark.* v, 1), pp. 97 ff., who has collected a vast amount of material in the notes; *B & WG*, pp. 60–1.

231. The piece illustrated is in Schimatari Mus. (see already *B & WG*, p. 61, with note 8). A pair of facing dolphins with bucranion between are placed in the pediment of a tombstone from Sagalassos(?), Pleket, *Leyden Inscr.*, no. 46.

232. See Stubbings, pp. 81–2; Cumont, *Symbol. funér. des Romains*, p. 155, note 4 (symbolism).

233. *Corinth*, I, iii, pp. 34–5, pl. 15, inscribed on the front of the base: *Cn. Babbius Philinus | Neptuno sacr(um)*. For other inscriptions relating to Cn. Babbius see ibid. VIII, iii, nos. 155, 241, 259 (a descendant). Apul. *Met.* iv, 31 refers to Palaemon as 'auriga parvulus delphini'. [See ADD.]

234. Agora 668. 6. R. 20 f. At Rhodes, Miss Grace informs me, the symbol occurs on stamps with the names of the fabricants Hipponikos, Hagesippos, and Dionysios: see Nilsson, *Troisième Rapport*, p. 168. For Thasos see Bon, *Les Timbres amphoriques de Thasos* (*Étud. Thas.* iv, 1957), Index, s.v. dauphin.

235. *IG* xii. 3, Supp. 1347: Ποσειδῶνι | Πελαγίωι· | πέτραι ἐν ἀκαμάτηι δελφῖνα θεοῖσιν ἔτευξεν | εὔνουν ἀνθρώποις νενομισμένον Ἀρτεμίδωρος.

236. UP (IGard.), provenance unknown. Beneath the body of the dolphin is a projecting piece which carries its fin (fig. 112, *b*). This could have surmounted an ordinary circular altar, like the hull of the ship, above, p. 32 and fig. 87, *c, d.* But the monument may very well have been of a different sort.

237. UP. Said to have been found in the neighbourhood of Ai Yanni during or shortly after the last war. It was not found at the same time, or in the same place, as the previous piece, which it is placed alongside in the Garden, so as to suggest the relationship of mother and young on a single monument; in fact they have no connection.

238. UP (Eph. Inner Ct.), H. 0·47 m, Th. of base 0·20 m. Rumpf, op. cit., p. 98, note 56, gives a long list of statues on which a dolphin appears as an attribute (e.g. the Medici Aphrodite, Bulle, *Sch. Mensch*, pl. 156; the Athens Poseidon, ibid. 73, and the Lateran Poseidon, ibid. 74, the last an excellent example). Our piece is paralleled by a very fine representation, *BMSculpt.* iii, 2132 (here fig. 112, *d*), which is of unknown provenance and, to judge by the stone, an almost fawn marble or limestone, is not Rhodian, and might be Italian. It too is resting on a cone, and probably formed part of a support for a statue or other object. The vigour and liveliness, as well as its streamlined poise, put it in a far higher class than its Rhodian counterpart which, nevertheless, has its own unsophisticated vigour. The dolphin is a very frequent symbol on coins, including those of the Rhodian area; for Rhodes see *BMCCaria*, 15 (iv a.C.); 119 (230–200 B.C.); 209, probably *c.* 200 (see Hackens, *Rev. Belg. Num.* 1971, pp. 37 ff.). It also occurs on coins of Nisyros (ibid., p. 222, and pl. xxxiv, 4–5; 350–300 B.C.), and on the archaic coins of Poseidion on Karpathos (ibid., p. 192, and pl. xxix, 14–15); see in general Imhoof-Blumer, *Tier- und Pflanzenbilder*, *passim* (Index, p. 164); Rumpf, op. cit., p. 98, note 53.

239. For an instance of *Δ* denoting the same name employed in direct line for four generations see *Ann.* 2, p. 168, no. 128: Θευφίλου *Ā* Νεισυρίου (IGard.) (Maiuri's comment, 'Il nesso *Δ* e il nesso *Γ* in luogo del patronimico indicano che il padre porta un nome eguale a quello del figlio' is inept); *IG* 4, line 7: Μενεκλῆς *Ā*; cf. also the Halicarnassian inscription quoted above, note 157, *init.* and Breccia, *Iscriz.* 156, Μίρτον / *Δαμο*/κρά/τους *Ā*, where the *Ā* presumably refers to the patronymic. [See ADD.]

240. See *B & WG*, p. 95.

241. See E. Loch, *De Titulis Graec. sepulchr.* (diss. Königsberg, 1890), pp. 57 ff.; id., *Festschrift L. Friedländer* (1895), pp. 276 ff.

242. In *IG* there is not one with patronymic as against a hundred without. Some instances are: *Ann.* 2, p. 163, no. 101: Διοσκουρίδης / 'Ηρακλείδου Τύριο[s] (*not* Τυρίου), χρηστὸς χαῖρε; *Cl. Rh.* 2, p. 219, no. 61, Ἀντίπατρος / Ἀσκληπιάδου / Κυρηναῖος πρόξενος / χρηστὸς χαῖρε, where the ethnic may refer rather to the following substantive (contrast *ILind.* 120: Ζήνων Ἀράδιος πρόξενος ὑπὲρ τῶν παιδίων / Βατοῦς καὶ 'Ηρακλείτου καὶ 'Ροδιάδος / Ἀθάναι Λινδίαι); ibid., p. 221, no. 71: Μελάνθιος / Σόλωνος / Βαργυλιήτης; ibid., p. 230, no. 113: Βόα Ἀπολλωνίου / Τενέδια χαῖρε; *NS* 94–8, esp. 96: Μενίσκος/Δράκοντος/ 'Ηρακλεώτ(η)s, and 98: 'Ιάσων 'Ιασωποῦ / Σιδώνιος.

243. See, for representative groups of such tombstones, *IG* 327–80; *NS* 100–33.

244. See *IG* ii². 10531–13084, which include both tombstones with single names and those with name and patronymic; cf. the discussion in *B & WG*, p. 95.

245. See, e.g., examples of the lists of magistrates, *IG* 49 (*AM* 20, 1895, pp. 377 ff., no. 3)–51; *AM* 20, p. 382, no. 4; *Supp. Rod.* 22. Cf. further Pugliese Carratelli, *Studi Arangio-Ruiz* 4 (1953), p. 486, with note 1. There are exceptions and contradictions of usage in honorific dedications; contrast, e.g., *IG* 53, Μοσχίωνα 'Εκάτωνος / τὸν Βράσιον πρύτανιν, with, e.g., ibid. 61, ὁ δᾶμος ὁ 'Ροδίων Φ[ι]λοκράτην / Ἀγητορίδα ἱερατεύσαντα Ἀθάνας Πολιάδος. In subscription-lists there is again variety: e.g. in *Ann.* 2, p. 134, no. 1, the demotic is regular, whereas in *Supp. Rod.* 58 it is not used once. Cf. Pugliese Carratelli, loc. cit., note 2.

246. A familiar example of this right is provided by the career of Poseidonius of Apamea, who migrated to Rhodes. According to Strabo 665, Ποσειδώνιος ἐπολιτεύσατο μὲν ἐν 'Ρόδωι καὶ ἐσοφίστευσεν, the first verb referring to public office. Documentary evidence for the practice is probably provided by the career of the sculptor Ploutarchos of Apamea, who held all the offices of state including that of prytanis: see Pugliese Carratelli, *Assoc.*, p. 151, no. 7 (cf. id., *Studi Arangio-Ruiz*, p. 486): Πλούταρχον 'Ηλιοδώρου / τὸ κοινὸν τὸ Ἀφροδισιαστᾶν Σωτηριαστᾶν ἐτίμασε χρυσέοις στεφάνοις. However, it is perhaps not certain beyond dispute that this is not a case of homonymity. That citizens of Rhodos remained outside the deme-system was, I believe, an inevitable consequence of the inherited right of citizenship being vested in the population of the three

old cities: see Hiller, *Rhodos*, col. 765, followed by Fraser, *Rhodian Peraea*, p. 79, etc. Pugliese Carratelli, *Stud. or. e class.* 2, 1953, p. 72, suggests that the Ialysian demotic Νεαπολίτας was that of the inhabitants of Rhodos. However, quite apart from the basic historical objection, Νεαπολίτας is among the rarest of all demotics (*Supp. Rod.* 5b, ll. 8, 16; *Ann.* 2, p. 156, no. 55; p. 158, no. 68; *NS* 343; one UP), and therefore unlikely to be that of the inhabitants of the city of Rhodos.

247. *IG* 544, Ἀφροδισίου / Τερμεσσέως / καὶ Ἀντιοχίδος / Ῥοδίας, where the ethnic of the woman may have been added to balance that of the man; *Ann.* 2, p. 168, no. 129, Ἀγαθόστρατος Ῥόδιος, an undecorated cylindrical altar, which may not be funerary. The absence of the patronymic is a further complication (cf. Pugliese Carratelli, *Studi Arangio-Ruiz*, p. 487, note 5). In *NS* 267, Ῥόδιος / θρεπτός, / [χρηστὸς χαῖρε], Ῥόδιος is evidently a proper name.

248. See the list of sculptors given in *ILind.* i, pp. 51 ff. The relationship between the sculptor, to whom ἁ ἐπιδαμία has been awarded, and his son, who is a Ῥόδιος, is clearly shown by the titles of Ἐπίχαρμος Σολεὺς ὧι ἁ ἐπιδαμία δέδοται, and of his son, Ἐπίχαρμος Ἐπιχάρμου Ῥόδιος (*ILind.* i, p. 54, no. 74). There are other examples which may be found in the same list. I do not enter here into the numerous problems concerning the significance of the title Ῥόδιος, save as it concerns the question at issue: see, however, Carratelli, *Stud. Arangio-Ruiz*, pp. 487–9, who maintains that since other instances of the use of Ῥόδιος in Rhodian documents occur entirely in the list of benefactors of a koinon, *IG* 137, the term is simply used there to distinguish the Rhodian citizens among the foreigners; see also *IG* 155, A, l. 2 (see note 354). If a Ῥόδιος and a demesman were to occur in the same document (as happens with the scarcely less enigmatic Ἀλεξανδρεῖς at Alexandria—see next note) that problem would be solved.

249. See Fraser, *Ptol. Alex.* i, pp. 47–9.

250. Blinkenberg, *ILind.* i, p. 54, no. 74, lists over 100 sculptors, of whom more than thirty are Ῥόδιοι, but it is difficult to evaluate the material in this respect, since it seems likely that Rhodian demesmen who were sculptors also signed themselves Ῥόδιος as a general practice, some of their works being destined for export.

251. For an exception, the only one I can record, see below, p. 52 and note 285; it is of the Roman period.

252. e.g. *Ann.* 2, p. 175, nos. 162, *a* and *b*; *a*, Ἱεροκλεῦς τοῦ Φιλιστίδα / Βρυγινδαρίου and *b*, Φιλιστίδα / Φιλίνου / Βρυγινδαρίου (fig. 26, *a*, *b*), the largest caskets known to me (cf. above, p. 12). Other caskets are: *Cl. Rh.* 2, nos. 65–6, 72, 77–81, 85 (all these, name+patron.+demot.), 96–100 (name +patron.), 110–24, excluding 121–2, (city-ethnics and ethnics), 131–2, 138–42 (single names). *NS* has a large and varied collection of caskets: 80, 94 (name+ patron.+demot.), 131–3 (name+patron.), 138, 140–1, 159, 169–71, 177,

180–1, 193, 202 (name+city-ethnic), 216, 218, 240–1 (name+ethnic), 301–36 excluding 335 (single names), 338, 351–4 (name+city-ethnic or ethnic), 355–9 (name+patron.+city-ethnic), 360–2, 365–8 (name+patron.+demot.), 369–72 (single names), 373 (name+patron.), 374–8 (name+patron.+demot.), 379 (single name), 380–1 (name+patron.+demot.), 382–3 (single names), 385–8 (name+patron.+demot.), 389 (name+patron.), 390–3 (name+patron. +demot.), 394 (name+patron.), 395 (name+patron.+demot.), 396 (single name), 397 (name+patron.), 398–9 (single name), 400 (name+patron.), 401 (name+city-ethnic), 402–4 (name+patron.+demot.), 405–14 (single names), 415 (name+city-ethnic), 416–17 (name+city-ethnic), 418–20 (name +patron.+demot.), 421–3 (single names), 424 (name+city-ethnic). This representative collection shows that (a) the single name and (b) the full name +patron.+demotic are about equally represented.

253. See, e.g., *IG* 552–65, *NS* 250–74 for two groups. The humble origin of the individual is clear in many cases from the name; cf. below, note 308. It is a notorious difficulty for purposes of identification that the eponymous officials on Rhodian amphora-stamps do not have the patronymic; for two exceptions see Grace, *Hesperia* 22, 1953, nos. 81 and 126, with her observations, p. 125, under no. 81.

254. See Hiller's rubric at the head of *IG* 556, altars, etc., with single names, which stood on lost bases: 'De his inscriptionibus dubitari potest sintne integrae an supplendae ex basibus, quae olim aras sustentaverint, et quibus patris et patriae nomina et nescio quid contineri potuisse nemo neget.' An obvious example of a surviving second part is *NS* 84, a complete base inscribed καὶ τᾶς γυναικὸς | Ἁγησιρόδης Τιμασάρχου Κρυασσίδος, with Maiuri's comment, 'essendo il basamento intero d'ogni lato è necessario supporre che l'altro nome fosse inciso sull'ara o sul cippo sovrimposto alla base'; further examples above, note 36. Another, rather different type of incomplete inscription is *Ann.* 2, p. 179, no. 187, a complete block inscribed on one side χρηστοὶ χαίρετε and on the other χαῖρε καὶ σύ. The names were on the upper member. Cf. below, p. 72.

255. See Wilamowitz, *Aristot. u. Athen*, ii, p. 179; Wilhelm, *Beiträge*, p. 2; Muehsam, *Berytus*, 10, 1952 (2), p. 65.

256. See *B & WG*, pp. 92 ff.

257. The only example in *IG* vii is 3458, Πυρίππου | Εὐφήμου, on which Ditt. commented 'Titulum integrum duobus nominum propriorum genitivis constare neutiquam probabile est . . .' The stone was not seen by Lolling.

258. The only example in *IG* xii. 9 is 965, Περίτου, which Papabasileiou took to be the genitive of Περίτας, but it is natural to doubt the termination. Ziebarth did not see the stone. *Diffido*, as Wilamowitz said of an equally uncertain dative in *IG* xii. 9, 1048. There are no genitive forms among the approximately 150 Eretrian tombstones in *IG* xii, Suppl. nos. 576–641, and

Arch. Delt. 23, 1968, Chron., pp. 99–116. There is a genitive from Chalkis, Μολπίδος, in *IG* xii, Supp. 676; is it complete (cf. 677)?

259. At the two Acarnanian cities which have yielded most tombstones, Palairos and Thyrreion, the figures are: Palairos, *IG* ix. 1² (2), nos. 460–572, the proportion of nominative to genitive is approximately 1:3; at Thyrreion, ibid. 257–361, it is about 10:1; cf. *B & WG*, pp. 160–1. In other parts of western Greece the evidence is less abundant, but we may note that elsewhere in Acarnania, at Anaktorion, the genitive is twice as common as the nominative, and at Stratos half as common. In many instances, however, the nominative is not a simple nominative, but forms part of the χρηστὸς χαῖρε formula. In Locris and Aetolia the evidence is slight, but equally divided between the two cases.

260. *Thera*: *IG* xii. 3, 822 ff., and Supp. 1617 ff.; nominatives slightly predominate, but the archaic tombstones, 802 ff., all have the genitive. *Paros*: *IG* xii. 5, 330–443, nominatives *c.* 5:1 against genitives. *Amorgos* (esp. Arkesine): *IG* xii. 7, 139–218, nominatives *c.* 8:1 against genitives, but many of the former are of late date, with the age of the deceased person.

261. E. Loch, *De Tit. Gr. sepulchr.*, pp. 61–2, already saw the frequency of the genitive at Rhodes. In my analysis of the material I confine myself, for reasons of space, to the two main collections, *IG* and *NS*, since these are characteristic of the whole. In these two collections, out of a total of 150 caskets, the genitive vastly preponderates, *c.* 6:1, the most frequent category being the full formula, name+patron.+demot., of which 11 are in the nominative and 50 in the genitive, while of those with name and city-ethnic or ethnic only, the ratio is about the same (*c.* 6:1). On the other hand, out of a total of 150 tombstones of all sorts, on which the deceased has name+patron.+demot., the nominative has a 3:2 superiority over the genitive. Later stelai with χρηστὸς χαῖρε are also a very numerous group. Rhodian islands: *Nisyros*: *IG* xii. 3, 108 ff., out of *c.* 35 items, 20 are in the nominative, 15 in the genitive; *Telos*: ibid. 50 ff., the genitive scarcely occurs in 25 examples, but there are several in Ἀρχ. Ἐφ., 1922, pp. 46 ff., and a further series in Ἀρχ. Ἐφ., 1913, pp. 8 ff. shows a proportion of 27:4 in favour of the nominative. In the *Peraea*, where the evidence is slight and scattered, the proportion is *c.* 4:3 in favour of the nominative on a variety of monuments.

262. *Cos*: nominative and genitive are represented in the approximate proportion of 3:5 in favour of nominative, out of a total of over 100 tombstones. The genitive predominates on the circular altars, the nominative on the rectangular blocks and stelai. These figures do not include stones with the χρηστὸς χαῖρε formula.

263. For *Cnidos* see the remarks of Hirschfeld, *BMI* iv, 1, p. 34, on the formula ὁ δᾶμος, followed by the genitive (nos. 833 ff.; cf. above, note 162), belonging mostly to a late date. The genitive is also usual on tombstones without the ὁ δᾶμος formula: see ibid., nos. 848–85, mostly of late date; Bean and Cook, *BSA*

47, 1952, pp. 189 ff., nos. 9 ff. Tombstones of a date earlier than the Roman period are so far rare at Cnidos.

264. *Halicarnassus*: see Newton, *Halic.* II, ii, pp. 694 ff.; Bean and Cook, *BSA* 50, 1955, pp. 104 ff.

265. For the rock-cut tombs of Telmessos see *TAM* ii, 1, nos. 30–42. Most have the plain genitive, but already by the early third century B.C. the tomb itself is mentioned (34–6: τοῦ δεῖνος μνημεῖον; 37–8: προγονικόν; 39: μνῆμα προγονικόν, etc.). Cf. Loch, op. cit., p. 8.

266. For the very numerous variants of this class see Kubińska, *passim*.

267. e.g. *IG* i². 998, 1002, 1004, and many other examples. For Rhodian instances see note 268 (a)–(c).

268. The early epitaphs from the Rhodian cities are discussed by L. H. Jeffery, *Local Scripts*, pp. 347 ff. The earliest are: (a) that of Idamenes (early sixth century), *IG* 737 (Jeffery, pp. 348 and 356, and pl. 67, no. 5), which, as Dr. Jeffery points out, may not be an epitaph, but it seems likely that it is; it begins Σᾶμα τόζ̓ 'Ιδαμενεὺς ποίησα; (b) that of Euthytidas (*c.* 550–525), *IG* 709 (Jeffery, pp. 349 and 356, no. 15; *Tit. Cam.* 160; Kern, *Inscr. Graec.*, pl. 10, above), beginning Εὐθυτίδα ἠμὶ λέσχα (=, uniquely, 'tomb'); both (a) and (b) are from Kamiros; (c) *IG* 887 ('end of sixth century?', Jeffery; see pp. 350 and 357, no. 24), 'Ιμασ(σ)άωλας ἠμὶ τᾶς Ἀπολ(λ)ω[ν]ίδα, from Lindos; and (d) from Rhodos (see above, note 20), *Ann.* 2, pp. 150 f., no. 27, Χαρωνίδας Ξηνοτίμω ('end of sixth century?', Jeffery; see pp. 349, 357, and pl. 68, no. 25, here fig. 14). The tombstone from Kumisala, with representation of birds in a circular field, *Ann.* 2, 296–8, fig. 14, M. Andronikou, *Arch. Delt.* 17 (1961/2), 1963, pp. 192–4 (bibliogr., p. 192, note 113), and fig. 88, α–γ, Bakalakis, 'Επιστ. 'Επετ. Φιλοσ. Σχολ. Θεσσαλον., ιγ', 1974, pp. 247–51, is of course, uninscribed, and probably incomplete; it is commonly regarded as of Geometric date, but doubts are expressed by Kurtz and Boardman, op. cit., pp. 219–20 (Bakalakis regards it as sub-Mycenean).

269. *NS* 127 (UG), a base for two stelai (ii a.C.); cf. *Cl. Rh.* 2, p. 219. no. 62, Τίτος 'Ορδιώνιος / "Ερως / καὶ Ζωσίμης τῆς / Καλλικράτου / Ἀλεξανδρίδος (Coan?).

269a. *Cl. Rh.* 2, p. 228, no. 101: Χαριξέναν / Ἀρχικλείδα.

270. e.g. *IG* vii. 1580–1645, 2000, 2124, 2126, 2130 (ἥρως ἀγαθός), etc.; cf. Wilhelm, *Beiträge*, pp. 67 ff.

271. e.g. *IG* ix. 2, 977: Θεοκλῆς Φιλίππου μνείας χάριν, ἥρωι (i p.C.); 1199, Πυθόδωρος Πρωταγόρου ἥρωι (ii a.C.?); cf. 1187, 'Ηρωίσσει / Παρμενίσκα Μενάνδρου Μελιβοΐσσα (ii a.C.).

272. See Kubińska, *passim*, for many examples.

273. See Larfeld, *Gr. Inschr.*, p. 436; Wilhelm, loc. cit.

274. *IG* 338 (Cova), on a plain circular altar of late iii a.C.

275. *Ann.* 2, p. 129, no. 15. For the expansion Καρ(πασιώτας?) see *B & WG*, p. 97, note 39 (*SEG* xvii. 360).

276. *IG* 649.

277. See Cagnat, *Cours d'épigr. lat.*⁴, pp. 282–3; Sandys–Campbell, *Latin Epigraphy*, pp. 60 ff. For instances of the very frequent use of the dative in the Roman period, which may reflect Roman practice, see the Macedonian epitaphs, *SEG* i. 270–5, 277, 279, 281; ibid. xii. 319 ff.; ibid. xvi. 401 ff.

278. *KF* 50.

279. *KF* 48. Cf. ibid. 51: Α(ὔλῳ) ῾Ρεννίῳ ᾿Ιούστῳ | Α(ὔλου) ῾Ρεννίου ὑῷ Μα/κεδόνι Πολε—.

280. See ad loc.: 'Zu dem Dativ am Schluss ist wohl in Gedanken zu ergänzen τὸν βωμὸν ἀνέθηκαν.'

281. For other examples from Cos see *PH* 165 (fig. 84, *d*): Δαμο[νί]κη | Νικάνδ[ρ]ῳ | Τυρίῳ | καὶ Νικάνδρῳ | τῷ υἱῷ· | χρηστοὶ καὶ ἄλυποι χαίρετε; cf. ibid. 307 and 313, datives with μνείας χάριν; *SEG* xv. 511, Πίστος Ἀπολωνίου [*sic*] | Πίσστι τῇ μητρὶ | καὶ τ⟨ῷ⟩ πατρί. For a dative of hellenistic date from Chios see *Archiv*, 16, pp. 169–70, no. 2: Μητρόδωρος ῾Ηγεῦς | τῆι μητρὶ Μητρίχηι Μητροδώρου, εὐχήν (*manu seriore*). For the use of ἀνέθηκε on tombstones see Fraser, *Ptol. Alex.* i, p. 578, with note 195. On *IG* ii². 7296, Θεογένης Γύλητος Προβαλίσιος ἀνέθηκεν. ᾿Ονητορίδης ἐπόησεν, Kirchner commented 'Et dedicationis formula (ἀνέθηκεν) et nomen artificis additum a titulis Atticis sepulcralibus alienum'. ἐπέθηκεν (ἐπέστησεν) followed by the dative is familiar from verse epitaphs from an early date: see Peek, *GVI*, nos. 137 ff., *passim*.

282. *IG* 355.

283. *NS* 276.

284. For ἥρως of the dead on Rhodian tombstones see below, pp. 76 ff.

285. *Cl. Rh.* 2, p. 229 no. 108. Note the absence of the patronymic with the demotic; cf. above, p. 48 and note 251.

286. Peek, *Inschr. dor. Inseln*, pp. 31–2, no. 78.

287. This series of tombs, with their inscriptions, is published in *NS* 347 ff. The line drawings on pp. 121, 124 (= fig. 5 here), 129, 130, show very clearly how the bodies and funerary furniture were disposed.

288. *NS*, p. 124, fig. 3, shows the caskets *in situ*, and fig. 5 here shows the loculus empty.

288a. *Ann.* 2, p. 163, no. 96 (*non vidi*); the inscription as printed by Maiuri is divided ῾Ρηγεί/νου Διο/δότου, | ὅπου ἐκάη, and at the end of lines 2 and 3 stand an isolated Α and Β (immediately below the Α). The significance of these letters escapes me; they can hardly represent filiation or a demotic (cf. note

139, end, for a similar enigma). *NS* 285, Βακχὶς / ἐγγενὴς / [ἐ]κάη, is also inscribed on a circular altar.

289. *NS* 192, a rectangular base, 'dalla necropoli orientale', Προτίμου Σιδωνίου εὐεργέτα τοῦ (*omisit* Maiuri) κοινοῦ· // Δώρου Μήδου; ibid. 193, the casket 'rinvenuta in una casa turca del quartiere *Enderûm* presso La Via dei Cavalieri', inscribed on two sides: (a) Δώρου Μήδου / καὶ / Προτίμου / Σιδωνίου, (b) εὐεργετᾶν. I have not located either the base or the casket to date. The inscriptions are considered in another context, p. 67.

290. See above, pp. 48–9, and note 252.

291. *NS*, pp. 124 ff., nos. 362–83 (cf. above, note 283), as indicated by number in the text.

292. See Fraser and Bean, p. 58, note 1.

293. Λέλος, the deme-centre of the Λέλιοι, is referred to in *Tit. Cam.* 84, in which an Ἄριος is honoured ὑπὸ Τρικτοίνων τῶν ἐν Λέλωι, and in *IG* 701, in which honours are bestowed by a koinon named Πυργαλιδᾶν κοινὸν ἐν Λέρωι, of which Hiller, *AM* 21, 1896, p. 62, said 'Λέλιος ist Demotikon von Kamiros und gehört zu dem *I.G. Ins.* i. 701, 12, erwähnten Orte Λέρος, der noch heute so heisst, und, wie ich kürzlich erfuhr, auch Λέλος gesprochen wird'; this was on the coast N. of Kretinia (see Hiller's map at the back of *IG*). Maiuri pointed out, *Ann.* 2, pp. 298 ff., that the locality referred to by Hiller was in fact called Λῆρος, while on the other hand a place named Λέλος existed in the centre of the island, 4 or 5 km west of Apollona, on the south slopes of Profiti Elia, where he excavated some Mycenaean tombs. This seems to be the more likely locality, and is accepted by Hiller, *Rhodos*, col. 750; Blinkenberg, *ILind.* ii, p. 982, note to no. 676; and Papachristodoulou, Τοπων. Ῥόδου, pp. 33–4.

294. That they formed a Kamiran deme is certain: see the summary of evidence in Fraser and Bean, p. 81, note 5(c).

295. See ibid., p. 152, note 1.

296. See, e.g., as a few examples out of many, *IG* 199, a Καττάβιος (L(indos)) and a Τυμνία (K(amiros)); 201, a Λαδάρμιος (L) and a Ποντωρηΐς (I(alysos)); 217, a Χαλκήτας (K) and a Κρυασσίς (I); *NS* 56, an Ἀμνίστιος (K) and a Κατταβία (L); 59, an Εὐριάδας (K) and a Κλασία (L).

297. *NS*, nos. 385–95. In 392 Maiuri restored Λυσά[νδρου]; but Πεδιάς is the feminine demotic (cf. 393; *ILind.* 252, l. 153; *AM* 25, 1900, p. 107, no. 106; in *IG* 215, Πεδιΐς).

298. Ibid., nos. 397–401: (397) Νικαγόρα Πυθοκλεῦς; (398) Πυθοκλεῦς; (399) Νικαγόρα καὶ Τιμοδίκας; (400) Νικαγόρα τοῦ Νικαγόρα; (401) Πειθοῦς Βαργυλ⟨ι?⟩ητίδος.

298a. An example of a family grave of foreign residents is provided by *AM* 23, 1898, pp. 392–3, nos. 56–9: 56: [Δ]α⟨μ?⟩άτριος(?) / Ἀσάνδρου / Μάγνης; 57: Μενεκράτης / Ἀσάνδρου; 58: Δρακοντὶς / Ἀσάνδρου / Μάγνησσα; 59: Ἀρτεμεισία / Ἀριστογένευς / Μάγνησσα. Note the absence of the city-ethnic in 57.

299. In the large group of citizen-tombstones, *IG* ii². 7000–881 the ratio of multiple to single graves is *c.* 1 : 7. Among foreigners they are much rarer.

300. From *IG* vii. 586–1163, all tombstones of Tanagra, only three, 1557, two brothers, 'Ολύμπιχος | Ἀναξίωνος, | 'Ηρόδωρος Ἀναξίωνος; 1577–8, Πίστις· || 'Επὶ Βαχχίωι (cf. above, note 176) ; 1615, 'Επὶ Κρι(το)βούλωι· || 'Επὶ Εὐφροσύνῃ Κριτοβού/λου Ἀθηναίᾳ, presumably father and daughter.

301. Ibid. 1890 (archaic, *c.* 510–500; see Jeffery, op. cit., p. 95, no. 14); 2116; 2118; 2121; 2153–4; 2160; 2166, combined with a construction-formula ('Επὶ Σωτηριχᾷ καὶ Εὐημέρῳ, τοῖς Μοσχᾶ τέκνοις. τὸ ἡρῷον τοῦτο Μοσχᾶς κατεσκεύασεν ἑαυτῷ καὶ τῇ γυναικὶ αὐτοῦ εἰς ἆ[ί]) ; Moschas does not mention his sons, already buried in the tomb. There are one or two further instances from Thespiai in *BCH*, 82, 1958, pp. 107 ff.

302. This is marked at Thespiai (1890–2222) and Thisbe (2247–368), and in west Greece (*B & WG*, pp. 161 ff.). For reuse at Athens see *IG* ii². 5228, 7061*a*, 7078, 7277, 7412, 7425, 7457, 8838.

303. I give a selection of these circular altars with joint inscriptions: *IG* 214, 217, 300, 412, 543, 545, 546, 579, 583, 648, 654; *NS* 150, 245; *Cl. Rh.* 2, pp. 219 ff., nos. 62, 63, 95; rectangular altars: *IG* 175 (or circular?), 382, 435, 447; *NS* 176, 198, 230, 342, 343. There are many more, and I give the evidence for individual variation in the following notes. There are, in all, over 100 relevant inscriptions.

304. Stelai: *IG* 539, *b*, 542, 652; *NS* 337, 339–40; *Cl. Rh.* 2, p. 222, no. 76; *Ann.* 2, p. 153, no. 37; p. 156, no. 57; p. 174, no. 157 (both stele-bases). Caskets: *IG* 393, 645; *NS* 193, 338; *Cl. Rh.* 2, p. 224, no. 85; *Ann.* 2, nos. 89, 120, 151, 168.

305. *IG* 176, Χρυσοῦς | Ἀστυμήδευς | Ποντωρηίδος | καὶ τοῦ ἀνδρὸς αὐτᾶς . . . ; 382, Ἀντιοχίδος Ἀντιοχίδος | ἀπὸ Δάφνας | καὶ | τοῦ ἀνδρὸς αὐτᾶς | Εὐκλείδα Σολέως μετοίκου; lines 3 ff. are in a different hand.

306. *IG* 539 a, Νικία Ἀντιοχέως | καὶ | Πρωτίου Κωίας; 544, Ἀφροδισίου | Τερμεσσέως | καὶ Ἀντιοχίδος 'Ροδίας (cf. note 238); 548, Ἄθως | Γαλάτας, | Ἀταλάντη | Σελγίς; *Ann.* 2, p. 169, no. 130, Ἀναξίδος Κωίας | καὶ Τίμωνος Αἰγιν[άτα], | ἀδελφῶν ἡρώων (see below, p. 74); *ILind.* 642 : Θευφάνης Σαρδιανός, | Μίκκη Ἀντιοχὶς | χρηστοὶ χαίρετε.

307. *Ann.* 2, p. 163, no. 97, Χαρίτα | Μακρώνισα· || Ἀπολλόδωρος ἐγγενής; *IG* 545, Παρθενίου | Θραίσσας || καὶ Φίλωνος | ἐγγενεῦς· | χρηστοὶ χαίρετε; 547, Ἀντίγονος Ἀντιοχεὺς καὶ ⟨Γλά⟩φυρον ἐγγενής; *Cl. Rh.* 2, p. 232, no. 124, Γοργία ⟨ἐ⟩γγενεῦς | καὶ | Εὐκλείας Φασηλείτιδος (casket). This last item is given as ΓΟΡ-ΓΙΑΘΓΓΕΝΕΥΓ, resolved by Jacopi as Γοργία τοῦ 'γγενεῦς, but the article is not right. However, Θ can hardly stand for nine generations of Gorgiases.

308. Servile status is not recorded in funerary inscriptions at Rhodes, or elsewhere, as a rule, and it is a notorious difficulty to determine whether persons were actually slaves, or simply humble members of the native or foreign population. One must be guided by various considerations, notably the type of

name (though this is fallacious at times: see Wilhelm, *JÖAI* 25, 1929, pp. 59–
64; Robert, *Noms indigènes, passim*), the absence of patronymic, and the ethnic
origin of the person concerned. But even so these three criteria can only create
a presumption, along with other factors, and I do not claim beyond doubt that
the persons commemorated in the next three notes were slaves. Morelli, in his
discussion of slaves at Rhodes, *Stud. Class. e Or.* 5, 1955, pp. 137–9, does not
consider the question how slaves are to be identified, but seems to accept the
principle of origin alone (p. 137): 'Il luogo di origine o di provenienza è, di
solito, segnalato accanto al nome proprio, sui brevi epitafi delle loro tombe.
There is a further complicating factor, that at Rhodes only one tombstone
refers explicitly to a freed slave, ἐξελεύθερος (*IG* 383: 'Επιγόνου 'Ροδιοπολίτα
μετοίκου ἐξελευθερω/θέντος ὑπὸ τᾶς πόλεως καὶ ξενωθέντος ὑπὸ / τᾶς βουλᾶς καὶ
τοῦ δάμου καὶ χοραγήσαν/τος δίς), and this particular individual was clearly
prominent in public life. It is therefore likely that many manumitted slaves are
concealed in the number of those recorded with single names; cf. above, p. 47.

309. *Cl. Rh.* 2, p. 232, no. 122, inscribed on a stele which I do not recall having
seen. The name Σαπις I cannot parallel, and its gender is doubtful. Zgusta,
Kleinas. Personennamen, p. 456, quoted a Lycian name Σαπια, but the link may
rather be with the Thracian tribe of the Σάπαι, for whom see Perdrizet, *Cultes de
Pangée* (1910), pp. 80–1.

310. *Ann.* 2, p. 153, no. 36, a cylindrical altar with bucrania and garlands.
Neither of these names is servile. Bithys, a Thracian name, was the name of the
father of the distinguished Ptolemaic administrator, Seleucus, described as
'Ρόδιος on one occasion, and as Αλεξανδρεύς on another: see Mitford, *Op.
Athen.* 1, pp. 131 ff. Εὐετηρία occurs also at Athens (*IG* ii². 11381, without patronymic, but 11382 is Εὐετηρὶς Ἀπατουρίου), and the masc. Εὐέτηρος in various
places; cf. Bechtel, *Att. Frauennamen*, p. 133, note 3.

311. *Ann.* 2, p. 153, no. 37, fragment of a stele. Φιλουμένη hardly needs a
parallel. 'Οπώρα is found at Athens as the title-personage of a play of Alexis,
CAF ii, p. 358, fr. 164 (Bechtel, op. cit., p. 128), of whom Athen. 443e says
ἑταίρας δ' ὄνομα τὸ δρᾶμα ἔχει; as the name of an Acanthian (*IG* ii². 7995,
'Οπώρα Στάχυος (!) Ἀκανθία (cf. Bechtel, *HP*, p. 610)), and also of a Heracleote
(*IG* ii². 8761, without patronymic).

312. *Ann.* 2, p. 161, no. 89, a casket. The simple Πλοῦτος, unlike its composite
derivatives, is uncommon; it occurs several times at Rhodes: (a) as the name
of a fabricant on Rhodian amphorae; *IG* 1375; *BSAAlex.* 9, 1907, p. 86, no. 28
(there wrongly attributed to Cnidos; *SB* 581, with patronymic Καλ⟨λ⟩ίστρα-
τος); (b) as the name of a three-year-old child, who fell off the shaft of a cart
carrying 'a heavy load of withies', and whose father was also named Πλοῦτος:
the child was commemorated on one of the most elaborate of late hellenistic
Rhodian stelai, *NS* 48 (Peek, *GVI* 1625; *Gr. Gr.* 217); cf. above, p. 34, and fig.
96, *b*; (c) on a casket, *NS* 327; and (d) as one of the non-demesmen of the
Amian group-burial, discussed above, p. 54, *NS* 372. It is quite impossible to
say that the bearer of the name was a slave (and (b) argues strongly against

the assumption), but the possibility remains. Outside Rhodes it occurs at e.g. Paphos, *BSA* 56, 1961, p. 39, no. 106 (grandfather and grandson). Πρόποσις occurs also at Athens, Bradeen, *Athen. Agora*, xvii (1974), no. 279 (*IG* ii². 7185).

313. *Cl. Rh.* 2, p. 235, no. 140, a casket. The similarity of names suggests a pair of female slaves or servants.

314. *IG* 540, a circular altar with bucrania and garlands.

315. Ibid. 550, a pedimental stele.

315a. *Ann.* 2, p. 166, no. 119, described by Maiuri as a 'lastra di marmo grigio'.

316. This practice must be distinguished from the reuse by others of a tombstone at a much later date, for which see above, p. 56 and note 302.

317. See note 302.

318. *IG* 647, last seen by Ross: Φιλάρχου Φιλάρχου καὶ | Εὐθρεπτίδα Φιλάρχου | καὶ Ποππηίας | Γοργίδος, | Μάρκου Πονπηίου Ἐπαφροδείτου | θυγάτηρ (sic) Σεβαστονείκου. Ross, *Hell.* i, 2, pp. 103 f., no. 30, commented (quoted by Hiller, ad loc.), 'Grosse quadratische Basis mit sculpturirten Ornamenten, im Hofe eines türkischen Hauses in den Gärten. Sie ist, wir mir Professor Heidenberg erzählt hat, seitdem ich (im Mai 1844) sie abgeschrieben, von den Eigenthümer zerschlagen worden, in der Hoffnung einen Schatz in Innern zu finden. Die Aufschriften dieses Steines sind in drei verschiedenen Handschriften [i.e. 'hands'] und wohl aus drei verschiedenen Zeiten, indem die genannten Personen nacheinander in demselben Gräbe beigesetzt worden sind.'

319. As the following examples show, it is not easy, in cases in which parents and children are all commemorated, to tell to which of them the ζώντων refers; (a) *IG* 648, two inscriptions on a cylindrical altar, (i) Γαίου Λικιννίου, Γαίου υἱοῦ, Βάσ/σου καὶ Λικιννίου Θεοδώρου ζώντων; and (ii) Λικιννί[ας] | Τύχης; it appears that the master and freedman named in (i) had seen to the erection of the monument in their lifetime, and that the daughter's(?) name was added subsequently; (b) ibid. 652, Τιβερίου Κλαυδίου | Δόνακος | ἐτ(ῶν) μεʹ καὶ τᾶς γυναικὸς αὐτ/οῦ Εὐτυχίας καὶ | τῶν τέκνων Γάμου | καὶ Μούσας Κνιδίων | ζώντων (ἐκ τῶν?) ἰδίων, the same uncertainty; (c) above, pp. 16–17 and note 69, the rectangular altar of late date, inscribed Καρποφό/ρου καὶ | τῶν αὐτοῦ ζώντων, in one hand. For the formula ζῶν (ζῶσα), ζῶντος, ζῶντες, see any of the large collections of tombstones from Roman Asia Minor, notably *TAM* and *MAMA*, where there are many hundreds of examples, and Kubińska, *passim*. On Latin tombstones no room for doubt was left in distinguishing between the living and the dead: see Cagnat, *Cours*⁴, pp. 291 ff. For ζῆι and ζῶσιν, which stand absolutely at the end of, or sometimes in the midst of, epitaphs, and fulfil the same purpose as the participial formula in a slightly different way, see Robert, *Étud. Anat.*, p. 225, and Index (p. 585), s.v.

320. An example of the difficulty of explaining such inscriptions is provided by *Cl. Rh.* 2, p. 224, no. 85, inscribed on the lid of a small casket, to which I have already referred above (note 47): Μάρ(κου) Αὐρ(ηλίου) | Ἑρμοκράτου | Ἐπαφρίωνος | καὶ Αὐρ(ηλίας) Ζωσίμης | καὶ τῶν τέκνων | αὐτῶν. I have unfortunately not found this casket, but Jacopi gives a detailed line drawing of it, which suggests that the hand is the same throughout. Evidently, literally understood, the inscription indicates that the ashes of at least four persons were accommodated in this small casket; easier, perhaps, to suppose that the inscription on the lid referred to interment, contemporary or future, in the same loculus, but not in the same casket.

321. *IG* 654. For (*faciendum*) *curavit* and similar formulae see Cagnat, op. cit., pp. 288–9. For προνοέω in a funerary formula see *IG* xiv. 1901 (προνοούσης) *SB* 5017 (προενόησε Ἑρμῆς). προνοέω is of course used regularly in both the active and middle voices in hellenistic documents for 'care for', of public acts, etc. (see *Syll.*[3] Index, s.v.); but the notion of the external 'care for' the burial is itself Roman, and in most cases the funerary formula reflects or translates the Roman formula.

322. See Kubińska, op. cit., *passim.* As an early example (ii a.C.; *IG*, sq.) of this practice note *AM* 21, 1896, p. 43, no. 11 (Peek, *GVI* 1256):

Εἴ τι μέλει φθιμένων τοῖς ζῶσιν, ὅρα τάφον ἀνδρός·
Χρήσιμος ἔσθ' ὅδε Κὰρ φιλοτιμότατος κατὰ πάντα,
ὃς καὶ ζῶν ἔτι τόνδε τάφον ποίησεν ἑαυτῶι
πολλὰ καμὼν τέχνηι καὶ πινυτᾶτι νόου

—inscribed on a rectangular base (from Mangavlí).

323. For such monuments see, e.g., *IG* 66 (ii a.C.), erected in honour of a priestess of Artemis Pergaea by a son, her grandson and granddaughter, and her great-grandchildren through their mother; ibid. 72, *a* (i a.C.), in honour of a victor in the Halieia, by his mother, his brother, two maternal uncles, and his maternal grandmother; *Tit. Cam.* 89 (i p.C.), in honour of a Camiran priest of Athana Polias and the Emperor Titus by his father, brother, nephew, sister-in-law, two uncles, and eight cousins; and *Cl. Rh.* 2, p. 188, no. 18 (ii/i a.C.), in honour of Pasiphon, a strategos, trierarch, etc., by his wife, his three sons, his brother, his five nephews, his daughter-in-law, two grandsons, and his great-nephew. One might compare the death notices in the newspapers in many European countries, including Greece, today, to which all relatives contribute.

324. These honorific family inscriptions are collected among the dedications in *IG* ii². 3822–4254. They are mostly of Roman date, though one or two are of the fourth century and early hellenistic (e.g. 3829; 3839; 3854). None equals the Rhodian dedications in respect of the range or number of relations participating; comparable examples are 3869 (ii a.C.), in honour of a man by his grandfather, mother, and daughter, and 4032, in honour of a woman by her mother and her brother. The relationship is at times not easily determined in

these examples, whereas the Rhodian dedications for the most part indicate the relationship of the different members of the family to the honorand in terms of his relationship to them: e.g. *Cl. Rh.* 2, p. 188, no. 18: [Πασιφῶντα Πασιφῶντος] ... τὸν ἄνδρα, ... τὸν πατέρα, ... τὸν ἀδελφόν, ... τὸν θίαν, ... τὸν τοῦ ἀνδρὸς πατέρα, ... τὸν πάππον, ... τὸν τοῦ πατρὸς θίαν, followed by the list of offices held by the honorand. The group of Lydian honorific tombstones of Imperial date, Buresch, *Aus Lydien* (Leipzig, 1898), nos. 25 ff., is comparable; e.g. 25: ἔτους σλε´ μ(ηνὸς) Δίου ζ´: | ἐτίμησεν Εὔμαχος | κὲ Ἄμμιον Ἀμαχιανὴν | τὴν ἑαυτῶν θυγατέρα, | Γάϊος τὴν γυνῖκα κὲ Ἀφι/άδες ἐ μάμμε, Νουμή/νιος ὁ μήτρων, | Φάνφιλα ἡ ἀδελφή, | οἱ πάτρως Νικόμαχος | Τρύφων Γάϊος κὲ ἡ πάτρα | Ἰουλία, Ἀμαχιανὴ ἡ τήθη, | Ἄλυπος ὁ μήτρων | κὲ οἱ συγγενῆς πάντες· | χαῖρε.

325. *Telos*: *IG* xii. 3, 40 (ii a.C.), to a woman by her husband, six children, and one grandchild; cf. 45, in honour of a woman by her husband, three sons, and her sister. *Nisyros*: ibid. 103 (ii a.C.; damaged), in honour of a man by his son (missing) and eight grandchildren; Peek, *Inschr. von Nisyros*, pp. 373 ff., no. 3, a dedication for a grandson of the honorand of 103, made by numerous other descendants. For the *Peraea*, Fraser and Bean, p. 45, no. 42 (Kedreai). For *Cos* see *Bull. Mus. Imp. Rom.* 3, 1932, p. 28, no. 25. The Rhodians did not suffer from ὀλιγανδρία.

326. See the sepulchral inscriptions in Dessau, *ILS* 7846 ff. Sometimes the *familia* is referred to collectively as such, e.g. 7849, *locus | familiae | Salvidienae | Q. f. Ruf.*, but more often the *liberti* and *libertae* are recorded alongside the *familia* within the same grave-complex, e.g. 7851, *libert. et | familiae | L. Arrunti L. f. | Ter.*; 7852, *libertorum | et libertarum | et familiae | C. Anni C. f. Cor. | Pollionis*. Cf. the remarks of Cagnat, op. cit., pp. 279 ff. The Roman practice of course extended even to the individual burial of slaves, who occur frequently with *liberti* in, for example, the 'Columbari di Vigna Codini', Nash, *Pict. Dict.* ii, pp. 333 ff., whose excellent photographs show the columbaria with the altars *in situ*, Toynbee, op. cit. (above, note 149), pp. 113 ff.; the inscriptions are *CIL* vi, 5179–538. The Roman caskets with bucrania, garlands, etc., very often contain the ashes of freedmen or slaves: see Altmann, op. cit., *passim*; cf. *CIL* vi, 5307 ff.

327. See the brief remarks of Kurtz and Boardman, op. cit., pp. 198–9. On p. 198 they write, 'No "slave cemeteries" have been identified, and it is likely that in the early period, before Classical class-consciousness had set in, they would have been buried in the family plot with other members of the household. If so, they would be difficult to identify and we have no reason to believe that all burials without offerings must be of slaves.' For tombstones of slaves in Attic inscriptions see Pfohl, *Untersuch.*, pp. 89–90; they are few, and almost the only unequivocal example seems to be of the second century A.D., *IG* ii². 12631, Σουροῦλα Π̊ Μουννατίου Ἀουείτου δούλη. Otherwise the word occurs infrequently save on the tombstones of Imperial slaves, whose status carried considerable prestige: e.g. *SEG* xxi, 1058 (Athens), *MAMA* ii, 114 (Lysias), [Ἄ]μίον Καίσαρος δούλη | τὸ ἡρῶον Διαδουμενῷ | τῷ ἰδίῳ ἀνδρὶ Καίσαρος δού/[λ]ῳ ἱππε[ῖ] μνε[ία]ς

χ[άρι]ν; ibid. i, 26 (Laodicea Combusta), Ἀσκληπιάδης / οὐέρνα τοῦ / Σεβαστοῦ, κ.τ.λ.; ibid. 27, Κόσμος οὐέρνας ἱππεύς; ibid. 28, Ἰουλιὰς δού/λη τοῦ κυρί/ου. In Roman Asia Minor the practice of interring adopted children, freedmen, and slaves in the family vault was common; in Lycia they were placed in the ὑποσόριον: see, e.g., *TAM* ii, 1, 437–8; and see in general Kubińska, pp. 81 ff. (For τὸ δουλικόν = τὸ ὑποσόριον see ibid., p. 90.)

328. *SGDI* iv, p. 851, no. ⁿ2; Schwyzer, *DGE* 792; Jeffery, *Local Scripts*, pp. 239 and 240, no. 12, with pl. 48; cf. Haussoullier, *Rev. Phil.* 1906, ppl 141–2; Cumont, *Rel. Or.*⁴, p. 197, fig. 12, and cf. p. 306, note 17; Bassi, *La scrittura greca in Italia* (Monum. ital. graph., Cremona, 1956), no. 44, pl. xiii, below. Wilamowitz, *Glaube*, ii, p. 64, points out the link with Euboea, an early source of Dionysiac legend.

329. Athens: Sokolowski, *Lois sacrées*, Suppl., no. 51 (*IG* ii². 1386; *Syll.*³ 1109).

330. Lines 163 ff.

331. προσ[[σ]]τα[φ]ιάζ[οντες] was suggested by Ramsay hesitatingly in the inscription of the Mystai from Amorion, *RÉG* 2, 1889, p. 20 (Laum, *Stiftungen*, ii, no. 175; Vermaseren, *Corpus Inscr. Mithr.* 22), with the same sense as ἐπιταφιάζειν, but Robert, *Étud. Anat.*, p. 308, rightly corrected this to προσσφα[γ]ιάζ[οντες].

332. Sokolowski, *Lois sacrées*, II, no. 126 (*IG* ii². 1275), ll. 4–7.

333. *IG* vii. 686. The whole group is 685–90 (all together as Schwyzer, *DGE* 463), of which 686 is the earliest. Note the example recently republished by J. Fossey in *AAA* 4, 1971, pp. 241 ff., from Vathy, N. of Tanagra: Εὐκλίδας· / οὗτον ἔθαμεν τὺ / σουνθούτη τὺ Ἀριστ[ι]/αστὴ κὴ Ἀφροδισιαστ[ὴ κ]ὴ τὺ φαρα-τρίτη (= *DGE* 463(3)). Fossey's conclusion (p. 245), that the practice of burial by sodalities was restricted, in Greece itself, to the area of the Tanagraean plain, should be modified in view of the stele from Chalkis, quoted in the next note; though the modification is only technical. [See ADD.]

334. *IG* xii. 9, 1151 (iii a.C.): Δημοσθένης / Λύσιος χρηστός· / τὴν στήλην ἔστησαν / Νουμηνιασταί. The epitaphs of the Roman period from S. Russia show the same feature: see below, note 339.

335. See Cumont, loc. cit.

336. *IG* vii. 685 (see note 333).

337. Ibid. 688.

338. Ibid. 689; cf. Fossey, loc. cit.

339. See in general Poland, *GGV*, pp. 503 ff. A group of such tombstones is that from Pantikapaion, *CIRB* 78–108, the synodos being regularly described as ἡ σύνοδος ἡ περὶ . . . The burial formula, when present, is τὴν στήλην (ἀνέστη-σεν): e.g. 89: ἡ σύνοδος ἡ περὶ συ/ναγωγὸν Ζοτουμᾶν / καὶ φιλάγαθον Παν/τάγαθον

καὶ γραμ/ματέα Δημήτριον / καὶ τῶν λοιπῶν θιασ/ειτῶν τὴν στήλ/ην Σωσίᾳ μνήμης χάριν. For Phanagoreia see *CIRB* 987–8.

340. For the *Collegia funeraticia* see especially De Rossi, *Comment. Mommsen* (1877), pp. 705–11; and also Waltzing, *Étude historique sur les corporations profess.* iv, pp. 177–80. For examples see De Rossi, loc. cit., and *CIL* vi, 10251–423, *ILS* 7344, 7363, 7375, 7945–7. The name of the *collegium* (in the form of a cognomen) is normally derived from that of the deceased testator who, by his testamentary act, creates the *collegium*: see *ILS* 7344, 7947. For such strictly funerary koina in the Greek world in the Roman period see Bean and Mitford, *Journeys in Rough Cilicia 1964–1968* (*Wien. Denkschr.* 102, 1970), p. 181, no. 201, an elaborate funerary text providing both for burial in the common tomb of the 'brothers' (ἀδελφοί) of the koinon, and also for the possibility of opting out on payment of a sum to the community and the koinon. Bean and Mitford publish other similar texts from the area (nos. 197, 198, 202, 205). Poland, op. cit., pp. 56, 503, had denied the existence of such koina. For the ταφικόν in Ptolemaic Egypt, a form of negotiable burial benefit of a member of a society, see *PEnt.* 20 and 21, of 221 and 219/18 B.C. respectively, and *PRyl.* 580 of (probably) 78 B.C. (in which no assignee for the benefit is named). Guéraud, on *PEnt.* 20 and 21, introd., refers to parallels for this burial benefit in Demotic texts.

341. See note 332. Observe especially lines 7–10 (in continuation of the passage quoted above, p. 59): καὶ ἄ/ν τις ἀδικῆται βοηθεῖν καὶ αὐτοὺς καὶ τοὺς φί/λους ἅπαντας, ὅπως ἂν πάντες εἰδῶσιν ὅτι καὶ / εἰς τοὺς θεοὺς εὐσεβοῦμεν καὶ εἰς τοὺς φίλους. Compare in general the provisions of a late Ptolemaic koinon, perhaps of Philadelphia, *HTR* 29, 1936, pp. 39 ff., ll. 15 ff., καὶ μὴι γ[ε]νεαλογ[ήσειν ἕ]τερος τὸν ἕτερον ἐν τῶι συμποσίωι μηδὲ κακο/λογ[ήσειν] ἕτερος [τὸν] ἕτερον ἐν τῶι συμποσίωι μηδὲ λαλήσειν μηι/δὲ ἐπ[ικα]λήσειν καὶ μὲ κατηγορή[σ]ειν [[α]] τοῦ ἑτέρου; and that of Tebtunis, *PMich.* v, 243 (reign of Tiberius), line 6: ἐάν τις παρίδη τινὰ ἐν ἀηδίᾳ καὶ μὴ συνεπισχύση ἐπὶ τῶ συλλῦσαι αὐτὸν τῆς ἀηδίας, δότω (δραχμὰς) η'; for other parallels from Egypt see Boak, *TAPA* 68, 1937, pp. 217–18.

342. xx, 6. 5 f.: οἱ μὲν γὰρ ἄτεκνοι τὰς οὐσίας οὐ τοῖς κατὰ γένος ἐπιγενομένοις τελευτῶντες ἀπέλιπον, ὅπερ ἦν ἔθος παρ' αὐτοῖς πρότερον, ἀλλ' εἰς εὐωχίας καὶ μέθας διετίθεντο καὶ κοινὰς τοῖς φίλοις ἐποίουν· πολλοὶ δὲ καὶ τῶν γενεὰς ἐχόντων ἀπεμέριζον τοῖς συσσιτίοις τὸ πλεῖον μέρος τῆς οὐσίας, ὥστε πολλοὺς εἶναι Βοιωτῶν οἷς ὑπῆρχε δεῖπνα τοῦ μηνὸς πλείω τῶν εἰς τὸν μῆνα διατεταγμένων ἡμερῶν. Cf. for the general state of Boeotia at this time Rostovtzeff, *SEHHW* ii, pp. 611–12.

343. The documents, found in the eastern necropolis (Dermen-dere: see above, note 13), were first published by Maiuri, *Ann.* 4–5, 1921/2, pp. 223 ff., thence with improvements in *SEG* iii, 674; subsequent bibliography in *Assoc.*, p. 161, note 2; Pringsheim, *Greek Law of Sale* (Weimar, 1950), p. 151, note 6; and republished by Pugliese Carratelli, *Assoc.*, pp. 156 ff., no. 18, with commentary by Carratelli and (on legal matters) V. Arangio-Ruiz. I have collated the texts myself, but my text differs only in small details from that established by Carratelli. The lettering of both documents, though quite different, is of the

second century B.C. The documents on side A of the inscription are dated by the eponymous priests of Halios, Aratophanes (line 2) and Agoranax (line 19). The eponyms are nos. 32 and 35 in Miss Grace's published list of eponyms, *Hesperia*, 22, 1953, pp. 122 ff. The ἀμφουριασμοί preserved on side B are dated by the eponym Archinos, who is no. 60 in Miss Grace's list. He must be earlier than Aratophanes and Agoranax, and since he is not represented in the Pergamon hoard of handles (see Grace, p. 119), a date in the third century is proposed for him (Carratelli, p. 154). Aratophanes is also the name of the eponym of the Rhodian decree of which a copy was found at Cyzicus (*SGDI* 3752). Note that in A iota adscript appears once only, in B invariably.

344. A, lines 3–7: ὅπως οἱ ἀμφουριασμοὶ | τῶν ἐγγαίων τῶν ὑπαρχόντων τῷ κοινῷ καὶ τᾶν ταφιᾶν | ἐνφανεῖς ὑπάρχωντι ὡς ἐν δυνατῷ πᾶσι τοῖς ἐρανισταῖς | εἰς πάντα τὸν χρόνον, καὶ μηθὲν ἀδίκημα γίνηται περὶ αὐτούς, | Ἀγαθᾶι Τύχαι· δεδό-χθαι τῷ κοινῷ κ.τ.λ. For ἀμφουριασμοί see the discussion by Arangio-Ruiz, loc. cit., and cf. Pringsheim, op. cit., pp. 151 ff., and briefly *Ptol. Alex.* i, pp. 111–12.

345. Lines 7 ff. (in continuation): κυρωθέντος τοῦδε τοῦ ψαφίσ/ματος, ἑλέσθαι τὸ κοινὸν παραχρῆμα ἄνδρα, ὁ δὲ αἱρεθεὶς | κατασκευάσθω στάλαν Λαρτίαν καὶ λαβὼν παρὰ τῶν ἀρχόν/των τοὺς ἀμφουριασμοὺς πάντων τῶν ὑπαρχόντων τῷ κοινῷ | ἐγγαίων καὶ τᾶν ταφιᾶν, ἀναγραψάτω αὐτοὺς εἰς τὰν στάλαν | καὶ ἀναθέτω τὰν στάλαν εἰς τοὺς τοῦ κοινοῦ τάφους εἰς τό/πον ὅς κα αὐτῷ δοκῇ εὐσαμότατος καὶ ἀσφαλὴς εἴμειν· | τοὶ δὲ ἄρχοντες δόντω τῷ αἱρεθέντι ἀνδρὶ ἀντίγραφον τῶν | ἀμφουριασμῶν πάντων ποτὶ τὰν ἀναγραφάν· δόντω δὲ | αὐτῷ ἐκ τοῦ κοινοῦ καὶ ὅ κα γένηται τέλεσμα εἰς τὰν κατασκευὰν | τᾶς στάλας καὶ τὰν ἀναγραφὰν τῶν ἀμφου-ριασμῶν.

346. Ibid., lines 20 ff.: Ζήνων Σελγεὺς εὐεργέτας εἶπε· ἐπειδὴ ψαφιξαμένου τοῦ κοινοῦ | κατασκευάξαι στάλαν καὶ ἀναγράψαντα εἰς αὐτὰν τὰ διατείνον/τα ποτὶ σωτηρίαν καὶ ἀσφάλειαν τοῦ κοινοῦ θέμειν εἰς τοὺς κοινοὺς | τόπους, συνβαίνει ἀσυν-τέλεστα γεγόνειν τὰ δεδογμένα τῷ κοι/νῷ διὰ τὸ τὸν αἱρεθέντα ἐπ' αὐτὰ ἄνδρα μεταλλάγειν, τὰ μὲν ἄλλα | πάντα γίνεσθαι περὶ τούτων κατὰ τὰ προδεδογμένα τῷ κοινῷ, | κυρωθέντος δὲ τοῦδε τοῦ ψαφίσματος, δεδόχθαι τῶι κοινῶι, ἑλέσθαι παρα/χρῆμα ἄνδρας δύο οἵτινες ἐπιτελεσεῦντι πάντα τὰ προδεδογμένα | τῷ κοινῷ περὶ τούτων, καθὼς ἐν τῷ προκεκυρωμένῳ ψαφίσματι | ποτιτέτακται, τοὶ δὲ αἱρεθέντες ἄνδρες ἐπιτελεσάντω | τὰ ποτιτεταγμένα ἐν τῷ προκεκυρωμένῳ ψα-φίσματι ἐν ἁμέ/ραις ἀφ' ἇς κα αἱρεθέωντι ἑξήκοντα, ὁ δὲ ἀρχερανιστὰς ὁ ἐν ἀρχᾶι . . .

347. See Carratelli, op. cit., p. 159, note 2, for various possibilities.

348. See Text B. Since the transaction recorded on the stele does not affect the present general discussion, I need not reproduce it here. It is sufficient to note that a plot of land is identified in line 10 as οἰκία ἐν τῶι ἄστει πᾶσα καὶ οἰκόπεδον τοῦ ποτὶ τᾶι οἰκίαι πᾶν ἇι γείτονες, and it seems to have no connection with the burial plots. For ἔγγαια at Rhodes see also Fraser, *BSA* 67, 1972, p. 117.

349. See the inscription quoted in note 351.

152 Rhodian Funerary Monuments

350. See *PH* 155–9 (156 = *Syll.*³ 1120); 155 runs: [ὅ]ρος θηκαίων / θιασοῦ Ἀφρο/διασιαστᾶν / τῶν σὺν Εὐ/τύχωι; 159, ὅρος θηκαί/ων Ἀθηνα/ϊστᾶν τῶν / σὺν Δράκο[ντι]. See also the group in *KF* nos. 38–44, in which the adjectival formulae ὅρος τόπου θηκαίου (38) and ὅρος θηκαῖος θιασοῦ (40–1) occur. As Herzog says, no. 38 is probably the official boundary stone of the whole necropolis of koina. θηκαῖον seems in this sense to be peculiarly Coan, and is evidently used of individual burial-plots of koina, all in close proximity to each other. In Athens we find ὅρος θήκης (*IG* ii². 2586–92), and also ὅρος μνήματος (2527–67) and ὅρος σήματος (2568–84), which almost always refer to individual, not collective, burial-plots, with legal rights of an individual attached (2552 has ὅρος μνημάτων; 2589–91, ὅρος θηκῶν, but 2591 seems to have ὅρος θηκῶν Λυσιμ[άχ]ο[υ]). For θήκη by itself see 12525 (iv a.C.), Προκρίτο θήκη; the same term occurs at Pherai, *IG* ix. 2, 426ᵇ–428, and at Eretria, *IG* xii. 9, 302 (v–iv a.C.) : see in general *Syll.*³ 1120, note 1 and Guarducci, *Epig. gr.* iii, pp. 241 ff.

351. *IG* 736 (*Syll.*³ 1118), of uncertain date, now lost : —εν— / [ἐ]ρανιστᾶν τῶι κοινῶι ἔ/δωκε δωρεὰν ἐς τάφια / τᾶς γᾶς τᾶς ἐν Ῥόγκχω[ι], / ὡς ἁ ὁδὸς ἁ φέρουσα ἐξ Ἀ/γυλείας εἰς Ἱππότειαν, / μᾶκος ὀργυᾶν εἴκοσι πέν/τε, πλάτος ὀργυᾶν δεκα/έξ, ὡς ὅροι κεῖνται· / δωρεὰν καὶ ἄλλον τόπον / ἐν τᾶι κτοίναι· δωρεὰν τὸ τέμενος τοῦ Ἀσκλαπ[ι]/οῦ καὶ τοῦ Ἀπόλ[λωνος καὶ] / τᾶς Ἀφροδίτα[ς —] / ποιούμενος — / [— τ]οὺ[ς] ὅρου[ς—]. The koinon was, as Hiller pointed out, evidently that of the Ἀσκλαπιασταὶ Ἀπολλωνιασταὶ Ἀφροδισιασταί, which is not independently attested, though there are numerous koina of each of the deities individually and in conjunction with other deities.

352. See note 350. Note that the ὅροι of the burial-ground of the ἐρανισταί are specifically referred to in the inscription quoted in note 351.

353. *IG* 155 (cf. *SGDI* 3836; *GDE* 290; Poland, *GGV* B, 267, a), re-edited with commentary by M. Guarducci, *Riv. r. Ist. arch. e stor. dell'Arte*, 9, 1942, pp. 16 ff., no. III. The excellent photographs in Miss Guarducci's article are reproduced here, fig. 113, a–d. The stone is in the Museo del Seminario patriarcale, Venice.

354. See especially Ziebarth, *Das gr. Vereinswesen* (Leipzig, 1896), pp. 45 ff., and Guarducci, loc. cit., with whose analysis of the texts, based on that of Hiller in *IG*, I agree. Hiller, when publishing *IG* 155, did not know the tombstone of Dionysodoros, which he subsequently published (see below, pp. 66–7), and which was republished by Maiuri as *NS* 46, and the relationship of which to *IG* 155 is discussed by Miss Guarducci. I repeat here the most probable sequence of the texts, as established by her, with reference to the plates, fig. 113, a–d.

A. (= d (I, 1 in *IG*); here 113, a). The decree of the koinon occupies one main face, which may be called the front. It is inscribed from the top of the stele, and stops about one fifth of the way from the bottom, in the middle of a sentence, but at the end of a line; it continues on the lower half of the right face, and then on the lower part of the back.

B. (= a (II, 40) ; here 113, b). On the upper half of the right face, below a representation of an olive wreath in relief, is inscribed a dedication made by

Dionysodoros, whose honours and titles in the koinon of the Haliastai and Haliadai and that of the Dionysiastai are recorded in full; the dedication is made τριετηρίσι καὶ τῶι κοινῶι, 'to the triennial festivals and to the koinon'.

C. (= *b* (III, 74); here 113, *c*). On the upper half of the back is inscribed a statement of a benefaction (ἐπαύξησε τὸν ἔρανον) by Dion., again with a full record of honours bestowed on him, this time by the koinon of the Paniastai. This text begins with the word καί, and seems to follow straight on from B.

D. (= *c* (IV, 105); here 113, *d*). On the upper part of the left face is inscribed another dedication by Dion. as εὐεργέτας of the koinon of the Haliastai and Haliadai, Διονύσωι Βακχείωι καὶ τῶι κοινῶι.

E. (= *e* (IV, 116); here fig. 113, *d*). On the lower part of the left face is a simple statement that Dion. had been honoured with various honours both in life and (potentially) posthumously; the koina bestowing the honours are not enumerated.

The front face of the block is undecorated, but the right face has at the top a crown of laurel in relief in a rectangular reserved field; the left face has one olive crown (with fillets) and one laurel crown; and the back also has one of laurel and one of poplar. These crowns correspond with those bestowed on Dion. during his lifetime, as recorded in the decree and in the honorific titles which he carries: see Guarducci, p. 24.

Dion.'s tombstone is preserved separately (see pp. 66–7), and this block is not a funerary monument. The references to his death and funerary ceremonies are in the future, and those in E, though not clearly expressed, may also look to the future. The question therefore arises how many, if any, of the separate documents were inscribed in his lifetime. That is the natural explanation of the 'dedicatory' texts, B, C, and D; there is no suggestion that he was dead at the time that they were composed. It is also clear that, though provision is made in A for honours to be bestowed on him at his death, he was still alive at the time that the decree was passed; the funerary honours are prospective. Equally, there is nothing in E to suggest that he was already dead. Thus we may conclude that the whole dossier records the honours bestowed on Dion. during his life, either by direct statement or in his own description of himself in the dedicatory texts, and that there is no reason to suppose either that the decrees were passed posthumously, or that they were inscribed posthumously. No doubt the block, with its emphasis on funerary rites, was erected in the funerary peribolos, probably in anticipation of Dion.'s death.

The chronological order of the texts is indicated internally, and by the method of their composition. A, the decree, was inscribed on the undecorated face of the stone, and continued where blank spaces were available; it was, then, clearly later than the dedicatory texts on the other faces, and these in turn were inscribed in the nineteenth (C) and twenty-fourth (D) years after Dion. became archeranistas of the koinon; the decree (A) covers his activities up to the thirty-fifth year. B carries no date, but is the first of the series.

Hiller, with Wilamowitz's help, determined the correct sequence of the various documents, but he believed the stone to be a funerary altar, and consequently, while rightly regarding A–D as inscribed during the lifetime of

Dion., he thought that E had been inscribed by his survivors. The discovery of Dion.'s tombstone made this hypothesis unnecessary (though Hiller, who first published it from a copy of Saridakis, *AM* 25, 1900, pp. 108–9, and established the fundamental connection between the honours recorded on the tombstone and those on the various documents of *IG* 155, maintained that the true chronological order was not B–C–D, but D–A–B: 'Dieses dürfte damit endgültig als die richtige Zeitfolge der drei Urkunden, *c, d, a* festgestellt sein'); it is possible that the tombstone itself was also inscribed before death (see below, note 380).

355. A, lines 15–25: ἐπα[ινέ]/σαι καὶ στεφανῶσαι Διονυσόδωρον Ἀλεξα[ν]/δρῆ εὐεργέταν τοῦ κοινοῦ εἰς τὸν ἀεὶ χρόν[ον] / χρυσέωι στεφάνωι τῶι ἐκ τοῦ νόμου μεγίστω[ι]· / καὶ ὁ γραμματεὺς ἀναγραψάτω τὰ δόξαντα, / ὁ δὲ ἀρχερανιστὰς καὶ τοὶ ἄρχοντες οἵ τε ἐν[ε]/στακότες καὶ οἱ μετὰ ταῦτα ἀεὶ αἱρούμενοι ἐπ[ι]/μέλειαν ποιείσθωσαν, ὅπως ἐξαιρῆται αὐτῶ[ι] / εἰς στέφανον καθ' ἑκάσταν σύνοδον τριώ/βολο[ν]. / ὑπαρχέτω δὲ αὐτῶι τὰ τίμια καὶ μεταλλάξα[ν]/τι τὸν βίον. The small sum of 3 obols, if understood to refer to a single payment, would not have gone far towards 'the largest gold crown permissible', and Miss Guarducci, p. 28, is no doubt right in assuming that the reference is to a contribution of 3 obols by each member of the koinon.

356. Ibid., lines 25–38, containing the text of the ἀναγόρευσις, which is to be made on the day of the synod after the sacrifices (τᾶι δεύτερον ἁμέραι μετὰ τὰ ἱερά).

357. Ibid., lines 38 ff.: ἐπε[ὶ] / δέ κα μεταλλάξῃ τὸν βίον, τὸ ἐξαιρούμενον / (rt. side) αὐτῶι εἰς τὸν στέφανον εἰς τὸν ἀ[εὶ] χρόνον λανβανόντω ὅ τε ἀρχε/ρανιστὰς καὶ τοὶ λογισταὶ καὶ ὁ ἐπι/στάτας, οἵ κα ἀεὶ ἐν ἀρχᾶι ἔωντι· καὶ / πριάσθων στέφανον καὶ διλήμνιον / καὶ ἀναγορεύσαντες τᾶι δεύτερον / ἁμέραι τᾶν συνόδων ἀποδόσθων κα[ὶ τ]ὸ εὑρὸν καταβαλέτω εἰς τὸ κοινὸν / ὁ ἐπιστάτας ἐν τῶι συλλόγωι ἐν τῶι / ἐχομένωι μηνὶ τᾶν συνόδων, καὶ ὁ / γραμματεὺς ἀναγραψάτω εἰς τοὺς / ἀπολόγους· "Διονυσοδώρου εὐεργέ/τα στεφανωθέντος χρυσέωι στε/φάνωι εἰς τὸν ἀεὶ χρόνον, στεφάνου / τοῦ πραθέντος".

358. Ibid., in continuation: ὑπάρχειν δὲ αὐτῶι / τὰν ἀναγόρευσιν καὶ στεφάνωσιν / καὶ ἐπὶ τῶν τάφων ἐμ μηνὶ Ὑακινθί/ωι καὶ μεταλλάξαντι τὸν βίον, καὶ / ποείσθων τὰν ἐπιμέλειαν ὁμοίως / ὅ τε ἀρχερανιστὰς καὶ τοὶ ἄρχοντες / οἱ μετὰ ταῦτα ἀεὶ αἱρούμενοι· τὸ δὲ ἐ/ξαιρούμενον αὐτῶι ἐν μηνὶ // (lower back) τῶι Ὑακινθίωι εἰς στέφανον εἰς τὸν ἀεὶ χρόνον / καταχρείσθων τοὶ ἄρχοντες καθ' ἕκαστον / ἐνιαυτὸν εἰς τὸν στέφανον τὸν ἀναγορευό/μενον ἐπὶ τάφοις μεταλλάξαντος αὐτοῦ / τὸν βίον, καὶ στεφανούντω αὐτοῦ τὸ μναμεῖον. / ὅτι δέ κα μὴ ποιήσωντι κατὰ τόδε τὸ ψάφισμα οἷς / ἕκαστα ποτιτέτακται, ὀφειλέτω τῶι κοινῶι ὁ μὴ / πράξας τι τῶν γεγραμμένων δραχμὰς ἑκατόν, / ἔνοχος δ' ἔστω καὶ τῶι νόμωι (ὃ)ς κεῖται, εἴ τίς κα / κοινὸν ἀδικῆι, καὶ ἐξέστω τῶι χρήζ(ο)ντι τῶν [ἐ]/ρανιστᾶν ἀπογράψαι αὐτὸν τὸ ἐπιτίμιον, τ[ὸ] / δὲ ψάφισμα τόδ[ε κ]ύριον ἔστω εἰς τὸν ἀεὶ χρό/νον, καὶ μὴ ἐξέστω μήτε ἄρχοντι μήτε ἰδι/ώται μήτε κινεῖν μήτε γνώμαν γράψασθαι / μήτε τοῖς ἄρχουσι προτιθέμειν, ὡς δεῖ τὰς δ[ε]/δομένας τιμὰς Διονυσοδώρωι ἀκύρους εἴμ/μειν· ἢ ὁ γράψας ἢ ὁ προθεὶς ἀποτεισάτω τὸ γε/γραμμένον ἐπιτίμιον δραχμὰς ἑκατόν, καὶ ἁ γνώμ[α / α]ὐτοῦ ἄκυρος ἔστω, καὶ ἔνοχος ἔστω τῶι νόμωι τῶι ἀκινήτωι. Cf. Guarducci, p. 28.

359. Ε: καὶ τιμαθεὶς εἰς τὸν ἀεὶ χρόνον | ἐπαίνωι, χρυσέωι στεφάνωι | [κ]αὶ λευκαίας στεφάνωι κα[ὶ] | ἀναγορεύσει τᾶν τιμᾶν | ἐν ταῖς συνόδοις καὶ ταῖς | ἐπιχύσεσι ἐπὶ τῶν τόπων | εἰς τὸν ἀεὶ χρόνον. The use of 'τόποι' where, as in the decree (note 358), τάφοι might be expected, is characteristic. It occurs in the decree of the Paniastai for Dion., C, l. 81, ἀναγορεύσει τᾶν τιμᾶν ἐπὶ τῶν τόπων, and his tombstone has the same phrase, *NS* 46, lines 6–7: ἀναγορεύσει τᾶν τι/μᾶν ἐπὶ τῶν τόπων καὶ στεφανωθέντος ἐπαίνωι | ἐπὶ τῶν τόπ(ω)ν. τόπος is frequently used of a burial-plot: see Konstantinopoulos, *Arch. Delt.* 21 (1966), pp. 59 ff., apropos of the inscription there published referring to the περιοικοδομὰ τῶν τόπων. Cf. Clem. Alex. *Protr.* iv, 48, 1, γειτνιᾶι δὲ τοῖς τόποις τὸ χωρίον.

360. See above, p. 59.

361. See above, p. 61 and note 350.

362. For εὐεργέτας (τοῦ κοινοῦ) see *IG* 384, Δημύλου Σαμίου | εὐεργέτα καὶ | τᾶς γυναικὸς | Ἀθανοκλείας Φασηλίτ[ιδος]; *AM* 21, 1896, p. 43, no. 12, Ἕρμων | Πτολεμαιεὺς | εὐεργέτας τοῦ κοινοῦ, | χρηστὸς χαῖρε; *Ann.* 2, p. 127, no. 4, Θεύφιλος | Κῶιος | εὐεργέτας τοῦ κοινοῦ; *ILind.* 251. For other examples see below, pp. 66 ff., with notes 380 ff.

363. The matter is not clear in the case of Dionysodoros. He appears to have been president (ἀρχερανιστάς) only of the koinon of the Haliastai and Haliadai, and it does not seem that he was *also* a member of the other two koina by which he was honoured, the Dionysiastai and the Paniastai; he held no office with them, and they are described by him in full, and not simply as συνερανισταί.

364. *PP* 5, 1950, p. 76, no. 2 (LG) (fig. 39, c): l.: Ἀριστόλα/Ἀριστόλα/τοῦ Ἀριστόλα | Λαδαρμίου | εὐεργέτα | τοῦ κοινοῦ; r.: καὶ Πύθωνος | Φιλοτίμου/Καρπαθιοπολίτα.

365. An exception has been seen in *IG* 385 (see above, p. 36, and fig. 98), the funerary monument of Aristoboulos of Termessos and his wife, Isigone of Ephesos, both Euergetai; Aristoboulos is described as εὐεργέτα χοραγήσαντος τρίς. Holleaux and Diehl, *BCH* 9, 1885, p. 121, no. 26, did not comment on the term when they published the inscription. Hiller, ad loc., pointed out that the duties of a χοραγός could be bestowed on a person of foreign birth by decree of the Assembly (see *IG* 127: Ἐπιγόνου Ῥοδιοπολίτα μετοίκου ἐξελευθερωθέντος ὑπὸ τᾶς πόλιος καὶ ξενωθέντος ὑπὸ τᾶς βουλᾶς καὶ τοῦ δάμου καὶ χοραγήσαντος δίς), and consequently that εὐεργέτα might also refer to the city and not to the koinon. The sculptor Phyles of Halicarnassos sometimes signed himself Φυλῆς Πολυγνώτου Ἁλικ. εὐεργέτας (see *ILind.*, p. 52, no. 24), and the title was perhaps bestowed by the city. Other uncertain instances are *IG* 114, Χρυσὼ Κεραμία εὐεργέτ[ις] | ὑπὲρ τοῦ ἀνδρὸς | Θαργηλίου Βαργυλιώτα εὐεργέτα | θεοῖς, and *ILind.* 78 (ca. 275 B.C.) [Ἀρισ]τοτίμα Σαλαμινία τὸν ἄνδρα | Κ[άσ]ανδρον Ἀσπένδιον εὐεργέταν | Ἀθάναι Λινδίαι; cf. Hiller, *IG*, Index, p. 238, § 3, and van Gelder, pp. 282–3. [See ADD.]

366. e.g. *Cl. Rh.* 2, p. 214, no. 53: [Ἑρ]μογένη Φασηλίταν | τὸ κοινὸν τὸ Ἀφροδισιαστᾶν Ἑρμογενείων | ἐτίμασε ἐπαίνωι καὶ θαλλοῦ στεφάνωι καὶ | χρυσέοις δυσί, εἰκόνι χαλκέαι, εὐεργεσίαι, | ἀναγορεύσει τᾶν τιμᾶν ἐν πάσαις ταῖς | συνόδοις εἰς τὸν ἀεὶ χρόνον, κ.τ.λ.; *Assoc.*, p. 147, no. 1: τὸ κοινὸν [τ]ῶν ἐρανιστᾶ[ν] | τῶν Ἀδωνιαζόντων ἐτίμασε Σωσικλῆ Σώσου Κρῆτα εὐεργεσίαι, ἀτελείαι, κ.τ.λ.; ibid.,

no. 11, quoted below, note 369. See also the funerary inscription of Dionysodoros, quoted below, note 380. *IG* 127, a list of victors in games instituted by
a koinon, ends with a list of [εὐεργέται καὶ εὐεργ]έτιδες τοῦ [κοινοῦ].

367. See the full text of the inscription as given in the editions listed above,
note 353, and the passages quoted in notes 355, 357.

368. *IG* 157 (plain circular altar; Ct.), Φιλοκράτευς ὦι ἁ ἐπιδαμία δέδοται,
followed by the list of honours awarded by the ᾽Ισιασταί, his συνερανισταί; 158
(rectangular base); 159; 160, Δαμᾶς Λυδὸς / τιμαθεὶς ὑπὸ / τοῦ κοινοῦ θαλλῶι
στεφάνωι, χρηστὸς χαῖρε. I would regard 161, in which the name of the
honorand is in the accusative, as wholly honorific, and not funerary. To the
same group as 157 belong 164–5; *NS* 39–41; *Cl. Rh.* 2, p. 203, no. 36; *Assoc.*,
p. 152, no. 8; p. 153, no. 11.

369. See, e.g., *IG* 156; *NS* 42, 43; *Assoc.*, p. 147, no. 1; p. 153, no. 11 (here fig.
113, *g*; *non vidi*), with three wreaths of olive above the inscriptions: (a) - - - /
[τιμ]αθέντος ὑπὸ . . . . . τᾶν / ―― στεφάνωι / [καὶ ὁ δεῖνα τιμαθεὶ(?)]ς ὑπὸ Διοσ-
σωτηριασ⟨τ⟩ᾶν / [χρυσ]έωι στεφάνωι· / [χρησ]τοὶ χαίρετε; (b) καὶ Κάρπου Γα-
λά[τα] τιμαθέντος ὑπὸ Δι[οσ]/σωτηρι[α]στᾶν χρυσ[έωι] / στε[φ]άνωι εὐεργεσία[ι]/
ἀτελείαι πάντων· χρηστὸς χ[αῖρε]; note that the valediction at the end of (a) is in
the plural, and also that both the persons commemorated in (a) are male; cf.
below, p. 67; *NS* 43 (IGard.): τὸ κοινὸν τὸ Σαμοθραικιαστᾶν / ἐτίμασε Μοσχίωνα /
Φασηλίταν χρυσέωι / στεφάνωι καὶ ὑπὸ / Παναθηναϊστᾶν / θαλλίνωι καὶ ὑπὸ Ἀφροδισιαστᾶν / θαλλίνωι. *IG* 156, a rectangular base of a circular altar, is betrayed
as funerary by the tense of the final verb: τὸ κοινὸν τὸ Ἁλιαδᾶν καὶ Ἁλιαστᾶν
ἐτίμασε καὶ ἐστεφάνωσε θαλλοῦ στεφάνωι ἐς τὸν ἀεὶ / χρόνον Στρατονίκαν Ἁλι-
καρνασσίδα εὐεργέτιν / εὐνοίας ἕνεκ[α καὶ φιλο]τιμίας ἃν ἔχουσα διετέλει ἐς τὸ
πλῆθος [τὸ Ἁλ]ιαδᾶν καὶ Ἁλιαστᾶν; ibid. 917, a large rectangular altar with
bucrania and garlands from Lartos (*non vidi*), with two inscriptions: in the
centre is a wreath of olive, in a rectangular sunk field, and to the left the
inscription (a) τὸ κοινὸν / τὸ Μηνιαστᾶν / ἐτίμασε / ῾Ηφαιστίωνα / Ἀντιοχῆ /
θαλλίνωι στεφάνωι; and to the right the epitaph of the son, (b): Διόδοτος /
ἐγγενής, / υἱὸς ῾Ηφαιστίωνος· / χρηστοὶ χαίρετε (cf. below, note 371). The Antio-
chene had evidently been a slave; cf. also ibid. 867 (Lindos), (a) [τὸ κ]οινὸν τὸ
Λαπηθιαστᾶν ἐτίμασε Ἀπολλόδωρον / [τοῦ δεῖνος] / θαλλίνοις στεφάνοις δυσίν,
χρυσέοις στεφάνοις δυσίν, / προεδρίαι, ἀτελείαι πάντων ἀρετᾶς ἕνεκα καὶ εὐνοίας ἃν
ἔ[χων] / διατελεῖ εἰς αὐτούς, and (b) of his wife, Νίκαια Λητο[δώρ]ου, / γυνὰ δὲ
Ἀπο[λλοδώρου] / στεφανω[θεῖσα] / ὑπὸ Λαπη[θιαστᾶν] / θαλλίνω[ι στεφάνωι]. The
crowns are not represented on this stone.

370. Peek, *Inschr. dor. Ins.*, no. 2, and pls. I–III, and fig. (here pl. 114, *a, b*); cf.
above, note 159.

371. Peek understands Μέροπος as a simple patronymic, and although on
common tombstones ἐγγενής almost invariably stands without patronymic (*IG*
483–9, 545, 711, 748, 751, 755, 873, 877, 881, 917; *Ann.* 2, p. 158, no. 66;
p. 160, no. 78; p. 163, no. 97; p. 174, no. 157; *NS* 242–8, 285, 428; *Supp. Rod.*
79; *ILind.* 641 (= *IG* 910; two instances; see below, p. 74, and note 431), 650,

658, 666, 689; Robert, *Étud. Anat.*, p. 222 (in Istanbul, recognized as Rhodian by Robert)), the patronymic might be used when the issuing body of a document is a koinon or the tombstone records the honours bestowed by a koinon: see *IG* 917, Διόδοτος ἐγγενὴς υἱὸς ʽΗφαιστίωνος; cf. above, note 369. An exception is *ILind.* 666 (from Mallona), Φρονίμιον / Σατύρου / ἐνγενής. This is an indication of the way in which membership of a koinon, which provided individual prestige, compensated for lack of status in public life.

372. Lines 4 ff.: ἐπὶ δὲ τᾶ[ς] ἐχφο/ρᾶς [τ]ᾶς Μηνοφίλου τοῦ ἰατροῦ γενομένου κωλύ/ματος ὑπομείνας πάντα κίνδυνον / εἰσελθὼν εἰς τὰν οἰκίαν μετὰ τῶν φορέ[ων] ἐ/ξήνεγκε τὸ κᾶδος, κ[αὶ] διαλαβόντες τὸ / ἀγγεῖον κατέστασαν ἐπὶ τὸν τά[φ]ον, κ.τ.λ. For κᾶδος = corpse see, as Peek points out, *ILind.* 487, line 14, ἀπὸ λούσεως κήδευς; cf. also *Syll.*³ 982, line 6: ἀπὸ κήδους καὶ τεκούσης γυναικὸς δευτεραῖος. *LS*⁹, s.v. κῆδος, I, does not make this sense clear. For ἐπὶ τᾶς ἐκφορᾶς (ἐπὶ τῆς ἐκκομιδῆς) see above, p. 59, L. Robert, *Rev. Phil.* 1959, pp. 218–19.

373. See Engelmann, *Ζ. für Pap. u. Epigr.* 6, 1970, pp. 279–82; Robb., *Bull. 1971*, p. 471, no. 466.

374. As, e.g., in *IG* 1032, quoted by Engelmann, λοιμικᾶς τε διαθέσιος γενομένας καὶ πολλῶν εἰς τοὺς ἐσχ[ά]τους κινδύνους ἐμπεσόντων; *ICret.* i, p. 249, no. 4, XIII, ll. 6 ff. (Olus), honours for a Casian doctor who had helped the city, ἐμπεπτω-κότος ἁμὶν καιροῦ σκληροῦ καὶ χρειῶν πολλῶν καὶ ἀναγκαίων διὰ τὰς φθορὰς τὰς τῶν ἀνθρώπων καὶ τὸν ἐμπεπτωκότα λοιμόν; *Syll.*³ 731, line 7 (Tomi): τῶν δὲ διὰ τὴν λοιμικὴν περίστασιν καὶ τὰς ἀρρωστίας μὴ δυναμένων [φυ]λάσσειν τὴν πατρίδα.

375. The phrase in line 12, περιθε[ῖ]σα[ν] (sc. τὴν σύνοδον) παρησίαν καὶ τοῖς ἄλλοις ἐράνοις, is indeed obscure, and Peek has no explanation to offer: 'Ich kann die ganze Ungereimtheit des Satzes nur als solche kennzeichnen, einen irgend überzeugenden Vorschlag, ihn umzuschreiben, habe ich nicht anzu-bieten.' My own suggestion as to the intended meaning of the phrase is sup-ported by the late lexical evidence given by *LS*⁹, e.g. Aristaen. ii, 7 (p. 77, Mazal, Teubner, 1971): οὐ γὰρ εἶχε παρρησίαν τῶν αὐτῶν μετασχεῖν τῆι δεσποί-νηι; Vett. Val., p. 6, line 3: ζωῆς καὶ θανάτου παρρησίαν ἔχοντες. The use is already foreshadowed in Isocr. ii. 3; see further the excellent article by Schleier, in *Theol. WB z. NT*, s.v. The phrase thus provides the documentary background for the practice already noted, by which a member of a koinon might be honoured by other koina.

376. Lines 15–18: ἀναθῆναί [τε Χρύσιππον καὶ] / στεφανῶσαι θαλλοῦ στεφάνωι κατὰ τὸν νόμον [κ]αὶ εὐεργε[σίαι· δότω δὲ τὸ ἀργύρι]/ον ἐπι τὸν ⟨στέφαν⟩ον ὁ λογιστὰς ὁ ἐν ἀρχᾶι ὤν, ἐς δὲ πι[νακίδα ἀναγράψαι αὐτὸν ὡς τιμαθέν]/τα μέγιστα ὑπὸ τοῦ κοινοῦ.

377. The Ἀθηνασταί are not recorded with this specific form of the title, but it may be only a variant of the Ἀθαναϊσταί, a koinon frequently referred to (see *Assoc.*, pp. 176 ff.).

378. See above, p. 64.

158   *Rhodian Funerary Monuments*

379. *NS* 46 (IGard.), cf. above, p. 62; figs. 42, *a*, and 113, *e* and *f*, from *NS*; unfortunately the altar is now cemented to the ground beneath a tree in continuous shade, and satisfactory photography is not possible.

380. Ἰάκχου καὶ Διονυσοδώρου Ἀλεξανδρέων εὐεργετᾶν, | τιμαθέντων ὑπὸ τοῦ κοινοῦ εὐεργεσίαι καὶ | ἀτελείαι πάντων διὰ βίου, καὶ στεφανωθέντων | ἐπαίνωι θαλλοῦ στεφάνωι, τιμαθέντος δὲ Διονυσοδώρου καὶ ὑπὸ τοῦ κοινοῦ τοῦ Ἁλιαστᾶν | ἀτελείαι πάντων διὰ βίου καὶ ἀναγορεύσει τᾶν τι|μᾶν ἐπὶ τῶν τόπων καὶ στεφανω-θέντος ἐπαίνωι | ἐπὶ τῶν τόπ(ω)ν εἰς τὸν ἀεὶ χρόνον· τιμαθέντος δὲ καὶ ὑπὸ τοῦ κοινοῦ τοῦ Διονυσιαστᾶν εὐεργεσί|αι καὶ ἀτελείαι πάντων διὰ βίου καὶ στεφανωθέν|-τος ἐπαίνωι χρυσέωι ἐπ' ἀρετᾶι. The wreaths represented on the two faces were identified as olive and oak by Maiuri, but Miss Guarducci, op. cit., p. 24, argues convincingly that the wreaths should correspond with those of the honorific monuments, which are laurel and poplar (see above, note 354).

381. See above, note 364.

382. I accept in this connection the arguments of Miss Guarducci, pp. 23–4. She is clearly right in maintaining, against Hiller, *AM* 25, 1900, p. 109, that the unidentified koinon of line 2 is that of the Πανιασταί, and that it was in the cemetery of this koinon that the altar was erected.

383. *NS* 193; cf. above, p. 53.

384. *NS* 192. I assume that Μῆδος is the ethnic, but it is not impossible that it is a patronymic.

385. Sufficient examples of this are to be found in the preceding notes, esp. note 362.

386. For example see the stele with epigrams referring to the στέφανος of the deceased noted in *B &WG*, Suppl. (*Op. Ath.* 10, 1971), p. 79 (on pp. 182 ff.), namely *GVI* 1881 and 1917. I may also call attention here to the circular altar with garland of oak leaves represented on the top of a decree from Selymbria, *SGDI* 3069 (*BCH* 36, 1912, p. 556, no. 13; the accompanying decree for a komarch refers only to the common act of crowning); and to that from Tomi, Michel, 1289 (Stoian, *Tomitana* (Bucarest, 1962), pp. 57–8, pl. 1), with in-scription Ἀργαδέων φύλη | ἐστεφάνωσε | Κερκίονα Τιμομάχου | φυλαρχήσαντα; though neither of these is funerary; see also L. Robert, *Rev. Phil.* 1959, pp. 218 ff., apropos of instances from Bulgaria. [See Add.]

387. The practice by which the crown is represented above the inscription, with the name of the issuing body, commonly the demos, inscribed within it, is extremely frequent, and needs no illustration here.

388. For examples on rectangular altars see fig. 39, *b*, with three wreaths of (apparently) olive, no bosses; fig. 42, *b*, olive, faint traces of two bosses; for circular altars with wreaths see figs. 58, *a*; 67, *b*; also *IG* 754 (Monolitho; *non vidi*; *IG*, sq.), a circular altar with three crowns above the inscription; *Assoc.*, p. 153, no. 11, and fig. vi (here fig. 113, *g*), described above, note 369. For the

crowns on the rectangular base see fig. 113, *h* (IGard.), with three wreaths of olive with fillets. Maiuri refers, in a note on the rectangular base with trochilus, *NS* 42, to 'un'altra base di βωμός circolare in marmo grigio . . . la quale recava sul lato principale il rilievo di tre ghirlande *oleaginae*' [his italics]. It is likely that this is the piece reproduced in fig. 113, *h*.

389. *IG* 656 (*BMI* 360; *Syll.*³ 1258), for the provenance of which it gives only 'Rhodes'; *BMSculpt.* iii, no. 2400. The full and apicated lettering combined with small omicron and pi with short right-hand stroke is characteristic of ii/i a.C.

390. *IG* 736 (*Syll.*³ 1118); cf. above, p. 61, and note 351.

391. See above, p. 39, and note 217.

392. The entry is οἱ συνηριστευκότες τὴν ἐλευθέραν δοῦλοι, which was emended by Steph. to τοῖς ἐλευθέροις (see Hiller, *Syll.*³ ad loc.).

393. = Deinarch. fr. xvi, 5, Bait.–Saup.

393a. [Lys.] ii, 66: Ἐκεῖνοι μὲν οὖν διὰ τοὺς ἐν Πειραιεῖ κινδύνους ὑπὸ πάντων ἀνθρώπων ζηλοῦνται· ἄξιον δὲ καὶ τοὺς ξένους τοὺς ἐνθάδε κειμένους ἐπαινέσαι . . . ἀνθ' ὧν ἡ πόλις αὐτοὺς καὶ ἐπένθησε καὶ ἔθαψε δημοσίαι, καὶ ἔδωκεν ἔχειν αὐτοῖς τὸν ἅπαντα χρόνον τὰς αὐτὰς τιμὰς τοῖς ἀστοῖς. Cf. Tod's comments, *GHI*, ii, pp. 9 ff., on no. 100 (*Syll.*³ 120; important new fragment, *BSA* 47, 1952, pp. 102–17 (*SEG* xii, 84)); cf. also Wilhelm, *Att. Urk.* iii, p. 9.

394. Hiller, *Syll.*³, 1258, understands the definition in Hesych. to indicate a source in which the lot of the slaves was deplored: 'ubi servi qui libertatis praemio proposito ad arma vocati fortissime pugnantes occubuerant deplorabantur, quia non una cum civibus honorificentissima sepultura efferrentur'.

395. The Palmyrene inscriptions in which the word ταφεών occurs are more numerous than they were in Newton's time: see Cantineau, *Inv. des Inscr. de Palmyre* vii (1931), no. 4 (= *LBW* 2619), line 5 (τὸ μνημεῖον ταφεῶνα ἔκτισεν, κ.τ.λ.); ibid. viii (1936), no. 55 (*LBW* 2621; *IGRR* iii, 1034) (τὸ μνημεῖον τοῦ ταφεῶνος ἔκτισεν, κ.τ.λ.); ibid. iv (1930), no. 13 (τὸ σπήλαιον τοῦ ταφεῶνος ὤρυξεν), restored from the Palmyrene; ibid. 14 (*LBW* 2625) (τὸ σπήλαιον τοῦ ταφαιῶνος); ibid. 25 (same formula). It does not seem to me that ταφεών in these instances means, as Newton and *LS*⁹ maintain, 'a burial ground', i.e. a plot of land containing a number of graves; its regular conjunction with a word meaning a tomb (μνημεῖον, σπήλαιον) indicates that it refers to a single plot or sometimes to the monument itself: see Gawlikowski, *Monum. funéraires de Palmyre* (Warsaw, 1970), pp. 193 ff., nos. 35, 50. The Palmyrene versions have their own formula.

396. For τοφιών see *DGE* 62 (Lex Heracl.), line 138: οὐδὲ τοφιῶνας ἐν τᾶι ἱαρᾶι γᾶι ποιησεῖ, on which see Buck–Petersen, *Rev. Index*, p. 253, s.v. ταφεών, and Fraser and Bean, p. 17, note 3; for ἐντόφιον see the Cyrenaean *lex sacra*, *SEG* ix, 72 (Sokolowski, II, 115), lines 47–9: τῶν δὲ χρημά/[τω]ν, ἇς κα δεκατὰ ἦι, ἐντόφιον οὐκ ἐνθησεῖ οὐδέ/[πω ο]ὐδὲ ἕν (for ἐντόφια = ἐντάφια see the Labyad

funerary law at Delphi, *Syll.*² 438, C, 1, Sokolowski, Suppl., 77, line 1: *Hόδ'* ό τεθμὸς πὲρ τῶ/ν ἐντοφηίων) ; as Buck, *Gr. Dial.*³, p. 20, §6, says, the explanation of the vocalization ο for α may not be the same in all cases.

397. See above, pp. 61–2.

398. The genitive probably represents an extension of the possessive sense found on votive altars, etc.; one may also compare the 'thematic' genitives standing as rubrics, for which see Nachmanson, *Göteborgs Högsk. Årsskr.* 48, 1942 (2), p. 40: e.g. the headings of *Dikaiomata*, ψευδομαρτυρίου (l. 24), [σι]δήρου ἐπαντάσεως (l. 186), μεθύοντος ἀδικιῶν (l. 193), etc. Cf. further, Turner, *JEA* 60, 1974, p. 241. It should be noted that, in fact, on horoi-stones from Attica the word ὅρος or ὅροι is never omitted in the phrases ὅρος θήκης, ὅρος μνήματος, ὅρος ἱερô, ὅρος χωρίο, etc. (cf. above, note 350).

399. xx, 100, 1.

400. *Mithrid.* 24–7. As in 305/4, there was considerable siege warfare, in which it would be natural to employ slaves, though Appian does not mention any.

401. *B & WG*, p. 158.

402. (a) *IG* 239: Ἱπποστράτη Ἀντιγένευς | Νισυρία | γυνὰ δὲ Ἀγία | χρηστὰ χαῖρε, no indication of date; (b) 266: Ἕρμων Εἰρηναίου Εὐθυνίτας χρηστὸς χαῖρε; (c) *NS* 72: Ὀνασὶς | Ἀρτωνίδα | Νισυρία, | γυνὰ δὲ Ἀριστογένευς | [χρ]ηστὰ χαῖρε, ii a.C.?; the presence of the patronymic in (a) and (c) indicates that Νισυρία is a demotic and not a city-ethnic (cf. pp. 46–7); (d) *NS* 99: [Κ]α[λλι]νίκα Πύθωνος | Τλωία | χρηστὰ | χα[ῖρε], where Τλωία is the demotic and not the city-ethnic; (e) *Ann.* 2, p. 130, no. 18: Λυσίας | Θρασυμβρότου | Νεττίδας /χρηστὲ χαῖρε.

403. It is not possible to quote all the instances of χ.χ. which appear in these categories of tombstones. In the various groups the approximate figures (based on the collections of tombstones in *IG, NS, Ann.* 2, and *Cl. Rh.* 2) are as follows: (a) out of a total of 128 relevant tombstones of persons denoted by name and patronymic only, 9 have (χρηστὸς) χαῖρε; (b) out of a total of 118 persons denoted by ethnics of race only, 40 have χ.χ.; (c) out of a total of 240 persons denoted by city-ethnics only, 65 have χ.χ.; and (d) out of a total of 135 persons denoted by name alone, 66 have χ.χ. Of these hardly one can be dated with any confidence to iii a.C., except *IG* 317 (class (c)), which is inscribed in a very elegant hand of the middle or later part of that century (*IG*, sq.).

404. Inevitably we lack the necessary series of tombstones from the home cities to establish this in any detail, but note, for Athens, *NS* 137, Ἀξιοθέα | Ἀθηναία | χρηστὰ χαῖρε, and three cases of Cyrenaeans with χ.χ., *IG* 437, 439, and, a piece of some interest, *Cl. Rh.* 2, p. 219, no. 61 (ii a.C.; *non vidi*), Ἀντίπατρος | Ἀσκληπιάδου | Κυρηναῖος | πρόξενος | χρηστὸς χαῖρε (cf. above, note 242); as at Athens there are enough tombstones surviving from Cyrene to indicate that the formula was not used there: see *SEG* ix, Index, p. 138, s.v. **Tituli Sepulcrales.**

405. Thus in the series from *Nisyros*, *IG* xii. 3, 108–66, the formula occurs only on late tombstones, or on those of people of humble status or foreigners (130, 140 (ἐγγενής), 147, 149, 159 (Μύνδιος), 162); other examples, Peek, *Inschr. Nis.*, p. 382, nos. 18, 22; p. 386, no. 34 (above, p. 24 and note 109, and fig. 54, *a*), [Ἀπολ]λώνιος Ἀστυπαλαιεὺς / χρηστὸς χαῖρε; id., *Inschr. dor. Ins.*, p. 31, no. 73; p. 32, no. 79; Ἄρχ. 'Εφ., 1913, p. 10, no. 10; p. 11, nos. 12 (χαῖρε alone), 16, 22 (Μένανδρε χρηστὲ χαῖρε, on the rectangular altar discussed above, pp. 18–19, and note 78; fig. 48, *a*, *b*); p. 13, nos. 27, 32; p. 14, nos. 39, 41, 42. *Telos*: *IG* xii. 3, 50–82, also of humble status (only present in 78 and 79, the second 'aetatis pravae'); also from Telos, Susini, *Supp. Epigr.*, p. 285, no. 15 (cf. above, p. 24, note 108, and fig. 53, *b*), which has the patronymic; Peek, *Inschr. dor. Ins.*, p. 25, no. 54; p. 26, no. 60. *Peraea*: Thyssanous; Fraser and Bean, p. 39, no. 25; Ἄρχ. 'Εφ., 1922, p. 48, nos. 39–40 (both late); ibid. 1911, p. 64, no. 57 (Φίλι[π]πε Ξάνθιε / π[α]τὴρ Μηνοφιλίας / χρηστὲ χαῖρε). None of the instances quoted here from the islands or the Peraea involves the use of the Rhodian demotic with χ.χ. There are one or two with patronymics.

406. *Ann.* 2, p. 157, no. 58: Στράτιος / Βρέττιος χαῖρε· καὶ σύ γε; ibid., no. 62: 'Ελάφιον / Χîα / χαῖρε· / καὶ σύ γε / πολλά; *IG* 565: —αρχος / χρηστ[ὸς] χαῖρε· / κα[ὶ σ(τ?)ύ]γε (ii a.C.; *IG*, sq.); ibid. 638: Καλλίκων / αὐτοκασίγ[νητε / χαῖρε· κ[α]ὶ σύ γ[ε]; ibid. 717 (*Tit. Cam.* 168, g): Κλεὼ χρηστὰ / καὶ πᾶσι ποθεινὰ χαῖρε· καὶ σύ γε (letters of ii/i a.C.; *IG*, sq.); ibid. 946 (nr. Lindos): 'Ρόδιππος / χρηστὸς χαῖρε· καὶ σύ γε; ibid. 1019 (Carpathos; i a.C.; *IG*, sq.): Εὔδημος Εὐδή[μου] / χρηστὸς χαῖρε· καὶ σύ γε.

407. *NS* 232 (IGard.), inscribed on a small stele in letters of ii/i a.C. The formula and approximations to it are, of course, very frequent within the general framework of the χαῖρε, παροδῖτα, παριόντες formulae; but ἀπότρεχε is a curious word in the context, and I cannot point to another instance of it.

408. *Ann.* 2, p. 179, no. 187, is the base of a stele, and the front of the base is inscribed χρηστοὶ χαίρετε, and on one side χαῖρε καὶ σύ. The front clearly contains the address *to* the deceased, and consequently χαῖρε καὶ σύ on the side, apparently written in the same hand, must be the address *of* the deceased. Further, in *NS* 232, just quoted, the dead woman *must* be the speaker of the reported second part, χαίρειν . . . ἀπότρεχε. In general, there seems no reason to attribute the χαῖρε of the first part of the formula to the deceased and the καὶ σύ γε to the living, as Pfohl, *Untersuch.*, pp. 69–70 (apropos of *IG* ii². 11552) does. Loch, *Festschrift Friedländer*, pp. 278 ff., takes χαῖρε καὶ σύ γε as *all* spoken by the deceased, and this is certainly sometimes so, when there are two χαῖρε (as in the instances noted by L. Robert, *L'Antiq. class.* 32, 1963, p. 13), but in the majority of cases it seems to go more naturally with the preceding χρηστ- or personal name, and I have adopted this solution in the relevant instances, quoted above, note 406 (as did Hiller, who in all such cases printed a stop after χαῖρε): see further G. Daux, *BCH* 98, 1974, p. 554; ibid. 99, 1975, p. 160. Note the passage of Plat. *Phaed.* 116 d: the janitor bringing the hemlock says νῦν οὖν . . . χαῖρέ τε καὶ πειρῶ ὡς ῥᾶστα φέρειν τὰ ἀναγκαῖα, καὶ ἄμα δακρύσας μεταστρεφόμενος ἀπῄει. καὶ ὁ Σωκράτης ἀναβλέψας πρὸς αὐτόν, καὶ σύ, ἔφη,

χαῖρε. Socrates speaks as already beyond the grave. For πᾶσι ποθεινός, not a description of the deceased, but reflecting the feeling of the survivors, see *Cl. Rh.* 2, p. 217, no. 58, ἰατρὸς πᾶσι ποθινός.

409. For ἐλεήμων see *NS* 110 (ii a.c.?): ʿΗράκλειτε / Ἀρτέμ[ω]νος / ἐλεήμων / χαῖρε. I cannot quote another instance of ἐλεήμων on a tombstone, though no doubt one exists.

410. For Arsinoe Eleemon see Fraser, *Ptol. Alex.* i, pp. 35, 237, and ii, note 276, and for the use of the epithet for Aphrodite in Cyprus see Jessen, *RE*, s.v. Eleemon. Tod, *BSA* 46, 1951, p. 189, quotes our instance of ἐλεήμων, and describes it as 'rare but significant'.

411. *IG* 584: Θύρσος / εὐδαίμων / χρηστὸς χαῖρε. Once more I can quote no exact parallel. The notion of the 'happiness' of the dead is of course as old as the notion of the νῆσοι τῶν μακάρων: see Rohde, *Psyche*, ii³, pp. 369–70, with 370, note 2 (= E.T., pp. 536–7, with p. 564, note 99), and for the later, epigraphical use of the notion, Lattimore, *Themes*, pp. 35–6, 52; but εὐδαίμων is not found in this context. G. Lejeune-Dirichlet, *De Veterum Macarismis* (*RVV* 14(4), 1914), pp. 22–3, says: 'Εὐδαίμων ab usu vulgari magis alienum fuisse ex ea re fortasse concludi potest, quod et a comoediae novae poetis rarius adhibetur et in sacra scriptura tam veteris tam novi testamenti non invenitur, contra philosophi hanc vocem vulgari adiectivo μακάριος aperte praetulerunt, nescio an Platonis atque Aristotelis exemplum secuti. Recentiores demum utraque voce aeque utuntur, immo iam adeo confundunt, ut μακάριος etiam de divitibus, εὐδαίμων nonnumquam de mortuis usurpetur' [ibid. fn. 2, 'Vox εὐδαίμων in titulis bis de mortuis usurpatur, *IG* xii. 1, 584; xii. 5, 389. Quam non ad aliquam sectam spectare, ut Hiller de Gaertringen ad *IG* xii. 5, 389 putabat, sed a simili mortuorum appellatione usitatissima μακάριος translatam esse puto']. *IG* xii. 5, 389 (Paros) is a late sarcophagus carrying six funerary reliefs in rectangular frames, each with an inscription beneath it; no. 6, the latest ('inscr. 6 serioris aetatis est, fortasse tertii p. Chr. n. saec.', Hiller) has beneath it Θάλλουσα Τροφίμης / εὐδέμων / εὐδαίμων; Hiller's comment is 'pravo εὐδέμων substitutum εὐδαίμων (id quod vix est nomen sed fortasse ad aliquam sectam spectat; cf. *IG Ins.* 1. 584...)'. The photograph is illegible, but Hiller prints late forms of majuscules. [See ADD.]

412. See Lattimore, op. cit., pp. 35–6, 56, where there are several examples of this phraseology.

413. *IG* 480, inscribed in good, apicated lettering of early ii a.c. The theta is Θ (*IG*, sq.).

414. It also occurs in the very late epitaph, *IG* 671, ending κατάκειμαι εὐσεβής. Other instances are given by Robert, *Hellenica*, ii, p. 81, and by Tod, op. cit., p. 188 (from *IG* xiv). The Rhodian example seems the earliest. An example from Perge, Bean, *Türk Tarih Bell.* 22, 1958, p. 86, no. 117 (*SEG* vi 656), here fig. 116, *b*, may be of the late hellenistic period. [See ADD.]

415. See *Ptol. Alex.* i, p. 264.

415a. We may compare *IG* 593, Εὐφροσύνα θεοσεβὴς / χρηστὰ χαῖρε where the epithet clearly points to a Jewish connection (cf. Robert, *Étud. anat.*, p. 411, note 5). In spite of the majuscule copy the lettering is probably of ii/i a.C. (*IG*, sq.).

416. For Rhodos the only evidence is *IG* 8 (ii/i a.C.): [ἱερεῖς – – – Σαρά]πιος· Στράτιππος Ἀσ[—, Ἀπο]λλόδοτος Β̄ ῾Ιστάνιος, but for Lindos it is abundant from iii a.C., since the priests of Sarapis occur in the dedications of priests, magistrates, etc., from 242 B.C., and they are always normal citizens of Lindos: see Fraser, *Op. Ath.* 3, 1960, p. 28, note 1, with ref. to *ILind.* 102, 166 (?), 167, etc.

417. See *WB*, and Foraboschi, *Supp. Pap. alt.* s.v.

418. *IG* 711 (= *Tit. Cam.* 168, *a*), from Kalavarda (but not still visible there, as Carratelli, after Hiller, says): Ἀφροδίσιος ἐγγενὴς / χρηστὸς χαῖρε· / καὶ κατὰ πᾶν ὅσιος. The inscription is in small, neat apicated lettering of i a.C. The pedimental stele on which it is inscribed had three acroteria of the type shown in figs. 19, *a*, 21, *d*, and 22. In the rubric to *Tit. Cam.*, taken from *IG*, the words 'tribus acroteriis' are omitted.

419. Tod, op. cit., p. 188, quotes *IG* xiv. 1480 (*IGRR* i, 227), lines 3–4: κεῖται δὲ οὖν σὺν αὐτῶι υἱὸς αὐτοῦ Αὐρήλιος ᾿Ιοῦστος, γλυκὺ πνε[ῦμα . . .] / καὶ ὅσιος, πράξας στρατείας τρεῖς, σεξαγηναρίας τρό[φων . . .], and Dörner, *Inschr. u. Denkm. aus Bithynien*, no. 121, in the phrase ζήσας ὁσίως. ὅσιος (καὶ δίκαιος) is of course very frequent in Jewish epitaphs: see Frey, *CIJ*, i, index, s.v., and Lifshitz, *ZDPV*, 78, 1962, p. 73.

420. Aesch. *Septem*, 1015: ἱερῶν πατρωίων δ᾿ ὅσιος ὢν μομφῆς ἄτερ. The phrase κατὰ πᾶν presumably means 'in every respect', but it is not common.

421. *NS* 163 (pl. 37, *b*).

422. *Ann.* 2, p. 163, no. 99. Maiuri restored ᾿Ιά[σωνος (*sic*)], but a feminine name is more probable, e.g. ᾿Ιά[δος]; cf. *IG* 901; *SEG* xvii, 607.

423. See, e.g., for Mylasa, *Syll.*³ 1246: δαιμόνων ἀγαθῶν / Ἀντέρωτος τοῦ Διο/νυσίου καὶ τῆς γυναι/κὸς αὐτοῦ Λεοντίου / καὶ τοῦ υἱοῦ αὐτῶν / Ἀντέρωτος καὶ ᾿Ισοχρύσου; *AM* 15, 1890, p. 276, nos. 23 (= *Syll.*³ 1246) –25, 27. The same formula is found at Iasos: see Bean and Cook, *BSA* 52, 1957, p. 205, no. 1 (*c.* 200 B.C.), heading a list of names of deceased mercenaries(?) of varied nationality; Carratelli, *Ann.* 39–40, 1961–2, p. 592, no. 23: Ἀγαθίνου / τοῦ ᾿Ιάσο/νος Ἀπα/μέως δα[ί]/μονος ἀγαθοῦ; ibid., no. 26, δαιμόνων ἀγαθῶν / Νικίου τοῦ ῾Εκαταίου, ζῇ, where the plural is not in agreement with the dead man, and may be a translation of *Dis Manibus* (see above, p. 51, below, p. 73).

424. See *ILind.* 252 (*c.* 115 B.C.), line 251.

425. See *IG* 161, line 5.

426. *Ann.* 2, p. 138, no. 7 (H. 0·14 m, W. 0·10 m, Th. 0·07 m), Ἀγαθοῦ / Δαίμο[νο]ς κα[ὶ] / Ἀγαθᾶς Τύχας. Ἀγαθὰ Τύχα appears with Εὐετηρία in *Tit. Cam.* 145, Ἀγαθᾶς Τύχας / [Ε]ὐετηρίας; cf. *Syll.*[3] 961 (Smyrna).

427. *Syll.*[3] 1044 (Sokolowski, I, no. 72), lines 9–10, the god, on the inquiry of Posidonios, enjoins sacrifices to the Ἀγ. Δαιμ. Ποσ. καὶ Γοργ., and at that time the couple were evidently alive; in the third document on the stone, headed ἔδοξεν Ποσειδωνίωι καὶ τοῖς ἐκγόνοις τοῖς / ἐκ Ποσειδωνίου, κ.τ.λ., it is decreed (ll. 34 ff.) τῆι μὲν π[ρ]ώτηι / θύειν Τύχηι Ἀγαθῆι πατρὸς καὶ μητρὸς Ποσε[ιδω]νίου / [κ]ριὸν καὶ Δαίμονι Ἀγαθῶι Ποσειδωνίου καὶ [Γο]ργίδος / κριόν, κ.τ.λ.

428. On *Syll.*[3] 1246: 'Sic Latina Dis Manibus Graece redduntur frequenter cum alibi tum in titulis Mylasensibus.'

429. For the date of the first occurrence of *Dis Manibus* see Sandys–Campbell p. 62.

430. *Ann.* 2, p. 169, no. 130 (*non vidi*); the letters are said to be well cut and apicated.

431. *IG* 910, republished from a copy of Kinch as *ILind.* 641. The stone is very worn (*IG*, sq.) and Hiller's text reads Ἕρμων ἐγγενὴς καὶ Θαῒς ἐγγενὴς / ἀδελφοί, while Kinch read for the second name ΝΟΛΗΣ, which he corrected to (Μ)ολῆς. The squeeze shows almost nothing. In any case it is very likely that the two ἐγγενεῖς are brother and sister or two brothers, and there is no reason to assign a transferred meaning to ἀδελφοί. I judge the lettering to be of ii a.C.

432. See briefly *Ptol. Alex.* i, pp. 117–18, and ii, p. 209, note 201.

433. See *LBW* 503, *a*, *b* (= *Ann.* 4/5, p. 472, no. 17); Newton, *Halic.* II, ii, p. 704, no. 120, a list of those admitted to the rank of ἄνδρες, ending ἱερῶν ἀδελφῶν; Bean and Cook, *BSA* 50, 1955, p. 103, no. 17: Γαίου καὶ / Λευκίου / τῶν ἀδελφ/ (ῶν); cf. Poland, op. cit., pp. 54–5. The possibility that the ἀδελφοί are Christian in these cases, as Poland suggests, p. 55, note ***, can probably be discounted. Ἀδελφός may also be used of a professional colleague, e.g. *IG* xiv. 2516 (Béziers): Φίλων Σωτάδου Μοψεάτης ῥήτωρ Ἀρτεμιδώρῳ τῷ ἀδελφῷ ῥήτορι.

434. See *CIRB*, Index, p. 909, and especially nos. 1281 ff. (εἰσποιητοὶ ἀδελφοί); cf. Poland, loc. cit.

435. *Syll.*[3] 1109, line 54: ἐὰν δὲ ἰόβακ/χον ἀδελφὸς ἰσέρχηται ψήφῳ δοκιμασθείς, / διδότω * ν'; cf. above, p. 59.

436. *IG* 986.

437. The inscription, inscribed on a rectangular base, is lost, and the supplement of the last line is uncertain, and depends on the interpretation of the relationship between the two parties. Hiller restored [τέκνων αὐτοῦ (?) ἡ]ρώων, indicating that, subject to the query, he regarded the relationship as that of blood brother and sister. [τέκνων αὐτῶν] is, however, equally possible epi-

graphically, if the two persons are regarded as husband and wife. If ἡρῴων is sound (the text is known only from a copy by Ross) a supplement along wholly different lines—e.g. [ἄλλων] ἡρῴων—does not seem likely. For *IG* 987 see below, p. 78.

438. For Romans on Cos see Herzog, *SBBerl. Akad.* 1901, pp. 470–94, esp. 490–2, 'Das Heiligthum des Apollo in Halasarna'; Degrassi, *Cl. Rh.* 10, pp. 203–13 (= *Scr. Var.* i, pp. 535–42); Pugliese Carratelli, *Synteleia Arangio-Ruiz* (1964), pp. 816 ff.

439. For recent discussions see Lattimore, op. cit., pp. 97 ff.; Nock, *HTR* 37, 1944, pp. 141–74 (= *Essays on Religion and the Ancient World* (ed. Z. Stewart, 1972), ii, pp. 575 ff.); Pleket, *Leyden Inscrs.*, pp. 28–31, a useful summary. Of the old accounts that of Rohde, *Psyche*, ii³, pp. 358 ff. (= E.T., pp. 531 ff.), contains the essentials of the matter in its correct perspective; Farnell, *Greek Hero Cults*, p. 367, has very little to say of this 'conventional' Heroization.

440. See Kurtz and Boardman, *Greek Burial Customs*, p. 301.

441. *IG* xii. 7, 515 (ll. 39 ff. only: *IGRR* iv, 1000; Sokolowski, II, 61). This important text must be studied in full, and small excerpts do not help much. The funds were provided by Kritolaos, the father of Aleximachos, but the entire responsibility was assumed by the state and organized by officials appointed by the Assembly. The document is of the late hellenistic period, and in line 57 οἱ παραγενόμενοι Ῥωμαῖοι are listed along with πολῖται and ξένοι among the beneficiaries.

442. *IG* xii. 3, 330 (Laum, *Stiftungen*, ii, 43; Sokolowski, II, 135, with references to earlier editions). See especially c, lines 2 ff.: Ἐπειδὴ Ἐπικτήτα Γρίννου ... ἐπιδέδωκε ἐς θυσίαν ταῖς Μούσαις καὶ τοῖς ἥρωσι ... (9) ὥστε γίνεσθαι τὰν συναγωγὰν ἐπ᾽ ἀμέρας τρεῖς ἐν τῶι Μουσείωι ... (13) καὶ θύεν τὸ[ν μ]ὲν τὰν πράταν ἐπιμηνιεύοντα ταῖς Μούσαι[ς, τὸ]ν δὲ τὰν δευτέραν τοῖς ἥρωσι Φοίνικι (E's husband) καὶ [Ἐπι]κτήται, τὸν δὲ τὰν τρίταν τοῖς ἥρωσι Κρατ[ησ]ιλόχωι καὶ Ἀνδραγόραι (her sons).

443. e.g. 889: Καλλικράτης | Θεομνάστου | ἥρως; 890: Χαρίλαος Ναυκρά/τους ἥρως. || Θευδοσία ἡρῷσσα.

443a. The circular funerary altars of Xanthos and area (Patara, etc.), of which regrettably I have no photographs, are regularly inscribed with formulae in which the deceased is called ἥρως, in either the accusative or the dative case: e.g. from Xanthos, *TAM*, ii, 1, 372: Σεῖμα Πάπου | Λεωνίδην | Ἱεροκλέους | Ἰοβάτειον | τὸν ἑατῆς ἄνδρα | ἥρωα; cf. 373–4; 375: Τληπόλεμος Στασιθέμιος | καὶ Λυκία Τειθωνοῦ | Τληπόλεμωι τῶι υἱῶι | ἥρωι; others have more elaborate formulae; from Patara, ibid. 471: Ἑρμαῖος Ἑρμα/ίου τοῦ Δαφνα/ίου Ἑρμαίωι τῶι | πατρὶ ἥρωι.

444. Note that *IG* xii. 3, 926, Φιλόξενος τὸν ἴδιον | θρεπτὸν | Ἀβάσκαντο/ν ἀφηρῴϊξε, from an Athenian private collection, is erroneously given as Attic

by Kirchner, *IG* ii². 10531, *a* (p. 886), and thence employed by Pfohl, op. cit., pp. 68, 69, as a basis for discussion of the Athenian Hero-epitaphs.

445. See Thönges-Stringaris, *AM* 80, 1965, pp. 48 ff.

446. *CAF* i, p. 622, fr. 75. The words are attributed to the *Menelaos* of Plato by Zenob. vi, 17, whose comment, φασὶ δέ, ὅτι ἐν Θήβαις οἱ ἑαυτοὺς ἀναιροῦντες οὐδεμιᾶς τιμῆς μετεῖχον, is based on a remark of Aristotle (= fr. 502 R). Zenob. says that the words are κατ' εὐφημισμόν.

446a. See below, note 451.

447. IGard., seemingly unpublished.

448. *IG* 986: see above, p. 74, and note 437; 987, now in Athens (cf. Susini, *Supp. Epigr.*, p. 236): Ξενοκρατέας / ᾿Εφεσίας / Καλικλέου[ς] / Κιδραμηνοῦ (cf. Wilhelm, *Beiträge*, p. 217, no. 207) ἡρώων (*IG*, sq.; the lettering is of a small, rather irregular cursive which I would date to ii/i a.C.; J. and L. Robert, *La Carie*, ii, p. 337, no. 181 (*SEG* xiv, 515) date it to 'l'époque impériale assez avancée sans doute'.

449. *Supp. Rod.* 84. Lines 6–14 are in larger letters than, but inscribed by the same hand as, lines 1–5. The lettering and the whole style and layout of the inscription are unlike anything I have encountered at Rhodes. Add to this that the ὁ δᾶμος formula, common at Cnidos, and attested elsewhere (see above, note 162), does not recur at Rhodes, and that the not very common name ῾Ιεροκλίων and the strange name Πορ—οσδέκτης do not reappear there, and one may wonder how just its claim to be Rhodian is. Πρόσδεξις, also at Cnidos (see note 213), tempts me to propose Π{ο}ροσδέκτης.

450. In Fraser and Bean, p. 43, no. 39, it is said to be 'a massive tomb' (not altar), and Bean says that he recalls it as a large inscribed block on the Acropolis hill; Chaviaras's description of it as βωμὸς μέγας ὀρθογώνιος ἐκ λίθου ὑπομέλανος may therefore be correct.

451. In general see Rohde, loc. cit. For Nicias see *PH* 76–80; *KF* 17–20; for Marcus of Side see Bean, *Inscriptions of Side* (Ankara, 1965), no. 117: —ιαν Γ. θυ/[γατέρ]α Μάγναν / [ἀδελφ?]ὴν Μάρκου ἥρω/ος (cf. no. 118). J. and L. Robert, *Bull. 1972*, p. 499, no. 525, say apropos of Bean and Mitford, *Journeys in Rough Cilicia*, no. 206, a dedication in honour of a ἥρως φιλόπατρις, 'Elle est exactement de la nombreuse catégorie des inscriptions honorifiques *post mortem*, dont nous avons parlé à mainte reprise … En réalité ἥρως est toujours le titre d'un défunt, même si celui-ci exerce une magistrature, notamment éponymique.' J. and L. Robert presumably restrict their observation here geographically and chronologically to the specific type of dedication of Imperial date under discussion, for there is of course no doubt that 'Heroization' occurred during life from the fourth century onwards, the best-known example being the ἡρωικαὶ τιμαί bestowed on Dion of Syracuse (Diod. xvi. 20, 6): see in general the excellent account by Nilsson *GGR* ii², pp. 136 ff. It seems perfectly

possible that Nicias of Cos was so honoured in his lifetime. According to Crinagoras, *AP* ix, 81, his body was taken from the grave and subjected to posthumous punishment by the citizens (ἀστοί) of Cos, so they are unlikely to have inaugurated Heroic rank and cult posthumously. The dedication to C. Vibius Postumus, procos. of Asia, A.D. 13–16 (*OGIS* 469; *Samos*, xii, no. 180; cf. Magie, *Roman Rule*, ch. 20, note 61), ὁ δῆμος Γαΐῳ Οὐιβίῳ Ποστόμ[ῳ] / τὸ τρὶς ἀνθυπάτῳ ἥρωι / εὐεργέτηι, might not be posthumous, though nothing is known of him after his proconsulship.

452. *IG* 687. Hiller thought that he saw φ as fourth letter on the squeeze (i.e. ʽΗροφῶν), whereas he had read iota on the stone. On the same squeeze iota seems to me much more likely, the cylindrical marks being subsequent damage. The letters are wide and apicated.

453. The Heroes of Rhodes are invoked in the civic oath at the head of the Rhodes–Hierapytna treaty, *ICret.* iii, pp. 31 ff., no. 3 (*Syll.*³ 581), ll. 2 ff.: ἀγαθᾶι τύχαι· εὔξασθαι μὲν τοὺς ἱερεῖς καὶ / τοὺς ἱεροθύτας τῶι Ἁλίωι καὶ τᾶι ʽΡόδωι καὶ τοῖς ἄλλοις θεοῖς / πᾶσι καὶ πάσαις καὶ τοῖς ἀρχαγέταις καὶ τοῖς ἥρωσι, ὅσοι ἔχοντι / τὰν πόλιν καὶ τὰν χώραν τὰν ʽΡοδίων; cf. the similar oath taken at Dreros to preserve the constitution, *ICret.* i, pp. 84 ff., no. 1 (*Syll.*³ 527), ll. 14 ff.

454. See *ILind.*, nos. 282, line 31 (restored); 294, line 22; 299, *c*, line 16, etc. (full list in Index, s.v. Λίνδος καὶ τοὶ ἄλλοι ἥρωες, col. 1179); the priest is recorded from 98 B.C. to the end of the century, in the full lists of the civic priests of Lindos. A plaque from Syme, *IG* xii. 3. 3, inscribed ἡρώων, was found inside the Acropolis, and is therefore unlikely to be funerary.

455. UP (Eph.).

456. Cf. Callimachus, *Ep.* 24:

ʽΗρως Αἰετίωνος ἐπίσταθμος Ἀμφιπολίτεω
ἵδρυμαι μικρῶι μικρὸς ἐπὶ προθύρωι,
λοξὸν ὄφιν καὶ μοῦνον ἔχων ξίφος· ἀνδρὶ δ' ἐφίππωι
θυμωθεὶς πεζὸν κἀμὲ παρωικίσατο.

For the various interpretations offered of this epigram see *Ptol. Alex.* i, p. 583, and ii, p. 827, note 225. For the god and his iconography see ibid., note 224, and the full collection of material in Kazarow, *Die Denkmäler des thrak. Reitergottes in Bulgarien* (Diss. Pannon. II, 14, 1938), and for the variations between ʽΗρως and ʽΗρων, Cumont, *Mél. Dussaud*, i (1939), p. 6; Will, *BCH*, 64/5, 1940/1, pp. 203–4.

457. *Ann.* 4/5, p. 479, no. 34.

458. *NS* 276 (*non vidi*). Maiuri says it was 'dalla necropoli orientale', but his subsequent comment is obscure: 'Questa iscrizione dedicatoria deve appartenere allo stesso recinto funebre in cui furono rinvenute le iscrizioni . . .'; but there is no indication to which inscriptions or which precinct he is referring. For the association of the Thracian Hero with chthonic cult see Picard, *Rev. Hist. Rel.* 150, 1956, pp. 24–5.

168   *Rhodian Funerary Monuments*

459. *ILind.* 184: Θαλῆς Ποσειδέρμου | Μασσαλιώτας | Ἀθάναι (Λ)ινδίαι | καὶ Ἑρμᾶι Ἁγεμόνι. Blinkenberg does not refer to the inscription from Rhodos for the cult of Ἑρμᾶς Ἁγεμών; it is also omitted from Morelli's *I Culti di Rodi*, s.v. Ἑρμᾶς Ἁγεμών.

460. *IG* ii². 1496 (*Syll.*³ 1029; 334–330 B.C.), line 20: ἐκ τῆς θυσ[ίας] τῶι Ἑρμῆι τῶι | Ἡγεμονίωι παρὰ [σ]τρατηγῶν; ibid. 2873 (*Syll.*³ 719; 95/4 B.C.), a dedication by στρατηγοὶ ἐπὶ τὸν Πειραιᾶ to Ἑρμῆς Ἡγεμόνιος. At Rhodes there is an incomplete reference to Hermes in *IG* 44, line 7: [᾿Εν]θάδ[ε——] καθηγητῆρα κελεύθου; cf. Hiller's note ad loc.; see also now the Rhodian dedication, *Arch. Delt.* 26 (1971), 1975, Chr. 2, p. 539, no. 2. Hermes' cult-title Ἡγεμόνιος was also borne by him in his role as leader of the dance of the Charites (see, e.g., Gruppe, *Gr. Mythol.* ii, p. 1330, note 3); but this is hardly likely to be relevant to the tombstone.

461. *PH* 337: [Αὖ]λος Πακώνιος, [Αὖ]/λου υἱός, Φλάμ[μ]ας, ἐτῶ(ν) / ξε̅· | [Α]ὖλος Πακώνιος Αὔλου | υἱός, Φλά[μ]μας ἥρως, ἐτῶν /—· | Λού[κ]ιος [Πακώνι]ος Αὔλου/ υἱός, Χείλω[ν, ἥ]ρως, ἐτῶν / κβ̅· | Μᾶρκος Πακώνιος, Αὔλου | υἱός, Παυλλεῖνος, ἥρως, ἐτῶν | [κζ̅]· | Οὐηδία, Ποπλίου θυ/γάτηρ, Παῦλλα, ἐτῶν | .η̅.

462. Peek, *Inschr. dor. Ins.* 72, Λικιννίου | Εὐποριστου | τραπεζειτοῦ | ἥρωος; ibid. 104, Εὐτυχία ἥ/ρως γλυκυ/τάτη φίλαν/δρε χαῖρε. For the slabs and stelai of Cnidos see above, note 162. In a wider context the same holds true: the designation ἥρως in central and northern Greece (cf. above, p. 77) occurs on stelai and similar markers, and not on altars.

ADDENDA

Pp. 29 ff. Ch. Börker, *AA*, 1975, pp. 244–50, has clarified the distinction in meaning between βουκράνιον (the naked skull) and βουκεφαλ(ι)ον (the full head), and examines the anatomy of the bovine cranium.

Note 23. See now Robertson, *History of Greek Art*, i (Cambridge, 1975), pp. [369]–370: 'The lettering of Krito's and Timarista's names has been thought to be of the mid fourth century. If this is correct one must, I think, conjecture that they were added later. Probably there was in any case a fuller inscription on the base into which the stele must have been fitted originally.'

Note 54. It seems possible that σωμακί, as recorded by Hiller, is an error for the Rhodian dialect-form τσασσούμακι (Turk. çakmak) = πυρόλιθος: see Papachristodoulou, Λεξικογραφικὰ καὶ λαογραφικὰ Ῥόδου (Λαογραφία, Παράρτ. 7, 1969), p. 277, s.v. Πυριόολο(ν). Papachristodoulou does not record σωμακί.

Note 67. For a fire kindled on an altar see also the Gnathia vase in the B.M., Forti, *La Ceramica di Gnathia* (*Mon. Ant. della Magn. Grec.* ii; Naples, 1965), fig. xxxvi, *a*.

Note 148 (i). For an example of a cylindrical altar with bucrania, garlands, and standing figures, probably from Rheneia, see Michaelis, *Anc. Marbles*, p. 564, no. 96 (here, fig. 82, *d*).

Note 151. The monuments of Rheneia have now been published as *Explor. de Délos*, xxx, 1974, M.-T. Couilloud, *Les Monuments funéraires de Rhénée*. The circular altars are published as nos. 492–9, with pls. 85–7. These include the funerary altars now on Delos, some of which I have listed in the note, namely: b(i) = *ED*, no. 493; b(iv) = ibid. 497.

Note 154. For the Charmyleion on Cos see now the full discussion by S. M. Sherwin-White, *ZPE* 24, 1977, pp. 207–17.

Note 176. This inscription was read by Hiller, when more legible, *AM* 21, 1896, p. 44, no. 15, as (a) . . αμ . . / Τύμνιος, (b) Ἐλ[έ]να / Θευδώρου / Ἀργεία, and this should probably be accepted for (b).

For a further example of two stelai on a single block see *IG* ix(1), 52–3, from Phokis (Stiris).

Note 193. This stele is also discussed by Clairmont, *Gravestone and Epigram* (Mainz, 1970), p. 161, no. 86 (and pl. 35). The inscription, which is barely visible on the photographs, is dated (on convincing grounds) by Guarducci to the early hellenistic period, but by Clairmont to the mid-fourth century. The head of the main figure is reworked.

Note 233. With the dolphin of Cn. Babbius Philinus compare now the dolphin-head gargoyle of the fountain recently uncovered at Ai-Khanoum, *CRAI* 1976, p. 311, fig. 16.

Note 239. I may refer here to the inscription on the cylindrical altar in Alexandria, of Imperial date, with bucrania and a crudely executed male figure in a niche, and a funerary dedication in the dative, Breccia, *Iscriz.* 327 (*SB* 3471):

Λυσίμαχος Γ̄ τοῦ Ξένωνος | καὶ Γλαφύρα Δημητρίου | Πάρεις Λυσιμάχῳ Δ̄ τοῦ Ξ|ένωνος Πάρει τῷ υἱῷ, | μνήμης ἕνεκεν. The inscription has caused mystification (see the notes in Breccia and *SB*), but unnecessarily. Evidently, the Lysimachoi, father and son, trace their descent back to a Xenon, through respectively three and four generations of Lysimachoi. The name Πάρεις is, I suspect, the common Egyptian name (Πάρεις, *et sim.*) bestowed as a secondary name on Glaphyra, and then on her son. I see no reason to suppose (with Néroutsos) that the genitives represent not filiation but emancipation from patrons.

Note 333. *DGE* 463(3) has now been discussed by A. Schachter, *Zeitschr. Pap. u. Epigr.* 23, 1976, pp. 251–4. He regards Ἀριστ[ι]ασταί as a military group (cf. ἄριστον), like the φαρατρίτη. H. Lloyd-Jones, ibid. 24, 1977 more aptly associates them with the cult of Aristaios, reading Ἀριστ[η]ασταί.

Note 365. Note also Fraser and Bean, *Rhodian Peraea*, p. 5, no. 5 (*SEG* xiv, 681), a dedication from Marmeris (Physkos), of Imperial date, by demesmen of the Ἄμιοι and Νεττίδαι demes, ὑπὲρ τῶν εὐεργ[ετῶ]ν. These εὐεργέται are probably public benefactors of the demes rather than of the individuals making the dedications.

Note 386. I may call attention also to the ring-stone from Amphipolis in Kavala Museum, Lazarides, ʿΟδηγὸς Μουσείου Καβάλας (Athens, 1969), p. 121, no. M 277, and pl. 40β, with a representation of a youth leaning on a staff and holding a lagobolon. Beside him is a cylindrical altar with upper and lower Ionic mouldings, round the centre of which is an olive wreath.

Note 411. The Parian series of sacrcophagi are now republished with photographs by M.-T. Couilloud, *BCH* 98, 1974, pp. 402–12. There are considerable difficulties as to their date (reuse within a family, addition of names, etc.), but all are Imperial. For a similar type of sarcophagus with inset reliefs see Fıratlı, *Stèles funér. de Byzance*, no. 206.

Note 414. Another instance of εὐσεβής occurs on the fragment (?) from Rheneia, *Explor. de Dél.* xxx, p. 197, no. 438. Mlle Couilloud regards this inscription as incomplete, and prints it thus: ʾΙσίας *APA* - - - | Ἀλεξανδρῖτι | Εὐσεβὴς καὶ - - | χρηστὴ χαῖρε. But the stone shows no superficial signs of damage, and the text is symmetrically engraved over the surface; ll. 2 and 4 are complete formulae that cannot be extended, and l. 3 is certainly not in need of extension. It is therefore difficult to believe that the inscription is not complete. *APA* is unlikely as the patronymic, and there is a gap between the sigma of 'Ισιας and the following alpha. Am I mistaken in believing that I can see the trace of a horizontal upper stroke in the gap, i.e. perhaps Τάρα; for Τάρας see *IG* v, 1, 2, 11, l. 43; 212, l. 41? But there are other possibilities.

I. GENERAL INDEX

Where specific geographical attribution of any entry is not given, it is to be understood to refer to Rhodes and Rhodian practices.

Acarnania, cities of, *see* Anaktorion; Palairos; Stratos; Thyrreion
Agathos Daimon: 73; nn. 426–7
Agoranax, eponymous priest of Helios: 61; n. 343
Ainetos of Rhodes, honoured by the Athenians: n. 15
Akrai, cylindrical altars with triglyph friezes at: n. 151
Alexandria:
citizens of:
Dionysios, brother(?) of Dionysodoros of Alex.: 67
Dionysodoros: 62 ff.
Iacchos, brother of Dionysodoros: 67
Cf. Index III (B), s.v. Ἀλεξανδρεύς
painted stelai of: 43
'Alexandrians' (Ἀλεξανδρεῖς), status in Egypt: 48
Aleximachos of Aigiale, 'heroization' of, and accompanying public ritual: 76–8, 81; n. 441
Alketas, supposed tomb of, at Termessos: n. 9
Altmann, W.: n. 146
Amorgos:
funerary inscriptions, case used for deceased: n. 260
(Aigiale), Hero-cult at: 76
Amphora-stamps, Rhodian:
Helios-heads on: 19; n. 82
'rose' on: 19; n. 81
Anaktorion, funerary inscriptions, case used for deceased at: n. 259
Ancestors, homonymous, represented by letters in epitaphs: 46; *see also* Index IV, s.vv. *B, Γ, Δ*
Aphrodisios, tombstone of, at Nisyros: 18–19
Apollodoros, of Perge:
rock-cut sanctuary dedicated by him at Thera: 40–1
representation of dolphin on: 41
'Apotheosis of Homer': n. 67
Appian: 70; *see also* Index V
Aratophanes, eponymous priest of Helios: 60; n. 343
Archinos, eponymous priest of Helios: 61; n. 343

Arideikes, a Platonist, commemorated in epitaph: 25; n. 203
Aristoboulos of Termessos, 'Benefactor': n. 365
Artemis Pergaea, dedication to priestess of, by descendants: n. 323
Arundel Collection: 44
Arundel House (Arundel), cylindrical altars at: 43–5
Arundel House (Strand, London): 43
Athana Polias, dedication in honour of Camiran priest of A. P. and Emp. Titus, by relatives: n. 323
Athens:
'Altar of the Twelve Gods' at: n. 145
cylindrical altar, from Agora; n. 148(v)
with standing figures, from Agora: n. 148(v)
with masks, in Theatre of Dionysos: n. 148(v)
votive, with bucrania, etc.: 31
of Roman period: n. 148(v)
rectangular altar at: 16
χρηστὸς χαῖρε formula at: 71
Augustus, dedication in honour of, from Thera: 16; n. 67

Bases, rectangular, of cylindrical altars: 25; nn. 119–23
Bean, G. E.: nn. 183, 450
Bearded man, archaic relief of: 9
Beazley, J. D., on origin of bucrania: n. 133
Benefactors (εὐεργέται) of koina: 36, 60, 62–3
normally foreigners: 64
burial of, in koina burial-plots: 63–4
funerary monuments of: 63–4
of state, possible instances: 64; n. 385
Birch, Samuel: nn. 105, 117
Blinkenberg, Chr.: nn. 57–8
Boeotia:
adverse effects of sodalities on family life in: 60
oblong tombstones of: 43
Bondelmonte, describes cylindrical altars on Rhodes: n. 150
Bosporan region (S. Russia), 'brothers' in koina at: 74
Bosses, circular, on rectangular altars, significance of: 15–16, 19–24, 42, 68

posthumous award of, by koina: 68
representations of, on tombstones, etc., of
members of koina: 68
'Cushion':
on tombstone of Asia of Seleucia: n. 67
on Athenian monument: 16; n. 67
on Theraean altar: 16
on altar in relief in Munich: n. 87
Cylindrical monuments:
funerary altars: 4, 25–33
on Chalke: 33; n. 177
on Karpathos: 33; n. 178
on Nisyros: 33; n. 181
on Kasos: 33; n. 182
on Syme: 33; n. 179
on Telos: 33; n. 180
decoration of: 26 ff.; *see also* Bucrania;
Frieze; Garlands
double, in one piece: 33; n. 176
mouldings of: 26
'Nike' group: 26, 31–2
undecorated: n. 128
represented on stelai: n. 386
two, of unknown provenance, in Venice:
n. 184
votive monuments (plain) at Kamiros:
25–6
at Lindos: 26
Cyme (Aeolis), public burial at: n. 162
Cyme (Campania), burial by koina at: 59;
n. 328
Cyprus, cylindrical altars at: n. 148(vi)
Cyrene, 'Ten Thousand' at: 48

Damocles, husband of Kalliarista, *see* Tombstone of Kalliarista
Dedications:
by families to relatives: 58; n. 323
at Athens: 58; n. 324
at Cedreae: 58; n. 325
at Cos: 58; n. 325
at Nisyros: 58; n. 325
at Telos: 58; n. 325
sepulchral, to Gods or Hero: 51–2
Deinarchus: 69; *see* Index V
Delos:
cylindrical altars:
votive and funerary, listed and discussed: 29, 31, 42; nn. 151, 161
naturalistic rendering of garlands,
bucrania, etc.: n. 151
reused as well-curbs, etc.: n. 151
omphaloid monuments at: n. 229
rectangular altar with skeletal bucrania:
n. 151
triangular base from: n. 222
Delphi, cylindrical altar with frieze of
women: n. 145

DEMES, of Rhodian state:
Amioi (Lindian): 54
Amnistioi (Camiran): 55
Histanioi (Camiran): 55
Karpathos (island) (Lindian): 55, 64; *see
also* Karpathos
Ladarmioi (Lindian): 64
Lelioi (Camiran): 54; n. 293
Neapolitai (Ialysian): n. 246
Nisyros (island) (Camiran): 54
Pedieis (Lindian(?)): 55
Plarioi (Camiran): 54; n. 294
Tloioi (Peraea) (Camiran): 54
Cf. also Index III (C)
Demetrias (–Pagasae), painted stelai of: 43
representation of fire on painted stele
from: n. 67
tombstones, reuse of as building material
at: 7
Demetrios of Phaleron, sumptuary legis-
lation of: 55–6
Demetrios, sculptor of funerary relief of
Hieronymos: 34; n. 198
Demotics, Rhodian:
absence from lists of magistrates, priests,
etc.: 47
occurrence in epitaphs:
at Athens: 46
at Rhodes: 46
Derveni (Macedonia), tomb with papyrus
roll at: n. 225
Diagoras, tomb of, in Peraea: 37; n. 211
Dialogues, funerary: 72; nn. 406–8; *cf. also*
Index IV, s.v. χαῖρε, etc.
Didyma, cylindrical altars, archaic, at: n.
145
Diodorus Siculus: 70; *see* Index V
Dion, of Syracuse, heroic honours for: n. 451
Dionysios, fabricant of Rhodian amphorae:
n. 234
Dionysios, of Alexandria, recorded on
funerary monument of Dionysodoros of
Alexandria: 67
Dionysodoros, of Alexandria:
funerary rites for: 12, 81; n. 354
honours, dossier of, relating to: 62–3, 64,
65; nn. 353 ff.
as benefactor of koina: 64
funerary monument of: 66–7; nn. 379 ff.
Diskoi: n. 96; *cf. also* Shields, votive
Dis Manibus: 73; nn. 423, 428–9
Dolphins:
on Rhodian amphora-stamps: 40; n. 234
on Thasian amphora-stamps: 40; n. 234
as attribute on statues: n. 238
on coins of Rhodes (hellen.); Nisyros (Archaic); Poseidion (Karpathos): n. 238
on cone, holding captured fish: 41; n. 238

H

182 *General Index*

Slaves:
burial of: 58
in Asia Minor: n. 327; in Athens: n. 327; in Rome: 58; n. 326
imperial, tombstones of: n. 327
status indicated on tombstone: n. 308
Smith, A. H.: n. 101
Snakes:
on altars, in act of drinking, at Crete: n. 162
at Delos: n. 162
at Mytilene: n. 162
at Paros: n. 162
at Pergamon: n. 162
apotropaic: 38; nn. 213–14
funerary: 4, 32, 38–40
at Cos: 39
at Halicarnassos: 39
encircling omphalos with dedication to Heros: 79
identification with deceased: 38
on casket-lids at Pergamon: n. 162
twined round figure in panoply: n. 205
'Snake-altars': 38; n. 213
at Cnidos: 38; n. 213
at Nisyros: 38; n. 213
Sperlonga group of sculpture: 43
Stag's head, decoration (as bucrania): 19, 27, 32; nn. 134, 169
Steer, Francis: 43
Stelai:
painted (?), stuccoed: 10; n. 37
plain, small: 9–11, 42
with representation of figures in parting embrace: 34; n. 196
Stele:
girl with bird: n. 193
warrior: 34; n. 191
youth with spear, from Rhodini: n. 192
Stratos, funerary inscriptions, case used for deceased: n. 259
Suda, the: 69; *see* Index V
Susini, G.: 20; nn. 120, 177, 178, 180
Sword, on funerary monument: 39
Sword-hilt, bird-headed: 39
on relief from neighbourhood of Byzantion: 39; n. 219
on façade of Bouleuterion of Miletus: 39; n. 221; on balustrade of precinct of Athena at Pergamon: 39; n. 220
in fresco of hypogaeum near Verria; in fresco in hypogaeum at Eretria; on Prima Porta statue of Augustus; on Attic relief from Agora: n. 221
Syme: cylindrical altars at: 33; n. 179
rectangular altars from: 24; n. 111
rectangular bases of circular altars on: n. 120

Tanagra:
columns on tombstones of: n. 191
double stelai at: n. 176
funerary stele from, with opposed dolphins: 40
Tebtunis, koinon at: n. 341
Telmessos, funerary inscriptions, case used for deceased: n. 265
Telos:
alliance with Rhodes: n. 112
cylindrical altars on: 33; n. 180
dedications in honour of two women by relatives: n. 325
funerary inscriptions, case used for deceased at: n. 261
incorporation of in Rhodian state: 24
links with Cos: n. 114
localities:
Ayios Antonios (bay of): n. 108
Megalochorio: nn. 87, 180
rectangular altars from: 20, 24; nn. 87, 116
rectangular bases of cylindrical altars on: n. 117
stele with representation of figures in parting embrace: n. 196
'Ten Thousand' (Μύριοι), at Cyrene: 48
Termessos: 36
Terraces:
in Rhodian landscape: 4
necropoleis in: 4
at Cnidos: n. 153
Texier, Ch. F. M.: n. 164
Thebes (Boeotia), cylindrical altars at: n. 148(v)
(Pyri), reuse of stelai at, as tomb-covers: n. 17
Theon, of Antioch, sculptor: n. 198
Thera:
cylindrical altars from: 16; n. 67
funerary inscriptions, case used for deceased: n. 260
votive cylindrical altars with bucrania, etc.: 31; n. 148(ii)
Thyateira, cinerary caskets from: n. 49
Thyrreion, funerary inscriptions, case used for deceased: n. 259
Tibur, cylindrical votive altar from: n. 149
Titus, Emp., Camiran dedication in honour of priest of Athana Polias and Titus: n. 323
Tlos, Rhodian (Peraean) deme: 34
Tombstones:
of Charonidas, s. of Xenotimos (*cf. also* RHODES (mod.), City area, s.v. Monte Smith): 8
of families, *see* Inscriptions, funerary, joint

II. INDEX OF INSCRIPTIONS AND PAPYRI

(A) INSCRIPTIONS

The abbreviations used in this index are those listed on p. 83, except that the opening entry of *IG* xii. 1 is not abbreviated to '*IG*'. Other abbreviations are those used in the notes. Large itemized groups of inscribed stones recorded solely as types of monuments (as, e.g., cinerary caskets in nn. 43, 252) are not listed in the index.

INSCRIPTIONS PREVIOUSLY UNPUBLISHED

(B) PAPYRI

III. EPIGRAPHICAL INDEX

(A) INDEX OF PROPER NAMES

1. The references throughout are to the pages and notes in which the inscriptions are quoted, and not to the inscription itself.
2. Names, etc., from non-Rhodian (incl. Island and Peraea) inscriptions are prefixed by an asterisk before the entry or individual reference.
3. Roman citizens with Greek cognomina are entered under the Greek cognomen.

*Ἀβάσκαντος, θρεπτός: n. 444
Ἀγάθανδρος, f. καθ. of Νίκων Φιλομβρότου, Νισύριος: n. 144
*Ἀγαθῖνος, s. of 'Ἰάσων, Ἀπαμεύς: n. 423
Ἀγάθιππος, s. of Φιλοκράτης, Ἀθηναῖος: 74
Ἀγαθόστρατος, s. of Ἀστυμήδης, Βράσιος: n. 89 (b)
'Ρόδιος: n. 247
Ἀγέλας: n. 32 (b)
Ἀγέστρατος, s. of Φιλίσκος, Κυμισαλεύς: n. 36
Ἀγήσανδρος, f. of Ἀπολλόδωρος, q.v.
s. of Σωσιγένης, Βράσιος: 32
Ἀγήσαρχος, Κνίδιος: n. 163
Ἀγησιρόδη, d. of Τιμάσαρχος, Κρυασσίς: n. 254
Ἀγησ—, s. of Ἀγήσανδρος: n. 81
Ἀγητορίδας, f. of Φιλοκράτης, q.v.
Ἀγίας: n. 402
*Μ. Οὔλπιος Κλαυδιανὸς Ἀγλαοφάνης: 77
Ἀγορακλῆς, s. of Ἀπολλόδοτος, Καρπαθιοπολίτας: n. 89 (d)
Ἀθανοκλεία, Φασηλῖτις: n. 362
Ἀθήναιος, f. of Ἀρτεμεισία, q.v.
Ἄθως, Γαλάτας: n. 306
Αἰσχίνας: n. 58
Αἴσχρων I, f. of Αἴσχρων II, Καρπαθιοπολίτας: 55 (390)
   II, s. of Αἴσχρων, Καρπαθιοπολίτας, f. of Αἴσχρων Γ̄ Καρπαθιοπολίτας: 55 (390)
   III, Γ̄, Καρπαθιοπολίτας, s. of Αἴσχρων II Καρπαθιοπολίτας, q.v.: 55 (391)
   f. of Φιλωνίδας, q.v.
Ἀλέξανδρος, s. of Φίλτατος, Φύσκιος: 57
Ἀλέξανδρος: n. 58
Ἀλεξίδαμος I, f. of Μικίων, Βρυκούντιος, q.v.
   II, f. καθ. of Μικίων, Βρυκούντιος, q.v.
Ἀλεξικράτης, f. of Στρατωνίδας, q.v.
*Ἀλεξίμαχος, s. of Κριτόλαος (Αἰγιαλεύς): 76; n. 223

Ἀλκικράτης, s. of Τιμαχίδας, Φύσκιος: 44 no. A (ii)
Ἀλκινόη: n. 107
*Ἄλυπος: n. 324
*Ἀμαχιανή, d. of Εὔμαχος: n. 324
*Ἀμαχιανή: n. 324
*Ἀμίον, Καίσαρος δούλη: n. 327
*Ἄμμιον: n. 324
*Ἀναξίλας: n. 155
*Ἀναξίς, Κωῖα: 74; n. 306
*Ἀναξίων, f. of 'Ὀλύμπιχος and 'Ηρόδωρος, qq.v.
*Ἀνδραγόρας, s. of Φοῖνιξ (Θηραῖος): n. 442
Ἀνδρότιμος, f. of Εὔφρᾶναξ, q.v.
*Ἀντέρως I, s. of Διονύσιος: n. 423
   *II, s. of Ἀντέρως I, q.v.
Ἀντιγένης, f. of 'Ἱπποστράτη, Νισυρία, q.v.
*Ἀντίγονος, f. of Σεραπιάς, q.v.
Ἀντιοχεύς: n. 307
Ἀντιοχίς, 'Ροδία: nn. 247, 306
Ἀντιοχὶς ἀπὸ Δάφνας: n. 305
Ἀντίπατρος, s. of Ἀσκληπιάδης, Κυρηναῖος: nn. 242, 404
Ἀντιφάνης, f. of Φαρνάκης, Μύνδιος: n. 404
Ἀξιοθέα, Ἀθηναία: n. 404
*Ἀπατούριος, f. of Εὐετηρίς, q.v.
Ἀπολλόδοτος, f. of Ἀγορακλῆς, Καρπαθιοπολίτας, q.v.
   I, f. of Ἀπολλόδοτος, 'Ἰστάνιος, q.v.
   II, s. of Ἀπολλόδοτος, 'Ἰστάνιος: n. 416
Ἀπολλόδοτος, s. of Ἀγήσανδρος: 51
   s. of —: n. 369
   ἐγγενής: n. 307
Ἀπολλωνίδας, f. of 'Ἰμασ(σ)αώλα, q.v.
Ἀπολλώνιος, f. of Ἀπολλώνιος, Μάγνης, q.v.
   f. of Βόα, Τενεδία: q.v.
   s. of Ἀπολλώνιος, Μάγνης: n. 155
   f. of Πίστος, q.v.
   f. of 'Ροδοφῶν, q.v.

Δημήτριος: 34
*Δημήτριος: n. 339
*Δημοσθένης, s. of Λῦσις: n. 334
Δημύλος, Σάμιος: n. 362
*Διαγόρας, s. of Τεῦκρος: n. 148 (vi)
Διαγόρας: n. 211
*Διαδουμενός, Καίσαρος δοῦλος, ἱππεύς: n. 327
Διόδοτος, f. of Ῥηγεῖνος, q.v.
  ἐγγενής, s. of Ἡφαιστίων: nn. 369, 371
Διομέδων, f. of Δημήτριος, Ῥόδιος, q.v.
Διονυσάριν, Μυνδία, μέτοικος: 57
*Διονυσᾶς I, f. of Διονυσᾶς II, q.v.
  *II, s. of Διονυσᾶς I: n. 157
*Διονύσιος, f. of Ἄντέρως, q.v.
  *f. of Γλαυκίας, q.v.
Διονυσόδωρος, Ἀλεξανδρεύς: 64, 67; nn. 355 f., 380
Διοσκουρίδης, s. of Ἡρακλείδης, Τύριος: n. 242
Διότιμος, f. of Τιμακράτης, Ἀμνίστιος, q.v.
  s. of Τιμακράτης, Ἀμνίστιος: 55 (387)
*Γ. Ἰούλ. Γ. Δίων: n. 155
Τ. Κλαύδ. Δόναξ, Κνίδιος, f. of Γάμος and Μοῦσα, qq.v.
Δρακοντίς, d. of Ἄσανδρος, Μάγνησσα: n. 298a
*Δράκων: n. 350
  f. of Μενίσκος, Ἡρακλεώτης, q.v.
Φλ. Δράκων: 51
Δῶρος, Μῆδος: 67; n. 289

*Ἐγνατία Σεκόνδα: 45
*Μ. Ἐγνάτιος Πρόκλος: 45
*Μ. Καστρίκιος Εἴκαρος: n. 95
*Εἰρηναῖος I, f. of Εἰρηναῖος II, q.v.
  *II, s. of Εἰρηναῖος I: 77
Εἰρηναῖος, f. of Ἕρμων, Εὐθηνίτας, q.v.
Εἰσίδωρος, Ἐφέσιος: n. 128
Ἑκαταῖος, f. of Νικίας, q.v.
*Ἑκατέα, d. of Θεύδα[μος]: n. 157
Ἑκάτων, f. of Μοσχίων, Βράσιος: n. 245
Ἐλάφιον, Χία: n. 406
*Ἑλλανίων, Ταρσεύς: n. 117
*Γ. Ἔλουιος Γαΐου Ῥωμαῖος: 51
Ἐλπίς, Κνιδία: n. 163
*Ἐλπίς: 59
Ἐπαφρίων, Μύ(ν)διος: n. 128
  f. of Ἡρώ, Μυνδία, q.v.
(Μ. Αὐρ. (?)) Ἐπαφρίων, f. of Μ. Αὐρ. Ἑρμοκράτης, q.v.
Ἐπαφρόδιτος: 54 (370)
Μ. Πονπ. Ἐπαφρόδιτος, f. of Ποππηία Γοργίς, q.v.
Ἐπίγονος, Ῥοδιοπολίτας, μέτοικος, ἐξελευθερωθείς: nn. 308, 365
Ἐπίγονος: n. 58
*Ἐπίκτησις: 77
*Ἐπικτήτα, d. of Γρίννος (Θηραία): n. 442

Αἴλ. Ἐπίκτητος, θρεπτός: n. 41a
*κογχυλιαβάφος, s. of Δημήτριος: n. 158
*Ἐπίνοια, τροφός: 51
Ἐπίχαρμος I, Ἐπιχάρμου, Ῥόδιος, f. of Ἐπίχαρμος Σολεύς, q.v.
  II, Σολεύς, ὧι ἁ ἐπιδαμία δέδοται, s. of Ἐπίχαρμος I, Ἐπιχάρμου, Ῥόδιος: n. 248
Ἐράτων, s. of Ἔρασις, Κεδρεάτας: n. 35
Ἐργοίτας, f. of Νικαινέτα, Κυμισαλίς, q.v.
*Ἑρμαῖος I, f. of Ἑρμαῖος II: n. 443a
  II, s. of Ἑρμαῖος I, q.v.
Καππάδοξ: n. 55
Ἑρμη⟨ί?⟩ς: see Φλ. Νεικασὼ Ἑρμη⟨ί?⟩ς
Ἑρμῆς: n. 321
Ἑρμογένης, Φασηλίτας: n. 366
Μ. Αὐρ. Ἑρμοκράτης, s. of Ἐπαφρίων: nn. 47, 320
Ἕρμων, s. of Εἰρηναῖος, Εὐθυνίτας: n. 402
Πτολεμαιεύς: n. 362
  ἐγγενής: n. 431
Τ. Ὁρδιώνιος Ἔρως: n. 269
Εὐαγόρας, s. of Εὔνικος, Ἄμιος: 54 (368)
Εὔδημος I, f. of Εὔδημος II, q.v.
  II, s. of Εὔδημος I: n. 406
*Εὐετηρίς: 56; n. 310
  d. of Ἀπατούριος: n. 310
*Εὐήμερος, s. of Μοσχᾶς: n. 301
Εὐθρεπτίδας, s. of Φίλαρχος: n. 318
Εὐθυντίδας: n. 268
Εὐκαρπία, Παλαιοπολῖτις, d. of Νείκων, Παλαιοπολίτας: 52
Εὐκλεία, Φασηλῖτις: n. 307
Εὐκλείδας, Σολεύς, μέτοικος: n. 305
*Εὐκλίδας: n. 333
*Εὔμαχος: n. 324
Εὐμοίρης, f. of Ἀριδείκης, q.v.
Εὔνικος, f. of Εὐαγόρας, Ἄμιος, q.v.
*Εὔνικος: n. 157
Εὐοδίων, f. of Χλόη, q.v.
*Εὐπορία: n. 213
Λικίννιος Εὐπόριστος: n. 462
Εὐταξία, Ἀπαμίς: 73
*Εὐτυχία, d. of Σωτήρ: n. 162
Εὐτυχία: n. 319
*Εὐτυχία: n. 462
*Εὔτυχος: n. 350
Εὐφάνης I, f. of Εὐφάνης II, Τύμνιος, q.v.
  II, s. of Εὐφάνης, Τύμνιος: n. 155
Εὔφρανξ, s. of Ἀνδρότιμος: 55 (394)
Εὐφράνασσα, d. of Δεξιναύτας, Ἰστανία: 55 (395)
Εὐφρανορίς, d. of Θεύφαντος, Πεδιάς: 55 (393)
Εὐφροσύνα, Ἐφεσία: 57
Σολίς: n. 128
Εὐφροσύνα: n. 415a
*Εὐφροσύνη, d. of Κριτόβουλος, Ἀθηναία: n. 300
*Εὐφροσύνη: n. 162

*Λεόντιον: n. 423
*Λεύκιος: n. 433
Λέων, f. of Θεύδωρος, Πλάριος, q.v.
Λέων: 54 (379)
*Λεωνίδης, s. of Ἱεροκλῆς, Ἰοβάτειος: n. 443a
Λητό[δωρ]ος: n. 369
Γ. Λικίννιος Γ̄. υἱ. Βάσσος: n. 319
*Λυκάων: 59
*Λυκία, d. of Τειθωνός: n. 443a
Λυσάνδρα, d. of Θεύφαντος, Πεδιάς: 55 (392)
Λυσίας, s. of Θρασύμβροτος, Νεττίδας: n. 402
*Λυσίμαχος Γ̄, τοῦ Ξένωνος: Add. to n. 239
*Δ̄ (ὁ καὶ Πάρις?), s. of Λυσίμαχος Γ̄, q.v.
Μαιώτης: 56
*Λῦσις, f. of Δημοσθένης, q.v.
*Λύσων: n. 95

*Μάγνα, d. of Μᾶρκος, ἥρως: n. 451
Μαδουσι-: n. 71
*Μᾶρκος, ἥρως, f. of Μάγνα, q.v.
Μέδων, s. of Νουμήνιος, Ἄμιος: 54 (366)
Μελάνθιος, s. of Σόλων, Βαργυλιήτης: n. 242
*Μέλισσα: n. 162
Μένανδρος, f. of Θεύδωρος, q.v.
s. of Θεύδωρος, Πλάριος: 54 (374)
*f. of Παρμενίσκα, Μελιβόϊσσα, q.v.
Μένανδρος: 19; n. 405
Μενέδαμος, f. of Ἀριστομένης, q.v.
Μενεκλῆς Δ̄: n. 239
Μενεκράτης, s. of Ἄσανδρος (Μάγνης): n. 298a
Αἰλία Μενέσθεια ἡ καὶ Καλλίκλεια, w. of
Φλάουιος Δράκων, q.v.
*Μενεσθεύς, see Βρίθιον, d. of Μενεσθεύς
Μενεστράτη, Κραγία: n. 89 (c)
Μένιππος Καρ(πασιώτας?): 51
Μενίσκος, s. of Δράκων, Ἡρακλεώτης: n. 242
Μέροψ, ?f. of Χρύσιππος, ἐγγενής, q.v.
*Μηνόδοτος, s. of Πίκανθις: 44, no. B (v) (ii)
Μηνοφιλία, d. of Φίλιππος, Ξάνθιος: n. 405
Μηνόφιλος: n. 372
*Μητρίχη, d. of Μητρόδωρος I, m. of Μητρό-
δωρος II: n. 281
Μητρόδωρος, Ἀπαμεύς, μέτοικος: 73
*I, f. of Μητρίχη, q.v.
*II, s. of Ἡγῆς: n. 281
Μικίων, s. of Ἀλεξίδαμος I and καθύ. of
Ἀλεξίδαμος II, Βρυκούντιος: n. 120
Μίκκη, Ἀντιοχίς: n. 306
Μιννίς: 54 (382)
*Μίρτον, d. of Δαμοκράτης Δ̄: n. 239
*Μνάσεας Δ̄: n. 157
Μνᾶσις, f. of Μνασίς, Ἐριναῖς, q.v.
Μνασίς, d. of Μνᾶσις, Ἐριναῖς: n. 32 (a)
*Μοσχᾶς, f. of Σωτηριχᾶς and Εὐήμερος,
qq.v.
Μοσχίων, s. of Ἑκάτων, Βράσιος: n. 245
Φασηλίτας: n. 369
*Π. Μουνάτιος Ἀουεῖτος: n. 327

Μοῦσα, d. of Τ. Κλαύδ. Δόναξ, Κνίδιος: n. 319
Μυρτίς: 57
Μυρτώ: 57

*Ναυκράτης, f. of Χαρίλαος: n. 443
Ναυτέλης, f. of Σωτώ, q.v.
Φλ. Νεικασὼ Ἑρμη⟨ι̇?⟩ς: n. 89 (b)
Νείκων, Παλαιοπολίτας, f. of Εὐκαρπία, Παλ.,
q.v.
Νικαγόρας I, f. of Νικαγόρας II, q.v.
II, s. of Νικαγόρας I: n. 298
f. of Ὀνασιφάνεια, q.v.
s. of Πυθοκλῆς: n. 298
Νικαγόρας: n. 298
Νίκαια, d. of Λητό[δωρ]ος: n. 369
Νικαινέτα, d. of Ἐργοίτας, Κυμισαλίς: n. 36
*Νίκανδρος, Τύριος, I, f. of Νίκανδρος II, q.v.
*(Τύριος), II, s. of Νίκανδρος, Τύριος, I: n.
281
*Νικίας, s. of Ἑκαταῖος: n. 423
Ἀντιοχεύς: n. 306
*Νικόμαχος: n. 334
Νίκων, s. of Φιλόμβροτος, καθύ. of Ἀγάθαν-
δρος, Νισύριος: n. 144
Νουμήνιος I, f. of Νουμήνιος, Ἄμιος, q.v.
II, s. of Νουμήνιος I, Ἄμιος: 54 (365)
f. of Τιμόθεος, Ἄμιος, q.v.
f. of Μέδων, Ἄμιος, q.v.
*Νουμήνιος: n. 334
Νῦσα, Αἰγυπτία: 72

Ξενόβουλος, f. of Ἀρτεμιδ[ώρα], Ποντωρεῖς,
q.v.
Ξενοκλῆς, ἐγγενής: 44, no. A (i)
Ξενοκρατέα, Ἐφεσία: n. 448
Ξενόχαρις: 54 (383)
*Ξένων, ancestor of Λυσίμαχος Γ̄, q.v.
Ξηνότιμος, f. of Χαρωνίδας, q.v.

Αἴλ. Οἰνοφόρος: n. 41a
Ὀλυμπιάς, Λυκαόνισσα: 57
*Ὀλυμπιόδωρος, Στειριεύς: n. 148 (v)
*Ὀλύμπιχος, s. of Ἀναξίων: n. 300
Ὀλυνπιὰς Ἀλεξάνδρα, Φυσκία: 57
Ὀνασίς, d. of Ἀρτωνίδας, Νισυρία: n. 402
Ὀνασιφάνεια, d. of Νικαγόρας: nn. 37, 194
Ὀνασιφῶν, f. of Σωσίς, Νισυρία, q.v.
*Ὀνήσιμος: 69
*Ὀνητορίδης: n. 281
*Ὀπίων, Ἡρακλεῶτις: n. 311
*d. of Στάχυς, Ἀκανθία: n. 311
Ὀπώρα: 56
*Ὀρδιωνία Διονυσία: n. 155
*Οὐηδία Ποπ. θυγ. Παῦλλα: n. 461
*Γ. Οὐίβιος Πόστομος: n. 451

*Αὖ. Πακώνιος Αὔλ. υἱ. Φλάμμα: n. 461
*Λ. Πακώνιος Αὔλ. υἱ. Χείλων: n. 461

Πῶλλα Τρύφαινα, Ῥωμαία: n. 47
*Τρύφων: n. 324
*Τρύφων: 51
*Τύχη, m. of Πρόσδεξις, q.v.
Λικιννία Τύχη: n. 319

*Φάνφιλα: n. 324
Φαρνάκης, s. of Ἀντιφάνης, Μύνδιος: 52
Φερενίκα, d. of Φερένικος: 50
Φερένικος, f. of Φερενίκα, q.v.
Φίλαρχος I, f. of Φίλαρχος II and Εὐθρεπτί-
δας, qq.v.
II, s. of Φίλαρχος I: n. 318
Φιλήρατος, f. of Καλλιαρίστα, q.v.
Φιλῖνος, f. of Φιλιστίδας Βρυγινδάριος, q.v.
Φίλιππος, Ξάνθιος, f. of Μηνοφιλία: q.v.
*Φίλιππος, f. of Θεοκλῆς, q.v.
*f. of Παρμενίσκος, q.v.
Φιλίσκος, f. of Ἀγέστρατος Κυμισαλεύς, q.v.
Φιλιστίδας, f. of Ἱεροκλῆς, Βρυγινδάριος, q.v.
s. of Φιλῖνος, Βρυγινδάριος (= preceding?),
nn. 46, 252
Φιλίων, f. of Πραξίων, q.v.
*Φιλόδαμος: n. 81
Φιλοκράτης, f. of Ἀγάθιππος, Ἀθηναῖος, q.v.
s. of Ἀγητορίδας: n. 245
ὧι ἁ ἐπιδαμία δέδοται: n. 368
Ἰλιεύς: n. 128
Φιλοκράτης: n. 71
*Φιλομάθης, s. of Σέλευκος: 51
Φιλόμβροτος, f. of Νίκων, Νισύριος, q.v.
*Φιλόξενος: n. 444
*Φιλόστοργος, f. of Φιλόστοργος Ᾱ, q.v.
Ᾱ, s. of Φιλόστοργος: n. 157
Φιλότιμος, f. of Πύθων, Καρπαθιοπολίτας, q.v.
Φιλουμένα: 56
Φίλτατος, f. of Ἀλέξανδρος, Φύσκιος, q.v.
Φιλτογένης, f. of Ἀριστοτέλης, Ἀμνίστιος, q.v.
Φίλων, Ἰλιεύς: n. 128
*s. of Σωτάδης, Μοψεάτης: n. 433
ἐγγενής: n. 307

Φίλων: n. 128
Φιλωνίδας, s. of Αἴσχρων: 55 (389)
Φλάουιος: 57
*Φοῖνιξ (Θηραῖος), f. of Κρατησίλοχος and
Ἀνδραγόρας, qq.v.
Φρονίμιον, ἐγγενής, d. of Σάτυρος: n. 371
Φυλῆς, s. of Πολύγνωτος, Ἀλικαρνασσεύς:
n. 365

Χαιρέας I, f. of Χαιρέας II, Πλάριος, q.v.
II, s. of Χαιρέας I, Πλάριος: 54 (381)
s. of Θεύδωρος, Πλάριος: 54 (380)
Χαιρέδαμος, f. of Πασιφάνεια, q.v.
*Χαρίλαος, s. of Ναυκράτης: n. 443
Χαριξένα, d. of Ἀρχικλείδας: n. 269a
Χαρίτα, Μακρώνισ(σ)α: n. 307
Χαρίτιμος, s. of Τιμαγόρας, Φαγαῖος: n. 189
*Χαρίτιον: n. 148 (iv)
Χαρωνίδας, s. of Ξηνότιμος: n. 268
*Χείλων, see Λ. Πακώνιος Αὖλ. υἱ. Χείλων
Χλόη, d. of Εὐοδίων: n. 108
*Αἴλ. Ἀγχαρηνὸς Χρήσιμος: n. 206
Χρήσιμος, Κάρ: n. 322
Χρύσιππος, ἐγγενής, ?s. of Μέροψ: 67; n. 376
Χρυσώ, d. of Ἀστυμήδης, Ποντωρηΐς: n. 305
d. of Τιμᾶναξ: 9
Κεραμία: n. 365

Ὠφελίων, Σύρος: n. 89 (c)

—άπτολις, Ἀλικαρνασσεύς, f. of ——, Ἀλικαρνασσεύς: n. 213
—κών, f. of Συρία, Βρυκούντισσα, q.v.
—μάνης, f. of ——, Τύμνιος: n. 176

*C. Annius C. f. Cor. Pollio: n. 326
*L. Arruntius L. f. Ter.: n. 326
*Cn. Babbius Philinus: n. 233
Hordionia Dionysia, see *Ὁρδιωνία Διονυσία
*familia Salvidiena Q. f. Ruf.: n. 326

(B) ETHNICS

Ἀθηναῖος: 74
Ἀθηναῖος: n. 404 (—αία)
*(Ἀθηναῖος) Προβαλίσιος: n. 281
*(Ἀθηναῖος) Στειριεύς: n. 148 (v)
*(Ἀθηναῖος) Χολλείδης: n. 148 (v)
Αἰγινάτας: 74; n. 306
Αἰγύπτιος: 72 (—οι)
*Ἀκάνθιος: n. 311 (—ία)
Ἀλεξανδρεύς: 64, 67; nn. 269, 355, 389
(—εῖς), *Add. to n. 414 (—ῖτις)
Ἀλικαρνασσεύς: nn. 213, 365, 369 (—ίς)
Ἀντιοχεύς: nn. 306 (m. and f.), 307, 369

Ἀντιοχεὺς ἀπὸ Δάφνας: n. 305 (—ίς)
Ἀπαμεύς: 73 (m. and f., —ῖτις); *n. 423
Ἀράδιος: n. 242
Ἀρκάς: n. 132
Ἀσπένδιος: n. 366
Ἀστυπαλαιεύς: nn. 109, 405

Βαργυλιήτης: nn. 242, 298 (—ῆτις), 365
(—ώτας)

Γαλάτας: nn. 80, 306, 369

'Εφέσιος: 57; nn. 128 (*bis*), 204 (—ία)

Ἡρακλεώτης: n. 242

Θρᾶιξ: n. 307 (—ισσα)

'Ιλιεύς: n. 127 (*bis*)
*'Ιοβάτειος: n. 443a

Καππάδοξ: n. 55
Κάρ: n. 322
Καρ(πασιώτας?): 51; n. 275
Κεράμιος: n. 365 (—ία)
Κιδραμηνός: n. 448
Κνίδιος: nn. 163 (m. and f.), 319
*Κνίδιος ἀπὸ Ῥόδου: n. 157
Κράγιος: n. 89 ([Κ]ραγία)
Κρής: n. 366
*(ἀπὸ) Κυ[π]ροβήλων: n. 158
Κυρηναῖος: nn. 242, 404
Κῶιος: 74 (—ία); nn. 306 (*bis* —ία), 362

Λαοδικεύς: n. 75
Λυδός: n. 89 (a) (—ή); n. 368
Λυκάων: n. 57 (—ισσα)

Μάγνης: nn. 155, 298a (m. and f.)
Μαιώτης: 56 (—ῶται)
Μάκρων: n. 307 (—ισ(σ)α)
Μασσαλιώτας: n. 459
*Μελιβόϊσσα: n. 271
Μῆδος: 67; n. 289

*Μοψεάτης: n. 433
Μύνδιος: 52 (m. and f.), 57 (—ία); nn. 128, 405
Μυρεύς: n. 71 (—ίς)

Ξάνθιος: n. 405

Πτολεμαιεύς: n. 362

Ῥοδιοπολίτας: nn. 308, 365
Ῥόδιος: nn. 15, 247 (m. and f.), 306 (—ία) (sculptors): nn. 198 (*bis*), 248, 250
*Ῥωμαῖος: n. 441 (—οι)

Σαλαμίνιος: n. 365 (—ία)
Σάμιος: nn. 128, 362
Σαρδιανός: n. 306
Σελγεύς: nn. 171, 306 (—ίς), 346
Σιδάτας: n. 35
Σιδώνιος: 67; nn. 242, 289
Σολεύς: 67; nn. 128 (—ίς), 248 (—ίς), 305
Σύρος: 72 (—α); n. 89 (c)

*Ταρσεύς: n. 117
Τενέδιος: n. 242 (—ία)
Τερμεσσεύς: nn. 204, 247, 306
Τύριος: nn. 242, *281

Φασηλίτης: 57 (one m., two f.); nn. 89, 307 (—ῖτις), 362 (—ῖτις), 366

Χαλκιδεύς: n. 89
Χῖος: n. 406 (—ία)

(C) RHODIAN DEMOTICS

(alphabetically under parent cities, Ialysos, Kamiros, Lindos)

(i) IALYSOS

Βρυγινδάριος: nn. 46 (*bis*), 252 (*bis*)

'Ερινεύς: n. 32 (—αῖς)

'Ιστάνιος: 55; nn. 395 (—ία), 416

Κρυασσεύς: nn. 254 (—ίς), 296 (—ίς)

Νεοπολίτας: n. 246

Ποντωρεύς: nn. 35 (—εῖς), 296 (—ητίς), 305 (—ητίς)

(ii) KAMIROS

Ἀμνίστιος: 55, nos. 385–8; n. 296

Εὐθυνίτας: n. 402
Εὐριάδας: n. 296

Κυμισαλεύς: n. 36 (m. and f. —ίς)

Λέλιος: 54 (376)
Λέλος: n. 293
Πυργαλιδᾶν κοινὸν ἐν Λέρωι: n. 293
Τρίκτοινοι ἐν Λέλωι: n. 293

Νισύριος: 54, no. 377, nn. 35 (m. and f.), 144, 239, 402 (—ία, *bis*)

Παλαιοπολίτας: 52 (m. and f. —ῖτις)
Πλάριος: 54, nos. 374, 378, 380–1

Τήλιος: n. 108
Τλώϊος: 34, 54, no. 375; n. 402 (—ία)
Τύμνιος: nn. 155, 176, 296 (—ία)

Φαγαῖος: 32 (—αία); n. 189

Χαλκήτας: n. 296

(D) DEITIES

IV. INDEX OF WORDS AND FORMULAE DISCUSSED

ἀδελφά: 74
ἀδελφοὶ ἥρωες: 74, 78
ἀδελφός: nn. 340, 433
ἀμφουριασμός: 61
ἀναγόρευσις τᾶν τιμᾶν (ἐπὶ τῶν τόπων): 67;
    nn. 356, 359
ἀνδρών: n. 58
ἀνέθηκε: 51; n. 281
    See also s.v. ἐπέθηκε
ἀπόταφοι: see s.v. ἀποτάφων ταφων
ἀποτάφων ταφων: 68–70
ἀφηροϊσμός: 76, 81
ἀφηρωΐζω: 77; n. 444

B (to denote homonymous descent): n. 416
βωμός: 12; n. 229

Γ (to denote homonymous descent): Add. to
    n. 239

Δ (to denote homonymous descent): nn.
    157, 239
δαίμονες ἀγαθοί: 73, 80; nn. 423–5
δᾶμος (δῆμος) (ὁ): 78; nn. 162, 449
δοῦλος (δούλη): n. 327
δοχεῖον: n. 58
(ἐπὶ τοῦ) δοχείου (ἐπὶ τῶι —ωι): 14; n. 58

ἔγγαια: 61; n. 348
ἐγγενής: 47, 56, 65; nn. 159, 371, 431
(ὅπου) ἐκάη: 53; n. 288a
ἐκφορά: n. 372
ἐλεήμων: 72; nn. 409–10
ἐντόφιον: 70; n. 396
ἐξελεύθερος: n. 308
ἐπέθηκε: 51
(ᾆι ἁ) ἐπιδαμία (δέδοται): 48
ἐπίπυρον: n. 91
ἐπιταφέω: 59
εὐδαίμων: 72; n. 411
εὐεργέτας: see Index I, s.v. Benefactors
εὐεργέτας τοῦ κοινοῦ: see Index I, s.v.
    Benefactors
εὐσεβής: 72: n. 414, and Add.

ζῆι: nn. 155, 158, 319, 423
ζώντων (ζῶν, etc.): 57–8; n. 319
ζῶσιν: n. 157

ἥρως (ἡρώϊσσα): 76 ff.; nn. 162, 442–62

See also Index I, s.v. 'Hero'
ἥρως ἀγαθός: n. 270
ἥρως δαίμων: 52

θεοῖς: 51–2, 65
θεοσεβής: n. 415a
θηκαῖον: n. 350

ἰσόθεος: 77, 80

κᾶδος: n. 372
κατὰ πᾶν ὅσιος: see s.v. ὅσιος
κατὰ τὸ ὅραμα: 79
κώλυμα: 66

λέων: n. 206
λοιμός (λοιμικὴ διάθεσις, περίστασις): 66

μακαρίτης: 77
μείλια: 23
μνείας χάριν: 52
μνῆμα: see s.v. μνημεῖον
μνημεῖον: 12; nn. 265, 395

ὀμφαλός: n. 229
ὄρος μνήματος (σήματος, θήκης, θηκαῖος):
    69–70; nn. 350, 397
ὅσιος (καὶ κατὰ πᾶν ὅσιος): 72–3; nn. 418–20

παρρησία: n. 375
πελανός: 23
ποθεινός: n. 408
πρατήνιος: n. 223
πρητήν: see πρατήνιος
πρητῆνας: see πρατήνιος
προνοέω: n. 321
πυραμίς: n. 100

σορός: n. 41a

ταφαίων (ταφέων): 69–70; n. 395
τάφια (ταφῖα) (ἐπὶ τῶν ταφιῶν): 61–2, 68, 70
ταφικόν: n. 340
τόποι: 12, 62, 67, 70; n. 359
τοφίων: 70; n. 396

χαῖρε: 71–2
χαῖρε καὶ σύ γε (πολλά): 72; nn. 254, 408
χοραγός: n. 365
χρηστὲ χαῖρε: 71–2; nn. 254, 261, 402–8

V. INDEX OF AUTHORS QUOTED

VI. INDEX OF MUSEUM INVENTORIES

This index does not include : (i) items from Rhodes and the other Dodecanesian islands which for the most part have no inventory numbers, and whose location is adequately described in the text; (ii) save by exception, inscribed stones, reference to which is to be found in Index II(A).

VII. INDEX TO PLATES

1. Monte Smith, stretch of city wall with earlier pit-graves

2. Graves with south edge of wall (top left)

3. Further graves in same area

4. Courtyard and tomb-entrance, Kizil Tepé

5. Façade of hypogaeum with loculi, Makry Steno

6. Chamber of main hypogaeum, Makry Steno

8. Cova necropolis, colonnaded hypogaeum

7. Cova necropolis, showing rock-terracing

11

9

10

9. Cova necropolis, Rider-tomb

10. Same, left section of rear wall

11. Cova necropolis, graves, etc. on shore

13. 'Ptolemaion', upper structure

12. Rhodini, 'Ptolemaion', main facade

14. Tombstone of Charonidas, *Ann.* 2, p. 150, no. 27

15. Stele from Rhodes (Istanbul; Mendel, i, no. 2)

16 (b). Relief from Rhodes (Copenhagen, Ny Carlsberg, Inv. 1996)

16 (a). Stele of Krito and Timarista, from Kamiros

7 (a). Stele of Kalliarista from Makry Steno

17 (c). Stele from Rhodes (Copenhagen, NM, Inv. 5622)

17 (b). Stele from Rhodes (Istanbul; Mendel, iii, no. 878)

18 (*a*). *NS* 113

18 (*b*). *NS* 103 (above)

19 (*a*). Stele of Mnasis

19 (*b*). Stele of Rhodokleia

20 (a). *NS* 108

20 (b). *NS* 102

21 (b). Stele of Praxion

21 (a). Stele of Stratonidas

21 (c). *IG* 1448 (Hanover; Kestner-Museum)

21 (d). *IG* 1459 (Hanover; Kestner-Museum)

22. *IG* 331 (Kunsthist. Mus. Vienna)

24. Sarcophagus, life-size

23 (b). Poros stele and base, Makry Steno

23 (a). Poros stele and base, Makry Steno

25 (a). Cinerary casket from Rhodes(?) (Istanbul)

25 (b). The same, interior

26 (a). Cinerary casket, *Ann.* 2, p. 175, no. 162ᵃ

26 (b). Cinerary casket, *Ann.* 2, p. 175, no. 162ᵇ

27 (a). Cinerary caskets

27 (c). Cinerary caskets

27 (b). Cinerary casket, NS 407

27 (d). Cinerary caskets

28. Cinerary casket, Rhodian Peraea (Büyükkaraağaç)

29 (a). Cinerary casket, Sardis (Berlin, *Beschr. ant. Skulpt.* 1123)

29 (b). Cinerary casket, Pergamon (Bergama, Museum)

29 (c). Cinerary casket, Pergamon (Bergama, Museum)

29 (*d*). Cinerary casket, Carthage (Parc archéol.)

29 (*e*). Cinerary casket, Carthage (Parc archéol.)

30. Cinerary casket, Sardis (*BMI* 1031)

1 (a). Upper member of rectangular altar

31 (b). Upper member of rectangular altar, Lindos

31 (c). Side of same

32 (b). Rectangular altar with base, single block

32 (a). Rectangular altar with base, single block, *NS* 219

33 (a). Epistatas-altar, Lindos (Copenhagen; *Inscr. Lind.* 209)

33 (b). Epistatas-altar, Lindos (Copenhagen; *Inscr. Lind.* 230)

34 (*a*). Epistatas-altar, Lindos (Copenhagen; *Inscr. Lind.* 149)

ΤΙΜΑΡΧΟΣ ΑΡΙΣΤΩΝΟΣ

ΤΙΜΑΘΕΙΣΥΠΟΤΟΥΚΟΙΝΟΥΤΩΝΑΙΤΩΛΩΙ
ΕΠΑΙΝΩΙ ΧΡΥΣΕΩΙΣΤΕΦΑΝΩΙ ΕΙΚΟΝΙ
ΠΟΛΙΤΕΙΑΙ ΑΡΕΤΑΣΕΝΕΚΑΚΑΔΙΚΑΙΟΣΥΝΑΣ
ΚΑΙΥΠΑΡΓΕΙΩΝ ΕΠΑΙΝΩΙ ΧΡΥΣΕΩΙΣΤΕΦΑΝΩΙ
ΕΙΚΟΝΙ ΑΡΕΤΑΣΕΝΕΚΑ ΚΑΙΥΠΟΔΕ/ΦΩΝ
ΑΘΑΝΑΣ ΣΤΕΦΑΝΩΙ ΤΟΙΣΠΑΡΑΤΟΥΘΕΟΥ
ΚΑΙΧΡΥΣΕΩΙ ΑΡΕΤΑΣΕΝΕΚΑΚΑΙΕΥΣΕΒΕΙΑΣ
ΚΑΙΕΠΙΣΤΑΤΗΣ

ΙΕΡΕΩΣΤΑΣΑΘΑΝΑΣ ΦΙΛΟΔΑΜΟΥ
ΤΟΥΑΡΙΣΤΟΒΟΥΛΟΥ
ΙΕΡΑΥΤΟΥΚΑΙΤΩΝ·ΝΣΤΡΑΤΕΥΣΑΜΕΝΩΝ
ΟΝΑΙ ΛΙΝΔΙΑΙ ΔΙΙΠΟΛΙΕΙ ΑΠΟΛΛΩΝΙ

34 (*b*). Epistatas-altar, Lindos (Copenhagen; *Inscr. Lind.* 195)

35 (a). Rectangular altar, Kamiros, *Tit. Cam.* 119   35 (b). Side of same

36. Shield with dedication, Kamiros (Louvre; *Tit. Cam.* 76)

35 (c). Rectangular uninscribed block, Kamiros

37 (b)

37 (a)

37 (d)

37 (c)

37 (a). Rectangular altar with two bosses

37 (b). Rectangular altar with two bosses, NS 163

37 (c). Rectangular altar with two bosses

37 (d). Rectangular altar with two bosses NS 384

38 (a)

38 (c)

38 (b)

38 (d)

38 (a). Rectangular altar with one boss, *IG* 549

38 (b). Rectangular altar with one boss, *NS* 342

38 (c). Rectangular altar with one boss

38 (d). Rectangular altar with one boss

39 (a)

39 (b)

39 (c)

39 (d)

39 (a). Rectangular altar without bosses

39 (b). Rectangular altar without bosses

39 (c). Rectangular altar without bosses, *Ann.* 2, p. 148, no. 67

39 (d). Rectangular altar without bosses, *Arch. Delt.* 18, 1963, p. 20, no. 31.

40 (b). Side of fig. 37 (b)

40 (a). Detail of bosses of fig. 37 (b)

40 (d). Circular altar with 'cushion', Thera *IG* xii. 3, 469

40 (c). Side of altar without bosses

41 (b)

41 (c)

41 (a). Rectangular altar with 'cushion', Athens (Athens, NM.
1971)

41 (b). Upper surface of same

41 (c). Rectangular altar with
'cushion', Arch. Delt. 25,
1970, p. 515

42 (b)

42 (a)

42 (c)

42 (d)

42 (a). Rectangular altar with wreaths, NS 46

42 (b). Rectangular altar with wreath, AM 23, 1898, p. 398, no. 81

42 (c). Rectangular altar, with bucrania

42 (d). Rectangular altar with bucrania

43 (b)

43 (d)

43 (a)

43 (c)

43 (a). Rectangular altar with bucrania, *Ann.* 2, p. 127, no. 3

43 (b). Rectangular altar with bucrania

43 (c). Rectangular altar with bucrania and stag's head (UP)

43 (d). Side of same

44 (a). Rectangular altar with relief, Rhodian Peraea (Karaca)

44 (b). Detail of fig. 43 c

44 (c). Detail of fig. 43 c

44 (d). Pediment of aediculate tombstone, Cos

45 (b)

45 (d)

45 (a)

45 (c)

45 (a). Rectangular altar with relief, *Cl. Rh.* 9, p. 100, fig. 66.

45 (b). Rectangular altar with relief

45 (c). Rectangular altar with 'Totenmahl'-relief, *Cl. Rh.* 5 (1), p. 96, no. 26

45 (d). Rectangular altar with relief

46 (c). Same (left face)

46 (a). Rectangular altar (front) with scene of parting (Vienna; *IG* 441)

46 (d). Same (right face)

46 (b). Same (back)

47 (a). Rectangular altar with relief, *Cl. Rh.* 2, no. 32

47 (b). 'Totenmahl'-relief from Rhodes (Copenhagen, N.M. Inv. 8630)

48 (a). Rectangular altar, Nisyros, *Arch. Dell.* 20, 1965, p. 602

48 (b). Same (left face)

49 (a)

49 (b)

49 (a). Same

49 (b). Unfinished rectangular (top), Telos

49 (c). Same (right face)

49 (d). Honorific base, Kamiros, *Assoc.*,
     p. 153, no. 12

50 (b). Relief with funerary scene and altar

50 (a). Votive relief (Munich; Glypt. 203)

51 (a). Funerary cone, Thebes, Boeotia, *BCH* 82, 1958, no. 258

51 (b). Funerary cone, Thebes, Boeotia, Wilhelm, *Beiträge*, pp. 72 f., fig. 36

52 (a). 'Totenmahl'-relief, Ainos (Istanbul; Mendel, iii, no. 1025)

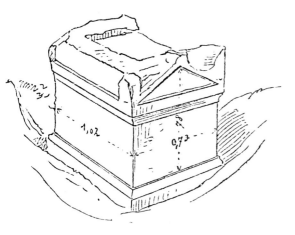

52 (b). Rectangular altar from Rhodian Peraea (Loryma)

53 (a). Rectangular altar with two bosses, Telos, *Suppl. Epigr.*, no. 12

53 (b). Rectangular altar with (remains of) two bosses, Telos, ibid., no. 15

53 (c). Rectangular altar with two bosses, Nisyros

53 (d). Same

53 (a)

53 (c)

53 (d)

54 (a). Rectangular altar with two bosses, Nisyros, Peek, *Inschr. Nis.* 34

54 (b). Rectangular altar without bosses, Syme (Chaviaras Coll.)

54 (c). Rectangular altar from Rhodian Peraea (Kasara), Ἀρχ. Ἐφ. 1913, p. 3, no. 87

54 (d). Rectangular altar with two bosses from Cos

55. Rectangular altar with two bosses from Iasos (?), *BMI* 445

56 (a). Same, upper surface

56 (b). Circular altar, Thera, *IG* xii. 3, 882

57. Parasema of Olbian decree for Rhodian, *Nadp. Olb.*, no. 24

58 (b). Double rectangular base with recessive moulding

58 (a). Simple rectangular base in two stages

58 (c). Double rectangular base with recessive moulding *Arch. Delt.* 1965, p. 598

58 (d). Double rectangular base with double recessive moulding, *NS* 69

59 (a). Cylindrical altar on circular base

59 (b). Cylindrical altar on circular base, *Cl. Rh.* 2, p. 200, no.32

59 (c). Cylindrical altar on rectangular base, *NS* 89*b*

60 (a). Cylindrical altar with multiple upper
moulding

60 (b). Cylindrical altar with multiple
moulding and cavetto cornice,
BCH 34, 1910, p. 246, no. 33

60 (c). Cylindrical altar with multiple moulding
and cavetto cornice, ibid., no. 40

60 (d). Cylindrical altar with painted lower
moulding

61 (*a*). Cylindrical votive altar, *Supp. Rod.* 51*a*

61 (b). Cylindrical votive altar, Kamiros, *Tit. Cam.* 16

61 (c). Cylindrical votive altar, Kamiros, *Tit. Cam.* 101

62 (a). Rectangular base, Kamiros, *Tit. Cam.* 39

62 (b). Rectangular base, Kamiros. *Tit. Cam.* 17

62 (*d*). Cylindrical base, Lindos, *Inscr. Lind.* 105

62 (*c*). Cylindrical base, Lindos, *Inscr. Lind.* 91

63 (b). Plain cylindrical funerary altar, *IG* 157

63 (a). Plain cylindrical funerary altar, *Supp. Rod.* no. 17

63 (d). Plain cylindrical funerary altar

63 (c). Plain cylindrical funerary altar, *IG* 541

64 (a). Upper moulding of large cylindrical altar

64 (b). Lower moulding of large cylindrical altar

64 (c). Upper moulding of large cylindrical altar (reversed)

64 (d). Cylindrical altar with rosette fascia and
cornucopiae

64 (e). Cylindrical altar (c. 200 B.C.), IG
243

65 (*a*). Metope block of 'Arsinoeion', Samothrace (Vienna)

65 (*b*). Architrave of portico of Antigonos, Delos

65 (*c*). Architrave of unidentified base, Delos

66 (a). Architrave of temple of Demeter, Pergamon, (Bergama, Museum)

66 (b). Block from unidentified monument, Pergamon (Istanbul)

66 (c). Section of fig. 66(a)

66 (d). Architrave from Ionic temple, Pergamon (Bergama, Museum)

67 (a). Cylindrical altar with pendent grape-cluster, *IG* 644

67 (b). Cylindrical altar with wreath above garlands, *NS* 431

68 (a). Cylindrical altar with tubular laurel wreath, *IG* 231

68 (b). Cylindrical altar with tubular laurel wreath (below), Ann. 2, p. 159, no. 70

69. Cylindrical altar, Mycenae (Athens, E.M. 221)

70. Cylindrical altar, Delphi

71 (a). Cylindrical altar, Pergamon (Berlin, Pergamon museum)

71 (b). Architrave of Ionic temple, Pergamon

71 (c). Cylindrical altar, Pergamon (Berlin, Pergamon museum)

71 (d). Votive altar, Pergamon (Berlin, Pergamon museum)

72 (b). Cylindrical altar, Delos (British Museum)

72 (a). Cylindrical altar, Delos (British Museum)

72 (c). Cylindrical votive altar, Delos, *Inscr. Délos* 2152

72 (d). Cylindrical votive altar, Delos, *Inscr. Délos* 1746

73 (b). Cylindrical altar, Asia Minor (Paris, Louvre, no. 2904)

73 (a). Cylindrical altar, Delos (British Museum)

73 (d). Cylindrical votive altar, Delos, *Inscr. Délos* 2153

73 (c). Cylindrical votive altar, Delos, *Inscr. Délos* 1747

74 (b). Cylindrical funerary altar, Delos, *BCH* 29, 1905, p. 244, no. 114

74 (a). Cylindrical funerary altar, Delos, *BCH* 34, 1910, p. 416, no. 76

74 (d). Well-curb, Delos, ibid., pl. xxxviii, no. 268

74 (c). Well-curb, Delos, Éd xviii, pl. xxxviii, no. 267

74 (e). Cylindrical funerary altar, Delos, *Inscr. Délos* 2480

74 (f). Rectangular altar, Delos

74 (g). Cylindrical funerary altar, Paros, *IG* xii. 5. 373 (Château Bordly, Marseilles)

74 (h). Cylindrical altar, Paros

75 (a). Cylindrical 'Dionysiac' altar, Athens

75 (*b*). Cylindrical altar, Athens, Agora (S 2525)

75 (d). Cylindrical funerary altar, Athens

75 (c). Cylindrical funerary altar, Athens (Venice, Mus. Arch.)

76 (b). Cylindrical altar, Thebes, Boeotia (Thebes Museum)

76 (a). Cylindrical altar, Thebes, Boeotia (Thebes Museum)

76 (*d*). Cylindrical altar, Salamis (Cyprus) (Nicosia Museum)

76 (*c*). Cylindrical altar, Corinth

76 (e). Cylindrical funerary cippus, Cyprus
(Nicosia Museum)

76 (f). Cylindrical altar, Chaeronea
(Chaeronea Museum)

76 (g). Cylindrical altar, Nehavend, Iran

77 (*a*). Group of Rhodian cylindrical altars

77 (*b*). Group of Coan cylindrical altars

78 (a). Cylindrical funerary altar, Cos, *NS* 450   78 (b). Cylindrical funerary altar, Cos

78 (c). Cylindrical funerary altar, Cos, *Cl. Rh.* 2, p. 225, no. 89

78 (d). Cylindrical funerary altar, Cos, *Cl. Rh.* 2, p. 233, no. 126

79 (a). Cylindrical funerary altar with cornucopiae, Cos, *NS* 564

79 (b). Cylindrical funerary altar with cornucopiae, Cos

79 (c). Cylindrical funerary altar with cornucopiae, Cos, *Cl. Rh.* 2, p. 224, no. 86

79 (d). Cylindrical funerary altar with Doric
frieze, Cos

80 (*a*). Cylindrical funerary Coan altar, Cos, *Cl. Rh.* 2, p. 226, nos. 90–3

80 (*b*). Cylindrical funerary altar, Cos

80 (*c*). Cylindrical funerary altar, Cos(?), (Rhodes, Castello)

80 (*d*). Cylindrical funerary altar, Cos

80 (*e*). Cylindrical funerary altar, Cos, *PH* 190 (Istanbul; Mendel, iii, no. 1151)

80 (*f*). Cylindrical funerary altar, Fener-burnu, *BSA* 50, 1955, p. 137, no. 47

81 (a). Cylindrical funerary altar, Halicarnassos

81 (b). Cylindrical funerary altar, Halicarnassos

81 (c). Cylindrical funerary altar, Halicarnassos

81 (d). Cylindrical funerary altar, Halicarnassos

1 (*e*). Cylindrical funerary altar, Halicarnassos   81 (*f*). Cylindrical funerary altar, Halicarnassos

(*g*). Cylindrical funerary altar, Halicarnassos   81 (*h*). Cylindrical funerary altar, Halicarnassos

81 (j). Cylindrical votive altar, Halicarnassos (British Museum)

82 (a). Cylindrical altar, Cnidos (British Museum)

82 (b). Cylindrical funerary altar, Cnidos, *SGDI* 3535 (British Museum)

82 (c). Cylindrical funerary altar with figures, Side, Mansel, *Side*, p. 96, no. 73

82 (d). Cylindrical funerary altar with figures, Cyclades (Oxford, Ashmolean Museum)

82 (e). Cylindrical votive altar, Delos, *Insc. Délos* 1791

83 (a). Cylindrical funerary altar, Mytilene, *IG* xii, 2, 286

83 (b). Other side of same altar

83 (c). Upper surface of same altar

83 (d). Cylindrical funerary altar, Cos, *PH* 165

83 (f). Cylindrical altar, Pergamon, Asclepieion

83 (e). Cylindrical funerary altar, Aeolic Cyme (Istanbul; Mendel iii, no. 1084)

83 (g). Circular casket-lid, Pergamon, Asclepieion

83 (h). Upper surface of cylindrical offertory-altar, Delos, *Inscr. Délos* 1898

83 (j). Cylindrical funerary altar, Mytilene, *SEG* xviii, 433

83 (k). Cylindrical funerary altar, Mytilene, *SEG* xviii, 434

84 (b). Other side of same altar

84 (a). Cylindrical 'Nike'-altar

84 (c). Cylindrical 'Nike'-altar

84 (d). Cylindrical 'Nike'-altar

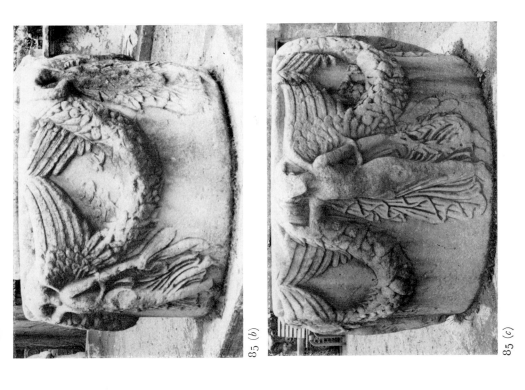

85 (b)

85 (c)

85 (a)

85 (a). Cylindrical 'Nike'-altar

85 (b). Cylindrical 'Nike'-altar, Cos (Istanbul; Mendel, iii, no. 1150)

85 (c). Other side of same altar

85 (e). Other side of same altar

85 (d). Cylindrical funerary altar (Marburg Univ., Arch. Inst.)

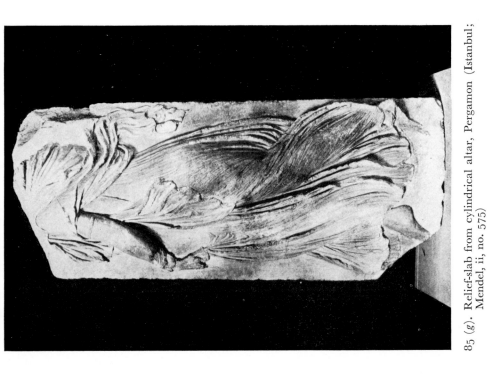

85 (g). Relief-slab from cylindrical altar, Pergamon (Istanbul; Mendel, ii, no. 575)

85 (f). Cylindrical 'Dionysiac' altar

85 (*h*). Cylindrical votive altar, provenance unknown (Istanbul; Mendel, ii, no. 564)

85 (*j*). Other side of same altar

86 (b). Cylindrical altar with inset relief, *IG* 574 (Vienna)

86 (a). Cylindrical altar with inset relief, *Cl. Rh.* 5 (2), pp. 9 ff.

86 (d). Cylindrical altar with inset relief, Cos

86 (c). Cylindrical altar with inset relief

87 (b). Cylindrical altar with inset panel

87 (a). Cylindrical altar with inset panel

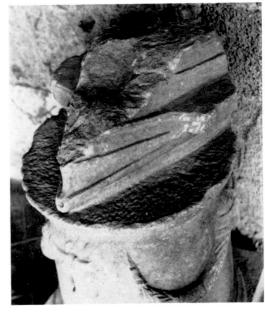

87 (c). Cylindrical altar with ship's prow

87 (d). Upper surface of same

88 (a). Cylindrical altar, Syme (Chaviaras Collection)

88 (b). Cylindrical altars, Telos

88 (c). Cylindrical altar, Telos

88 (d). Cylindrical altar, Telos

89 (a). Cylindrical altar, Nisyros 89 (b). Cylindrical altar, Nisyros

89 (c). 'Bench-altar', Cos (Museum)

89 (d). Side of same 'bench-altar', Cos

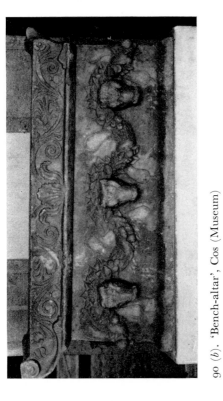

90 (*a*). Inscribed 'bench-altar', Cos, *NS* 571 (Castello)

90 (*b*). 'Bench-altar', Cos (Museum)

90 (*c*). 'Bench-altar', Cos ('Casa Romana')

90 (*d*). 'Bench-altar'. Cos ('Casa Romana')

91 (a). Double cylindrical altar and base in one piece

91 (b). Twin stelai in single block, Tanagra

91 (c). Twin stelai in one piece, Tanagra

91 (d). Architrave of Gymnasion, Olympia

91 (e). Cylindrical altar, unknown provenance (Venice, Mus. Arch.)

91 (g). Cylindrical altar, unknown provenance (Istanbul. Inv. 6275)

91 (f). Cylindrical altar, unknown provenance (Venice, Mus. Arch.)

91 (h). Cylindrical altar, Nicomedia (Istanbul)

92 (a). Stele with inset parting scene, *Cl. Rh.* 5
(2), pp. 28 ff., no. 37

92 (b). Stele with inset parting scene, *Cl. Rh.* 5
(1), p. 90, no. 23

92 (c). Stele with inset parting scene, *SGDI* 3988 (Vienna)

92 (e). Stele with inset figure, *IG* 481 (Berlin, Pergamon-museum)

92 (d). Stele with inset parting scene (Copenhagen, NM, Inv. 8629)

93 (a). Stele with inset figure (Copenhagen, NM, Inv. 2620)

93 (b). 'Ionic' style stele with Doric frieze, *AAA* 6, 1973, (1), p. 117, fig. 5

93 (c). Stele with relief on ledge, *Cl. Rh.* 5 (1), p. 92, fig. 61

94. 'Helmet' stele (Copenhagen, NM, Inv. 5619)

93 (d). 'Warrior' stele with relief on ledge, Πρακτ.
Αρχ. Ἐτ. 1954. pp. 357 ff.

95. Stele of youth holding hare, with dog (Copenhagen, Ny
    Carlsberg Glypt.)

96 (a). Stele of youth with dog, *Cl. Rh.* 2, p. 66, no. 29

96 (b). Stele with inset parting scene, *NS* 48

96 (c). Stele with female figure and child, *Rend. Linc.* 1946, pp. 432 ff. (Naples, Mus. Naz.)

97. Funerary relief of Hieronymos (Berlin, Pergamon museum)

98. Block of funerary monument of Aristoboulos, *IG* 385

97

98

100 (a)

100 (b)

99. Lion-monument of Cnidos (British Museum)

100 (a). Lion from tomb at Ialysos

100 (b). Lion from tomb at Ialysos

101 (c)

101 (d)

101 (a)

101 (b)

101 (a). Lion from funerary monument

101 (b). Lion from funerary monument, Rhodian Peraea (Turgut)

101 (c). Fragment of lion's head

101 (d). Same from side

101 (g)

101 (f)

101 (e)

101 (e). Trunk of lion

101 (f). Lion with prey, Kaunos

101 (g). Lion with prey, Pergamon
(Bergama, Museum)

102 (b). Snake-altar, Nisyros

102 (a). Snake-altar

104. 'Snake-altar', Cnidos (British Museum)

103. Snake-altar, Cnidos (British Museum)

105 (a). Bell-kantharos with snake, front

105 (b). Same, side view

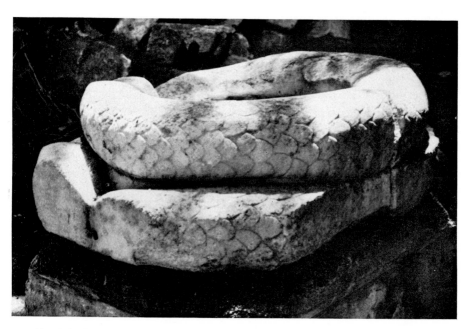

105 (c). Coiled snake

106 (c). Stele with shield and skyphos, Halicarnassos

106 (b). Stele with shield and skyphos, Halicarnassos

106 (a). Stele with shield and skyphos, Halicarnassos

107 (b). Same, showing graves

107 (a). Shield on wall of necropolis area, Dokuz Sokak

108 (a). Block with ram's head and snake

108 (b). Same

109 (b). Epithema with snake curled over papyrus-rolls

109 (a). Relief with sword and scabbard (Istanbul; Mendel, ii, no. 1080)

110 (a). Altar with omphaloid cone and base in one piece

110 (b). Omphaloid cone

110 (c). Reticulated omphaloid monument

110 (d). Cone-epithema with olive wreath

111 (a). Pediment of funerary monument, Tanagra (Schimatari Museum)

111 (b). Dolphin of fountain of Cn. Babbius Philinus, Corinth

111 (c). Rhodian stamped amphora handle, Athens (Agora, 668.6 R 20)

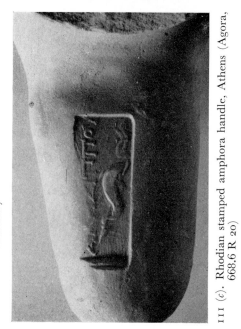

111 (d). Dolphins on altar of Artemidoros of Perge, Thera

112 (d). Plunging dolphin, unknown provenance
(British Museum)

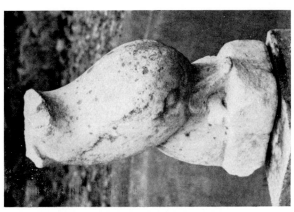

112 (c). Plunging dolphin

112 (a). Dolphins, large and small

112 (b). Large dolphin, other side

113 (a). Dossier of Dionysodoros of Alexandria, front, *IG* 155 (Venice, Museo del Seminario Patriarcale)

113 (b). Same, right side

113 (c). Same, back

113 (d). Same, left side

113 (*e*). Tombstone of Dionysodoros of Alexandria, *NS* 46

113 (*f*). Same, back

113 (*g*). Rectangular funerary altar with wreaths, *Assoc.*, p. 153, no. 11

113 (*h*). Rectangular base of cylindrical altar, with wreaths

114 (a). Cylindrical altar with decree and epitaph

114 (b). Same

115 (b)

115 (c)

115 (a)

115 (a). Inscribed solid stone skyphos, IG 656 (British Museum)

115 (b). Same

115 (c). Same

116 (a). Cylindrical altar of 'hero' Kallon

116 (b). Cylindrical altar, Perge (Antalya Museum)

116 (c). Well-curb, Pompeii

116 (d). Cylindrical altar with relief figures, Perge (Antalya Museum)

117 (a). Cylindrical altars at Arundel House

117 (b). Cylindrical altars at Arundel House

118 (b). Cylindrical altar, Arundel House, A (ii)

118 (a). Cylindrical altar, Arundel House, A (i)

118 (c). Detail of 118 (a)

118 (e). Cylindrical altar, Arundel House, A (iv)

118 (d). Cylindrical altar, Arundel House, A (iii)

118 (g). Detail of 118(f)

118 (f). Cylindrical altar (Coan?), Arundel House, B (v)

118 (*h*). Cylindrical altar (Cycladic), Arundel House, C (vi)